Shojo Beat

ANONYMOUS NOISE

Ryoko
Fukuyama

D0943303

Anonymous Noise
Volume 4
Volume 4

CONTENTS

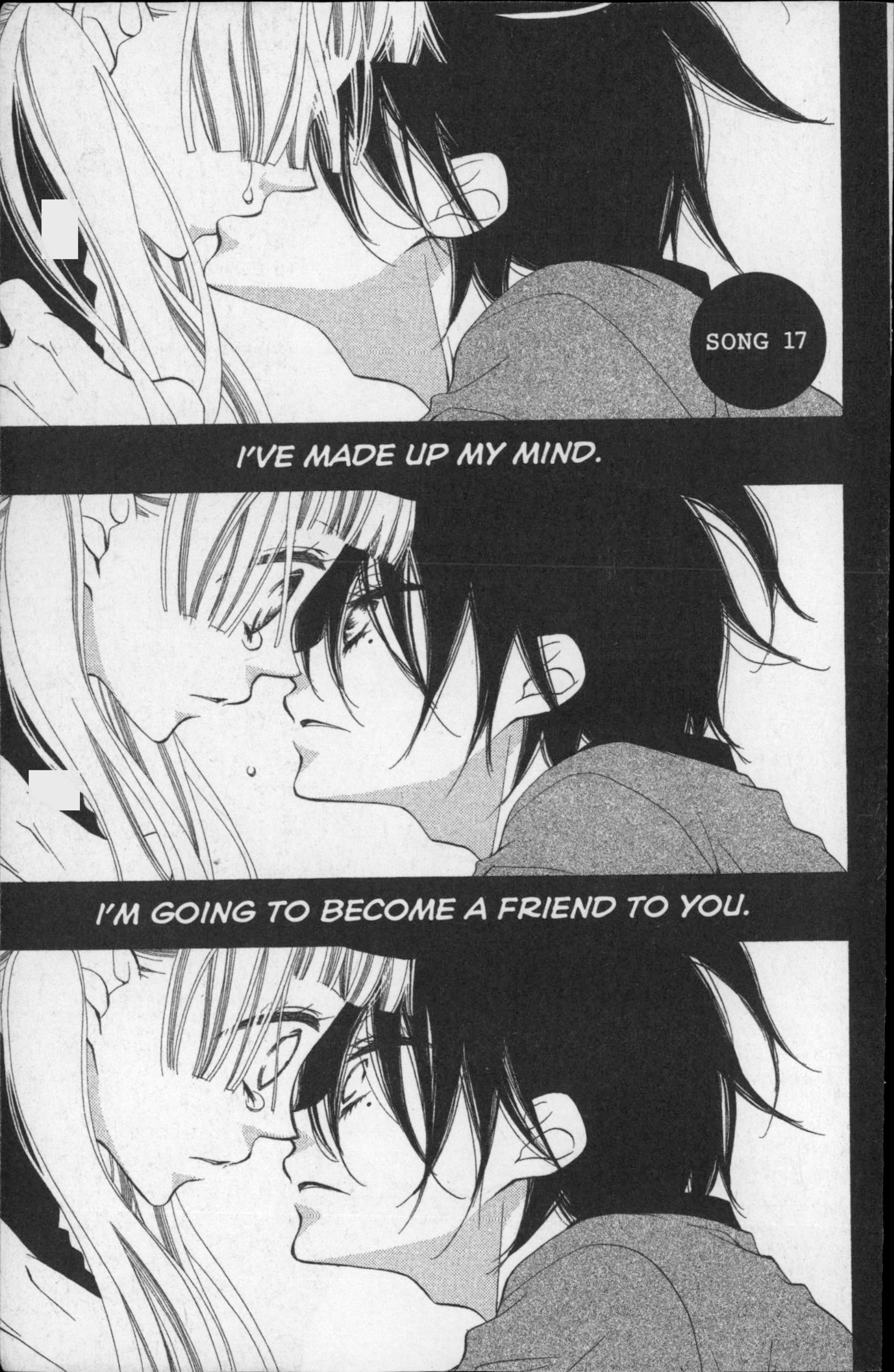
SONG 17
I'VE MADE UP MY MIND.
I'M GOING TO BECOME A FRIEND TO YOU.

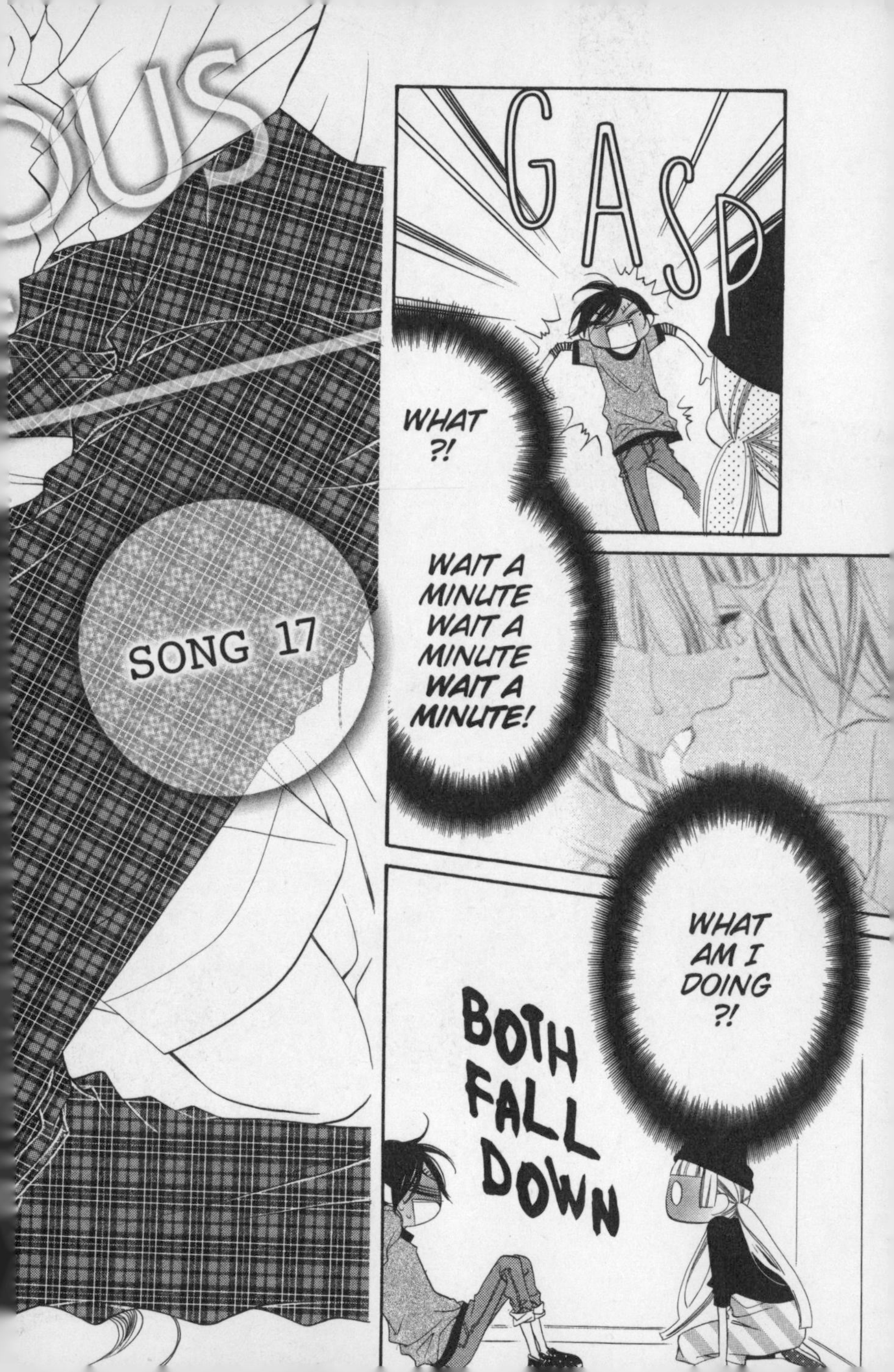
GASP
WHAT ?!
WAIT A MINUTE WAIT A MINUTE WAIT A MINUTE!
WHAT AM I DOING ?!
BOTH FALL DOWN
OUS
SONG 17

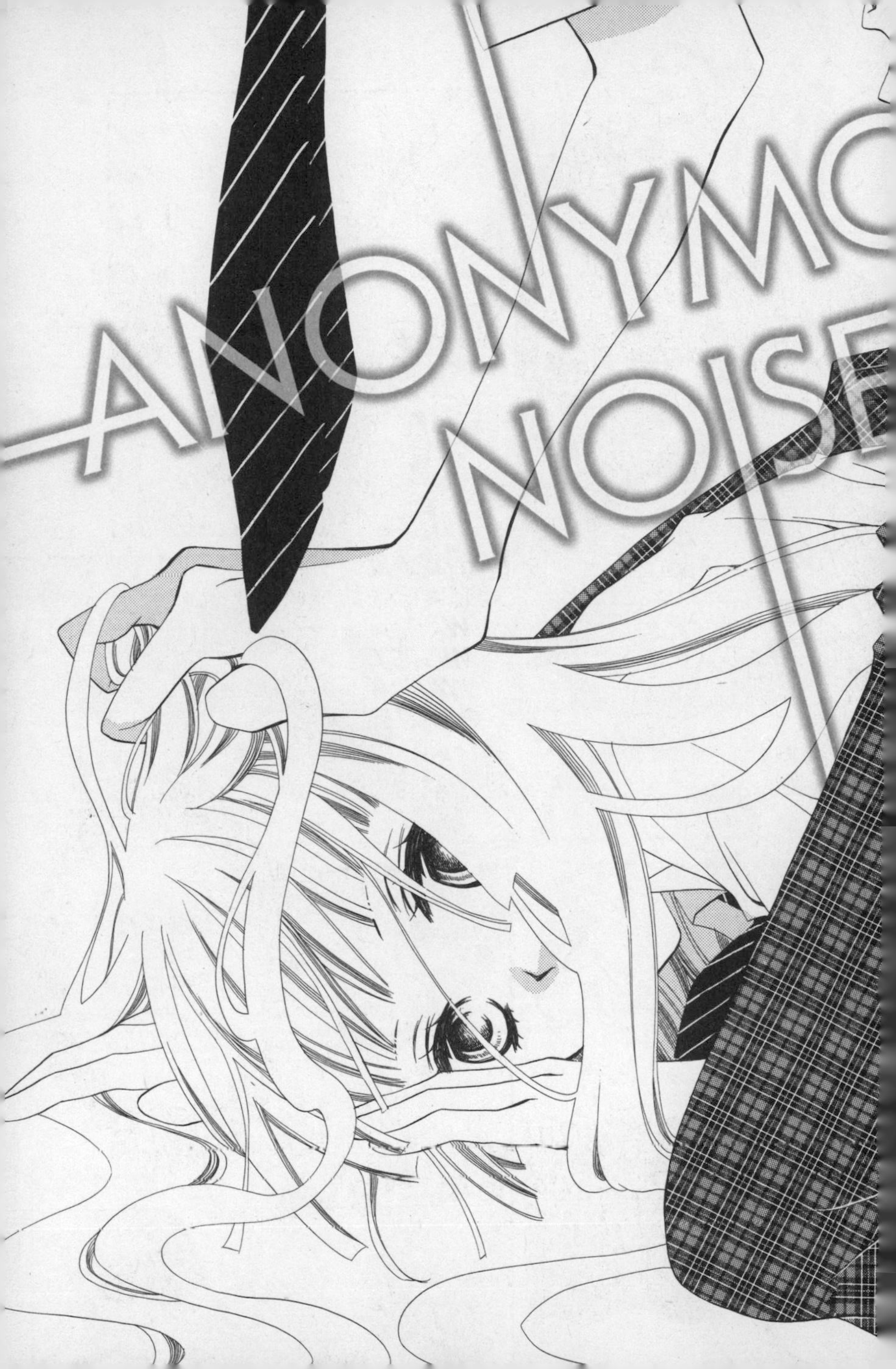
ANONYMO
NOISE

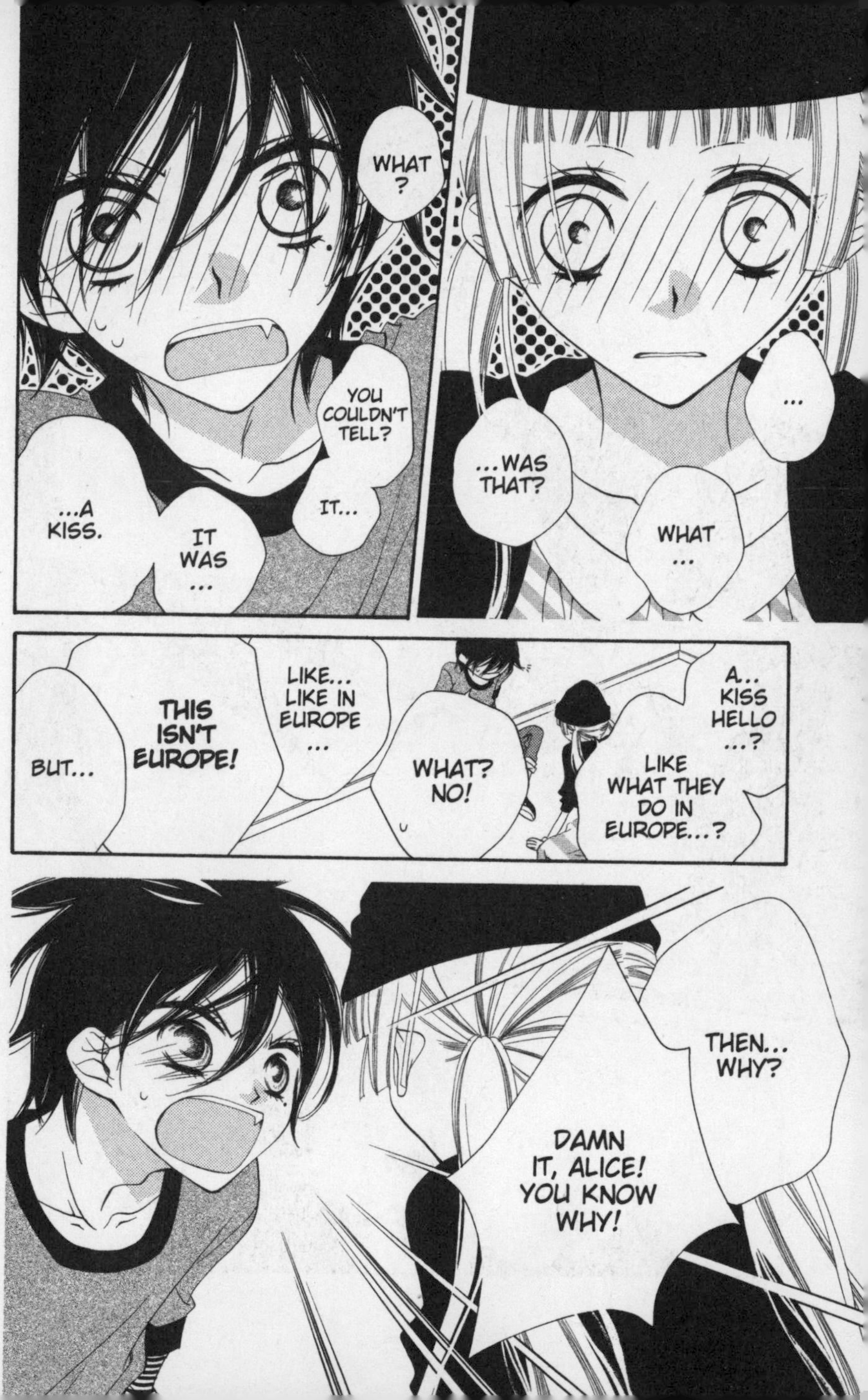
...
WHAT ...
...WAS THAT?
WHAT ?
YOU COULDN'T TELL?
IT...
IT WAS ...
...A KISS.
A... KISS HELLO ...?
LIKE WHAT THEY DO IN EUROPE...?
WHAT? NO!
LIKE... LIKE IN EUROPE ...
THIS ISN'T EUROPE!
BUT...
THEN... WHY?
DAMN IT, ALICE! YOU KNOW WHY!

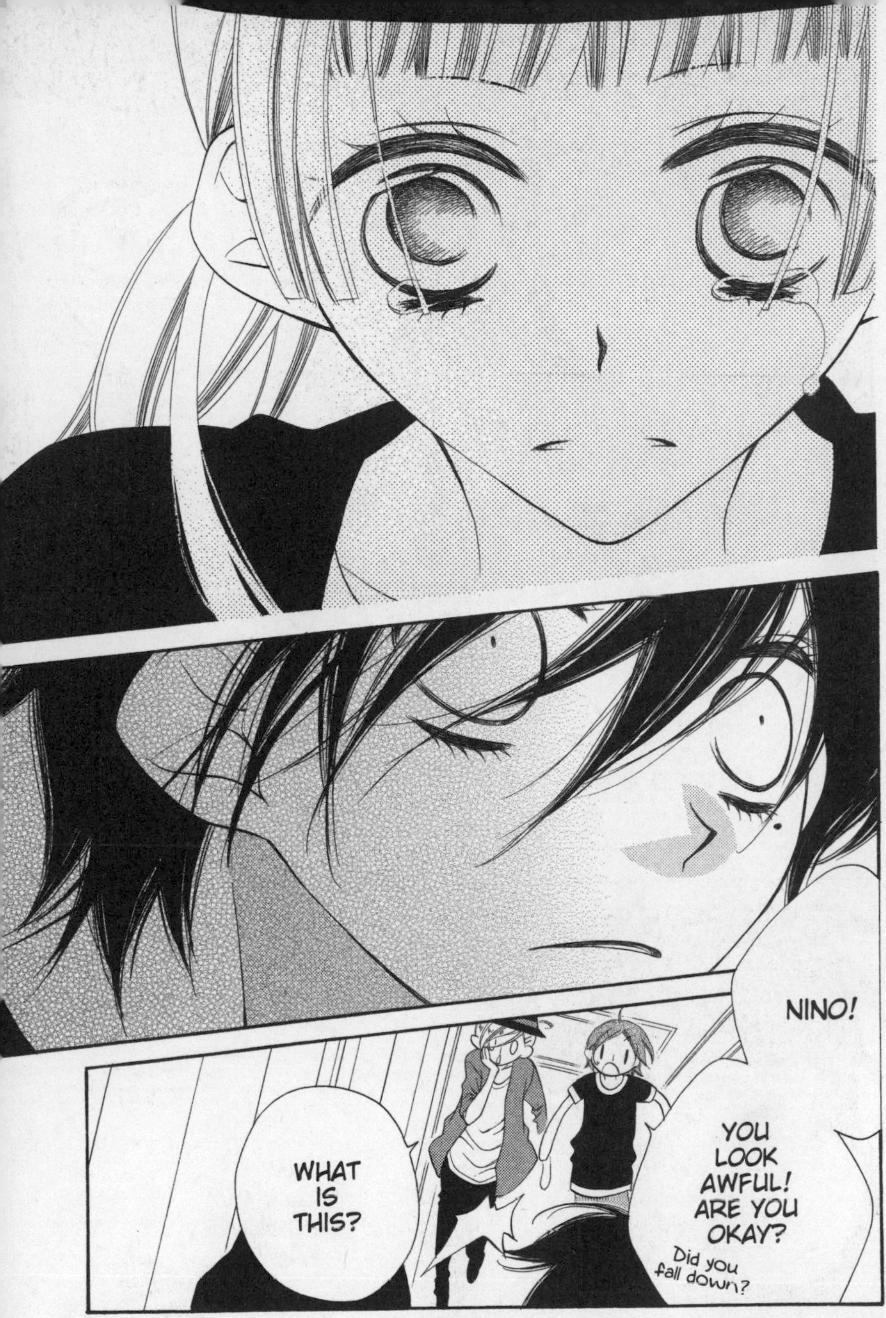
NINO!
YOU LOOK AWFUL! ARE YOU OKAY?
Did you fall down?
WHAT IS THIS?

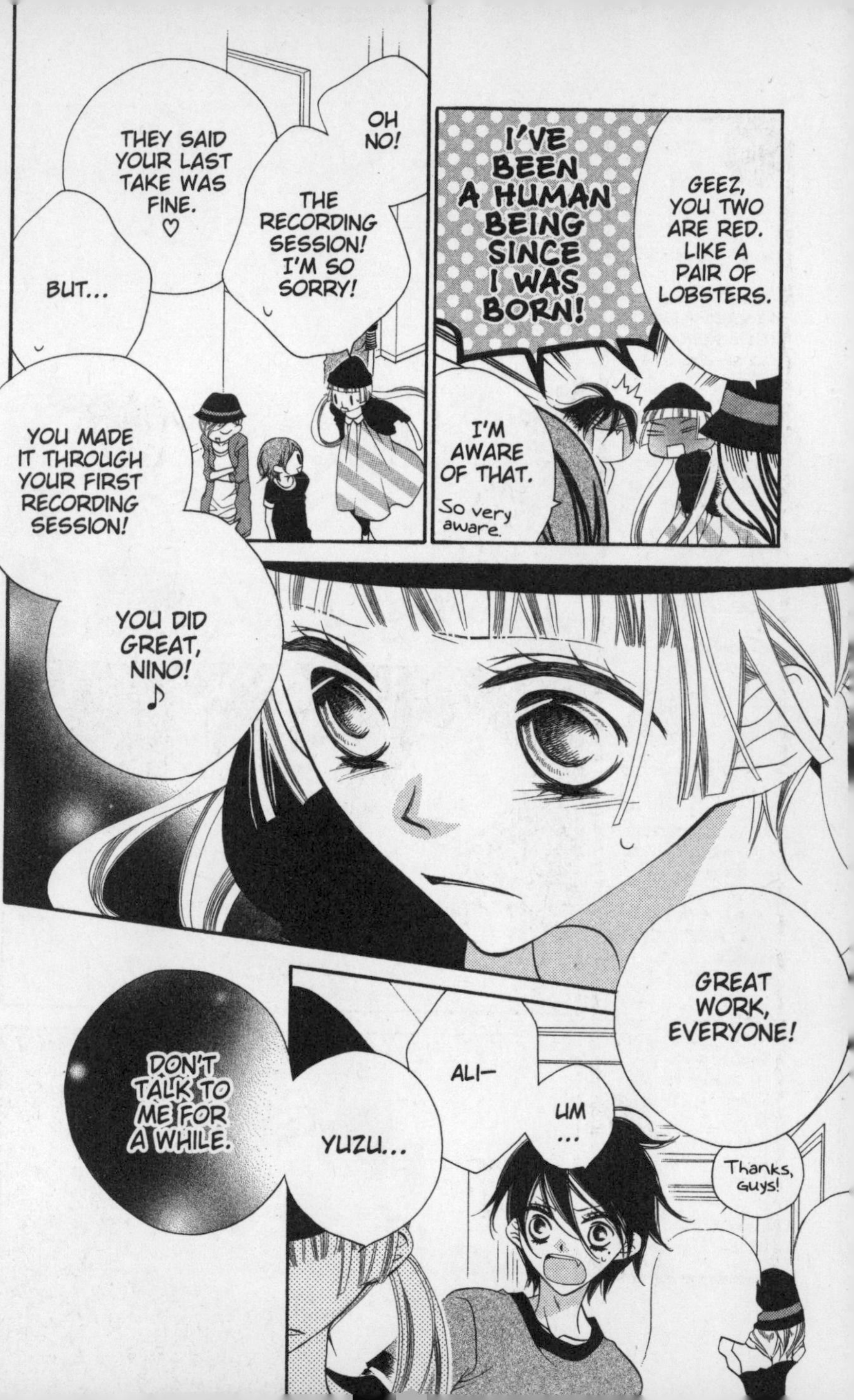
GEEZ, YOU TWO ARE RED. LIKE A PAIR OF LOBSTERS.
I'VE BEEN A HUMAN BEING SINCE I WAS BORN!
I'M AWARE OF THAT.
So very aware.
OH NO!
THE RECORDING SESSION! I'M SO SORRY!
THEY SAID YOUR LAST TAKE WAS FINE. ♡
BUT...
YOU MADE IT THROUGH YOUR FIRST RECORDING SESSION!
YOU DID GREAT, NINO! ♪
GREAT WORK, EVERYONE!
Thanks, Guys!
UM...
ALI—
YUZU...
DON'T TALK TO ME FOR A WHILE.

WHAT HAVE I DONE?

1

Hello, everyone!

Ryoko Fukuyama here. It's a pleasure to see you!

Thank you so much for picking up volume 4 of Anonymous Noise!

The cover of volume 4 is our blond, effeminate upperclassman Haruyoshi!

Haruyoshi is so delightfully easy to draw—I had to redo the covers for volumes 2 and 3, but I got volume 4 on the first try!

This volume finds both our heroes in trouble—in a variety of ways.

I hope you enjoy it!

YAAAY!

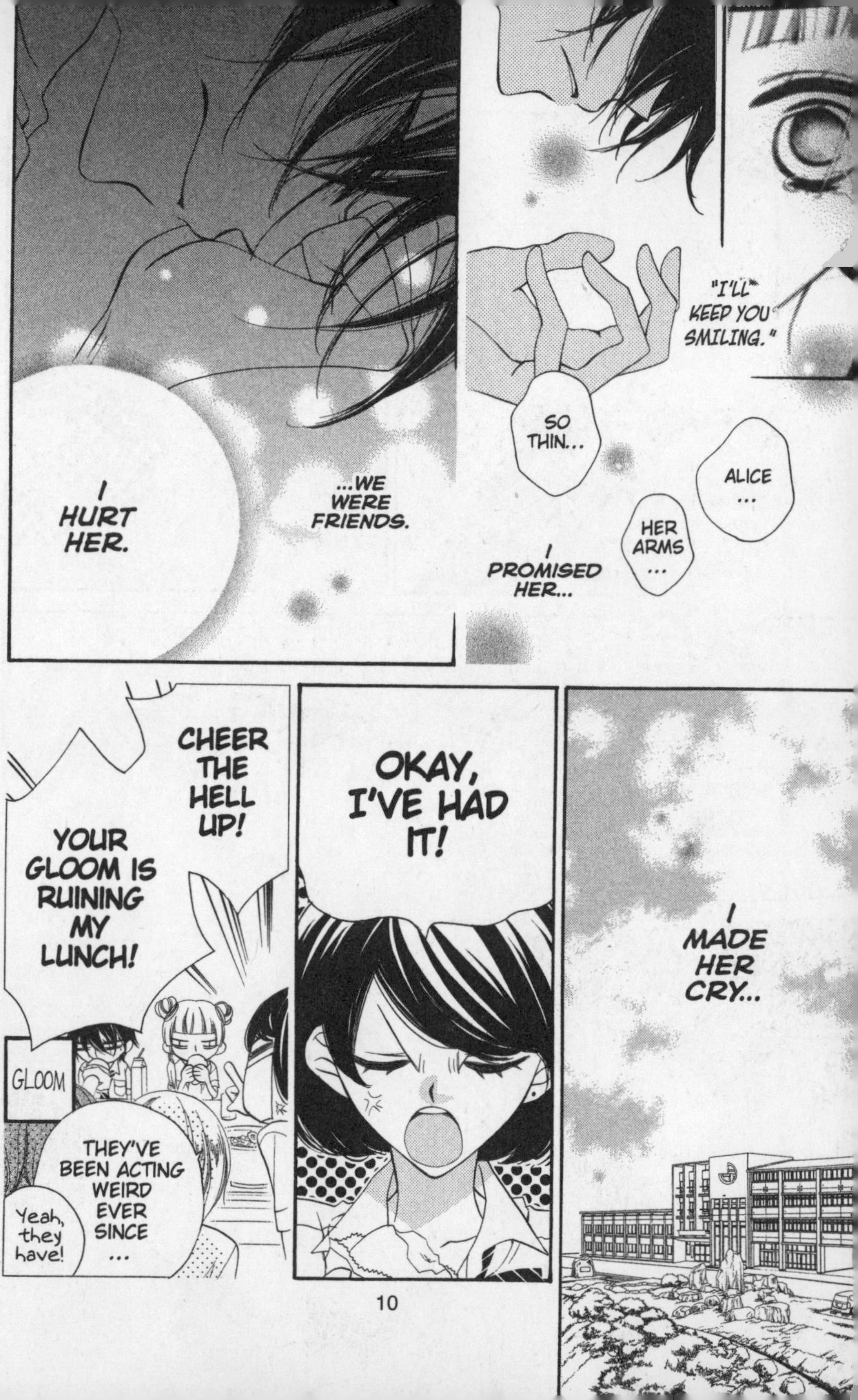
"I'LL" KEEP YOU SMILING."
ALICE ...
HER ARMS ...
SO THIN...
I PROMISED HER...
...WE WERE FRIENDS.
I HURT HER.
I MADE HER CRY...
OKAY, I'VE HAD IT!
CHEER THE HELL UP!
YOUR GLOOM IS RUINING MY LUNCH!
GLOOM
THEY'VE BEEN ACTING WEIRD EVER SINCE ...
Yeah, they have!

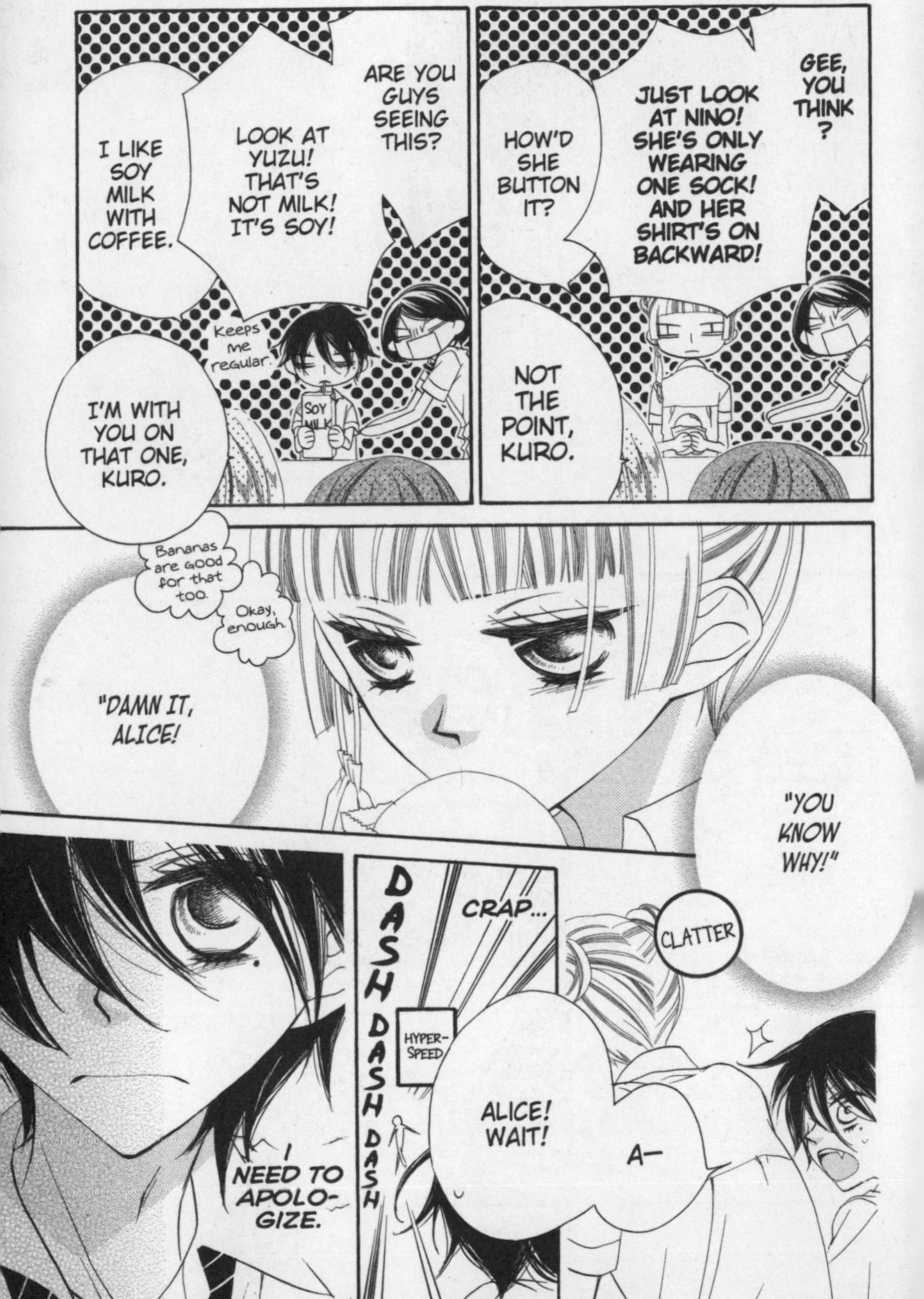
GEE, YOU THINK?
JUST LOOK AT NINO! SHE'S ONLY WEARING ONE SOCK! AND HER SHIRT'S ON BACKWARD!
HOW'D SHE BUTTON IT?
NOT THE POINT, KURO.
ARE YOU GUYS SEEING THIS?
LOOK AT YUZU! THAT'S NOT MILK! IT'S SOY!
I LIKE SOY MILK WITH COFFEE.
Keeps me regular.
SOY MILK
I'M WITH YOU ON THAT ONE, KURO.
Bananas are good for that too.
Okay, enough.
"DAMN IT, ALICE!
"YOU KNOW WHY!"
CLATTER
A—
ALICE! WAIT!
CRAP...
DASH DASH DASH
HYPER-SPEED
I NEED TO APOLOGIZE.

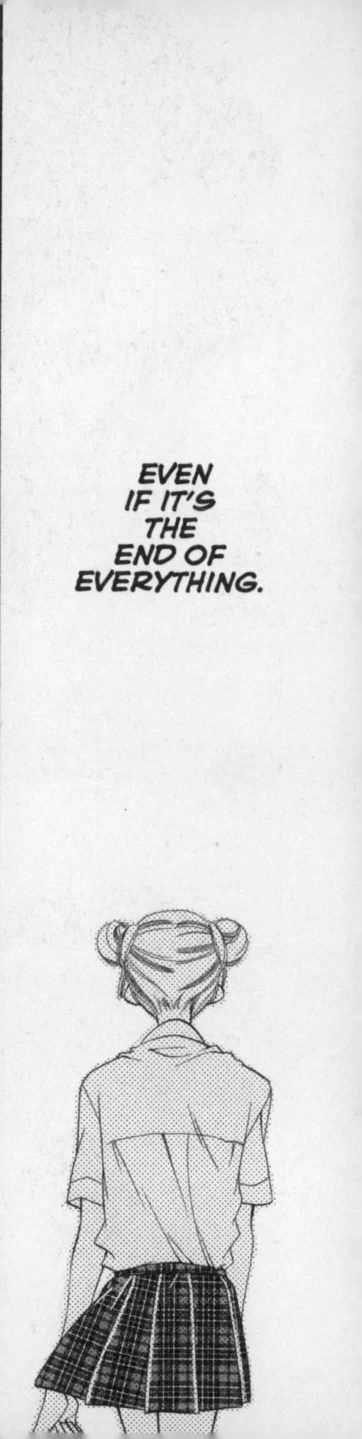
EVEN IF IT'S THE END OF EVERYTHING.

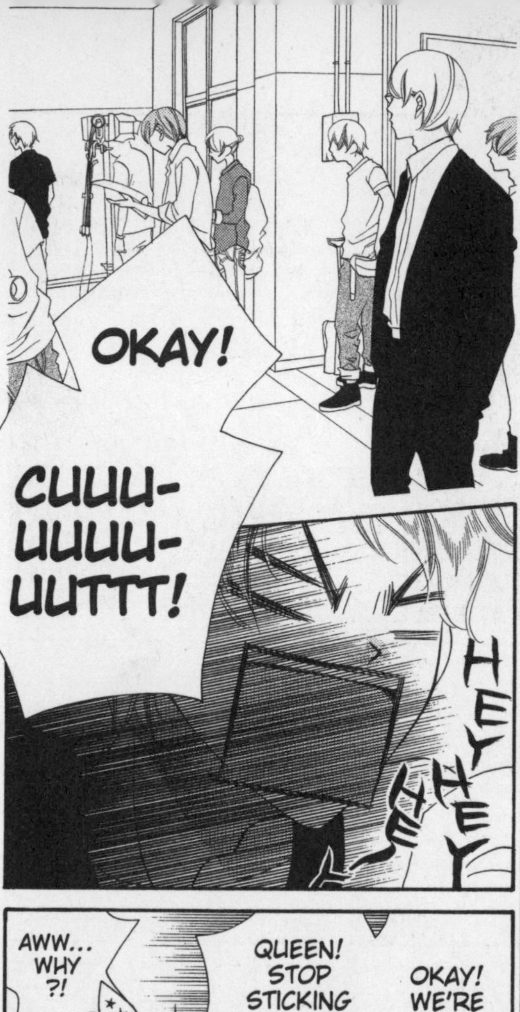
OKAY!
CUUUU-UUUUU-UUTTT!
HEY HEY HEY
OKAY! WE'RE DOING SCENE 35 NEXT!
QUEEN! STOP STICKING OUT YOUR PINKIE FINGER!
AWW... WHY?!
Hee Hee
I SEE DIRECTOR MUKAI IS AS ENTHUSIASTIC AS EVER.
VIDEO DIRECTOR MUKAI
And running a tight ship...

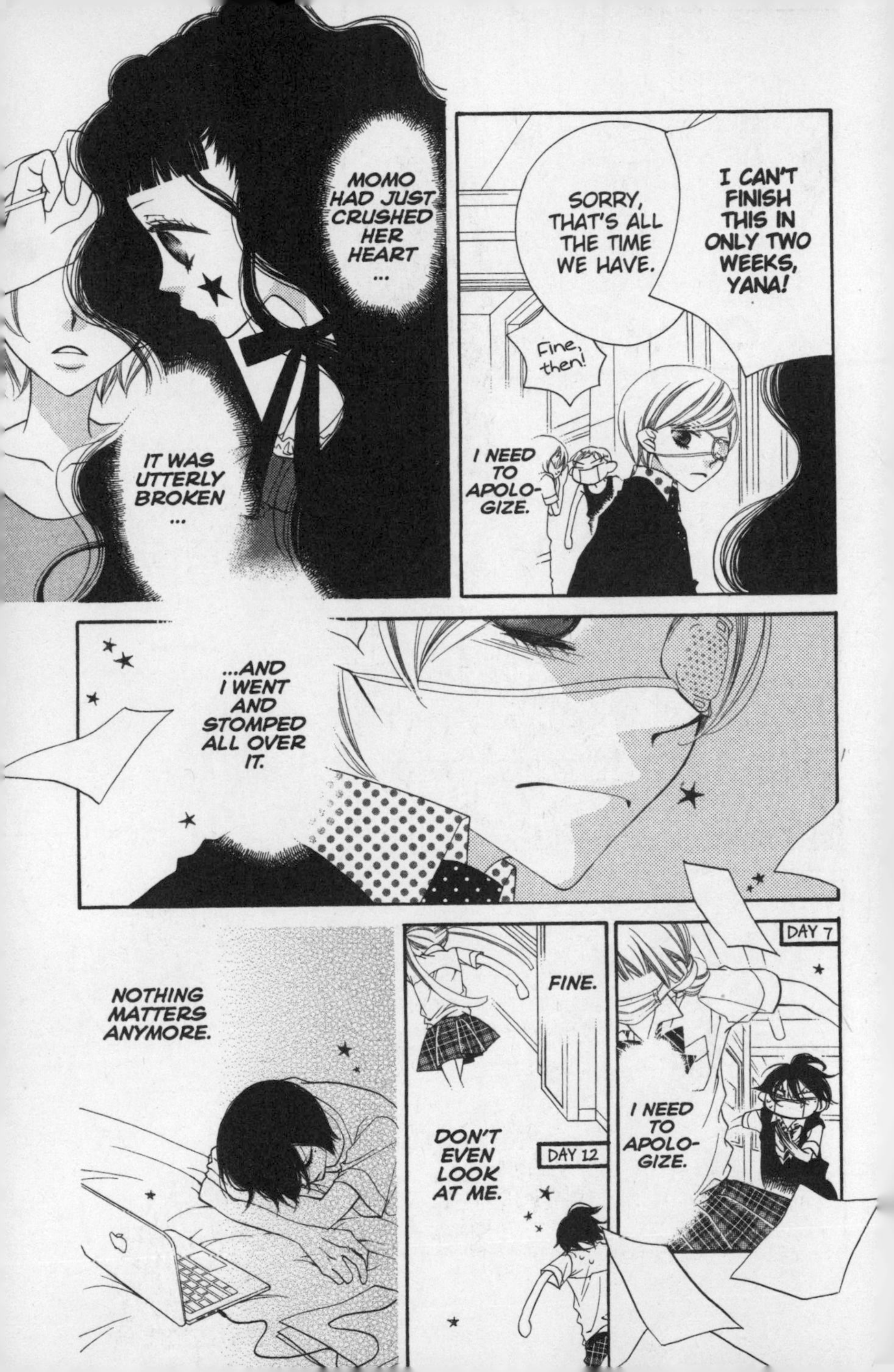
I CAN'T FINISH THIS IN ONLY TWO WEEKS, YANA!
SORRY, THAT'S ALL THE TIME WE HAVE.
Fine, then!
I NEED TO APOLOGIZE.
MOMO HAD JUST CRUSHED HER HEART ...
IT WAS UTTERLY BROKEN ...
...AND I WENT AND STOMPED ALL OVER IT.
DAY 7
I NEED TO APOLOGIZE.
FINE.
DAY 12
DON'T EVEN LOOK AT ME.
NOTHING MATTERS ANYMORE.

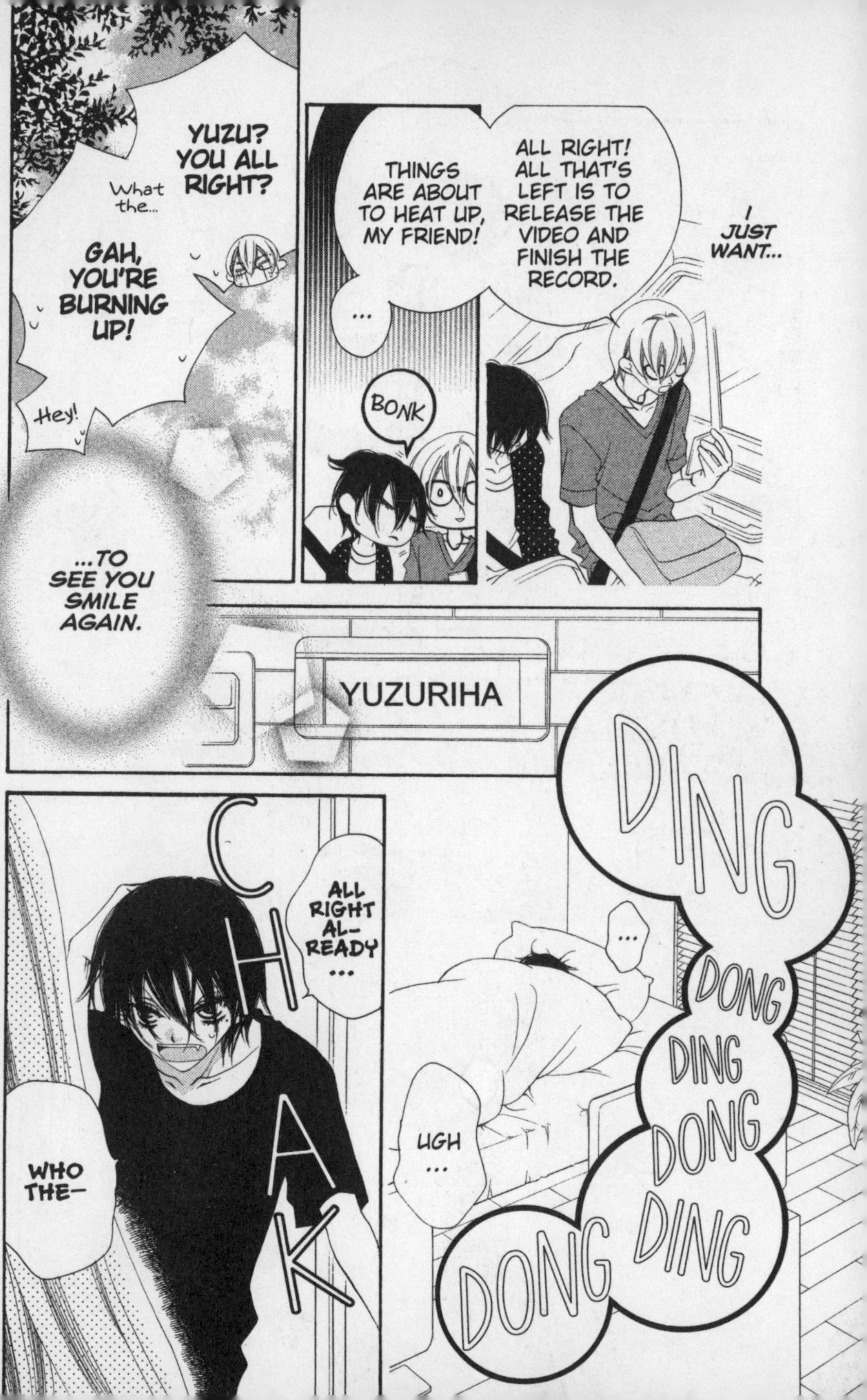
ALL RIGHT! ALL THAT'S LEFT IS TO RELEASE THE VIDEO AND FINISH THE RECORD.
THINGS ARE ABOUT TO HEAT UP, MY FRIEND!
...
BONK
I JUST WANT...
YUZURIHA
YUZU? YOU ALL RIGHT?
What the...
GAH, YOU'RE BURNING UP!
Hey!
...TO SEE YOU SMILE AGAIN.
DING DONG DING DONG DING DONG
...
UGH ...
CHAK
ALL RIGHT AL-READY ...
WHO THE-

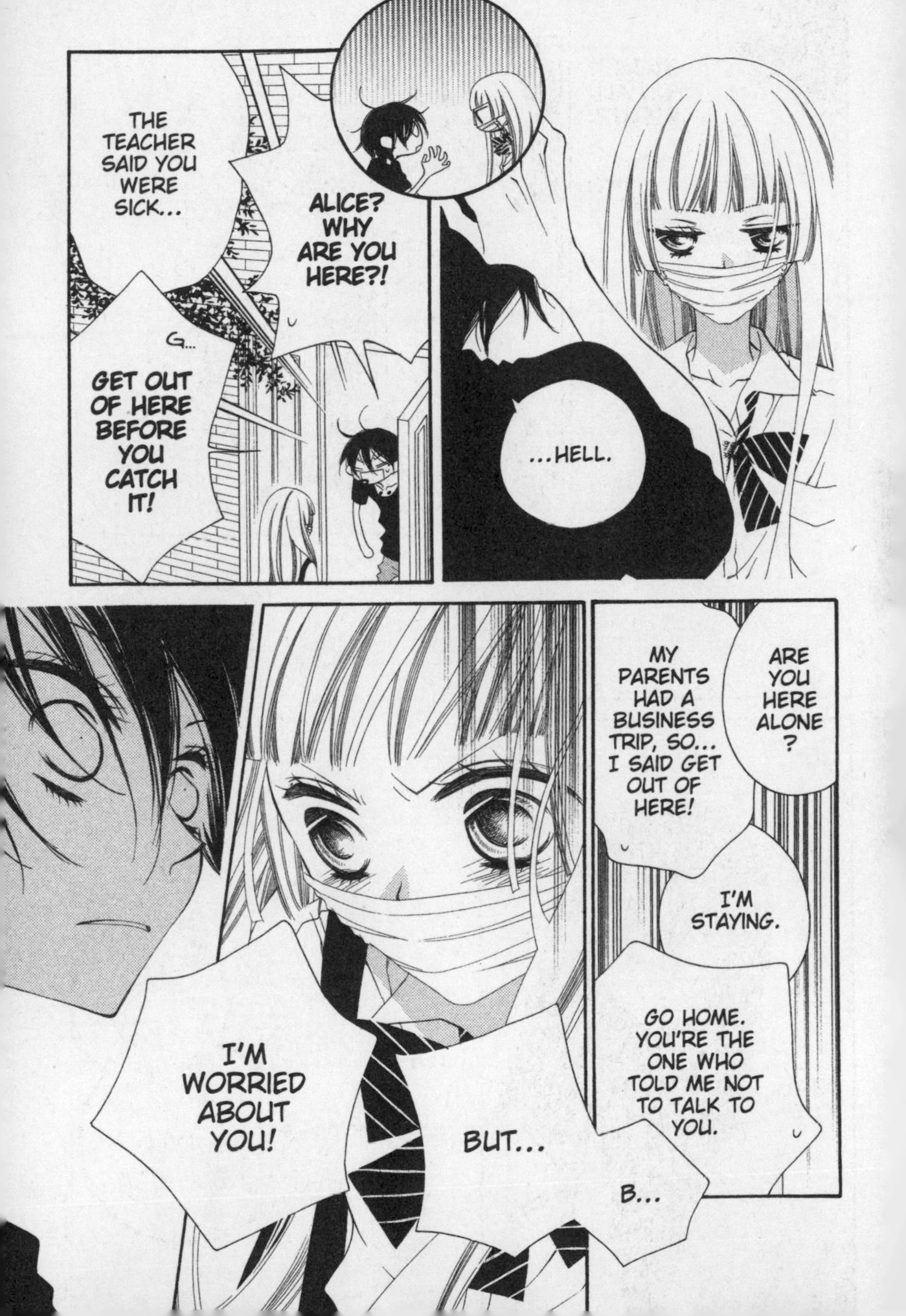
...HELL.
ALICE? WHY ARE YOU HERE?!
THE TEACHER SAID YOU WERE SICK...
G...
GET OUT OF HERE BEFORE YOU CATCH IT!
ARE YOU HERE ALONE?
MY PARENTS HAD A BUSINESS TRIP, SO... I SAID GET OUT OF HERE!
I'M STAYING.
GO HOME. YOU'RE THE ONE WHO TOLD ME NOT TO TALK TO YOU.
B...
BUT...
I'M WORRIED ABOUT YOU!

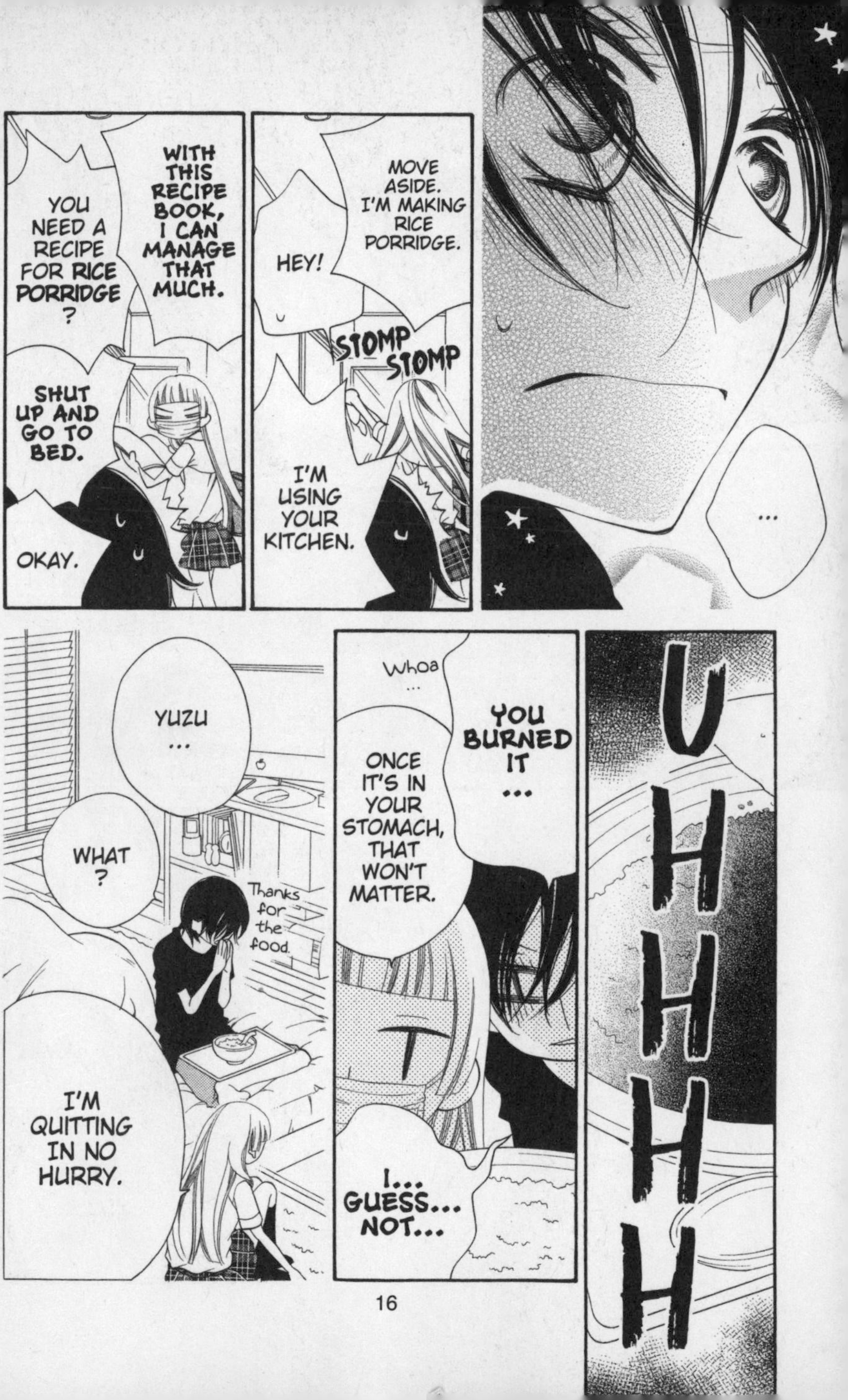
...
MOVE ASIDE. I'M MAKING RICE PORRIDGE.
HEY!
STOMP STOMP
I'M USING YOUR KITCHEN.
YOU NEED A RECIPE FOR RICE PORRIDGE?
WITH THIS RECIPE BOOK, I CAN MANAGE THAT MUCH.
SHUT UP AND GO TO BED.
OKAY.
UHHHHH
YOU BURNED IT...
Whoa...
ONCE IT'S IN YOUR STOMACH, THAT WON'T MATTER.
I... GUESS... NOT...
YUZU...
WHAT?
Thanks for the food.
I'M QUITTING IN NO HURRY.

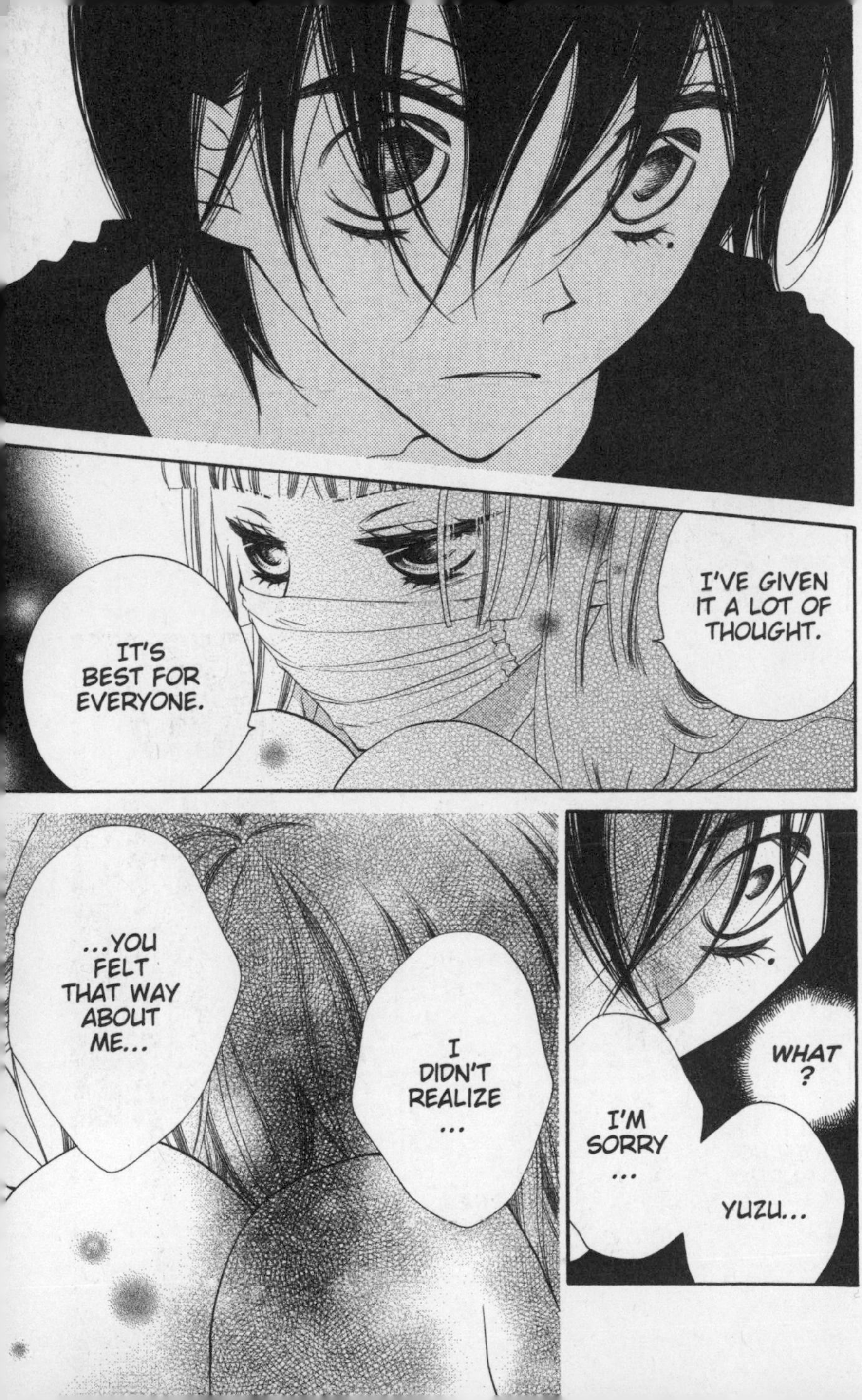

I'VE GIVEN IT A LOT OF THOUGHT.
IT'S BEST FOR EVERYONE.
WHAT?
YUZU...
I'M SORRY...
I DIDN'T REALIZE...
...YOU FELT THAT WAY ABOUT ME...

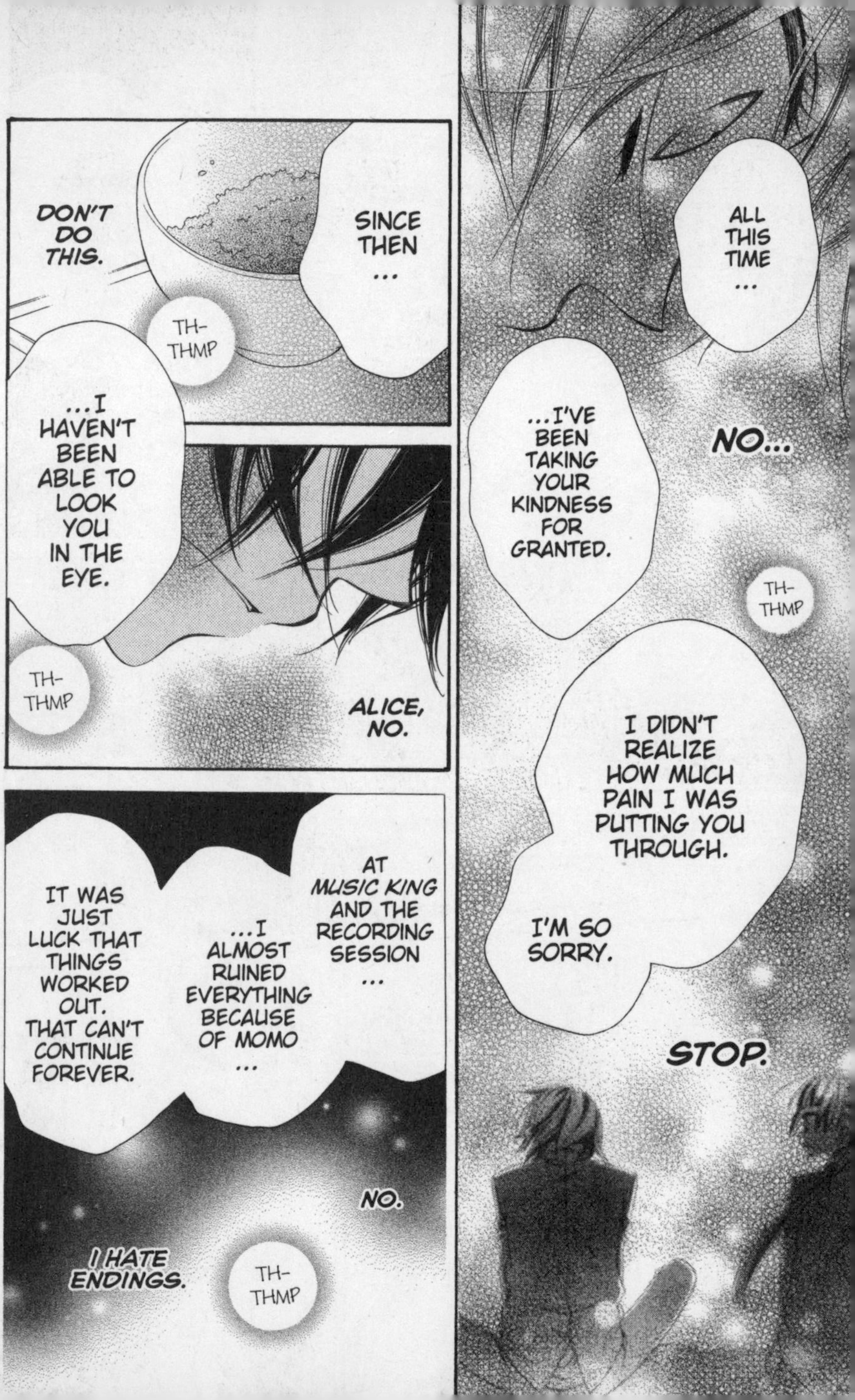
ALL THIS TIME...
NO...
...I'VE BEEN TAKING YOUR KINDNESS FOR GRANTED.
TH-THMP
I DIDN'T REALIZE HOW MUCH PAIN I WAS PUTTING YOU THROUGH.
I'M SO SORRY.
STOP.
SINCE THEN...
DON'T DO THIS.
TH-THMP
...I HAVEN'T BEEN ABLE TO LOOK YOU IN THE EYE.
ALICE, NO.
TH-THMP
AT *MUSIC KING* AND THE RECORDING SESSION...
...I ALMOST RUINED EVERYTHING BECAUSE OF MOMO...
IT WAS JUST LUCK THAT THINGS WORKED OUT. THAT CAN'T CONTINUE FOREVER.
NO.
TH-THMP
I HATE ENDINGS.

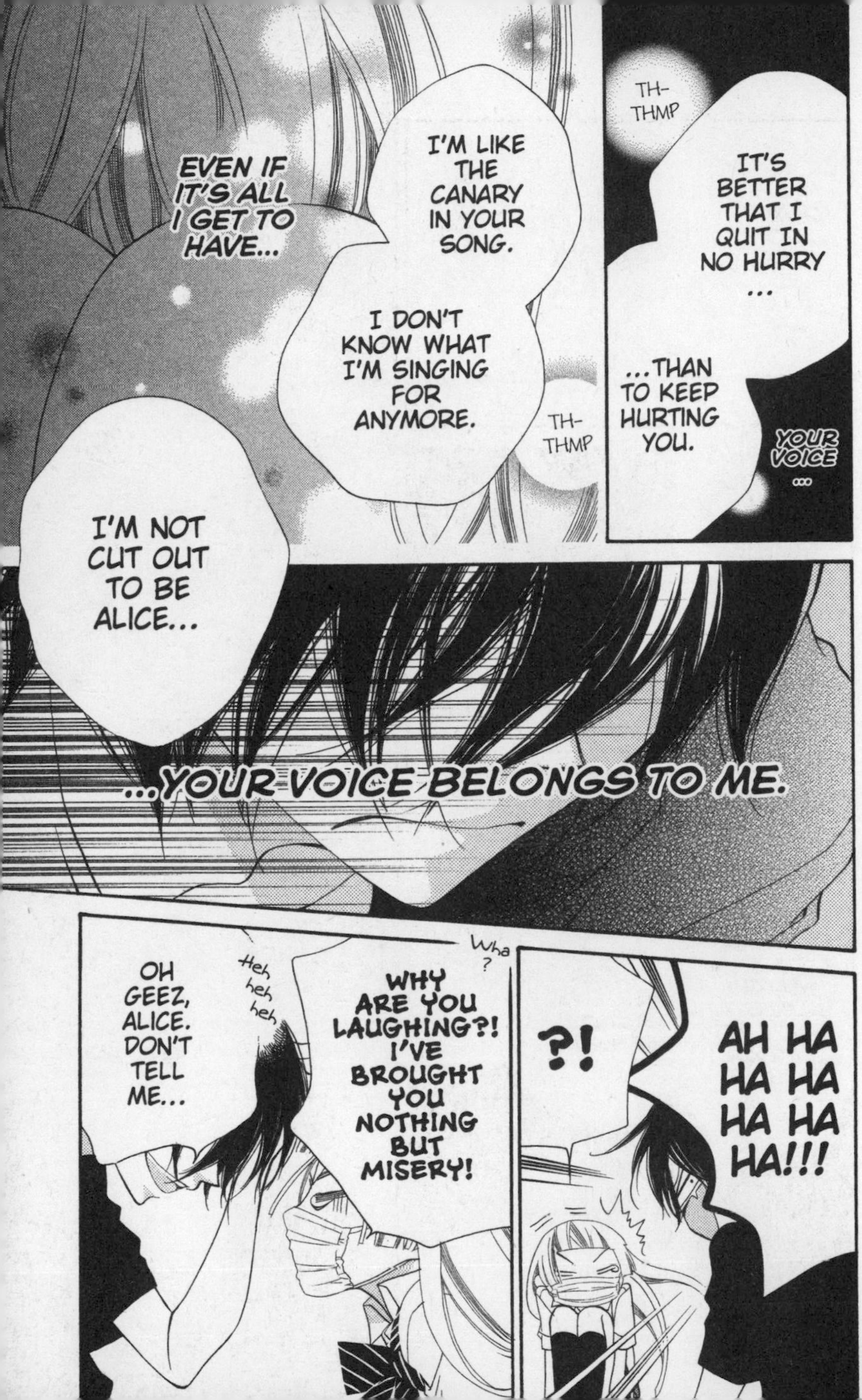

TH-THMP
IT'S BETTER THAT I QUIT IN NO HURRY ...
...THAN TO KEEP HURTING YOU.
YOUR VOICE ...
I'M LIKE THE CANARY IN YOUR SONG.
EVEN IF IT'S ALL I GET TO HAVE...
I DON'T KNOW WHAT I'M SINGING FOR ANYMORE.
TH-THMP
I'M NOT CUT OUT TO BE ALICE...
...YOUR VOICE BELONGS TO ME.
?!
AH HA HA HA HA HA HA!!!
Wha ?
WHY ARE YOU LAUGHING?! I'VE BROUGHT YOU NOTHING BUT MISERY!
Heh heh heh
OH GEEZ, ALICE. DON'T TELL ME...

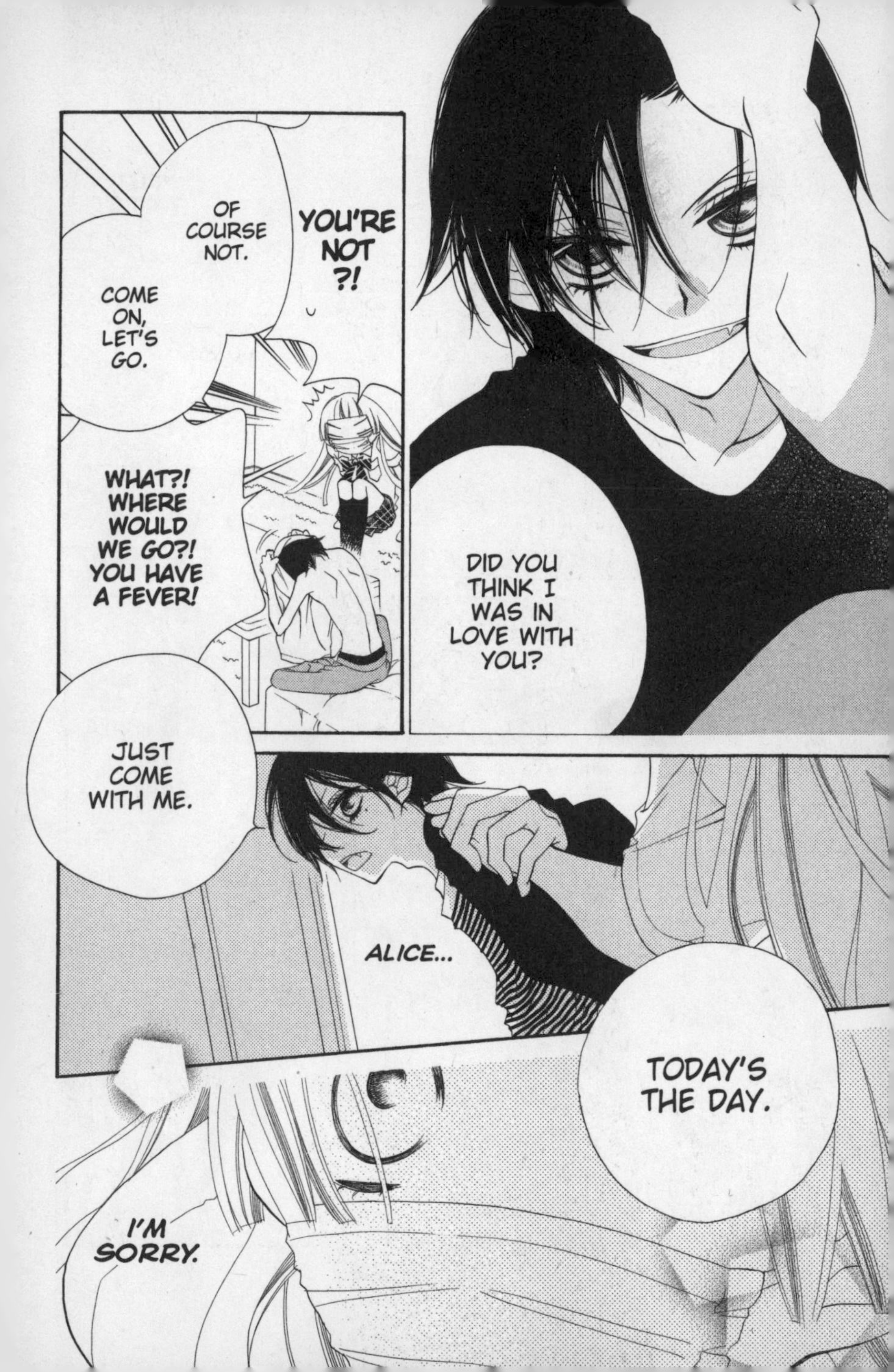
DID YOU THINK I WAS IN LOVE WITH YOU?
YOU'RE NOT?!
OF COURSE NOT.
COME ON, LET'S GO.
WHAT?! WHERE WOULD WE GO?! YOU HAVE A FEVER!
JUST COME WITH ME.
ALICE...
TODAY'S THE DAY.
I'M SORRY.

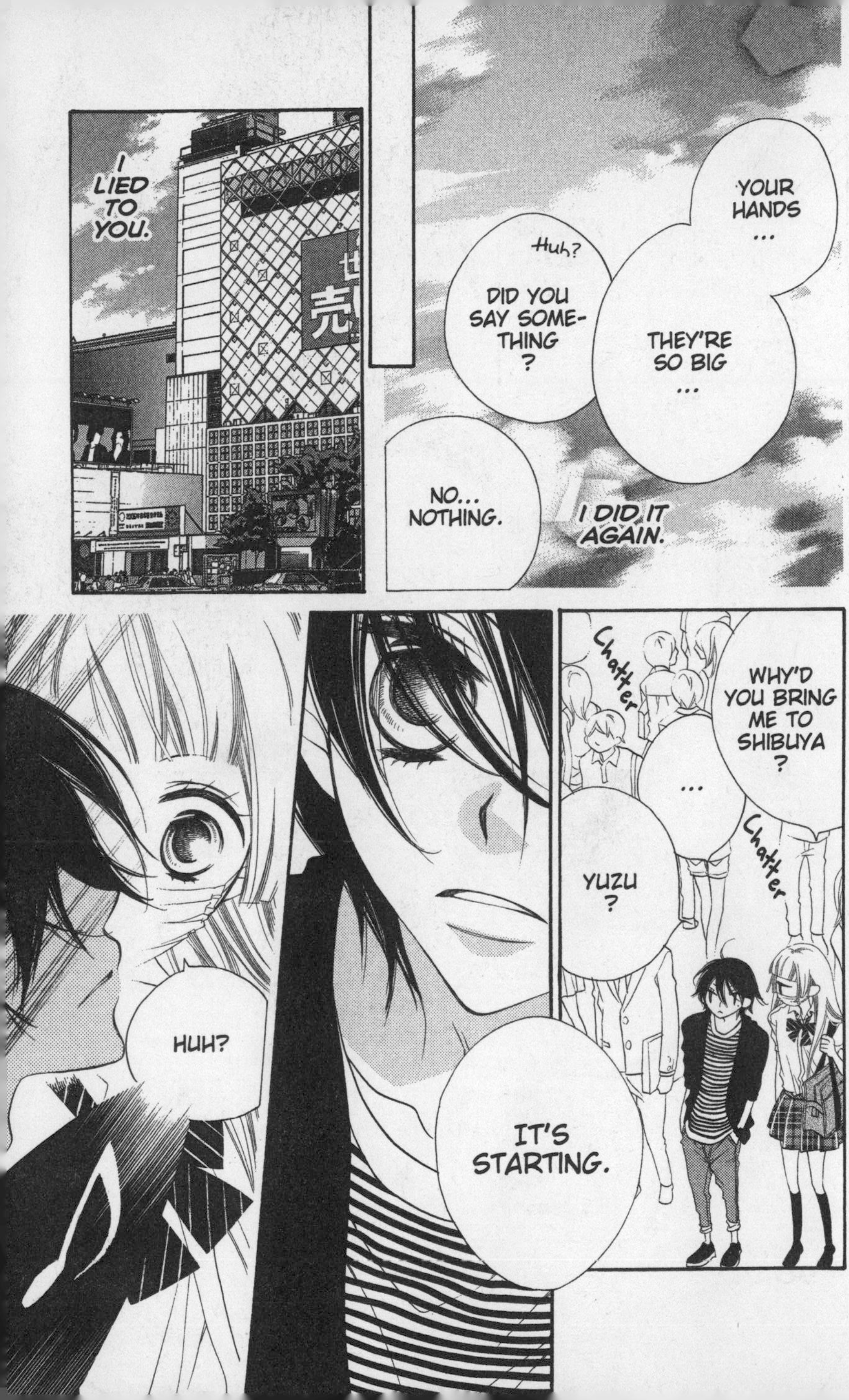

YOUR HANDS ...
THEY'RE SO BIG ...
Huh?
DID YOU SAY SOMETHING?
NO... NOTHING.
I DID IT AGAIN.
I LIED TO YOU.
Chatter
WHY'D YOU BRING ME TO SHIBUYA?
...
Chatter
YUZU?
IT'S STARTING.
HUH?

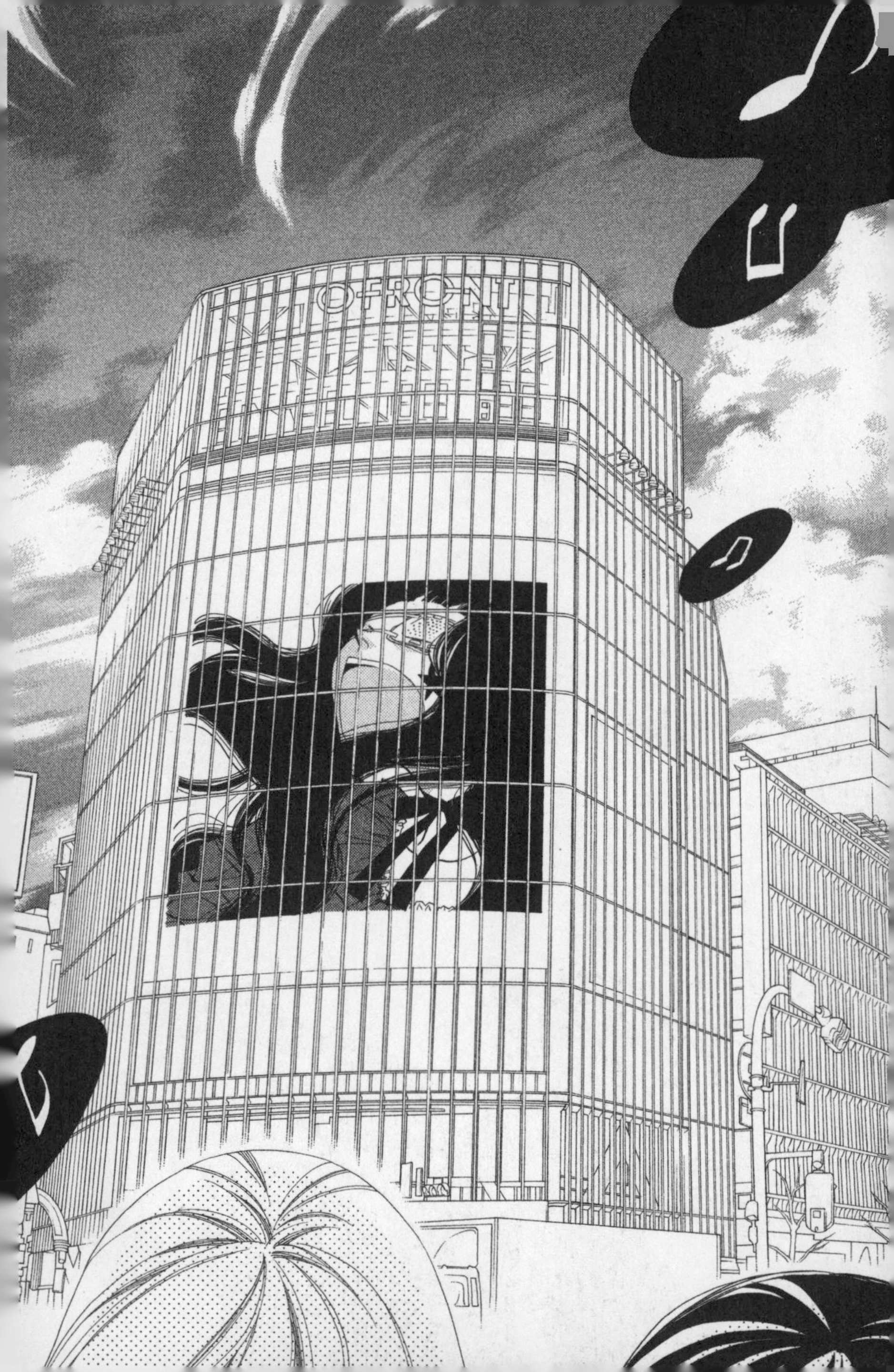
QFRONT

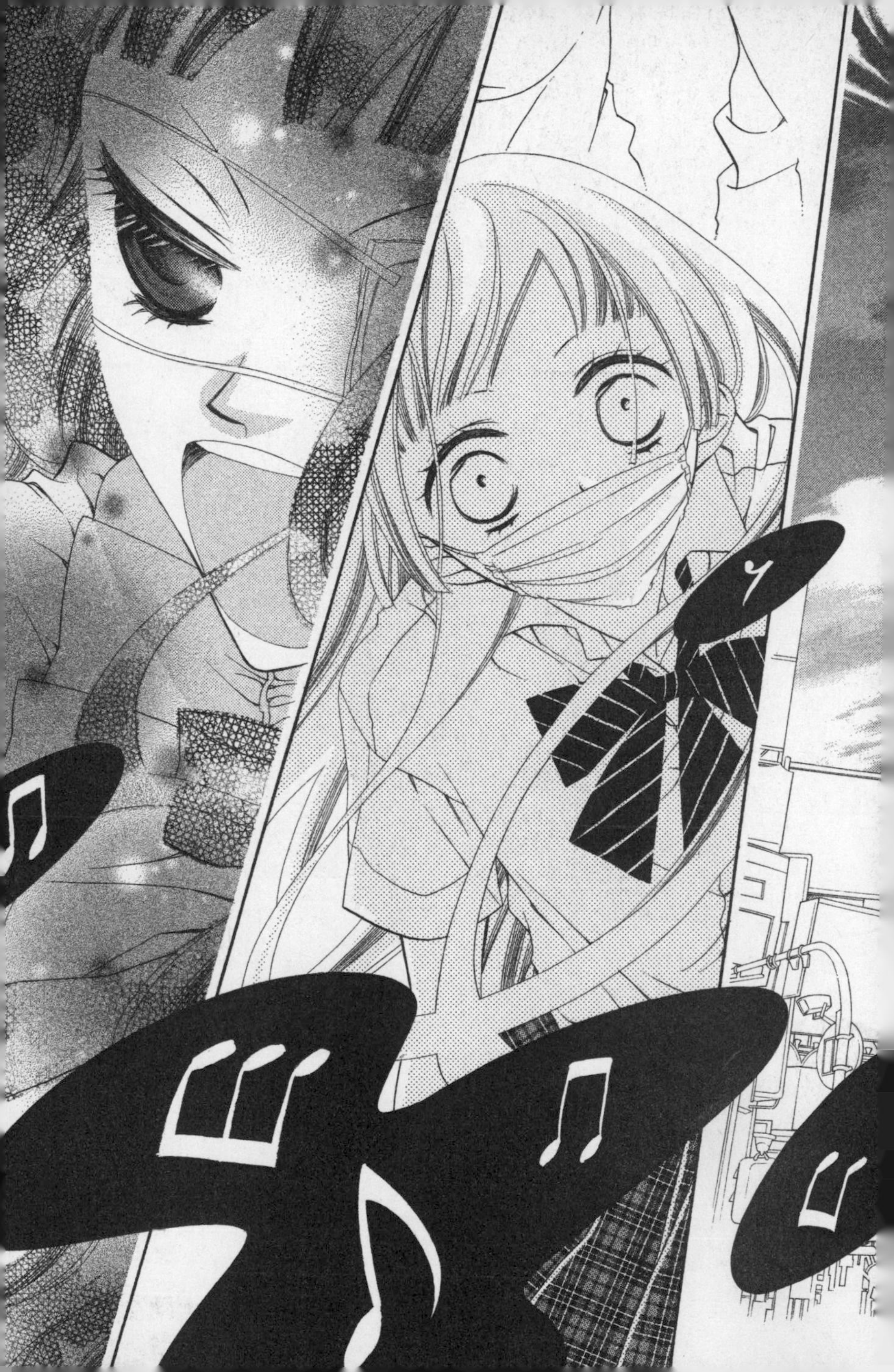

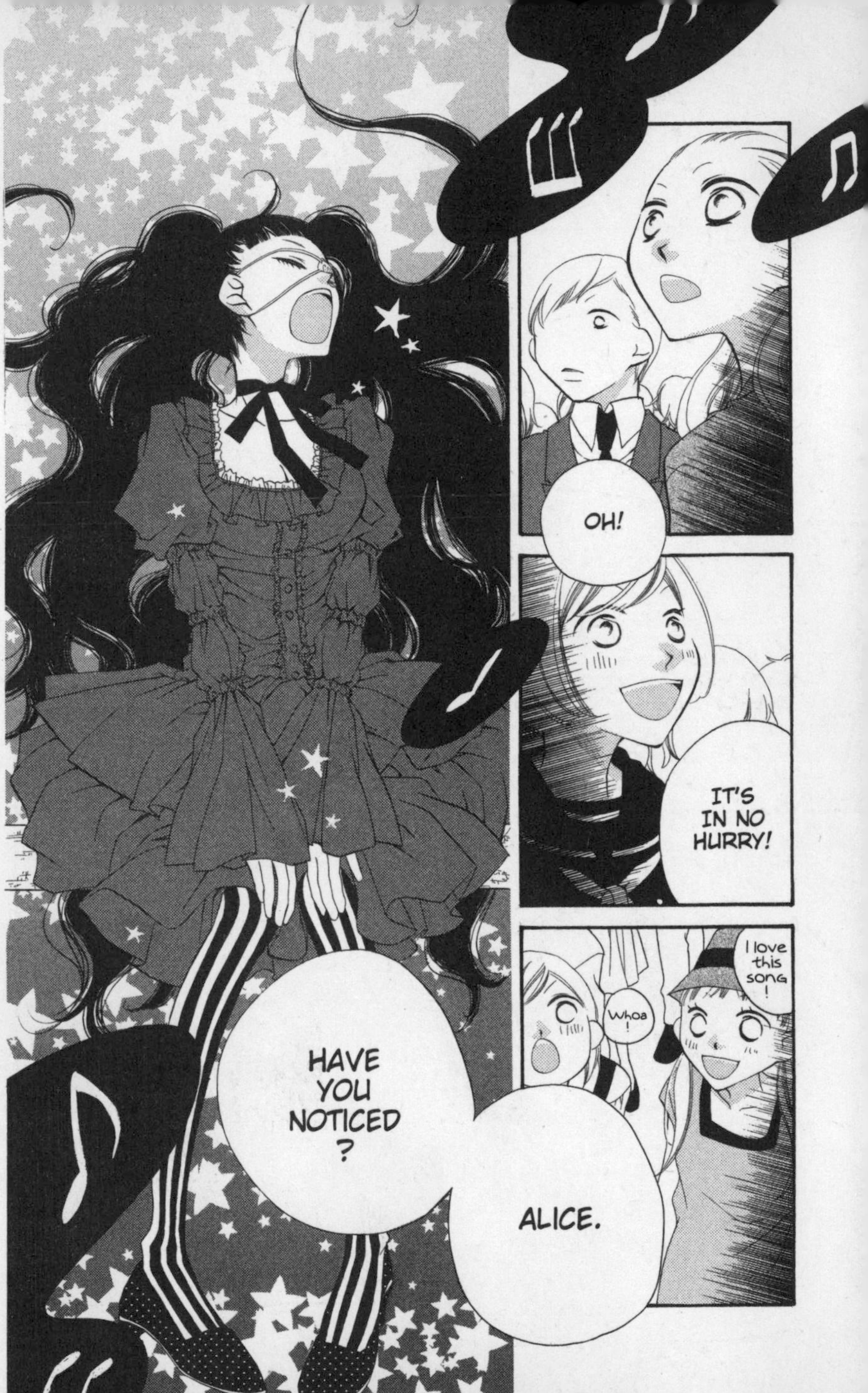
OH!
IT'S IN NO HURRY!
I love this song!
Whoa!
HAVE YOU NOTICED?
ALICE.

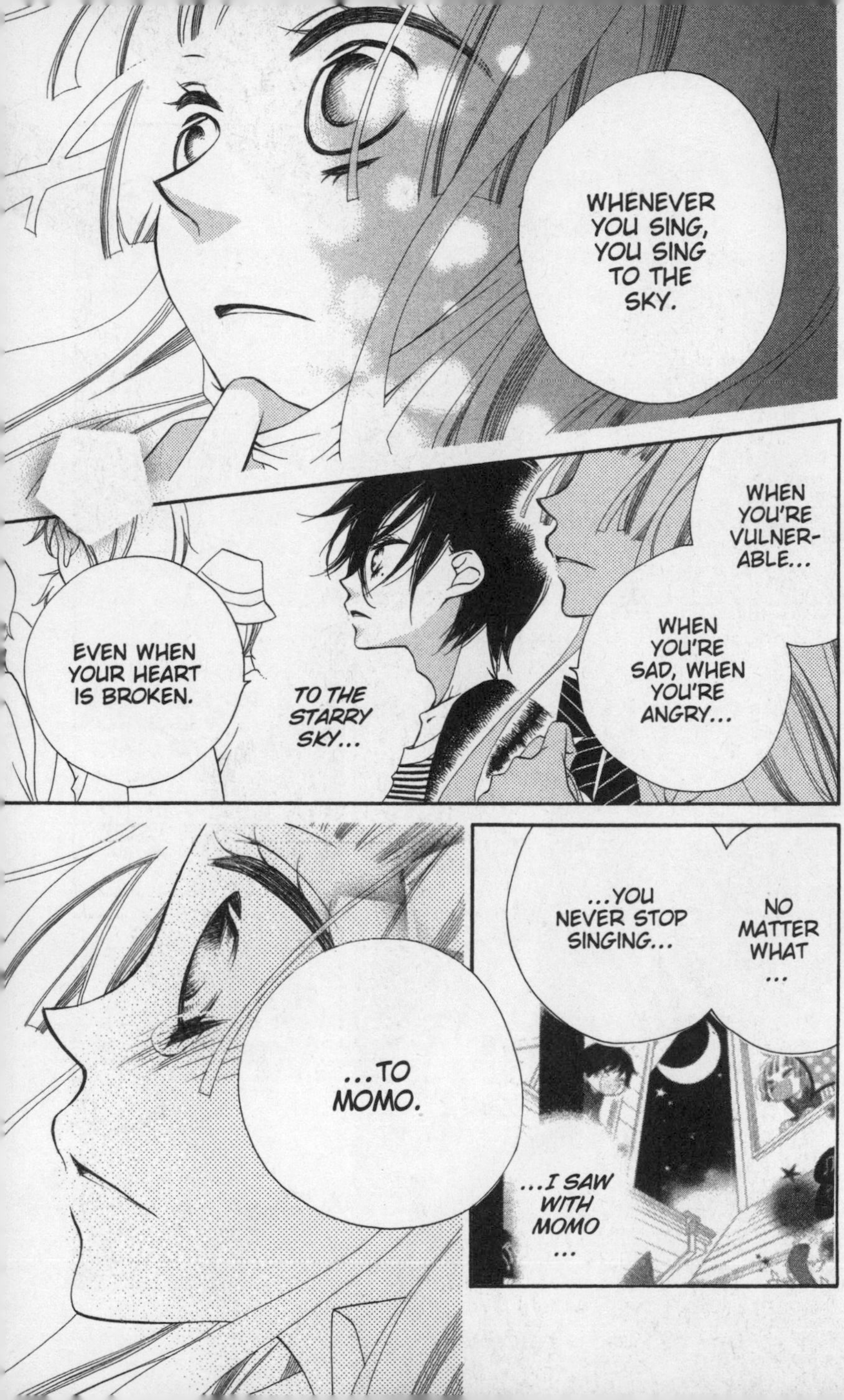
WHENEVER YOU SING, YOU SING TO THE SKY.
WHEN YOU'RE VULNER-ABLE...
WHEN YOU'RE SAD, WHEN YOU'RE ANGRY...
TO THE STARRY SKY...
EVEN WHEN YOUR HEART IS BROKEN.
NO MATTER WHAT ...
...YOU NEVER STOP SINGING...
...I SAW WITH MOMO ...
...TO MOMO.

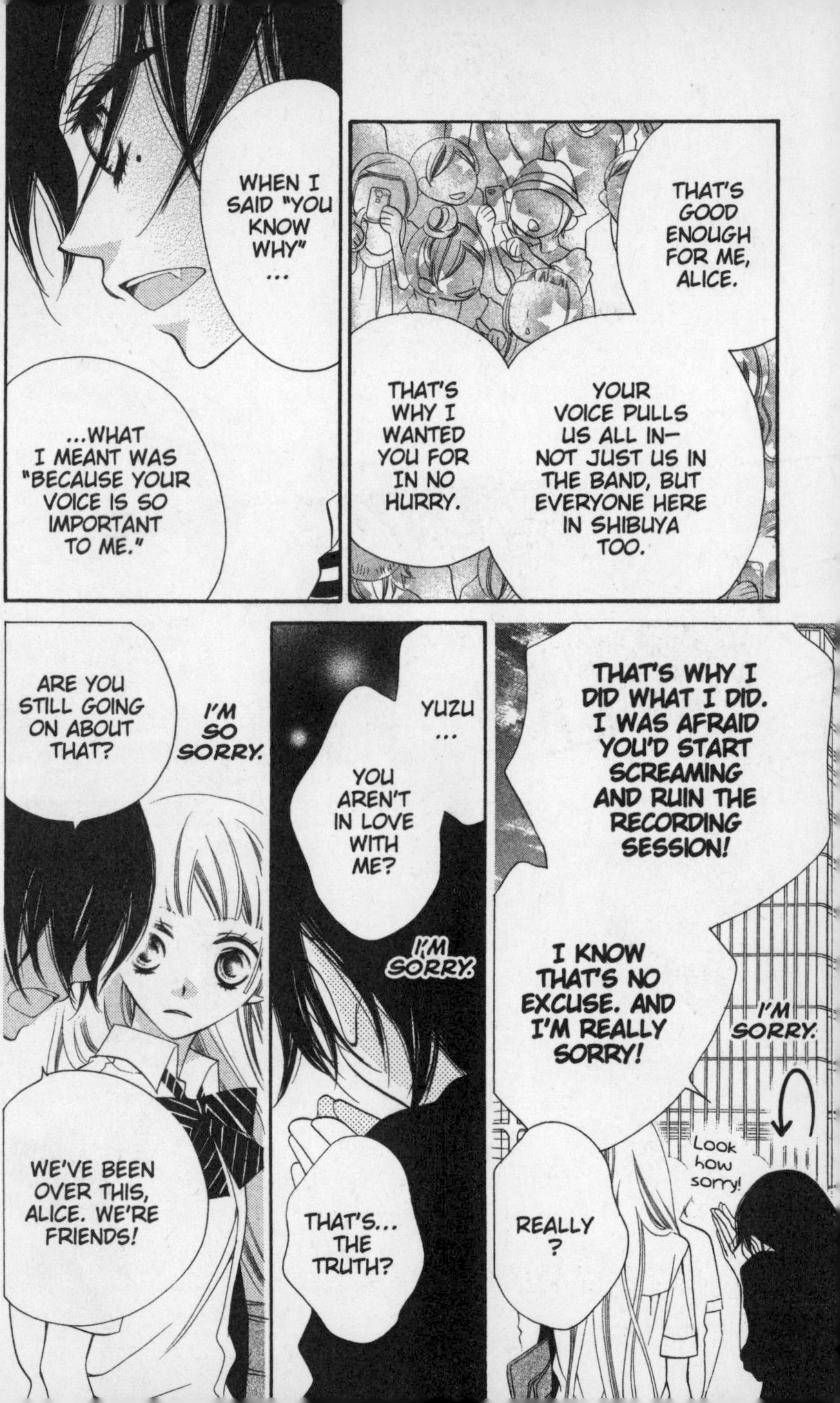
THAT'S GOOD ENOUGH FOR ME, ALICE.
YOUR VOICE PULLS US ALL IN— NOT JUST US IN THE BAND, BUT EVERYONE HERE IN SHIBUYA TOO.
THAT'S WHY I WANTED YOU FOR IN NO HURRY.
WHEN I SAID "YOU KNOW WHY" ...
...WHAT I MEANT WAS "BECAUSE YOUR VOICE IS SO IMPORTANT TO ME."
THAT'S WHY I DID WHAT I DID. I WAS AFRAID YOU'D START SCREAMING AND RUIN THE RECORDING SESSION!
I KNOW THAT'S NO EXCUSE. AND I'M REALLY SORRY!
I'M SORRY.
Look how sorry!
REALLY ?
YUZU ...
YOU AREN'T IN LOVE WITH ME?
I'M SORRY.
THAT'S... THE TRUTH?
ARE YOU STILL GOING ON ABOUT THAT?
I'M SO SORRY.
WE'VE BEEN OVER THIS, ALICE. WE'RE FRIENDS!

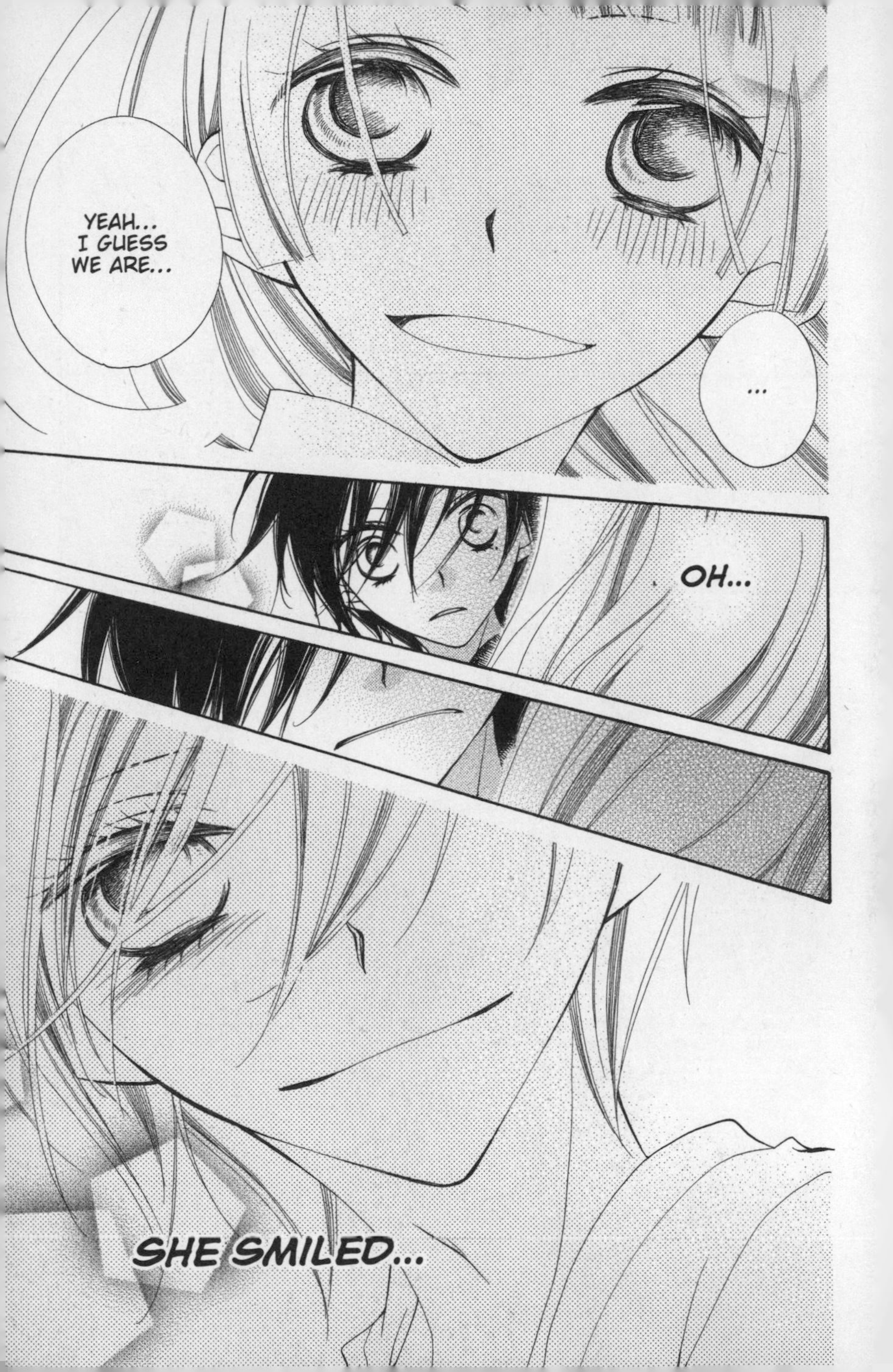
YEAH... I GUESS WE ARE...
...
OH...
SHE SMILED...

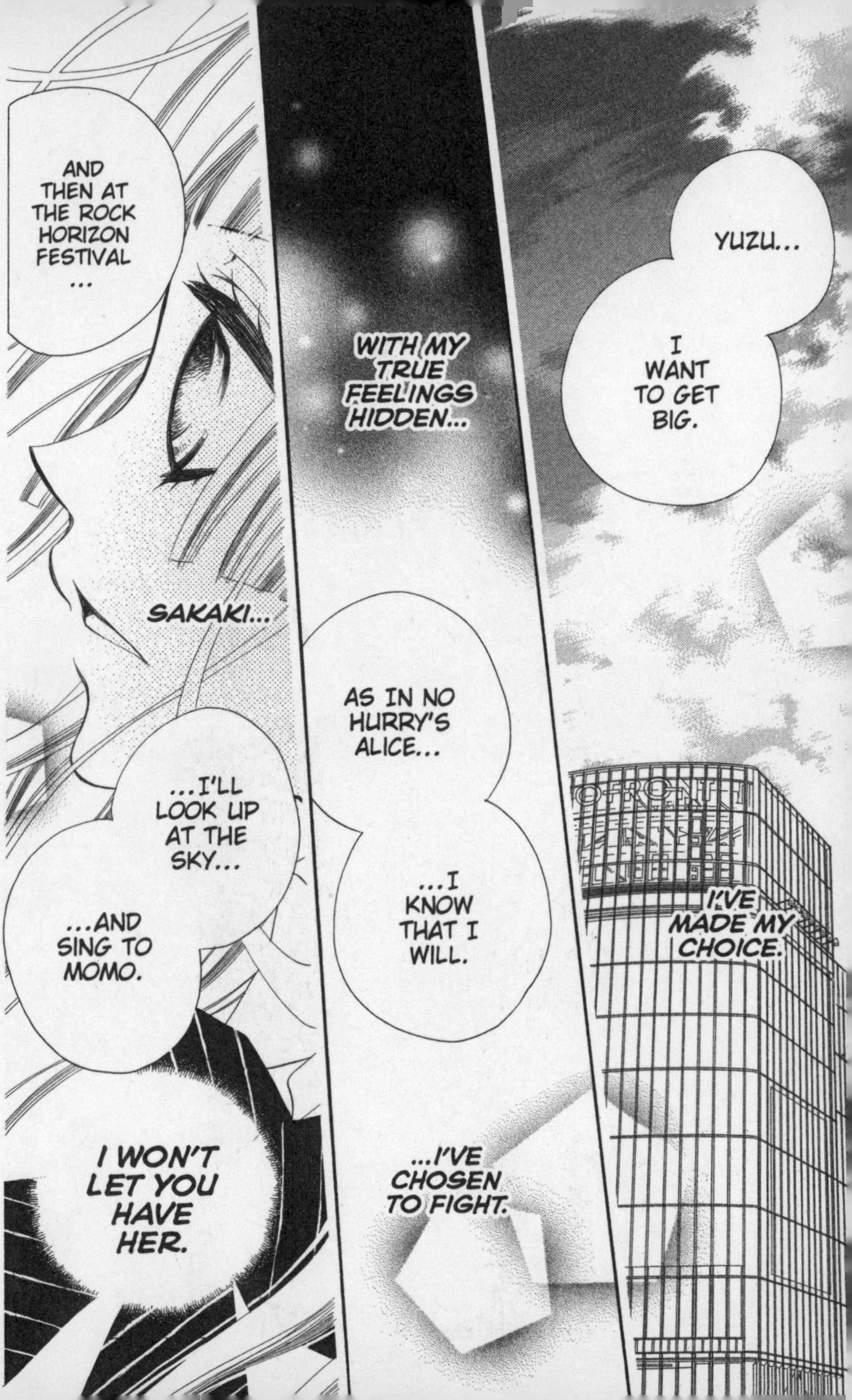
YUZU...
I WANT TO GET BIG.
I'VE MADE MY CHOICE.
WITH MY TRUE FEELINGS HIDDEN...
AS IN NO HURRY'S ALICE...
...I KNOW THAT I WILL.
...I'VE CHOSEN TO FIGHT.
AND THEN AT THE ROCK HORIZON FESTIVAL ...
SAKAKI...
...I'LL LOOK UP AT THE SKY...
...AND SING TO MOMO.
I WON'T LET YOU HAVE HER.

I WON'T LET YOU LAY ONE FINGER ON MY ALICE.

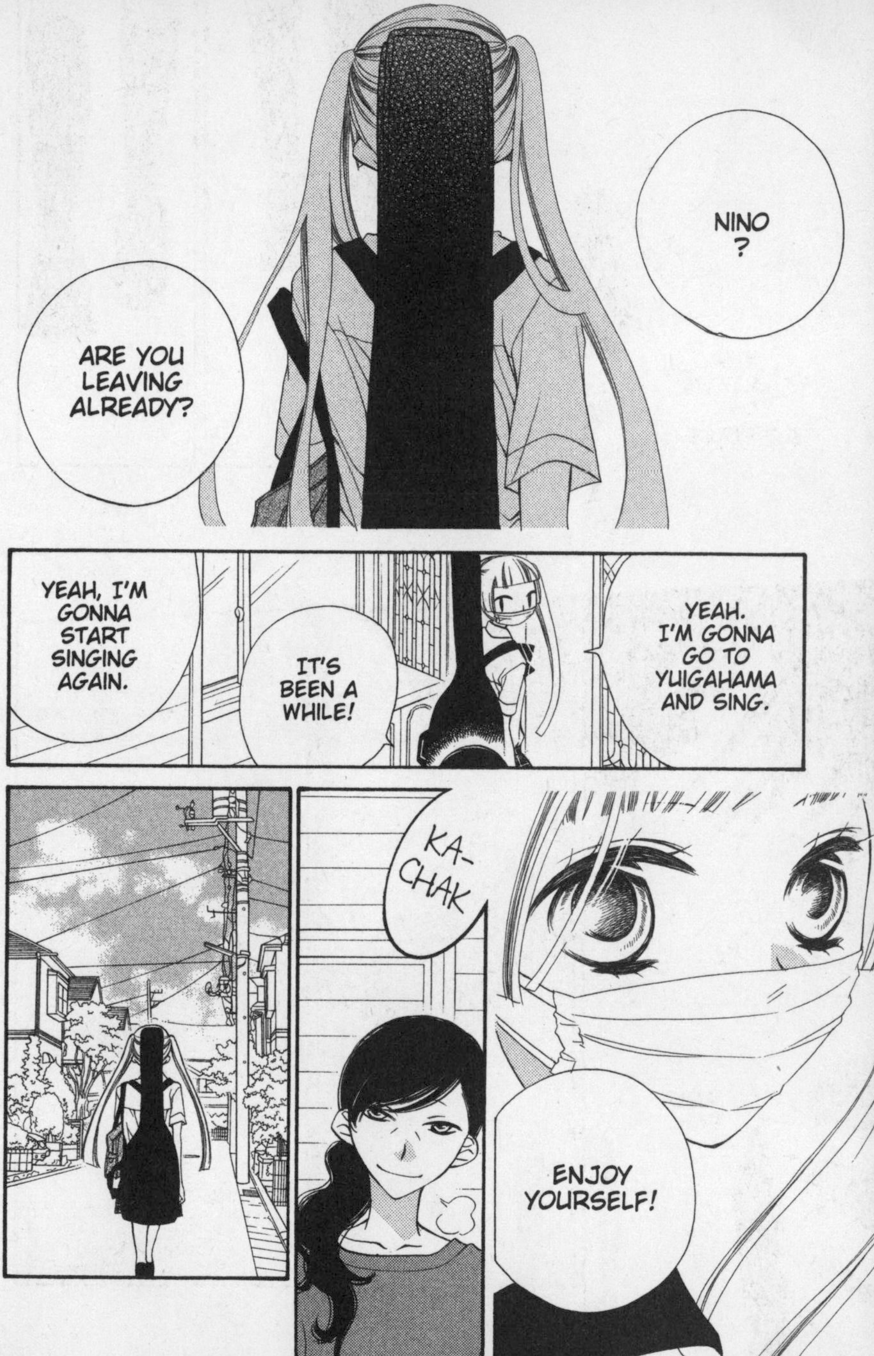
NINO ?
ARE YOU LEAVING ALREADY?
YEAH. I'M GONNA GO TO YUIGAHAMA AND SING.
IT'S BEEN A WHILE!
YEAH, I'M GONNA START SINGING AGAIN.
ENJOY YOURSELF!
KA-CHAK

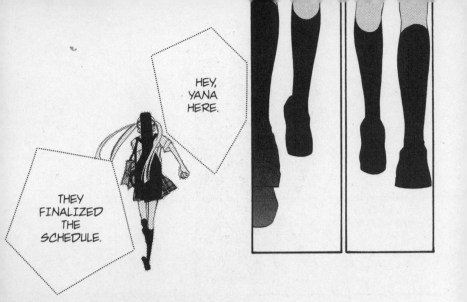

HEY, YANA HERE.

THEY FINALIZED THE SCHEDULE.

WE'RE PLAYING THE SAME DAY AS BLACK KITTY, ON THE SAME STAGE.

I'LL CALL BACK.

KLAT

BEEEEP

AND SO...

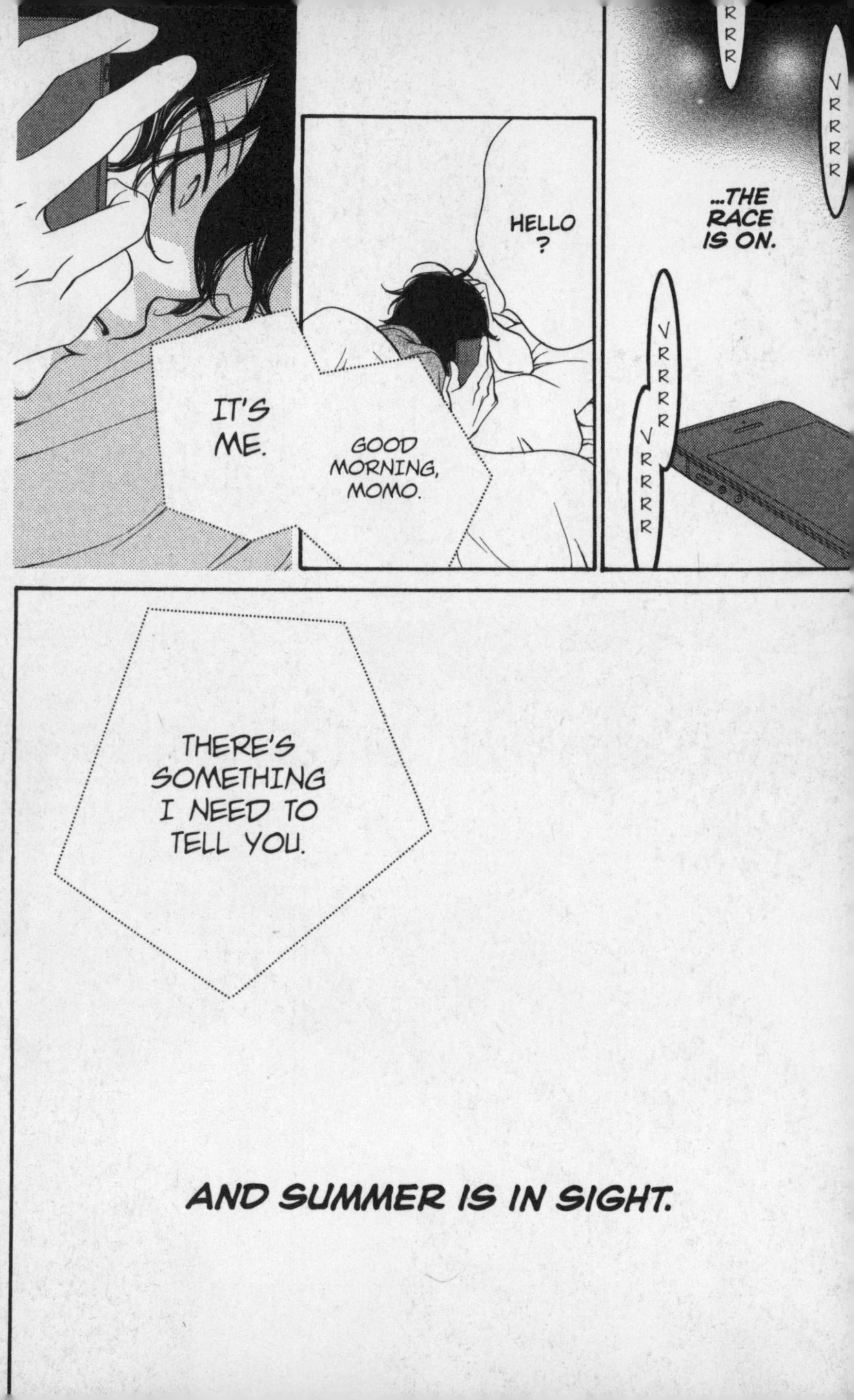
VRRRR
RRR
...THE RACE IS ON.
VRRRR VRRRR
HELLO?
GOOD MORNING, MOMO.
IT'S ME.
THERE'S SOMETHING I NEED TO TELL YOU.
AND SUMMER IS IN SIGHT.

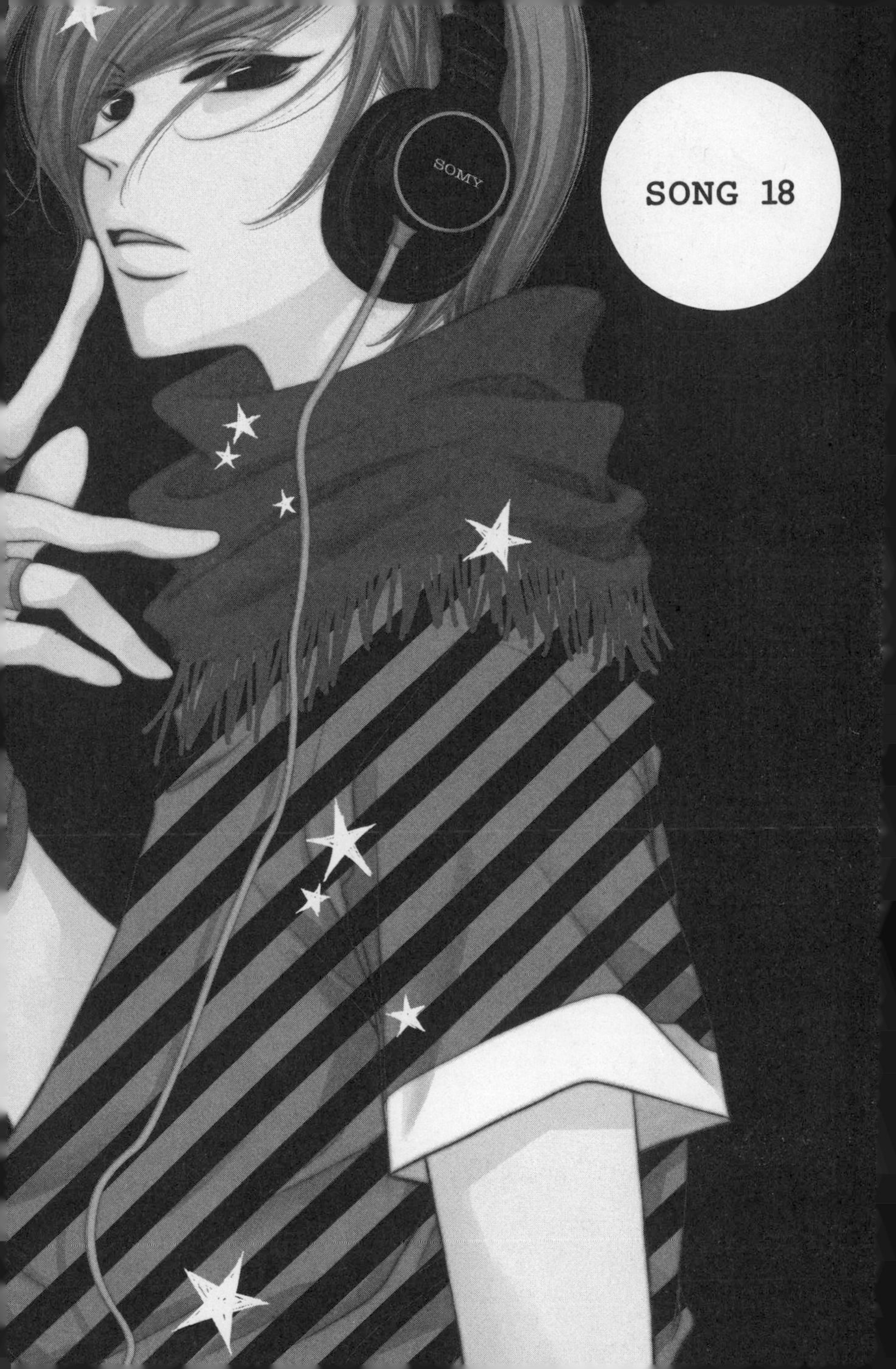
SOMY
SONG 18

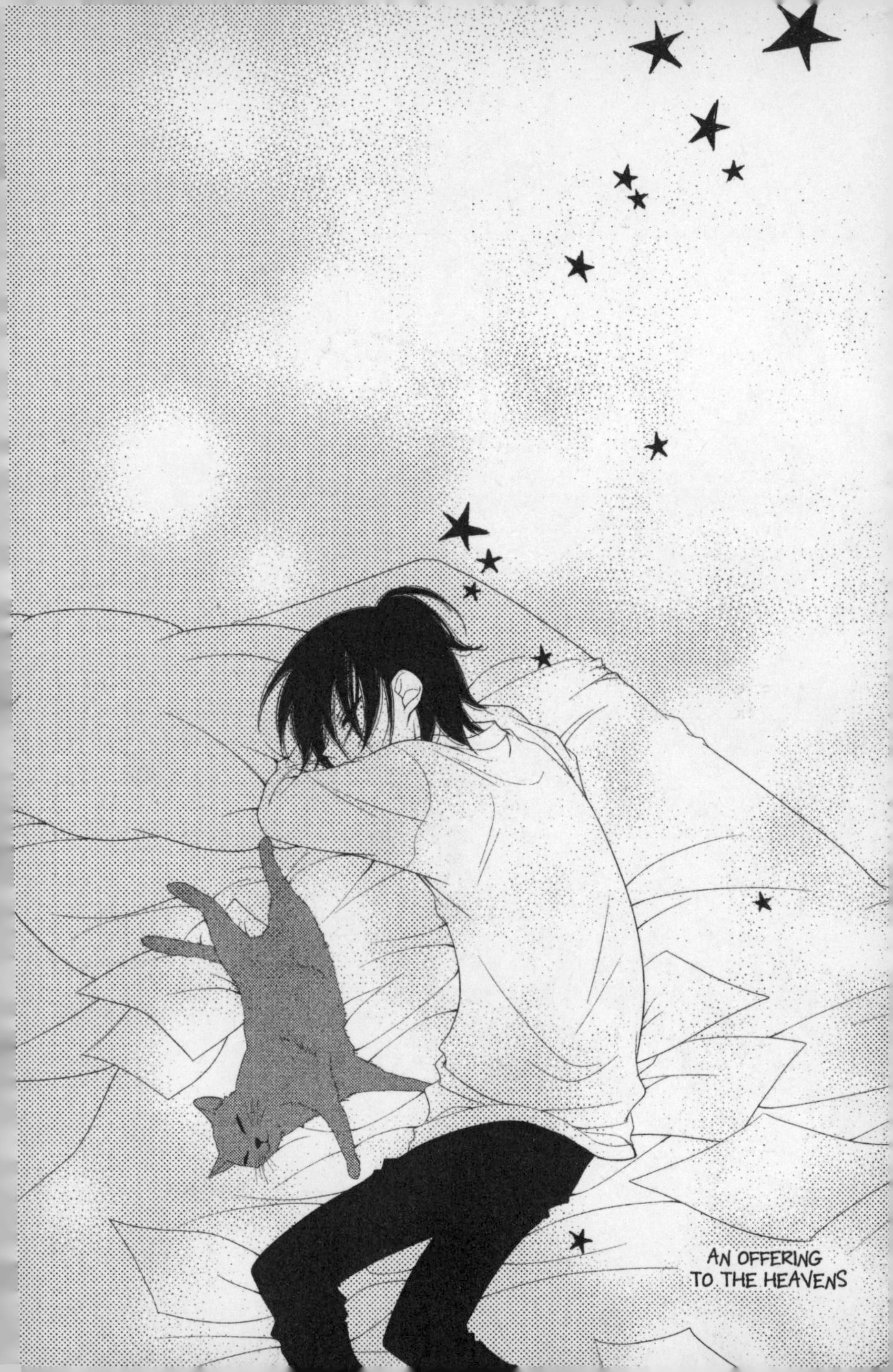
AN OFFERING
TO THE HEAVENS

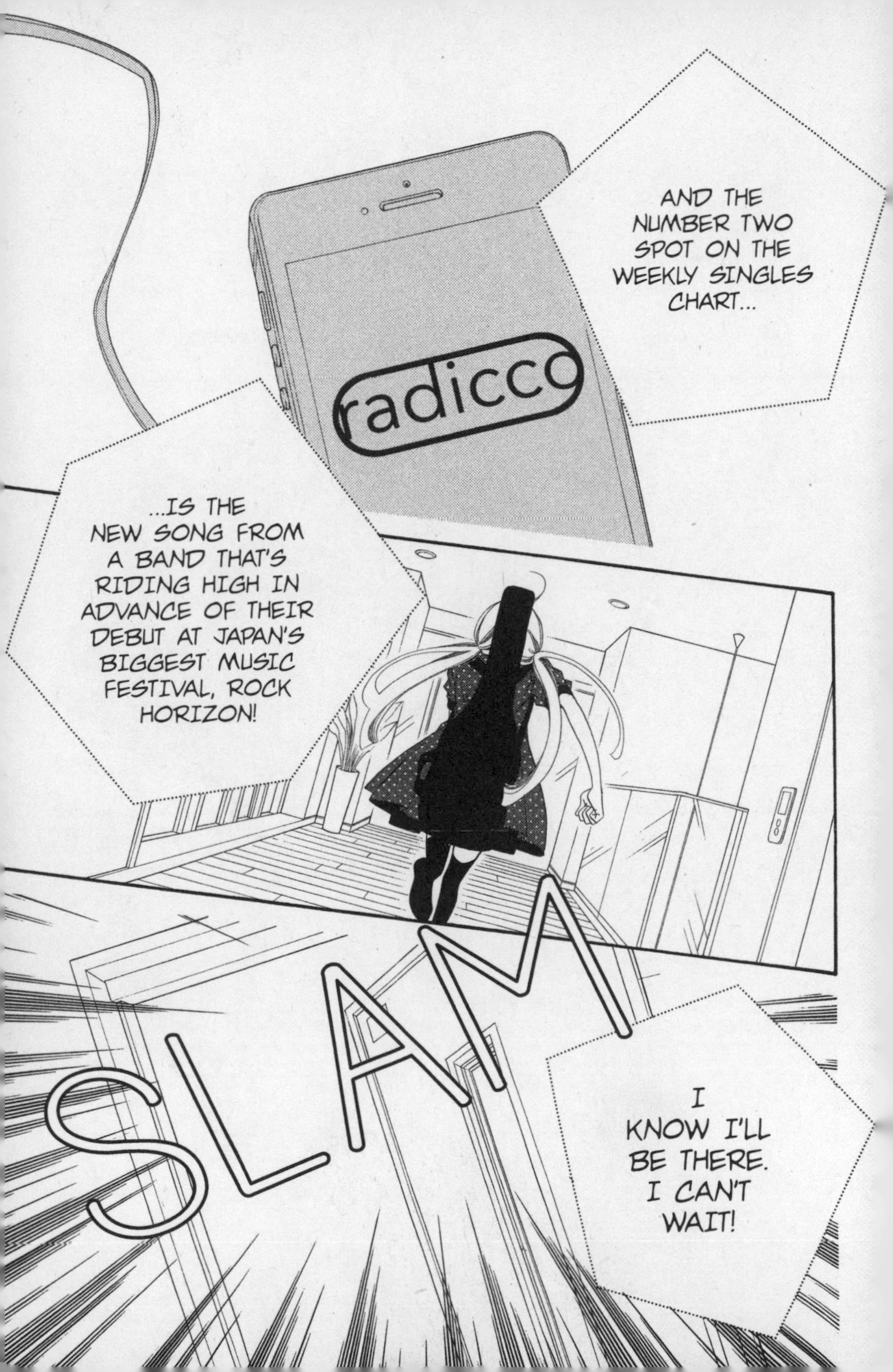
AND THE NUMBER TWO SPOT ON THE WEEKLY SINGLES CHART...
radicco
...IS THE NEW SONG FROM A BAND THAT'S RIDING HIGH IN ADVANCE OF THEIR DEBUT AT JAPAN'S BIGGEST MUSIC FESTIVAL, ROCK HORIZON!
I KNOW I'LL BE THERE. I CAN'T WAIT!
SLAM

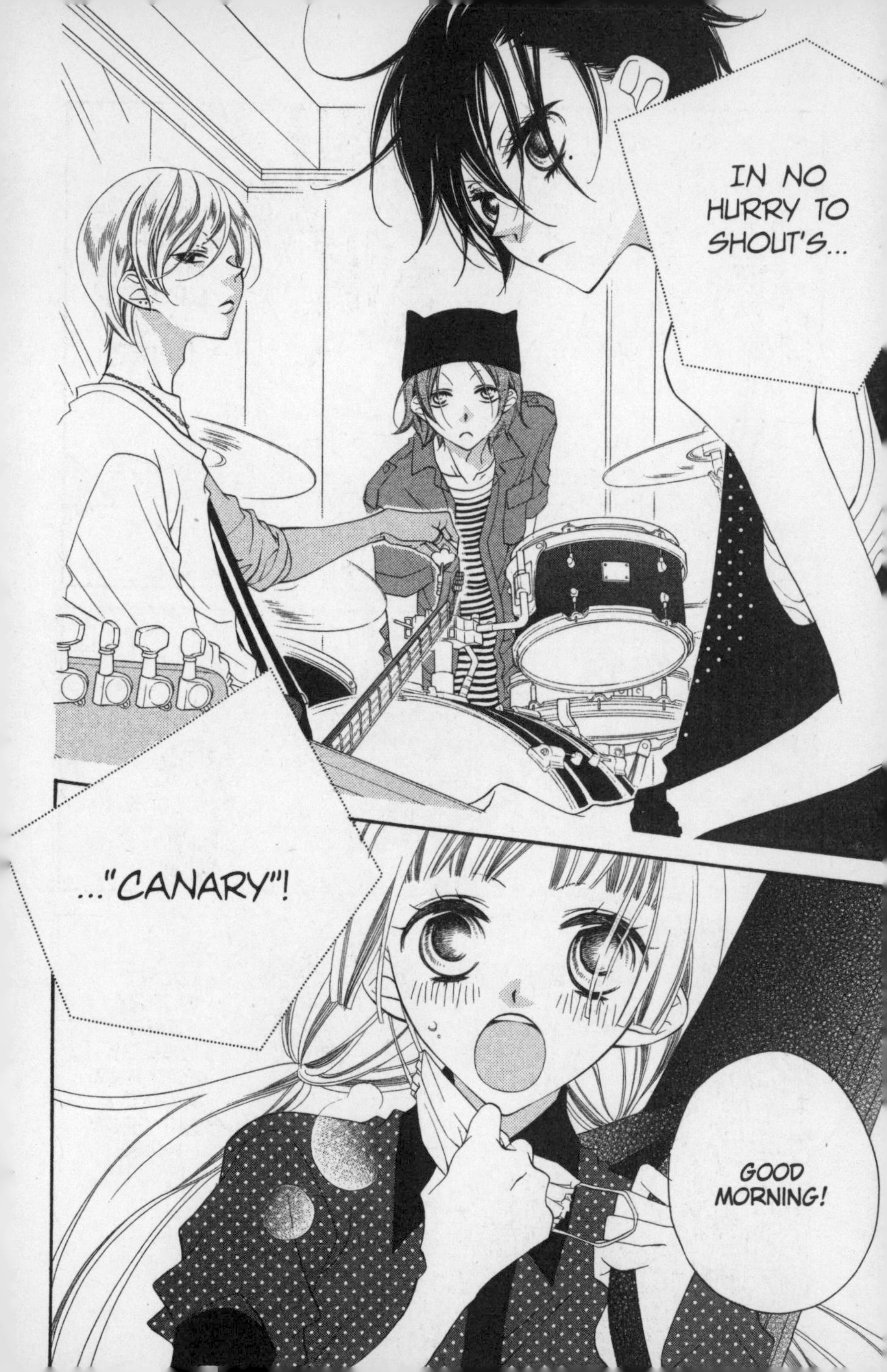
IN NO HURRY TO SHOUT'S...
..."CANARY"!
GOOD MORNING!

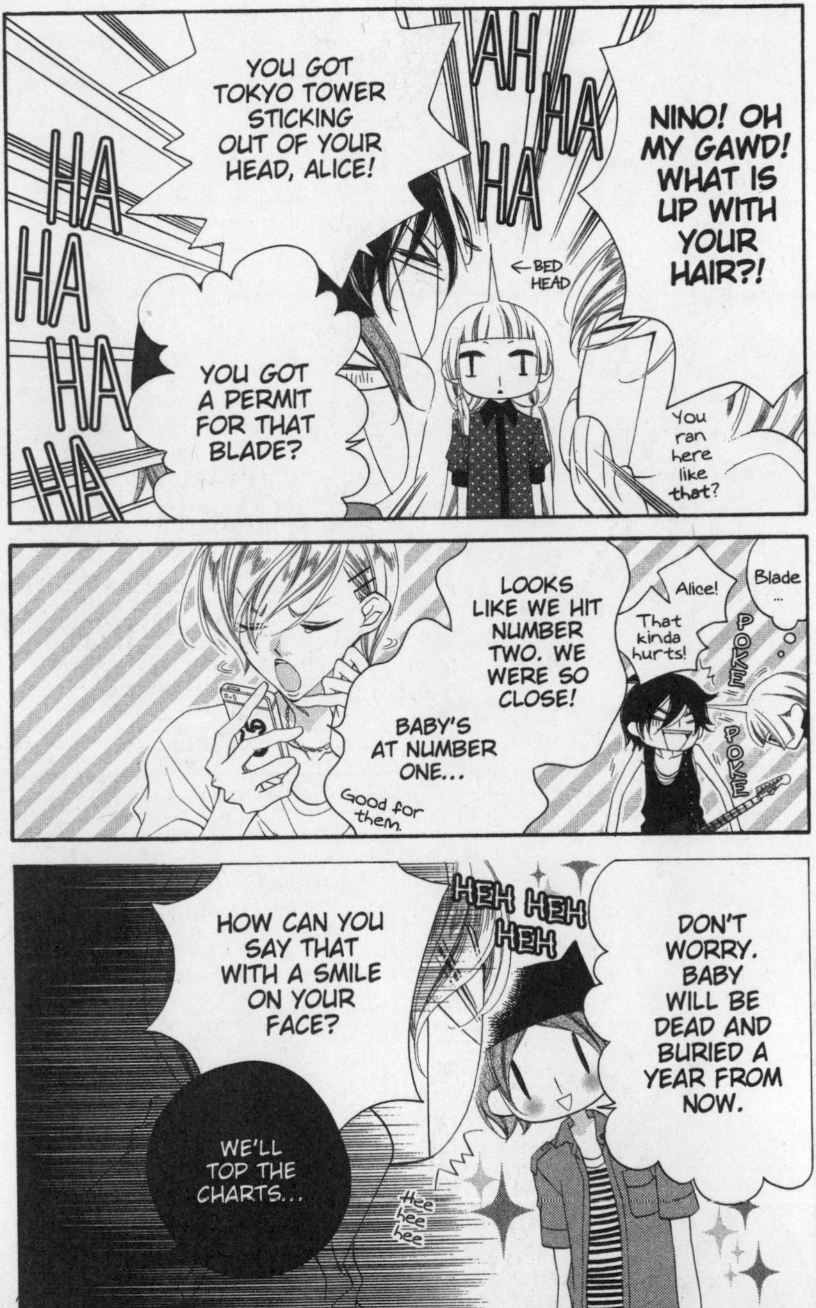
NINO! OH MY GAWD! WHAT IS UP WITH YOUR HAIR?!
You ran here like that?
AH HA HA HA
←BED HEAD
YOU GOT TOKYO TOWER STICKING OUT OF YOUR HEAD, ALICE!
HA HA HA HA HA HA
YOU GOT A PERMIT FOR THAT BLADE?
Blade ...
Alice!
That kinda hurts!
POKE POKE POKE
LOOKS LIKE WE HIT NUMBER TWO. WE WERE SO CLOSE!
BABY'S AT NUMBER ONE...
Good for them.
DON'T WORRY. BABY WILL BE DEAD AND BURIED A YEAR FROM NOW.
HEH HEH HEH
HOW CAN YOU SAY THAT WITH A SMILE ON YOUR FACE?
Hee hee hee
WE'LL TOP THE CHARTS...

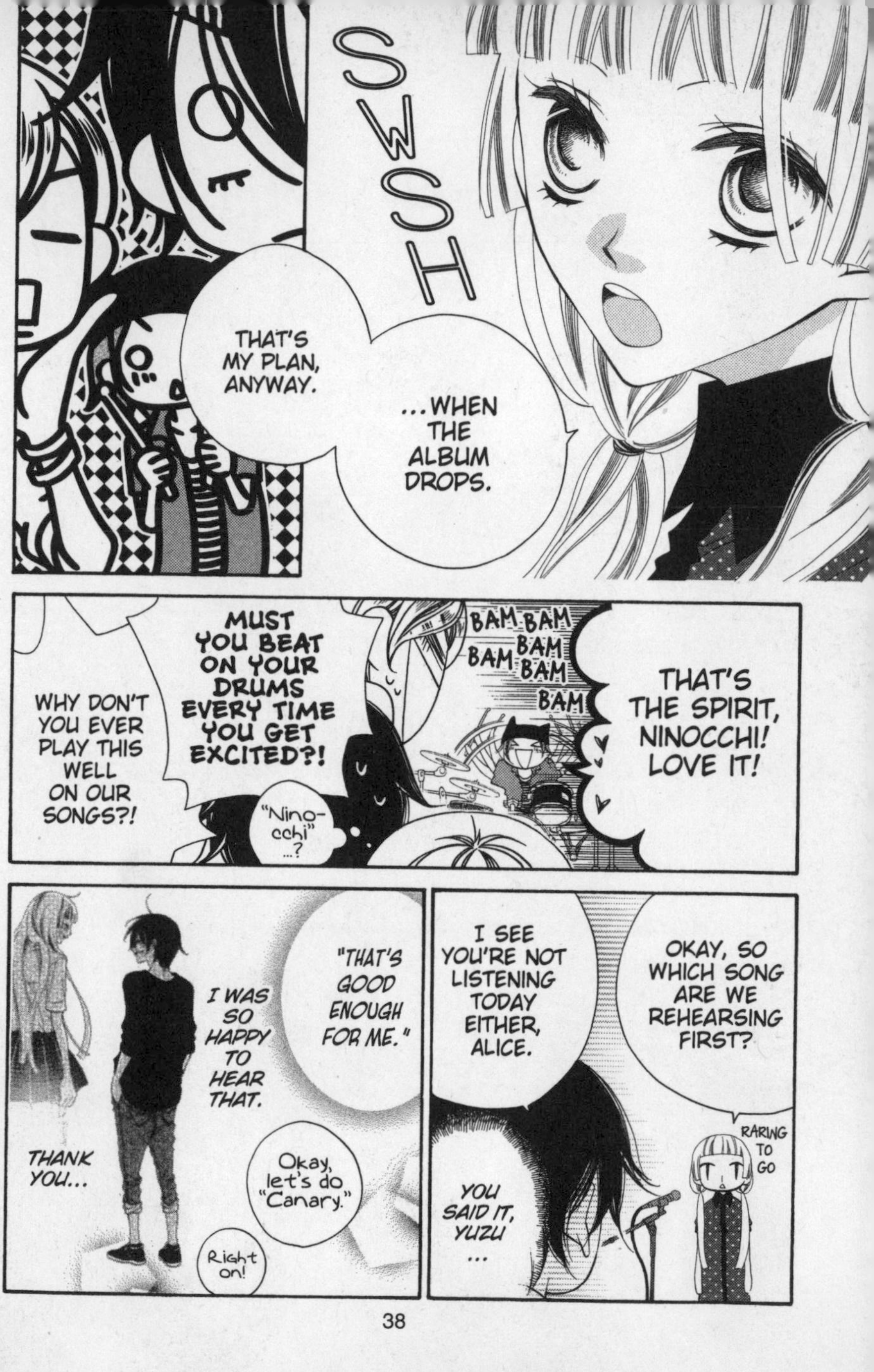
SWSH
...WHEN THE ALBUM DROPS.
THAT'S MY PLAN, ANYWAY.
THAT'S THE SPIRIT, NINOCCHI! LOVE IT!
BAM BAM BAM BAM BAM BAM
"Nino-cchi" ...?
MUST YOU BEAT ON YOUR DRUMS EVERY TIME YOU GET EXCITED?!
WHY DON'T YOU EVER PLAY THIS WELL ON OUR SONGS?!
OKAY, SO WHICH SONG ARE WE REHEARSING FIRST?
RARING TO GO
I SEE YOU'RE NOT LISTENING TODAY EITHER, ALICE.
YOU SAID IT, YUZU ...
"THAT'S GOOD ENOUGH FOR ME."
I WAS SO HAPPY TO HEAR THAT.
Okay, let's do "Canary."
Right on!
THANK YOU...

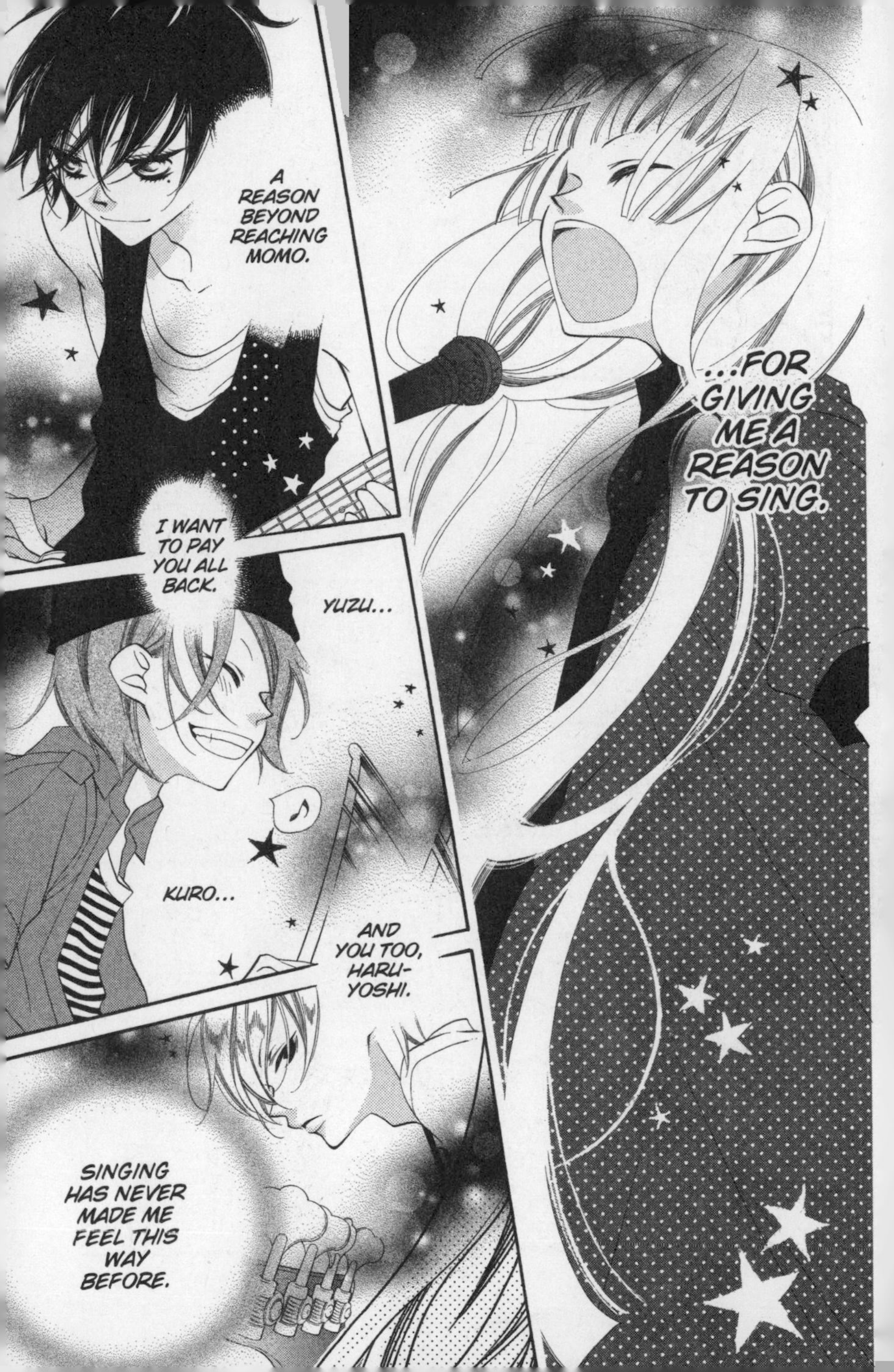
...FOR GIVING ME A REASON TO SING.
A REASON BEYOND REACHING MOMO.
I WANT TO PAY YOU ALL BACK.
YUZU...
KURO...
AND YOU TOO, HARU-YOSHI.
SINGING HAS NEVER MADE ME FEEL THIS WAY BEFORE.

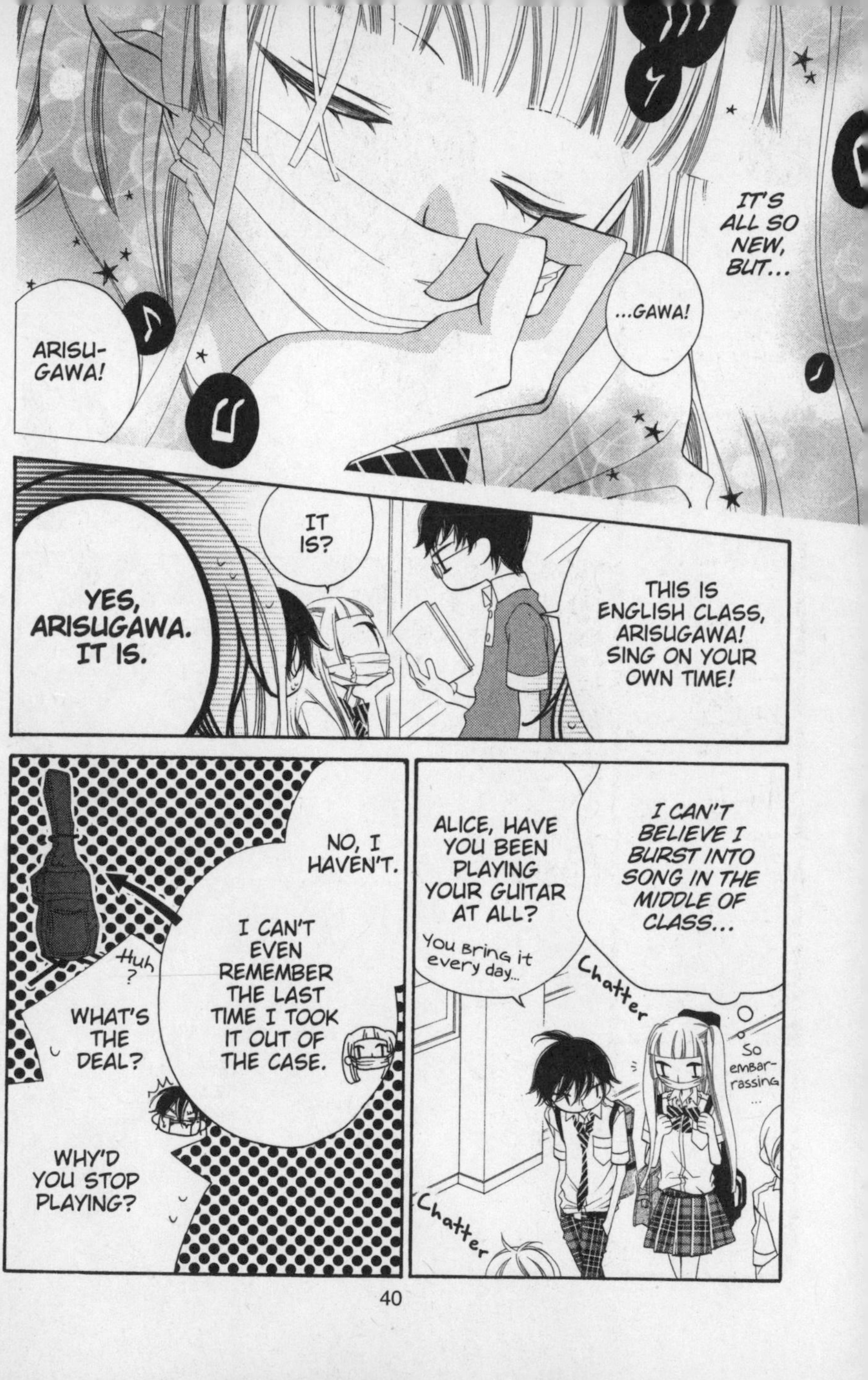
IT'S ALL SO NEW, BUT...
...GAWA!
ARISU-GAWA!
THIS IS ENGLISH CLASS, ARISUGAWA! SING ON YOUR OWN TIME!
IT IS?
YES, ARISUGAWA. IT IS.
I CAN'T BELIEVE I BURST INTO SONG IN THE MIDDLE OF CLASS...
So embar-rassing ...
ALICE, HAVE YOU BEEN PLAYING YOUR GUITAR AT ALL?
You bring it every day...
Chatter
Chatter
NO, I HAVEN'T.
I CAN'T EVEN REMEMBER THE LAST TIME I TOOK IT OUT OF THE CASE.
Huh?
WHAT'S THE DEAL?
WHY'D YOU STOP PLAYING?

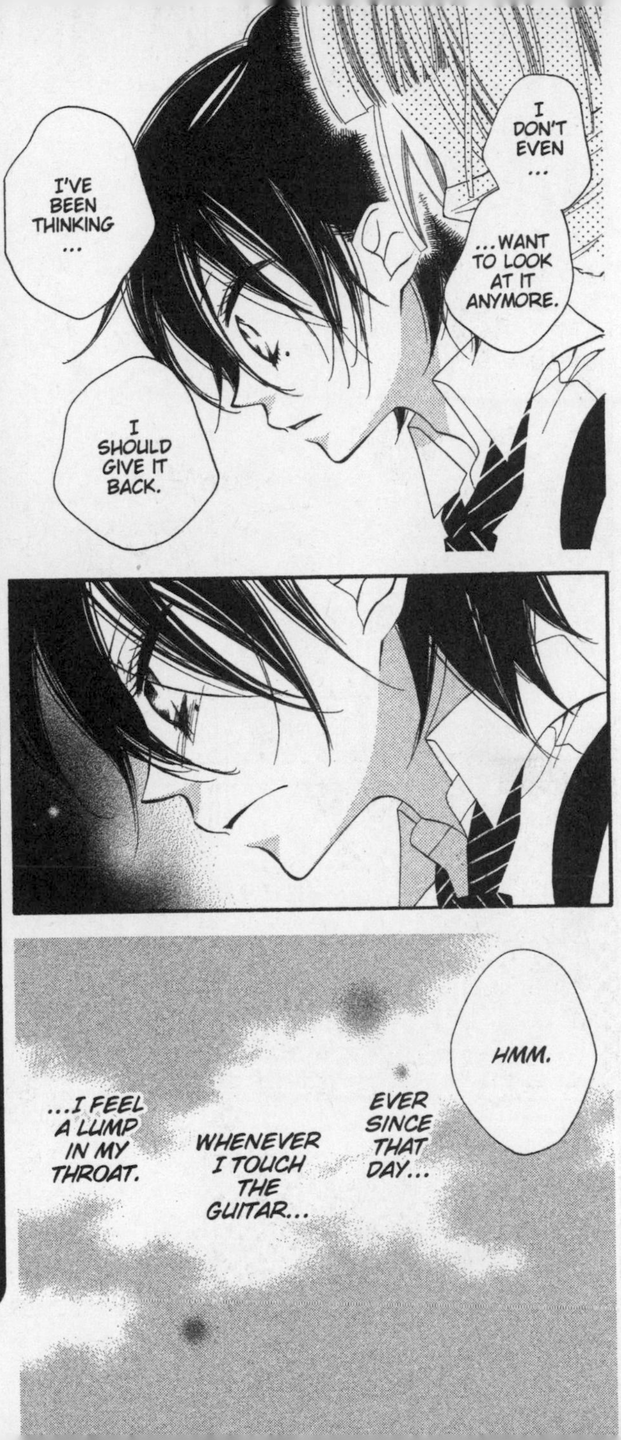
I DON'T EVEN ...
...WANT TO LOOK AT IT ANYMORE.
I'VE BEEN THINKING ...
I SHOULD GIVE IT BACK.
HMM.
EVER SINCE THAT DAY...
WHENEVER I TOUCH THE GUITAR...
...I FEEL A LUMP IN MY THROAT.

2

With the Rock Horizon summer festival playing a part in this story, I was desperate to get my hands on some reference photos of rock festivals.

Thankfully, my editor was able to arrange for us to attend Rock in Japan 2014!!

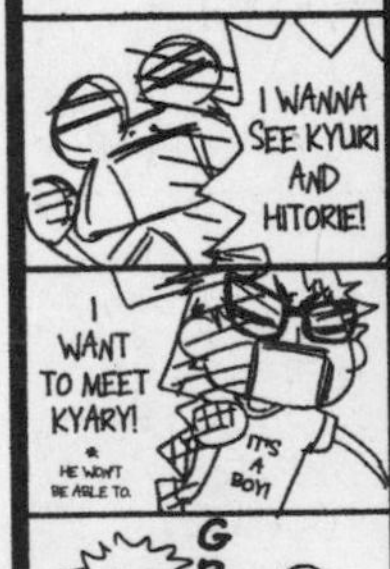
I WANNA SEE KYURI AND HITORIE!
I WANT TO MEET KYARY!
* HE WON'T BE ABLE TO.
IT'S A BOY!
GRIN

And so, with impressively similar goals, we set out to Hitachinaka in Ibaraki Prefecture on August 9.

(TO BE CONTINUED!)

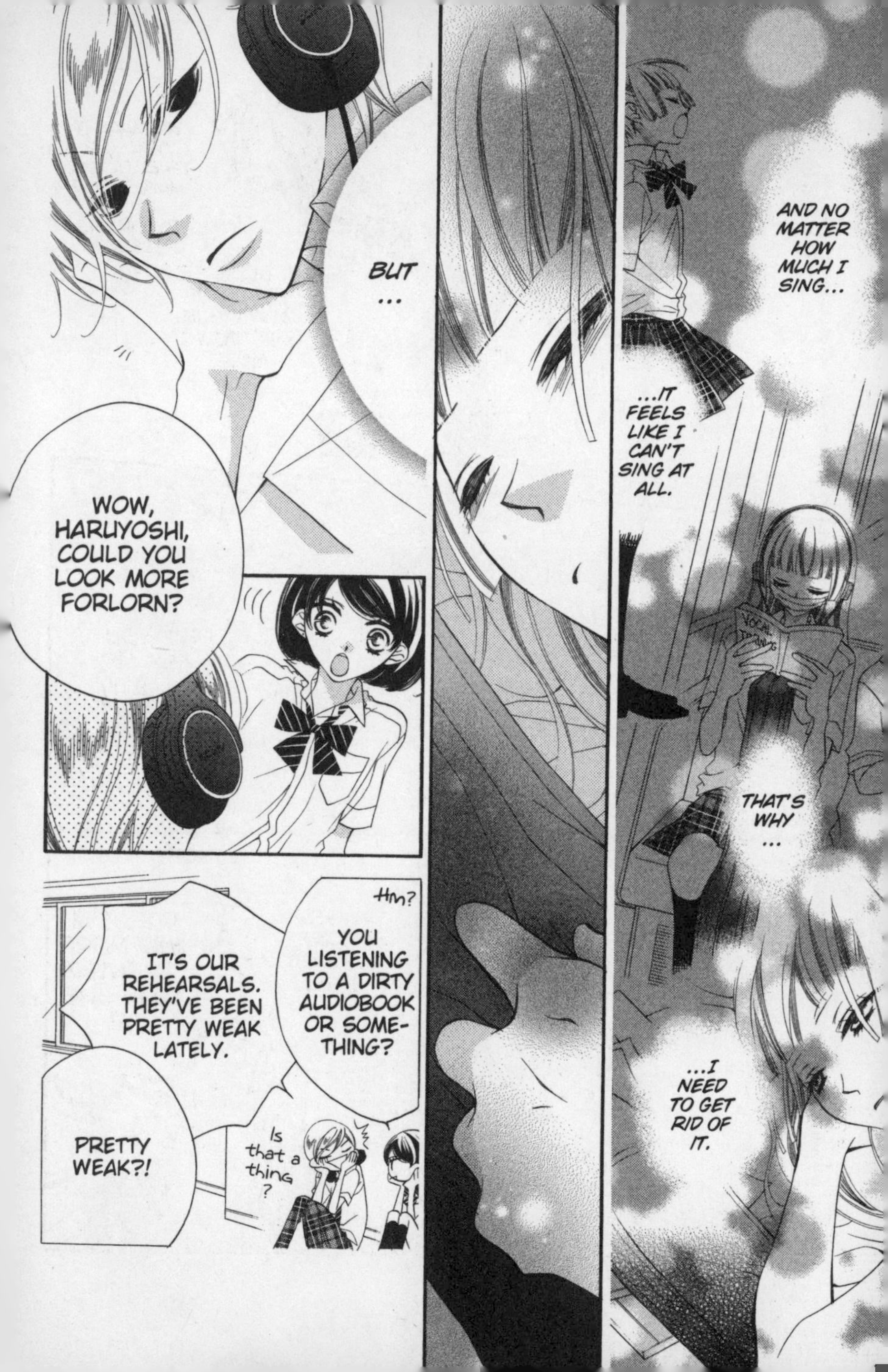
AND NO MATTER HOW MUCH I SING...
...IT FEELS LIKE I CAN'T SING AT ALL.
THAT'S WHY...
...I NEED TO GET RID OF IT.
BUT...
WOW, HARUYOSHI, COULD YOU LOOK MORE FORLORN?
Hm?
YOU LISTENING TO A DIRTY AUDIOBOOK OR SOME-THING?
IT'S OUR REHEARSALS. THEY'VE BEEN PRETTY WEAK LATELY.
PRETTY WEAK?!
Is that a thing?

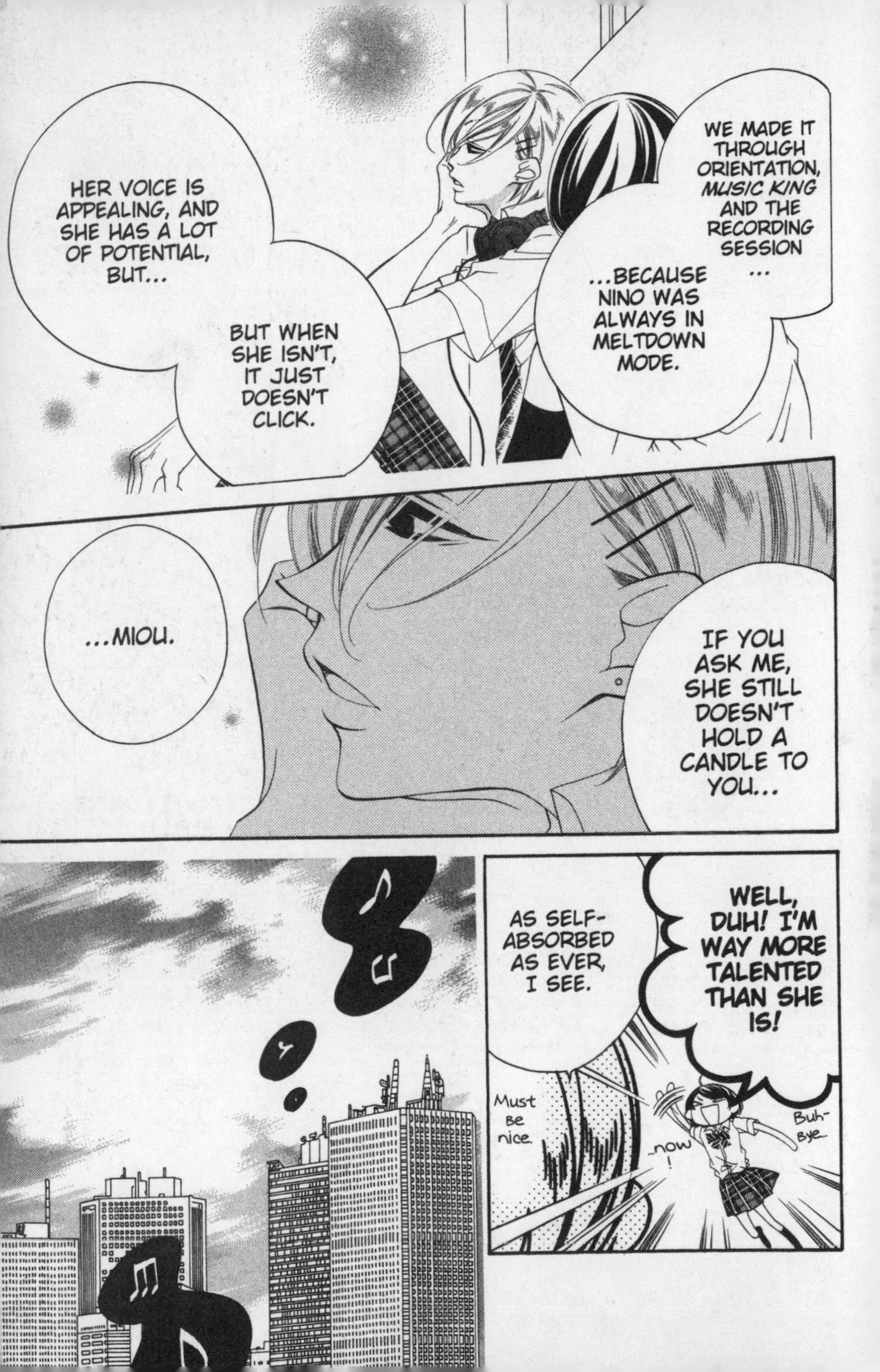
WE MADE IT THROUGH ORIENTATION, MUSIC KING AND THE RECORDING SESSION...
...BECAUSE NINO WAS ALWAYS IN MELTDOWN MODE.
HER VOICE IS APPEALING, AND SHE HAS A LOT OF POTENTIAL, BUT...
BUT WHEN SHE ISN'T, IT JUST DOESN'T CLICK.
IF YOU ASK ME, SHE STILL DOESN'T HOLD A CANDLE TO YOU...
...MIOU.
WELL, DUH! I'M WAY MORE TALENTED THAN SHE IS!
Buh-bye...
AS SELF-ABSORBED AS EVER, I SEE.
Must be nice.
...now!

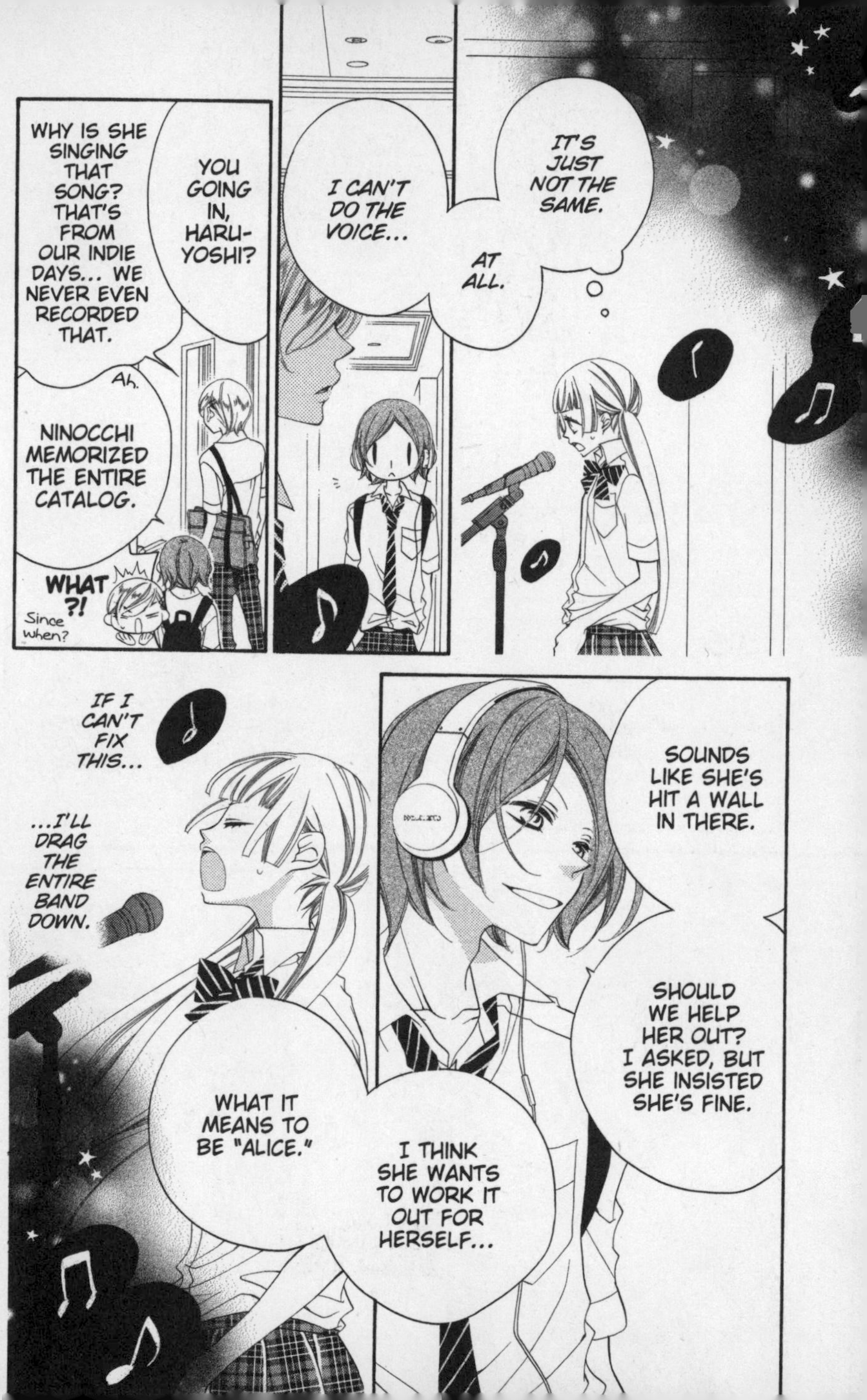
IT'S JUST NOT THE SAME.
AT ALL.
I CAN'T DO THE VOICE...
YOU GOING IN, HARUYOSHI?
WHY IS SHE SINGING THAT SONG? THAT'S FROM OUR INDIE DAYS... WE NEVER EVEN RECORDED THAT.
Ah.
NINOCCHI MEMORIZED THE ENTIRE CATALOG.
WHAT?!
Since when?
SOUNDS LIKE SHE'S HIT A WALL IN THERE.
SHOULD WE HELP HER OUT? I ASKED, BUT SHE INSISTED SHE'S FINE.
I THINK SHE WANTS TO WORK IT OUT FOR HERSELF...
WHAT IT MEANS TO BE "ALICE."
IF I CAN'T FIX THIS...
...I'LL DRAG THE ENTIRE BAND DOWN.

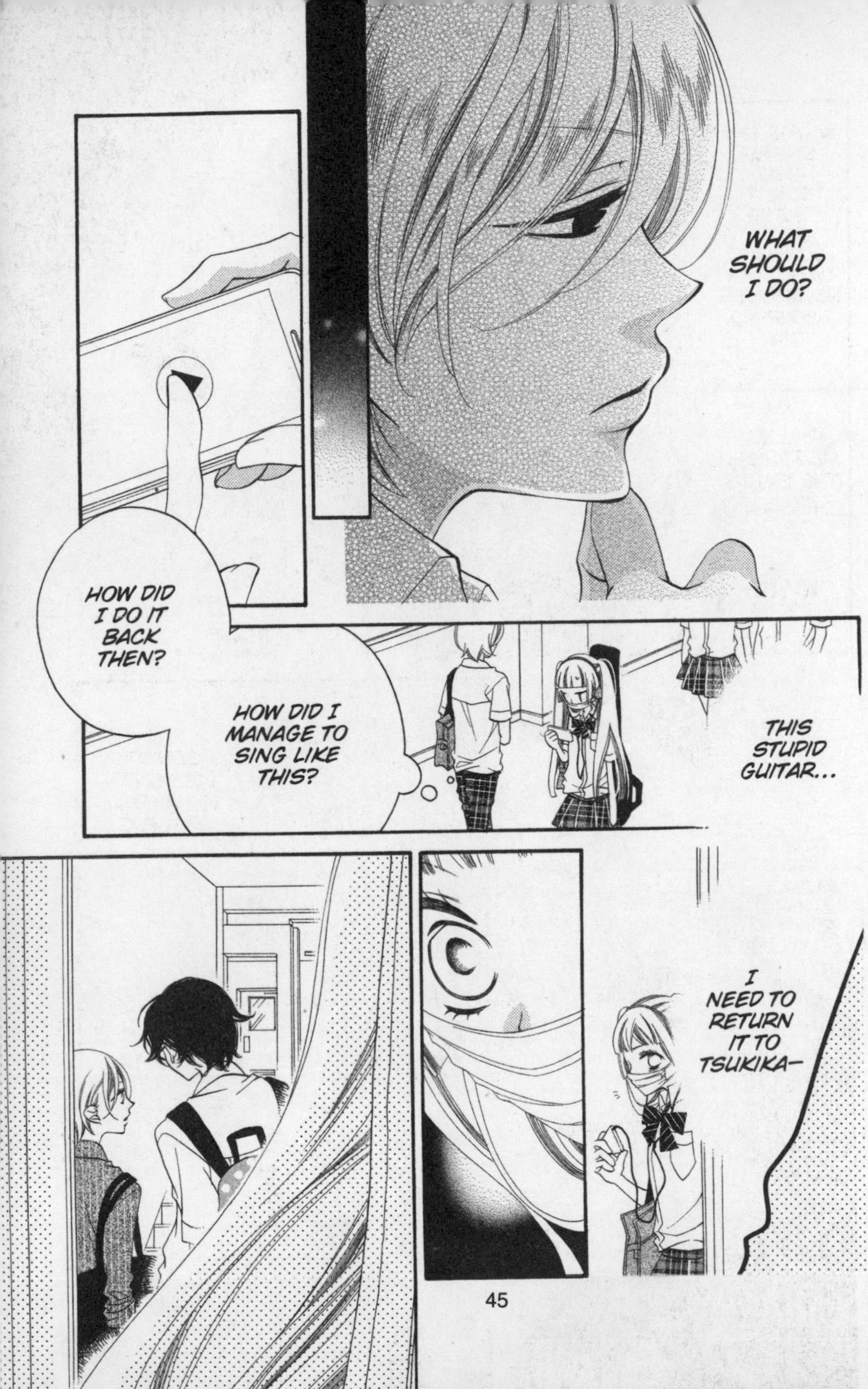
WHAT SHOULD I DO?
HOW DID I DO IT BACK THEN?
HOW DID I MANAGE TO SING LIKE THIS?
THIS STUPID GUITAR...
I NEED TO RETURN IT TO TSUKIKA-

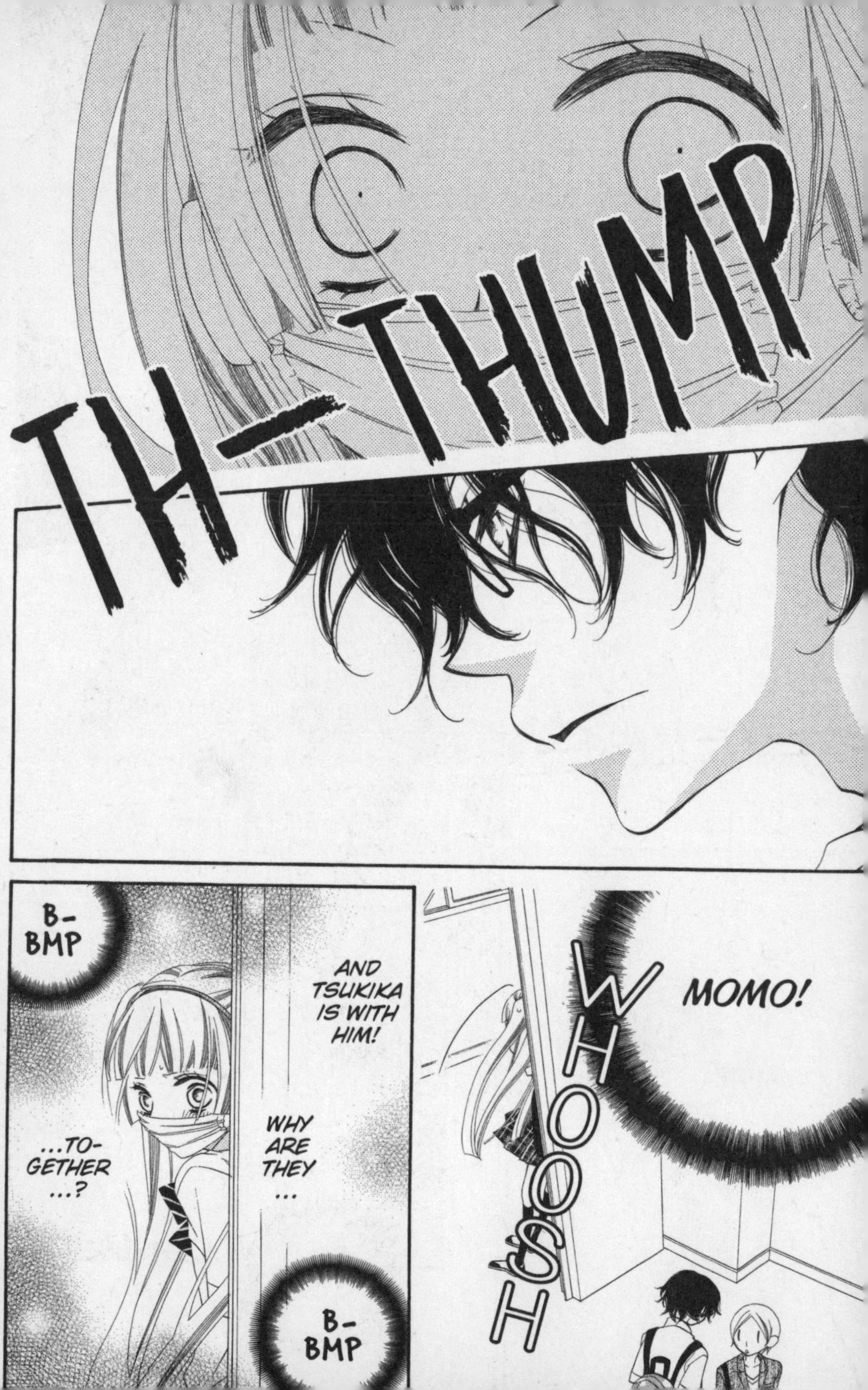
TH-THUMP
MOMO!
WHOOSH
AND TSUKIKA IS WITH HIM!
B-BMP
WHY ARE THEY ...
...TO-GETHER ...?
B-BMP

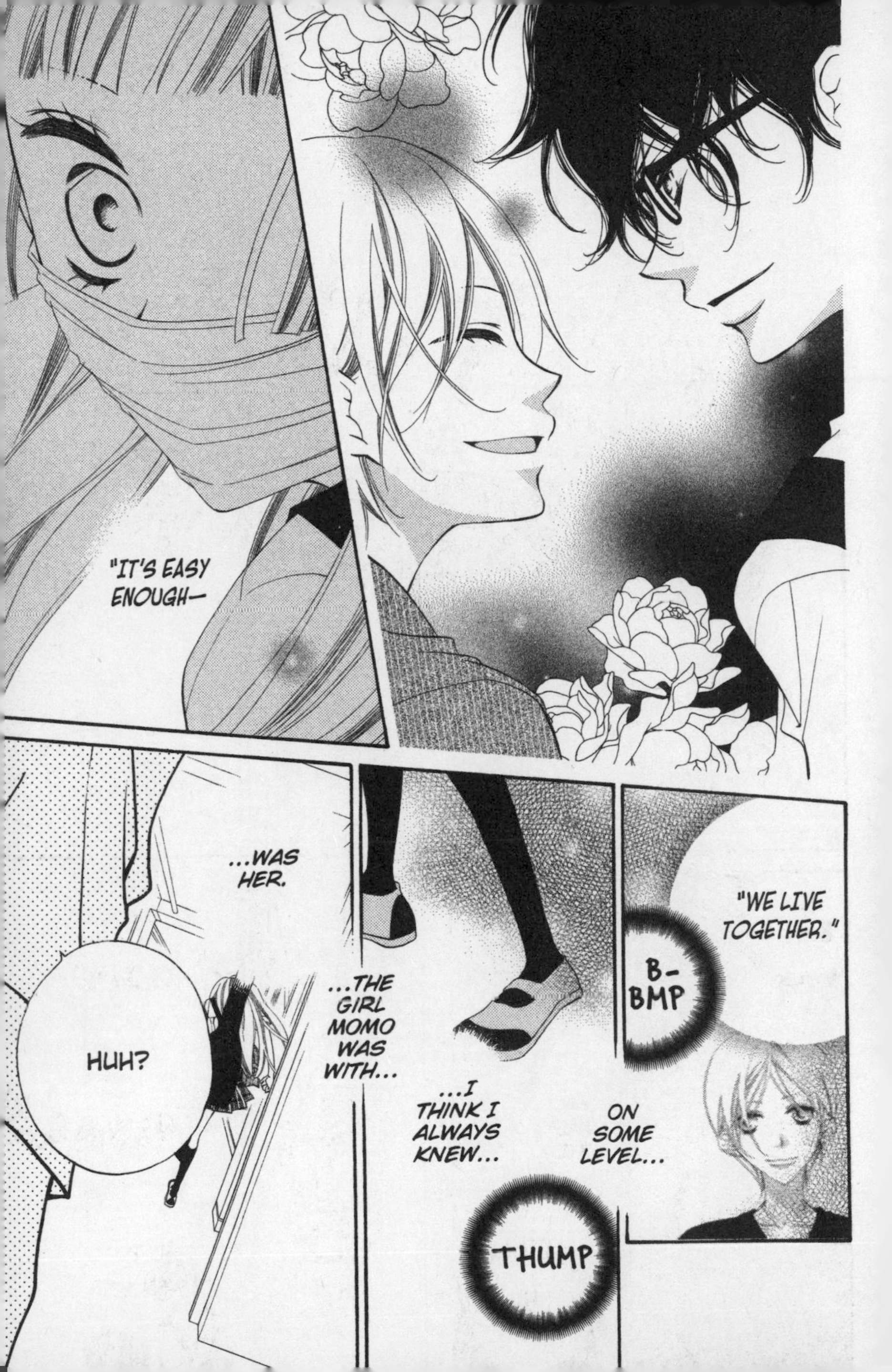
"IT'S EASY ENOUGH—
"WE LIVE TOGETHER."
B-BMP
ON SOME LEVEL...
...I THINK I ALWAYS KNEW...
THUMP
...THE GIRL MOMO WAS WITH...
...WAS HER.
HUH?

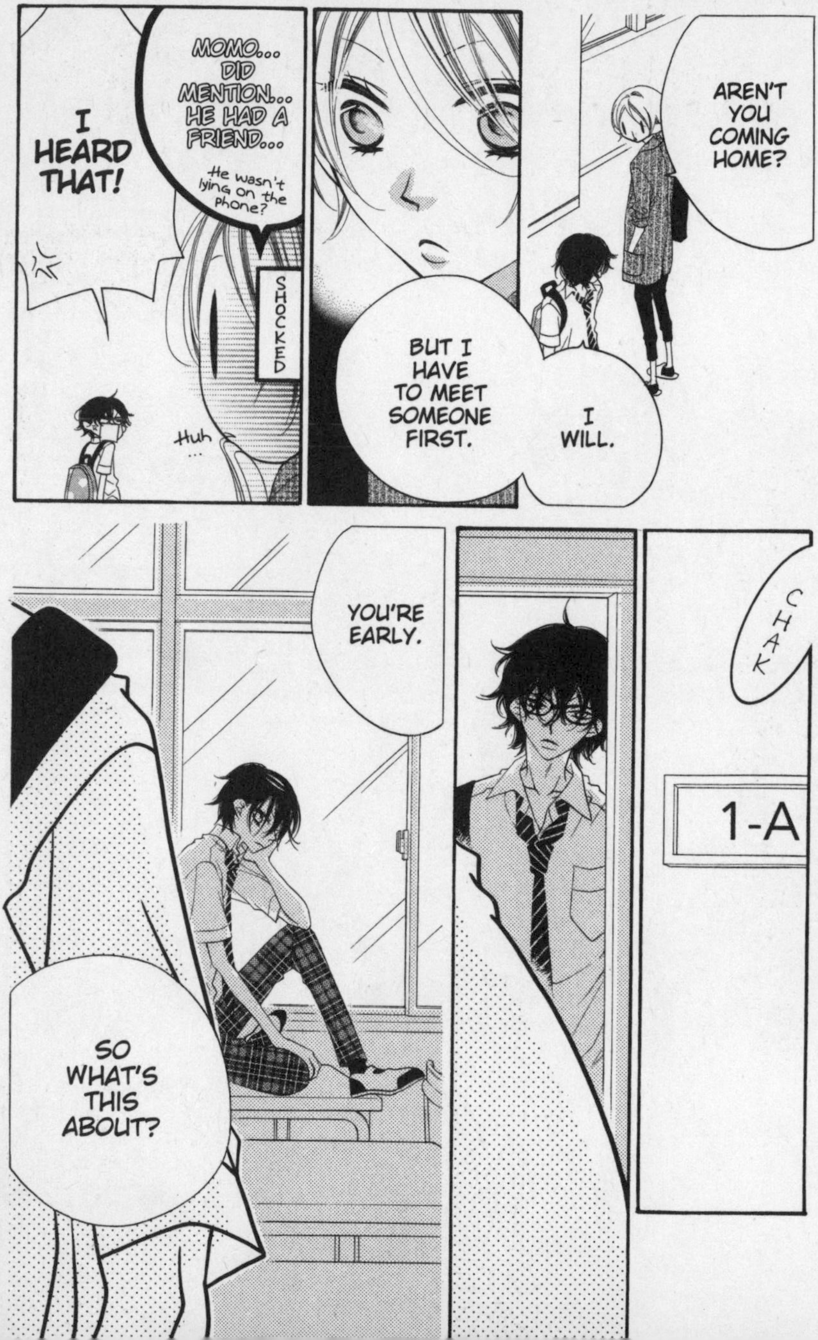
AREN'T YOU COMING HOME?
I WILL.
BUT I HAVE TO MEET SOMEONE FIRST.
MOMO... DID MENTION... HE HAD A FRIEND...
He wasn't lying on the phone?
SHOCKED
I HEARD THAT!
Huh...
CHAK
1-A
YOU'RE EARLY.
SO WHAT'S THIS ABOUT?

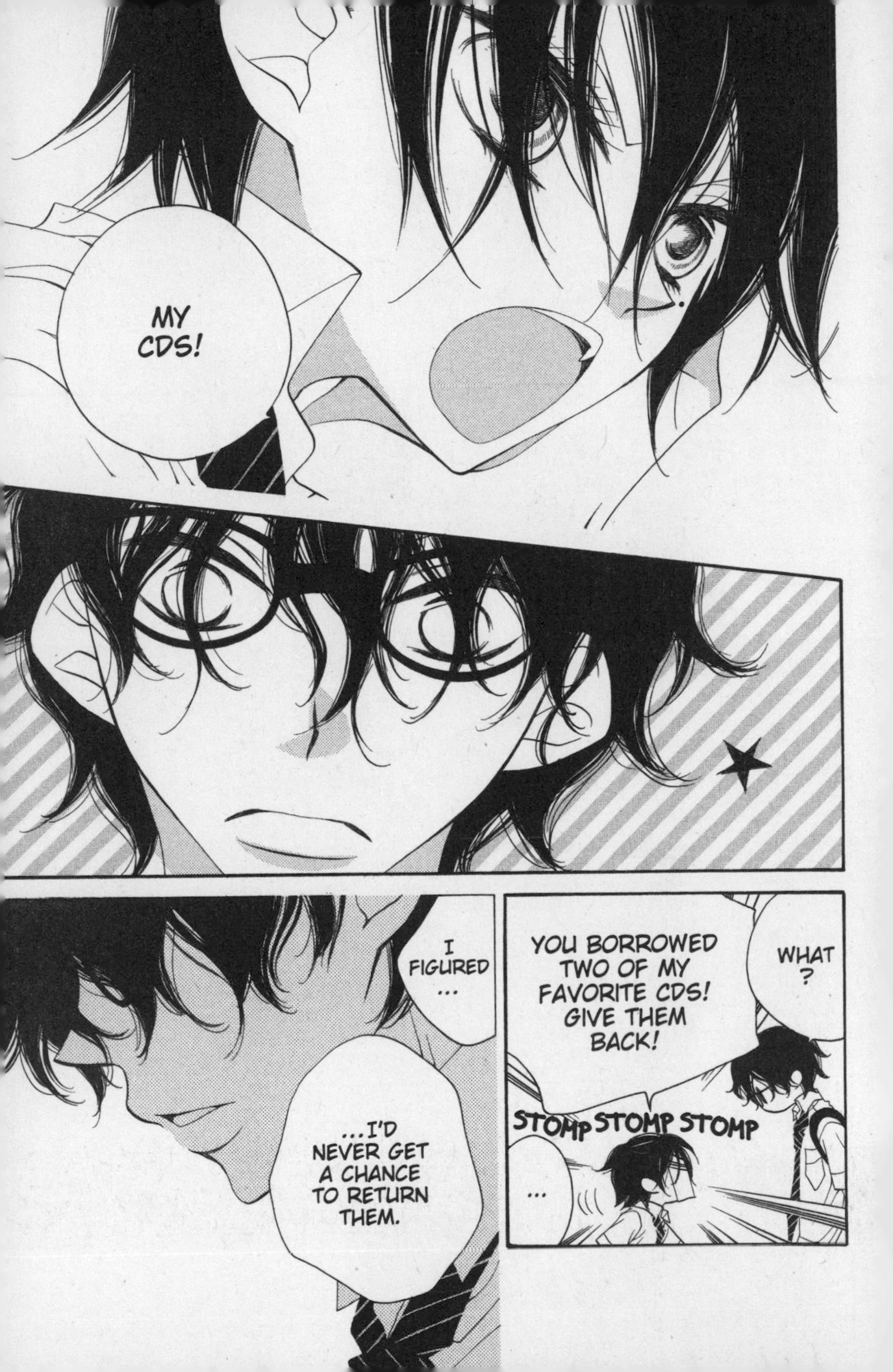
MY CDS!
WHAT?
YOU BORROWED TWO OF MY FAVORITE CDS! GIVE THEM BACK!
STOMP STOMP STOMP
...
I FIGURED...
...I'D NEVER GET A CHANCE TO RETURN THEM.

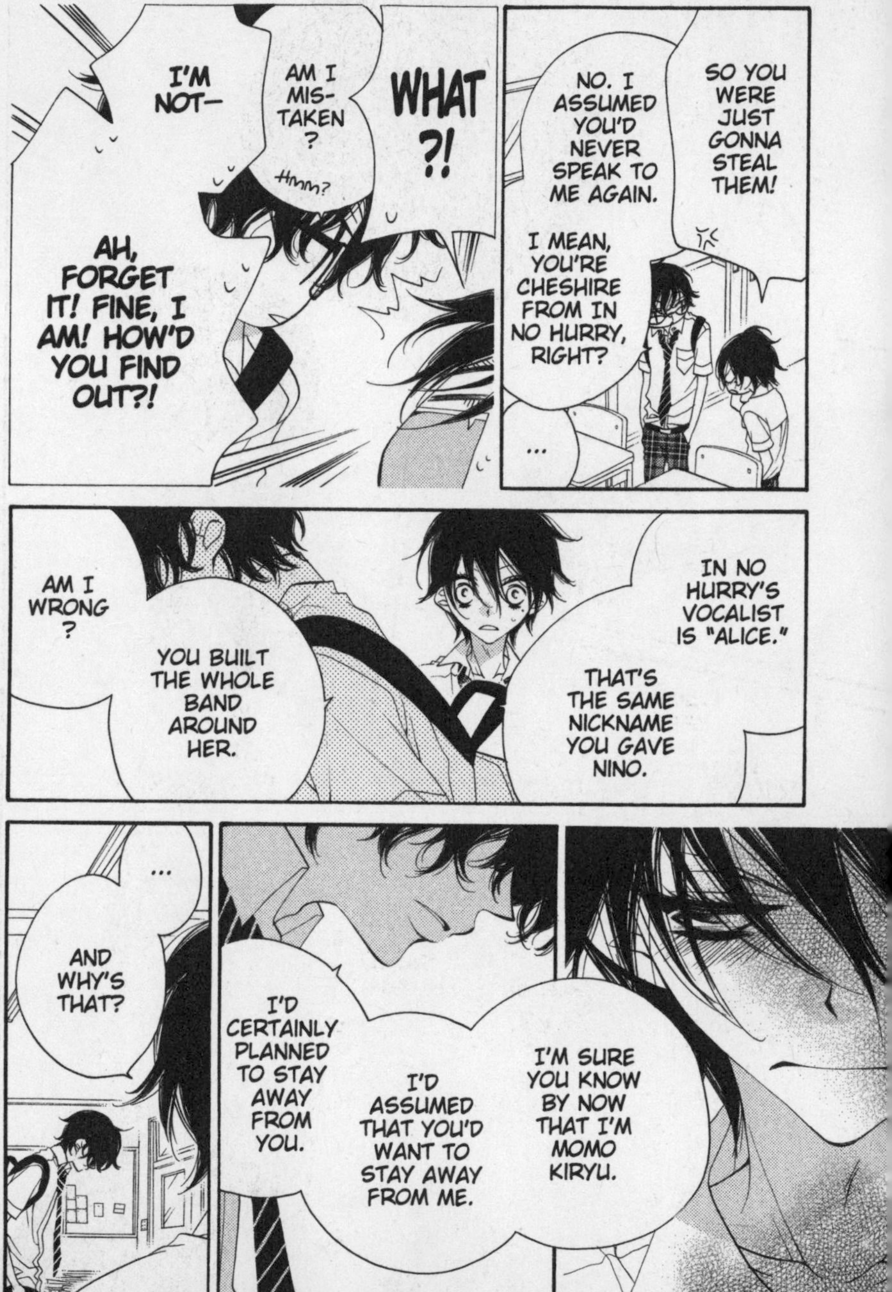
SO YOU WERE JUST GONNA STEAL THEM!
NO. I ASSUMED YOU'D NEVER SPEAK TO ME AGAIN.
I MEAN, YOU'RE CHESHIRE FROM IN NO HURRY, RIGHT?
...
WHAT?!
AM I MIS-TAKEN?
Hmm?
I'M NOT—
AH, FORGET IT! FINE, I AM! HOW'D YOU FIND OUT?!
IN NO HURRY'S VOCALIST IS "ALICE."
THAT'S THE SAME NICKNAME YOU GAVE NINO.
YOU BUILT THE WHOLE BAND AROUND HER.
AM I WRONG?
I'M SURE YOU KNOW BY NOW THAT I'M MOMO KIRYU.
I'D ASSUMED THAT YOU'D WANT TO STAY AWAY FROM ME.
I'D CERTAINLY PLANNED TO STAY AWAY FROM YOU.
...
AND WHY'S THAT?

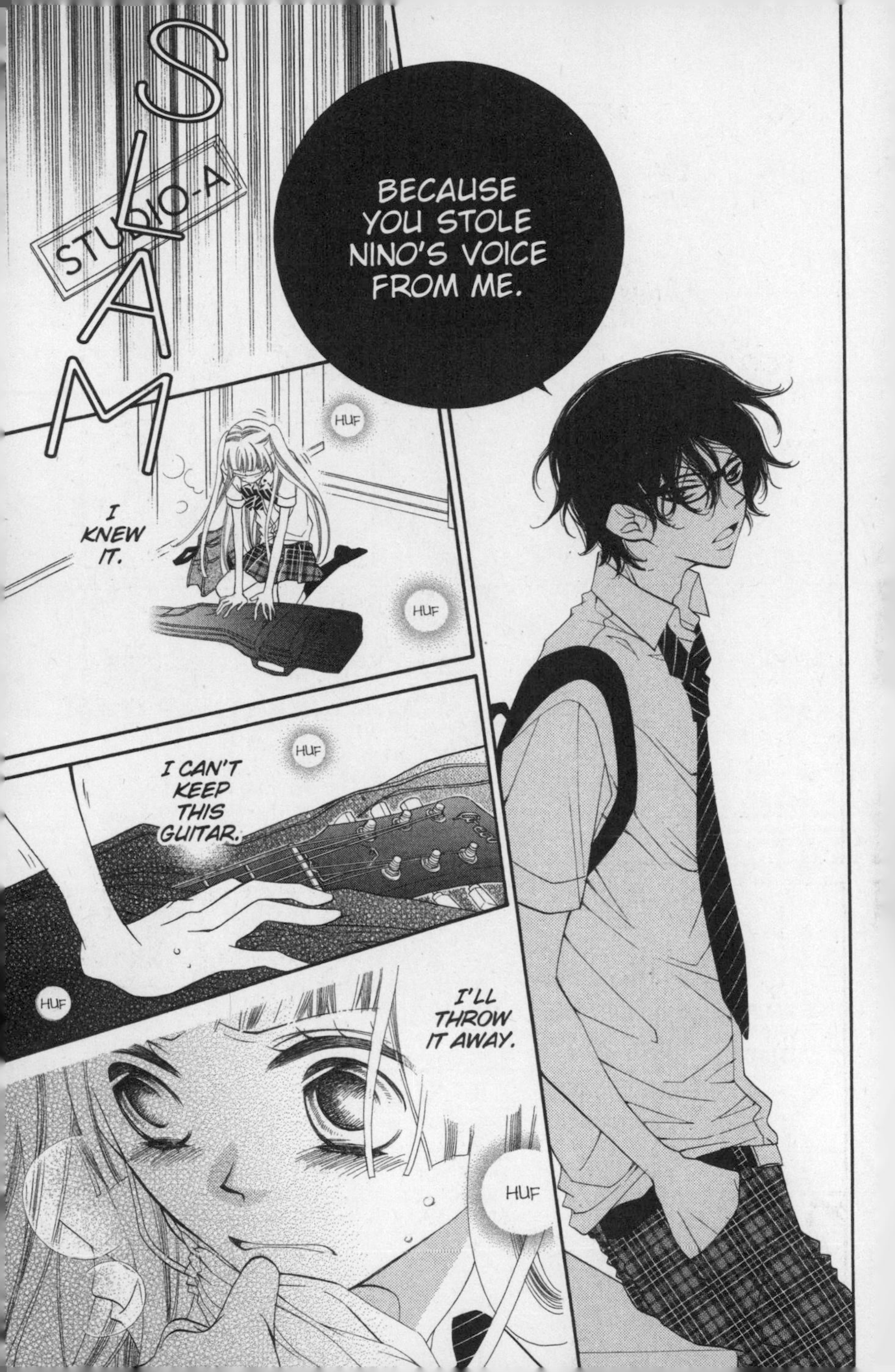
BECAUSE YOU STOLE NINO'S VOICE FROM ME.
SLAM
STUDIO-A
HUF
I KNEW IT.
HUF
HUF
I CAN'T KEEP THIS GUITAR.
HUF
I'LL THROW IT AWAY.
HUF

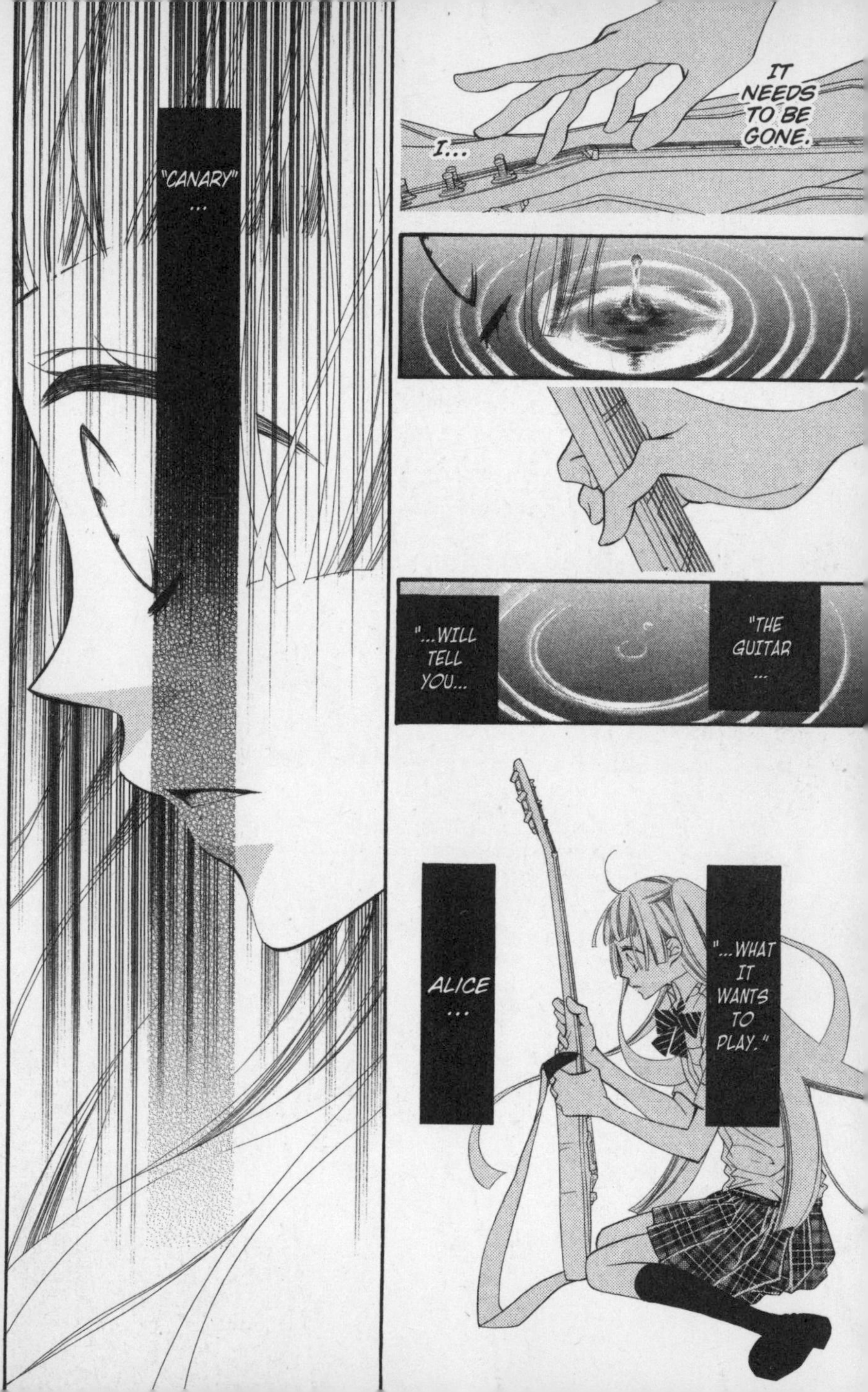
IT NEEDS TO BE GONE.
I...
"THE GUITAR ...
"...WILL TELL YOU...
"...WHAT IT WANTS TO PLAY."
ALICE ...
"CANARY" ...

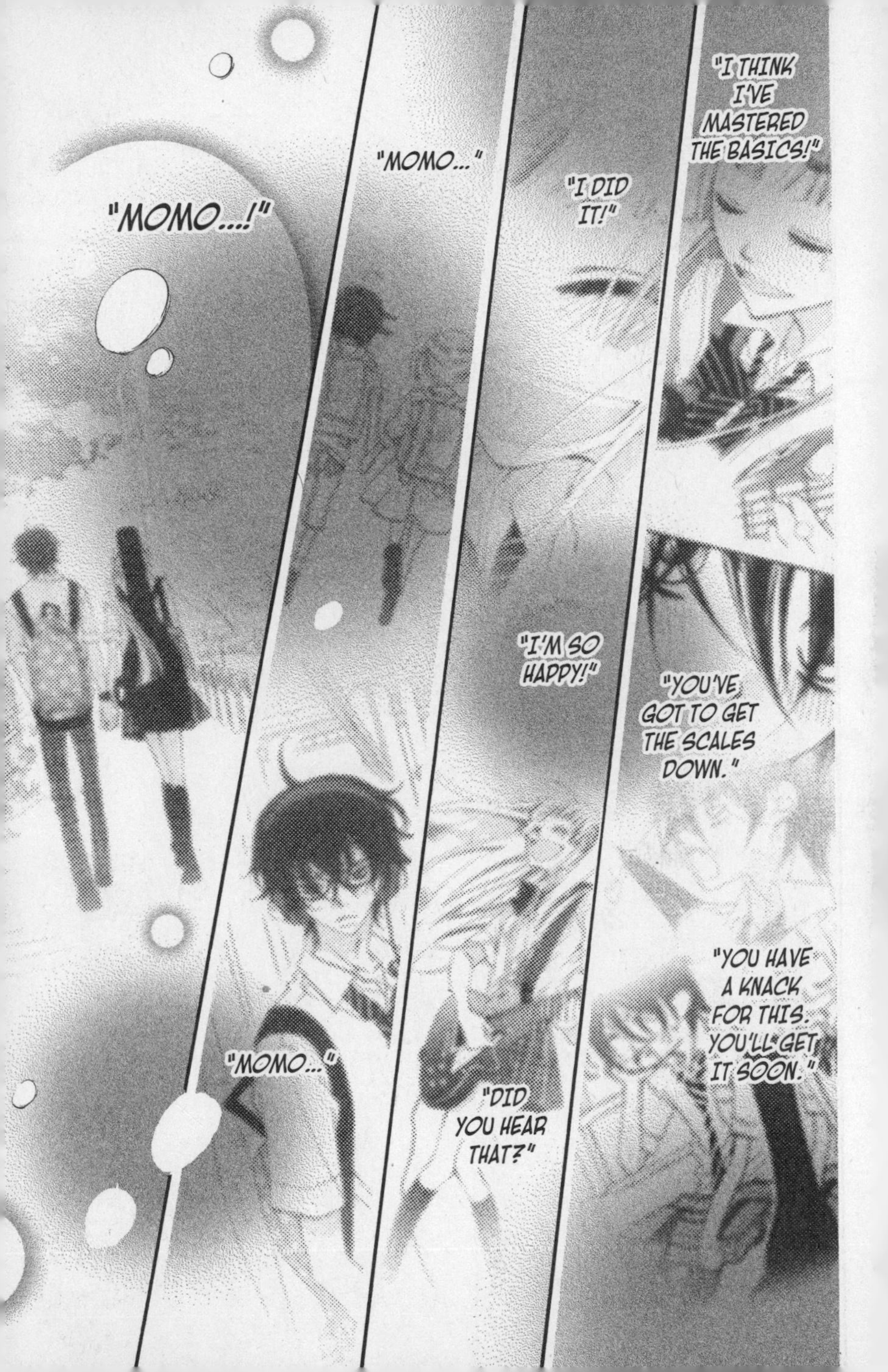
"I THINK I'VE MASTERED THE BASICS!"
"YOU'VE GOT TO GET THE SCALES DOWN."
"YOU HAVE A KNACK FOR THIS. YOU'LL GET IT SOON."
"I DID IT!"
"I'M SO HAPPY!"
"DID YOU HEAR THAT?"
"MOMO..."
"MOMO..."
"MOMO...!"

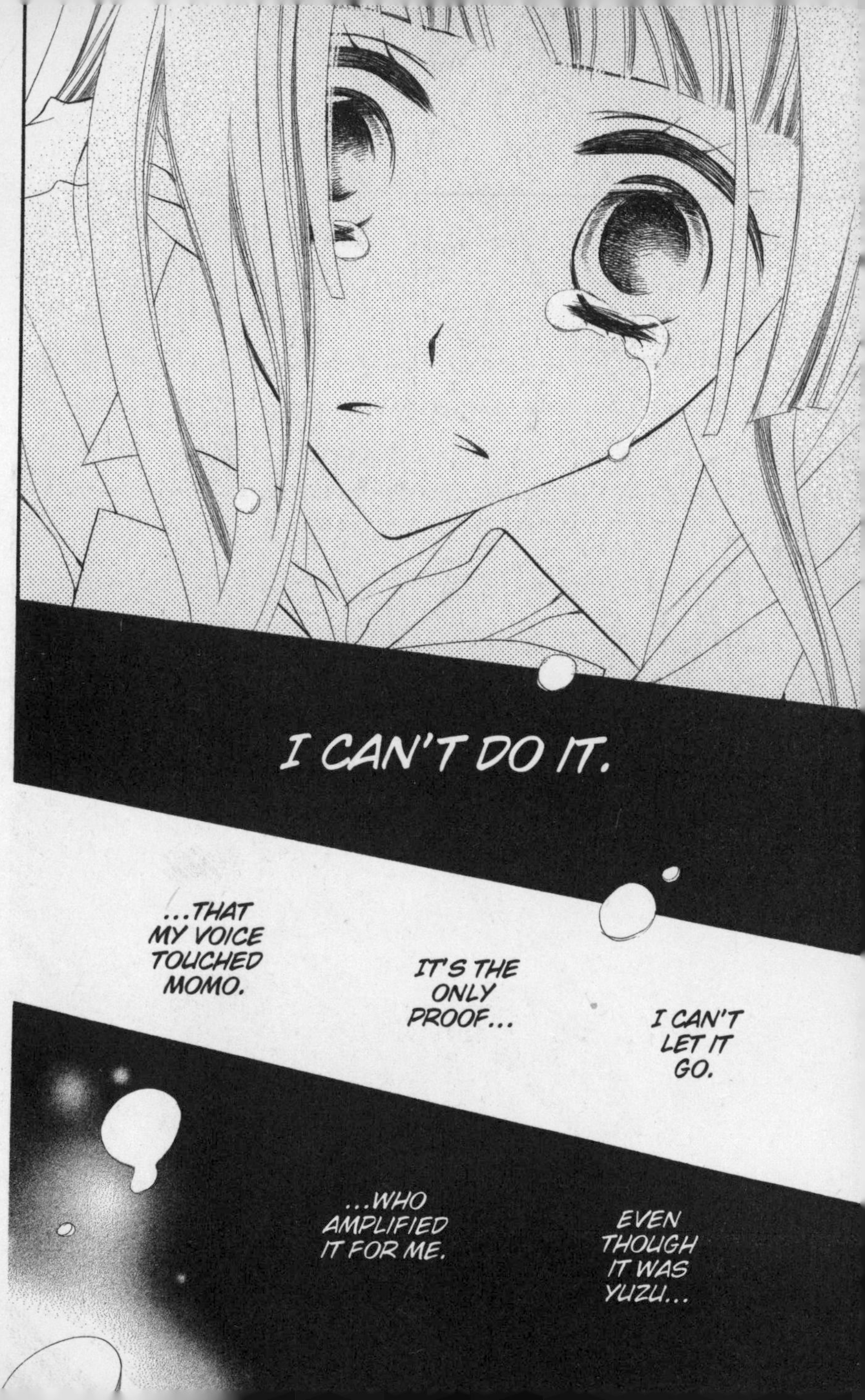
I CAN'T DO IT.
I CAN'T LET IT GO.
IT'S THE ONLY PROOF...
...THAT MY VOICE TOUCHED MOMO.
EVEN THOUGH IT WAS YUZU...
...WHO AMPLIFIED IT FOR ME.

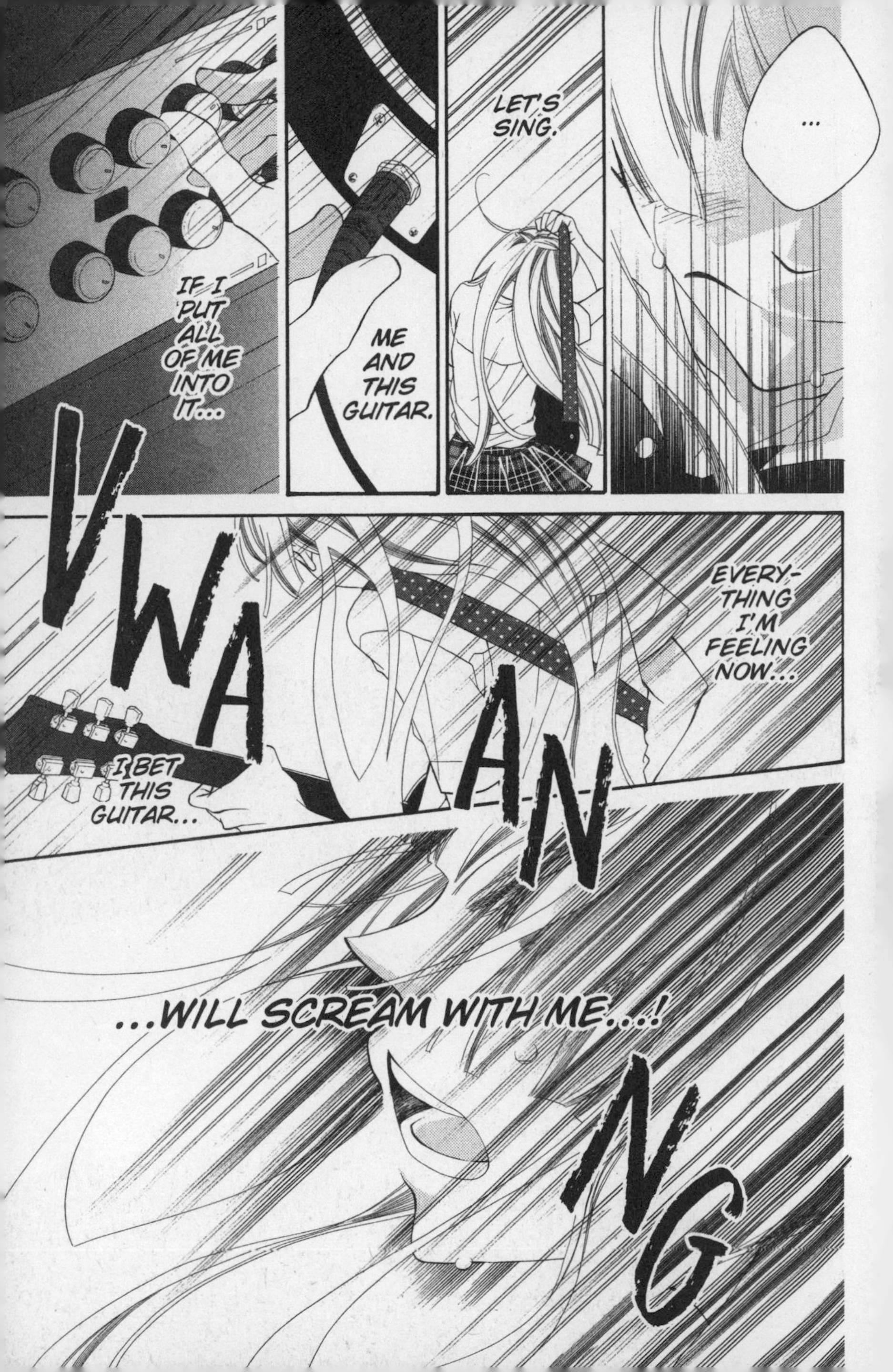
...
LET'S SING.
ME AND THIS GUITAR.
IF I PUT ALL OF ME INTO IT...
EVERYTHING I'M FEELING NOW...
I BET THIS GUITAR...
...WILL SCREAM WITH ME...!
VWAANNG

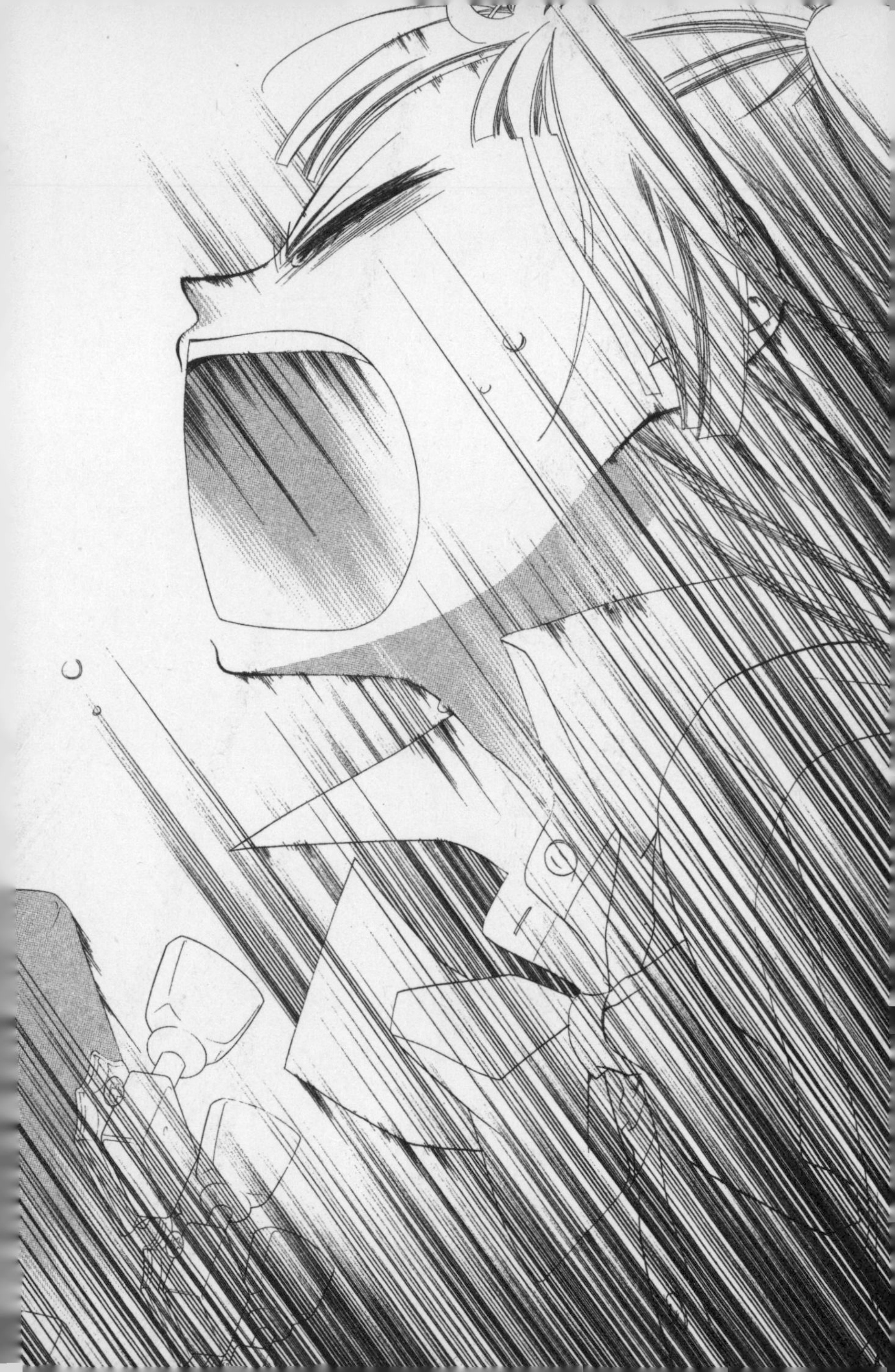

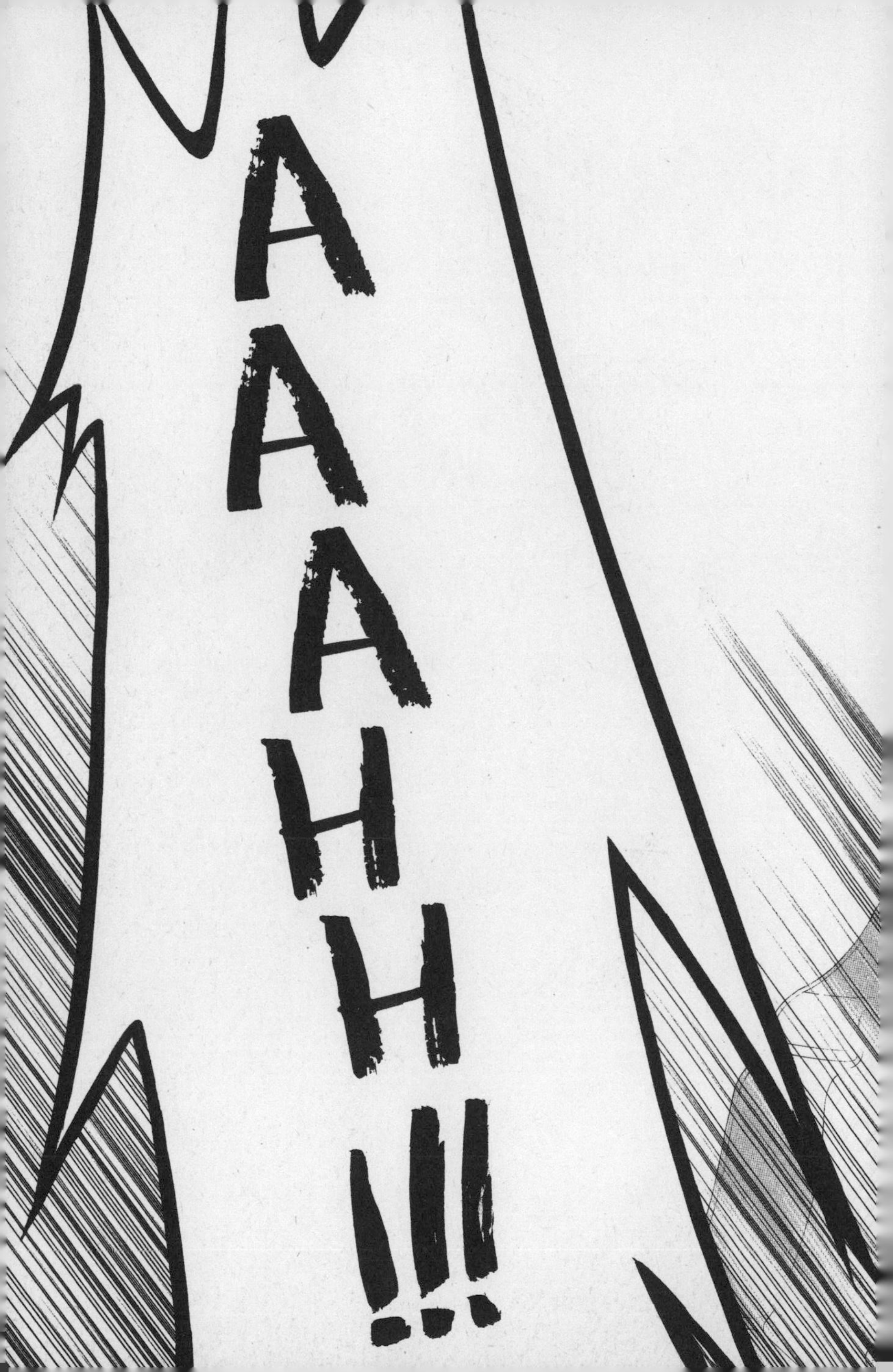
AAAHH!!!

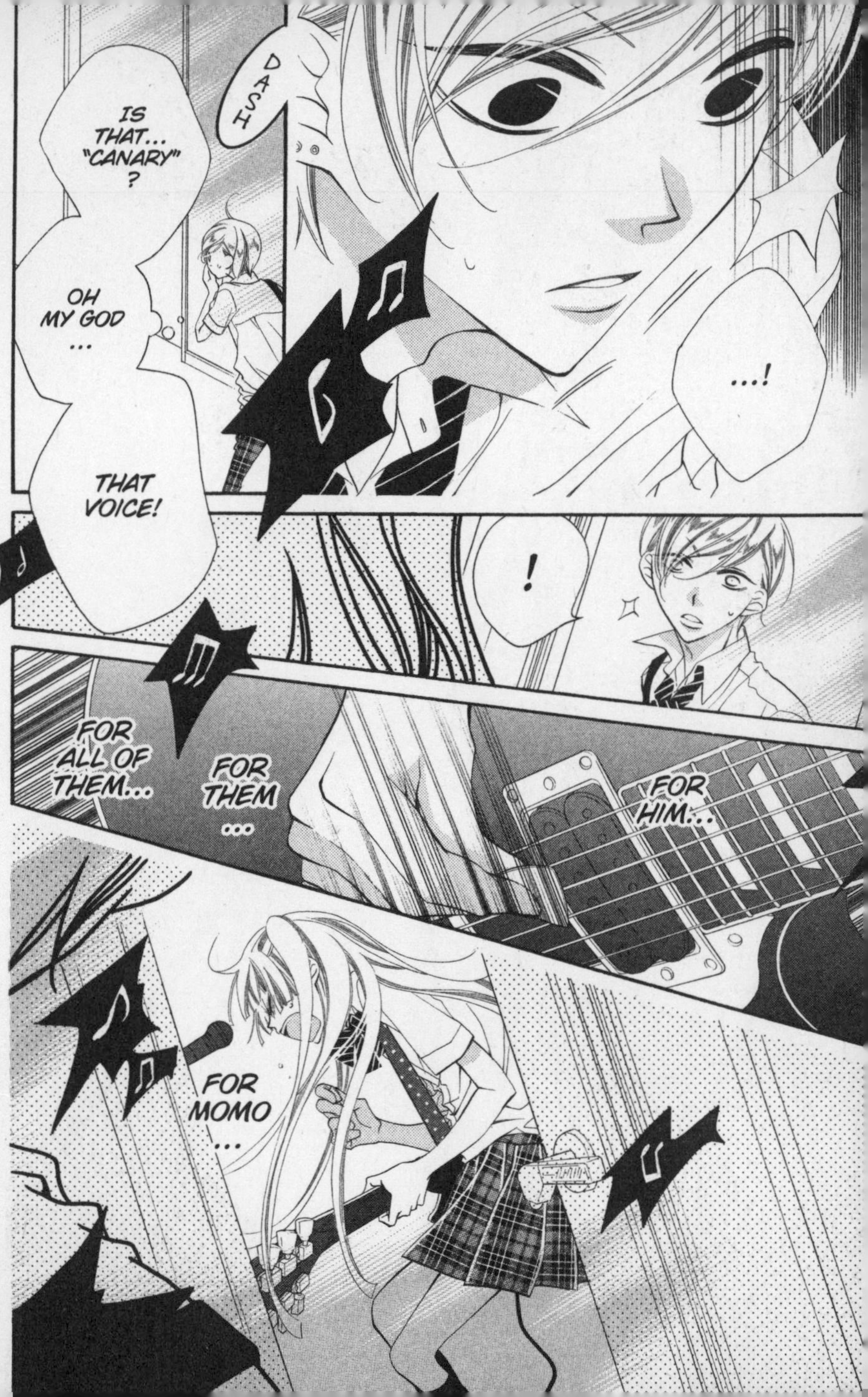
DASH
...!
IS THAT... "CANARY" ?
OH MY GOD ...
THAT VOICE!
!
FOR HIM...
FOR THEM ...
FOR ALL OF THEM...
FOR MOMO ...

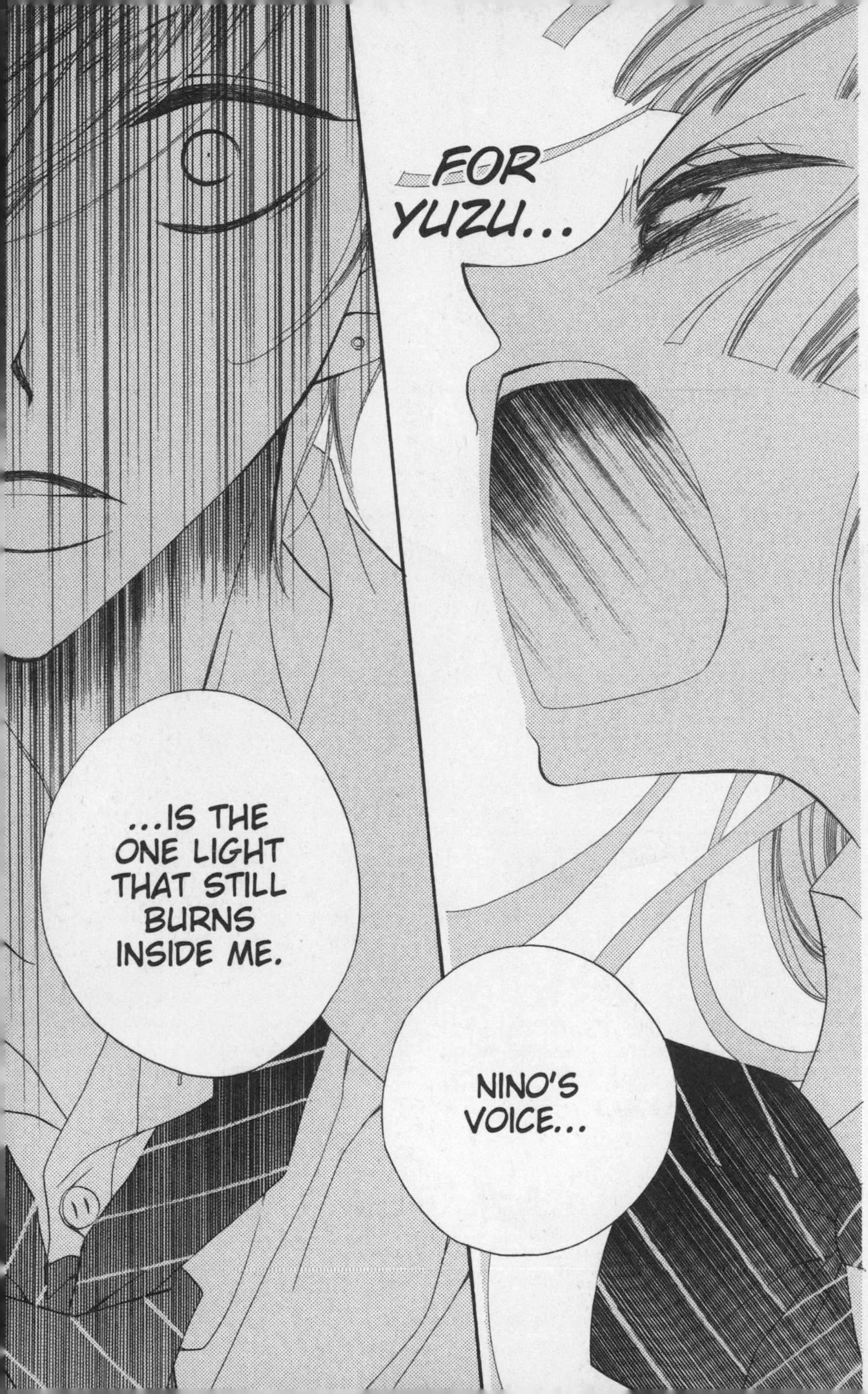
FOR YUZU...
NINO'S VOICE...
...IS THE ONE LIGHT THAT STILL BURNS INSIDE ME.

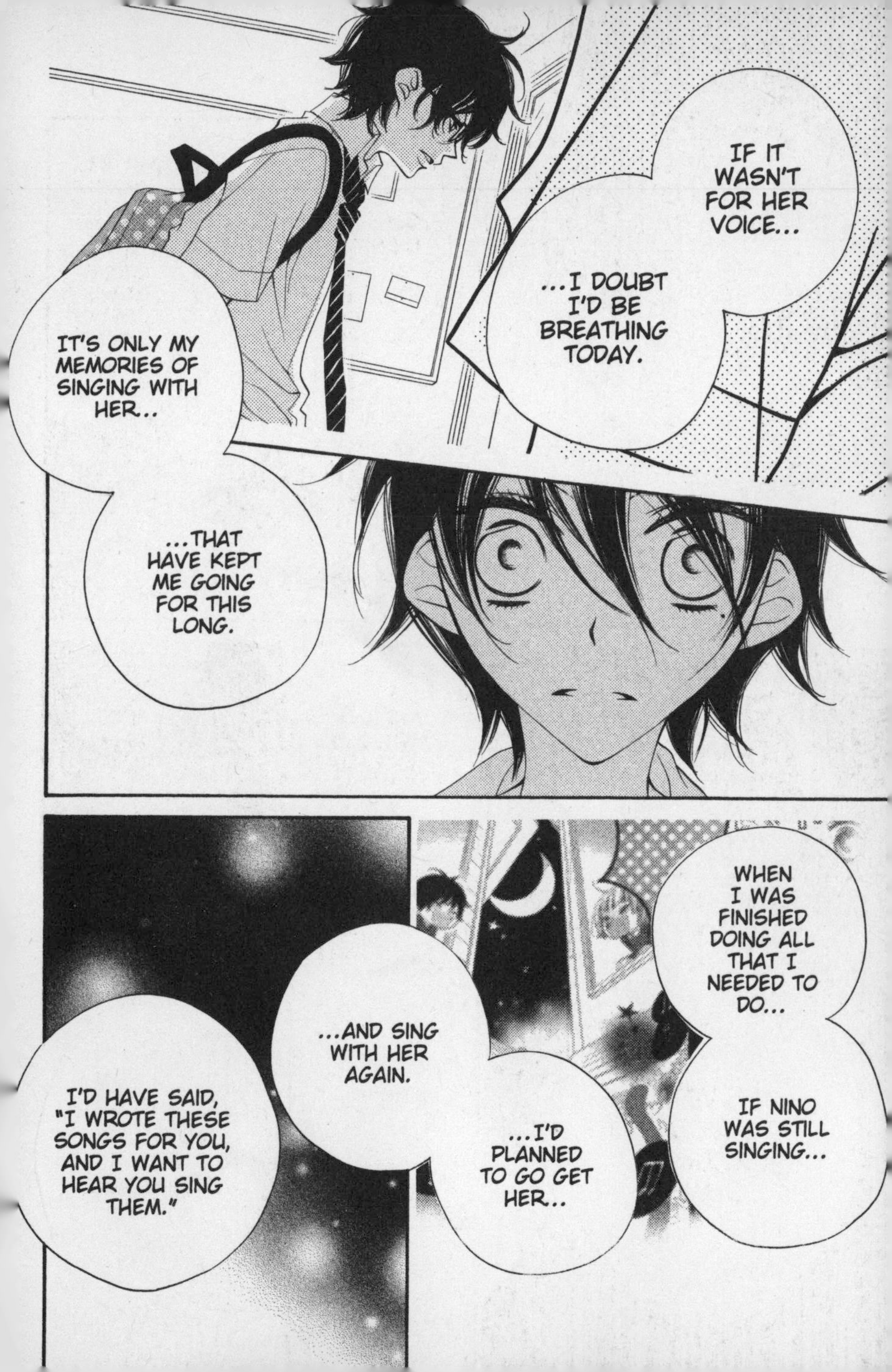
IF IT WASN'T FOR HER VOICE...
...I DOUBT I'D BE BREATHING TODAY.
IT'S ONLY MY MEMORIES OF SINGING WITH HER...
...THAT HAVE KEPT ME GOING FOR THIS LONG.
WHEN I WAS FINISHED DOING ALL THAT I NEEDED TO DO...
IF NINO WAS STILL SINGING...
...I'D PLANNED TO GO GET HER...
...AND SING WITH HER AGAIN.
I'D HAVE SAID, "I WROTE THESE SONGS FOR YOU, AND I WANT TO HEAR YOU SING THEM."

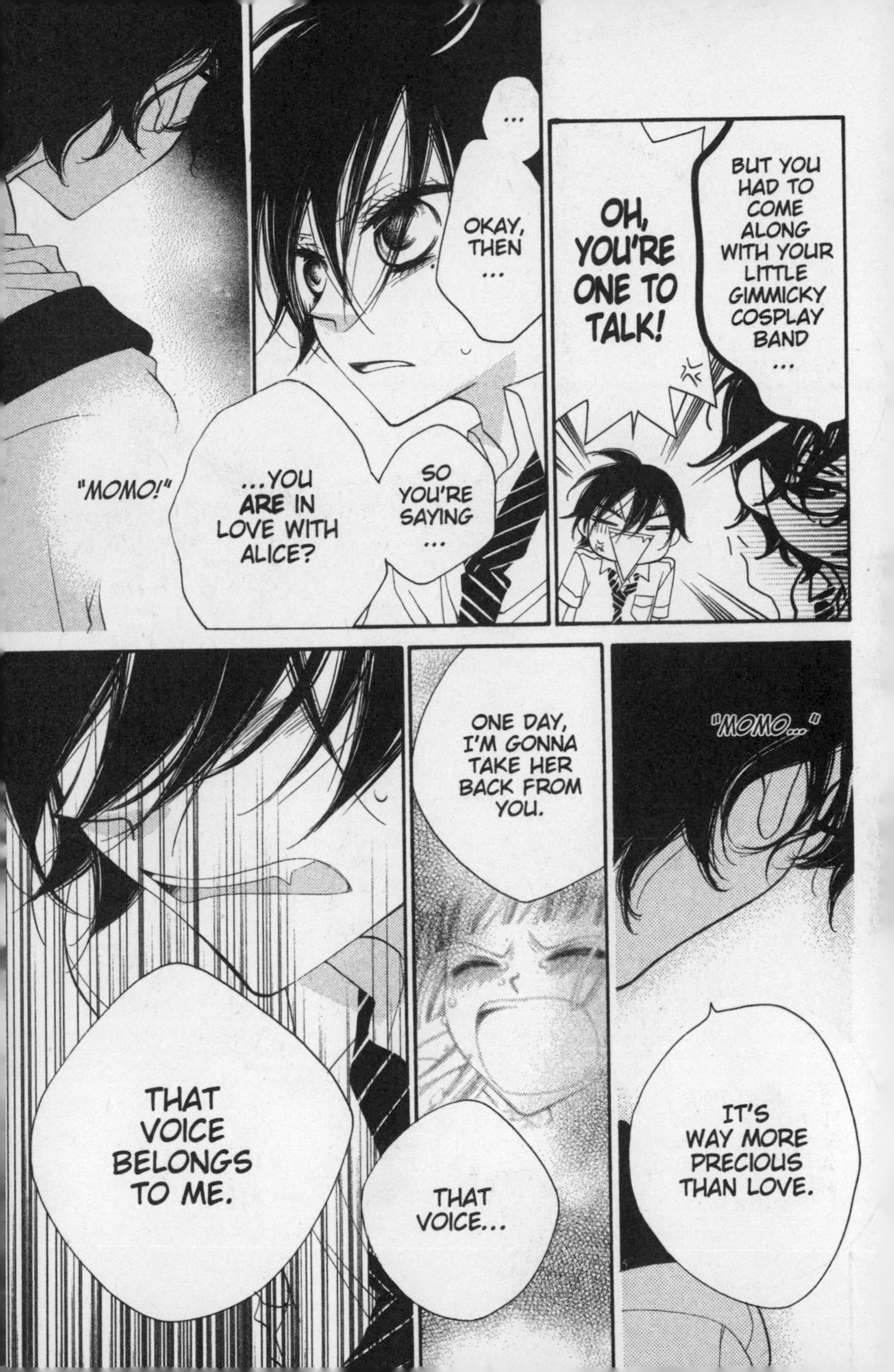
BUT YOU HAD TO COME ALONG WITH YOUR LITTLE GIMMICKY COSPLAY BAND ...
OH, YOU'RE ONE TO TALK!
...
OKAY, THEN ...
SO YOU'RE SAYING ...
...YOU ARE IN LOVE WITH ALICE?
"MOMO!"
"MOMO..."
IT'S WAY MORE PRECIOUS THAN LOVE.
ONE DAY, I'M GONNA TAKE HER BACK FROM YOU.
THAT VOICE...
THAT VOICE BELONGS TO ME.

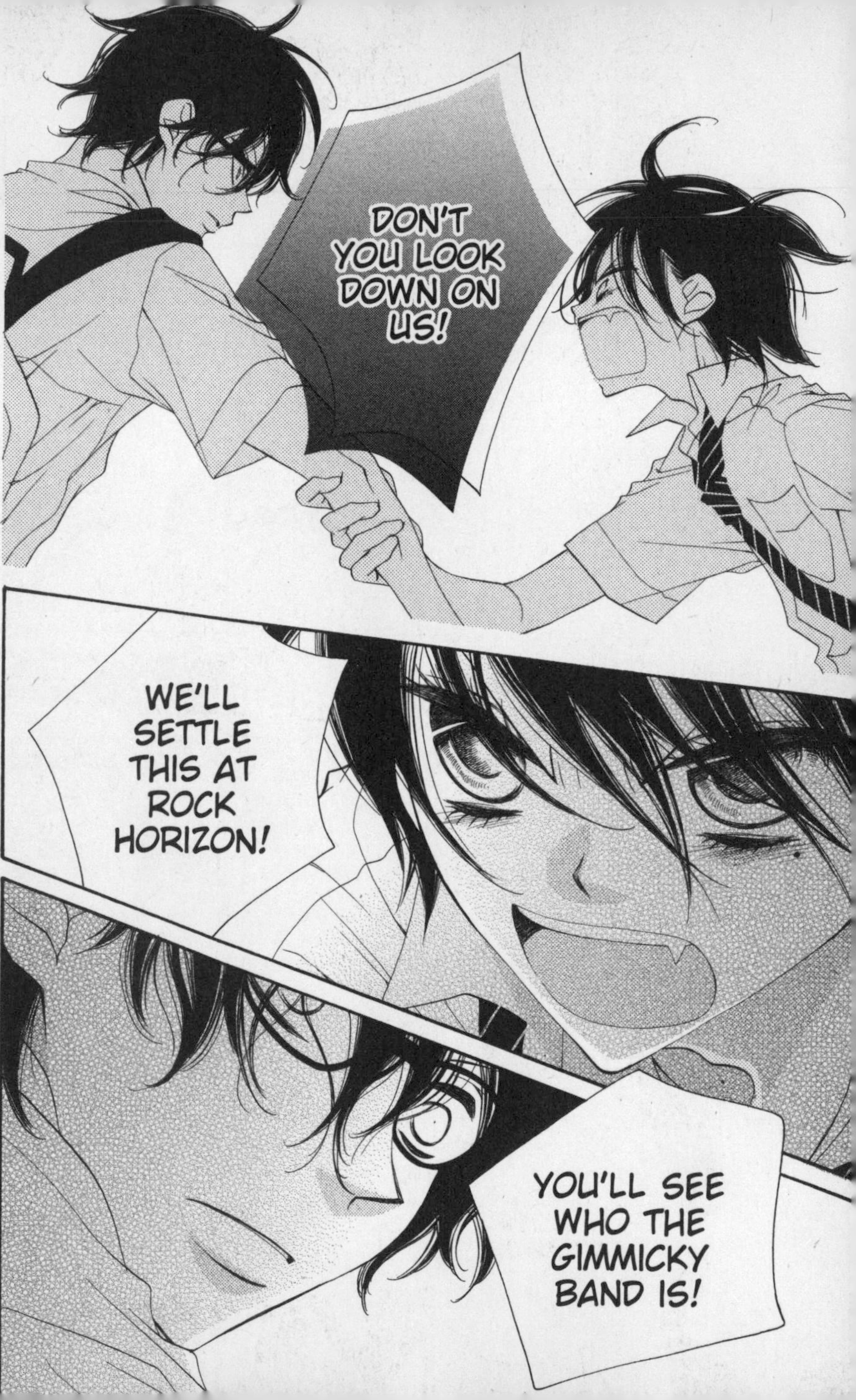
DON'T YOU LOOK DOWN ON US!
WE'LL SETTLE THIS AT ROCK HORIZON!
YOU'LL SEE WHO THE GIMMICKY BAND IS!

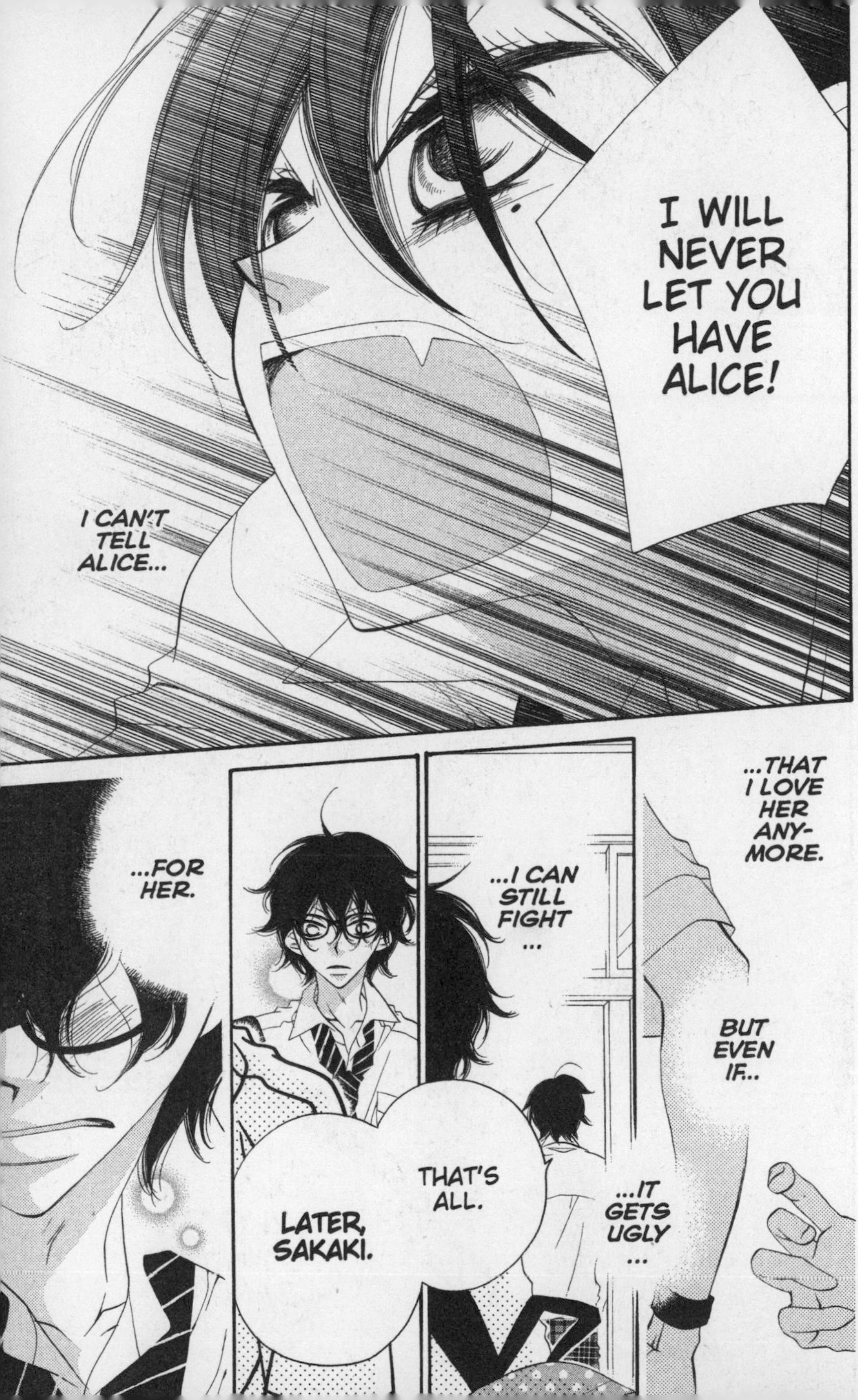
I WILL NEVER LET YOU HAVE ALICE!
I CAN'T TELL ALICE...
...THAT I LOVE HER ANYMORE.
BUT EVEN IF...
...IT GETS UGLY...
...I CAN STILL FIGHT...
THAT'S ALL.
LATER, SAKAKI.
...FOR HER.

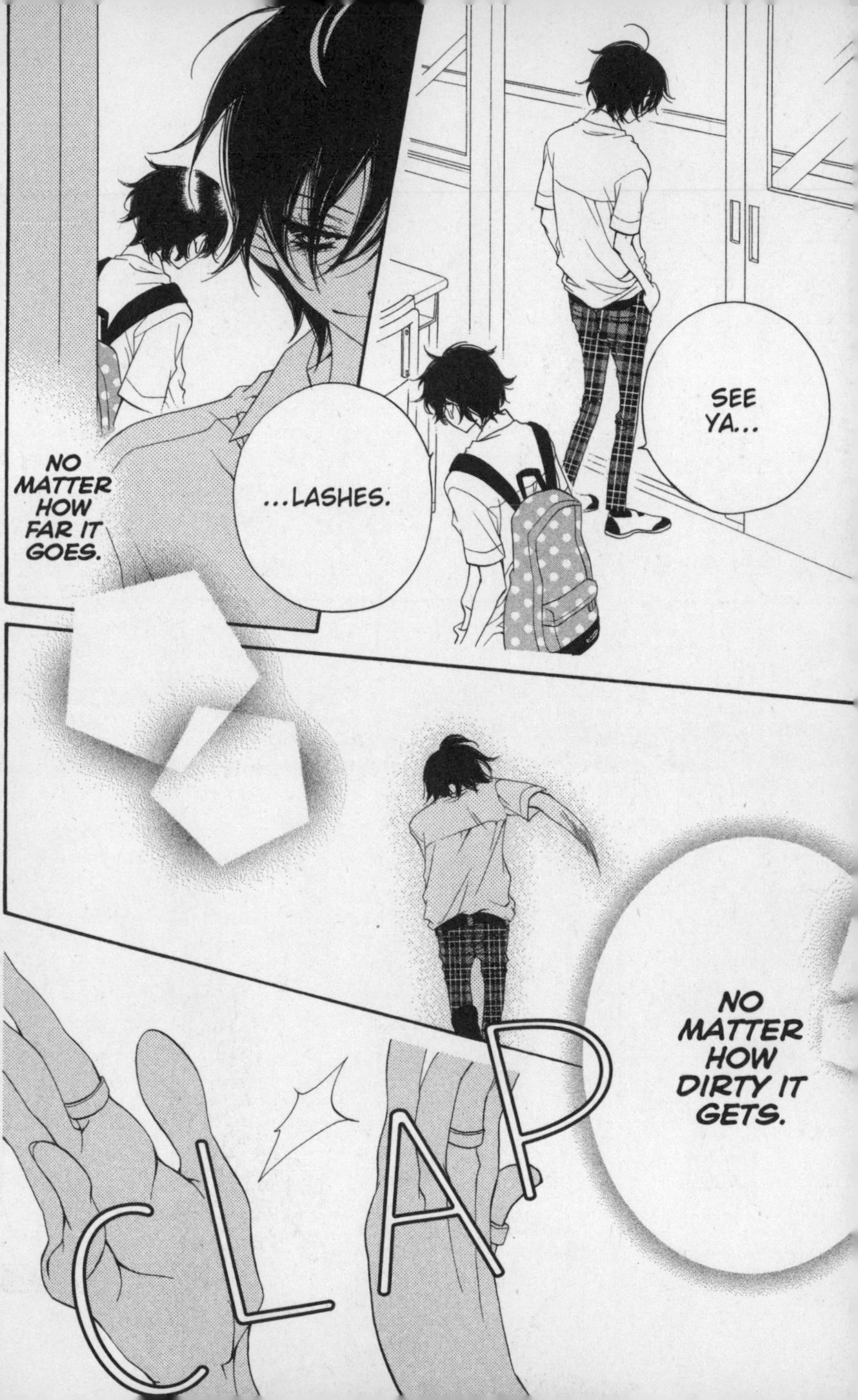
SEE YA...
...LASHES.
NO MATTER HOW FAR IT GOES.
NO MATTER HOW DIRTY IT GETS.
CLAP

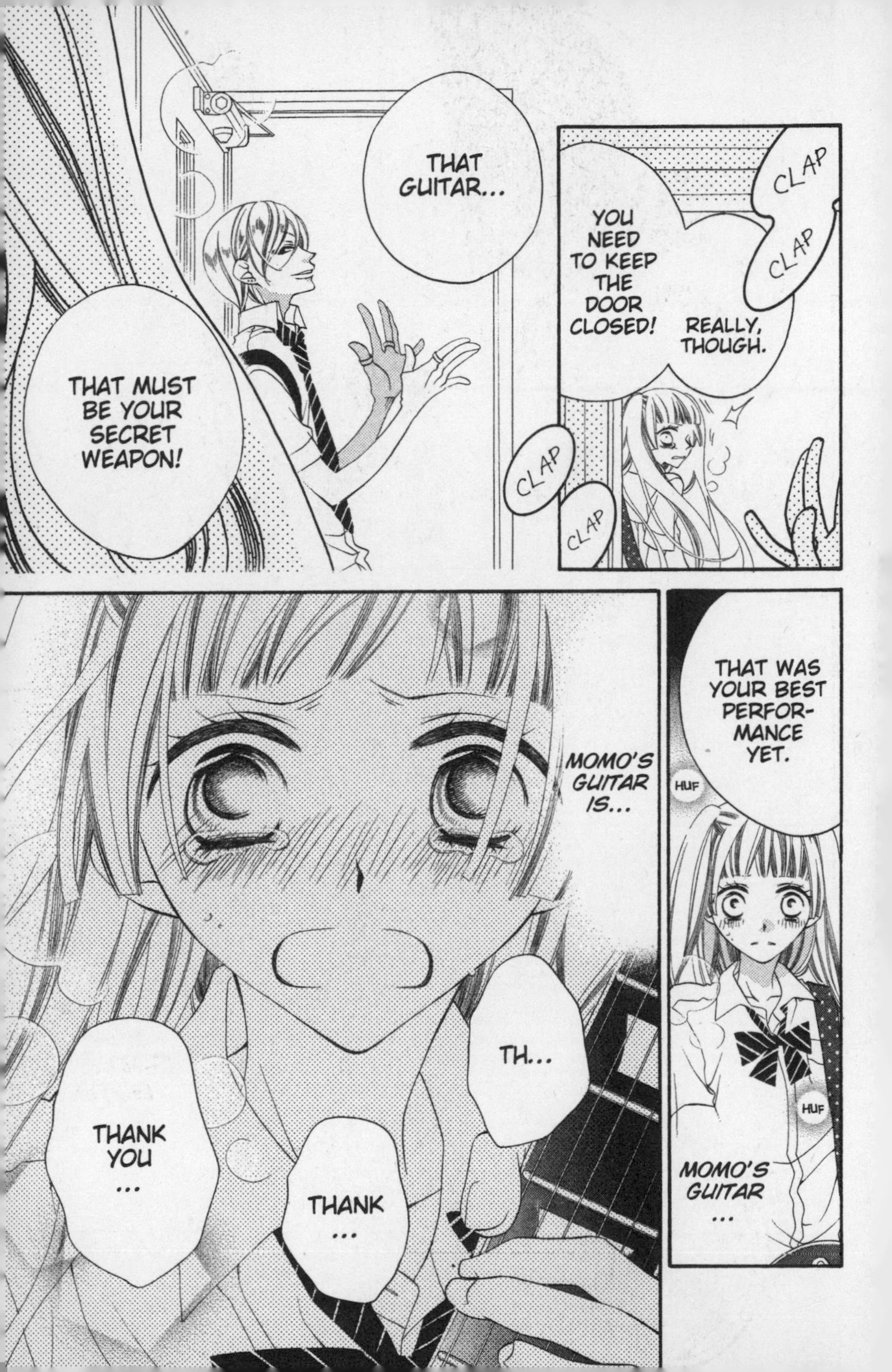
CLAP
CLAP
REALLY, THOUGH.
YOU NEED TO KEEP THE DOOR CLOSED!
CLAP
CLAP
THAT GUITAR...
THAT MUST BE YOUR SECRET WEAPON!
THAT WAS YOUR BEST PERFORMANCE YET.
HUF
HUF
MOMO'S GUITAR ...
MOMO'S GUITAR IS...
TH...
THANK ...
THANK YOU ...

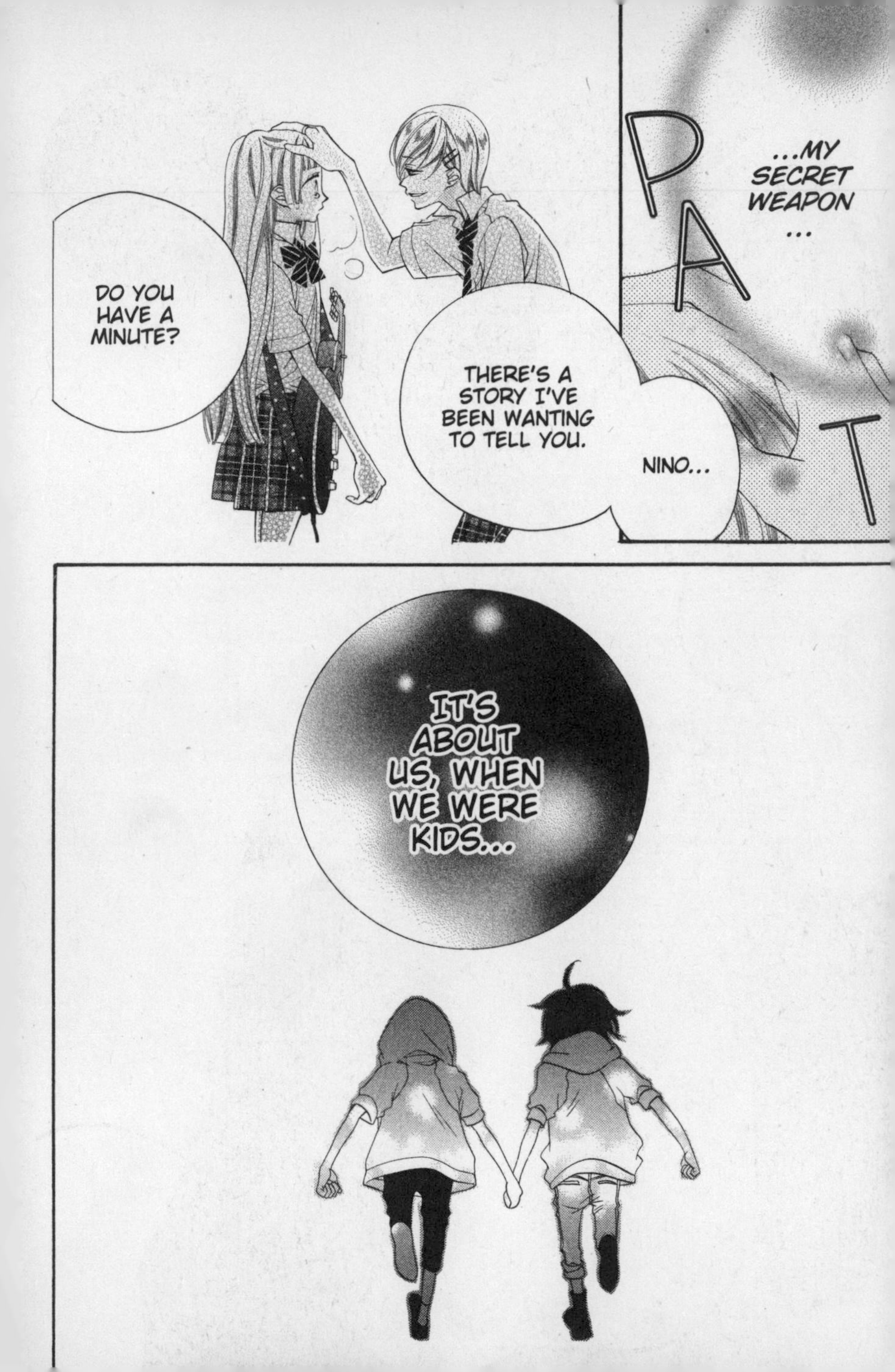
PAT
...MY SECRET WEAPON ...
NINO...
DO YOU HAVE A MINUTE?
THERE'S A STORY I'VE BEEN WANTING TO TELL YOU.
IT'S ABOUT US, WHEN WE WERE KIDS...

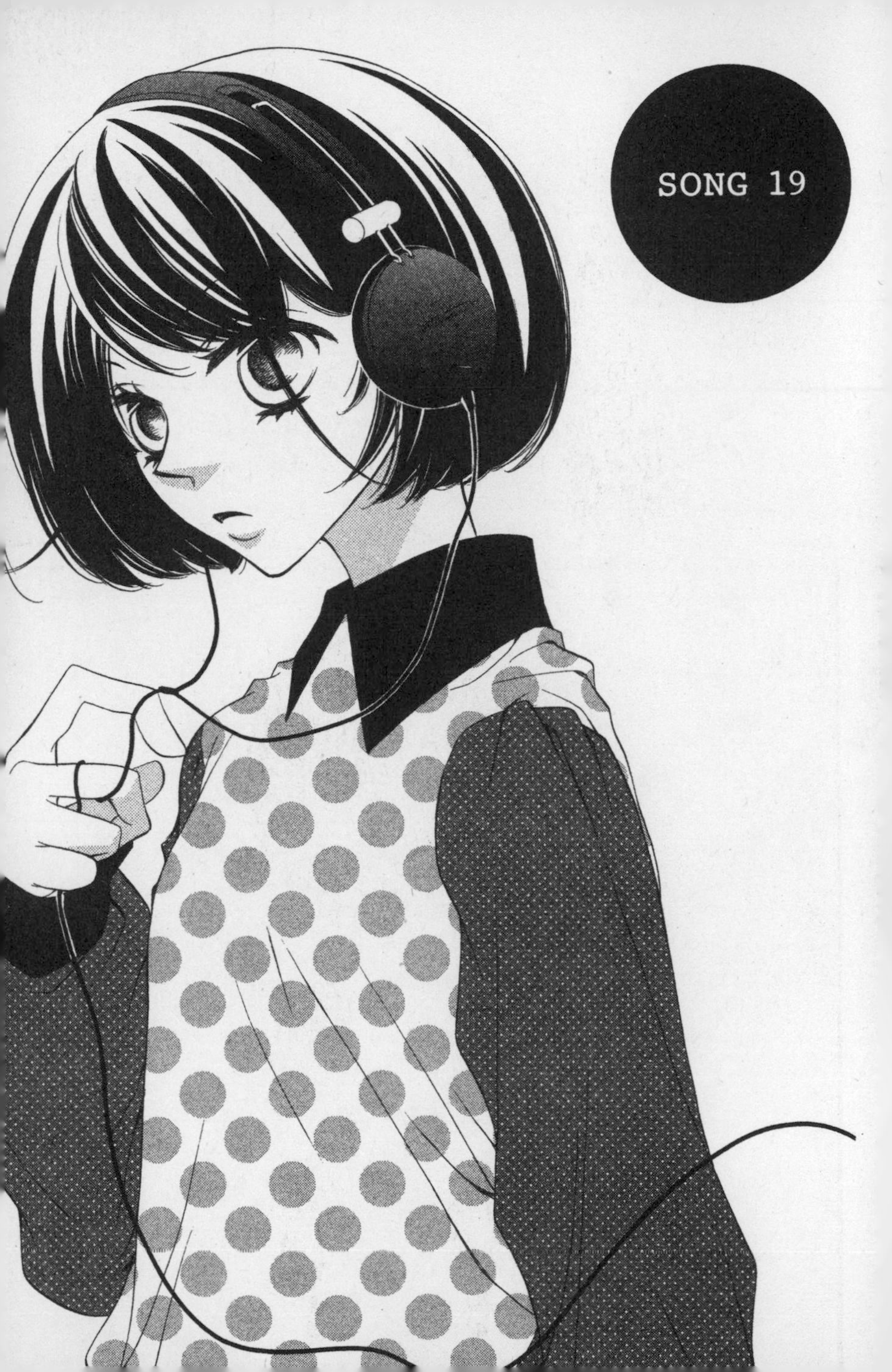
SONG 19

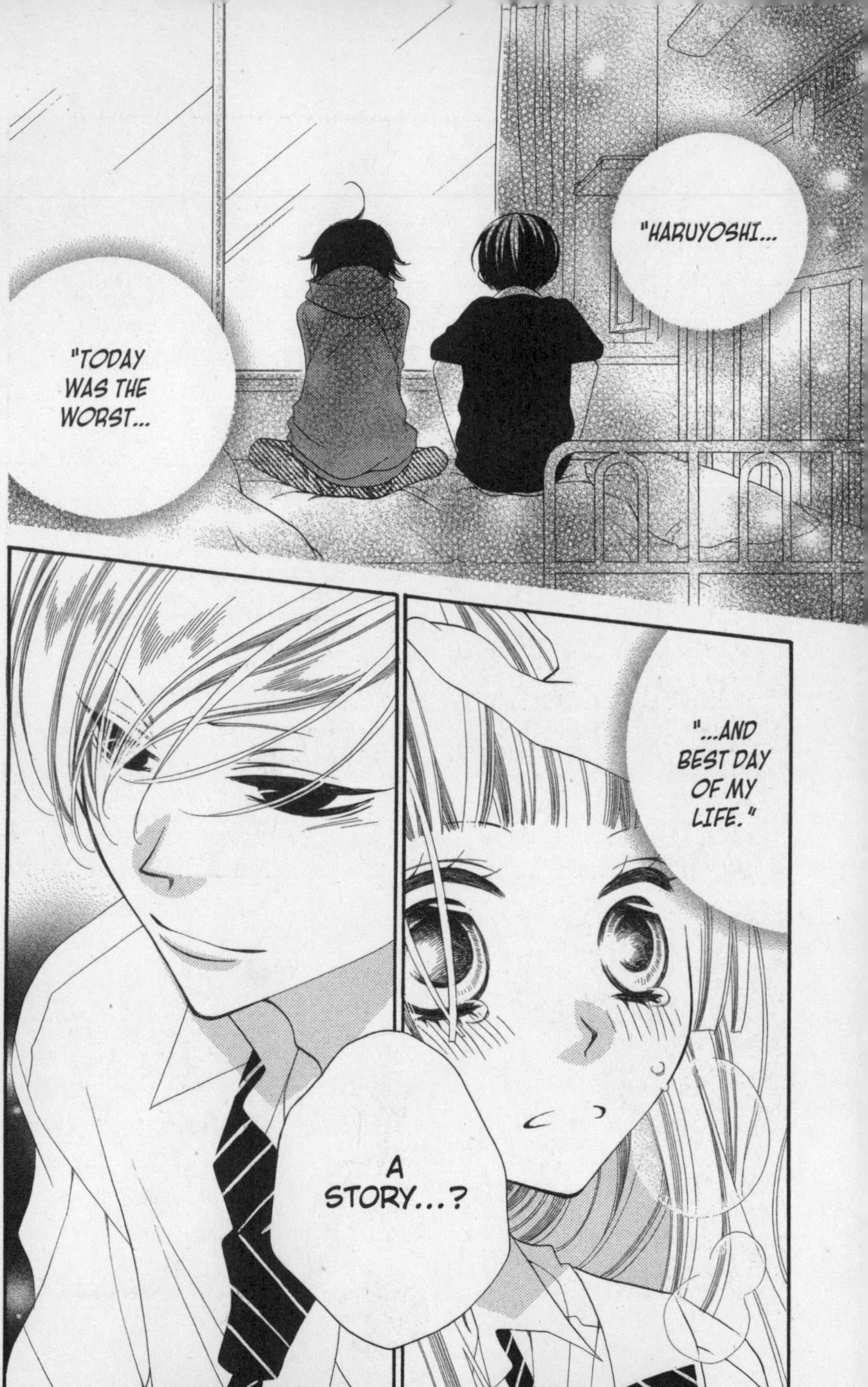
"HARUYOSHI...
"TODAY WAS THE WORST...
"...AND BEST DAY OF MY LIFE."
A STORY...?

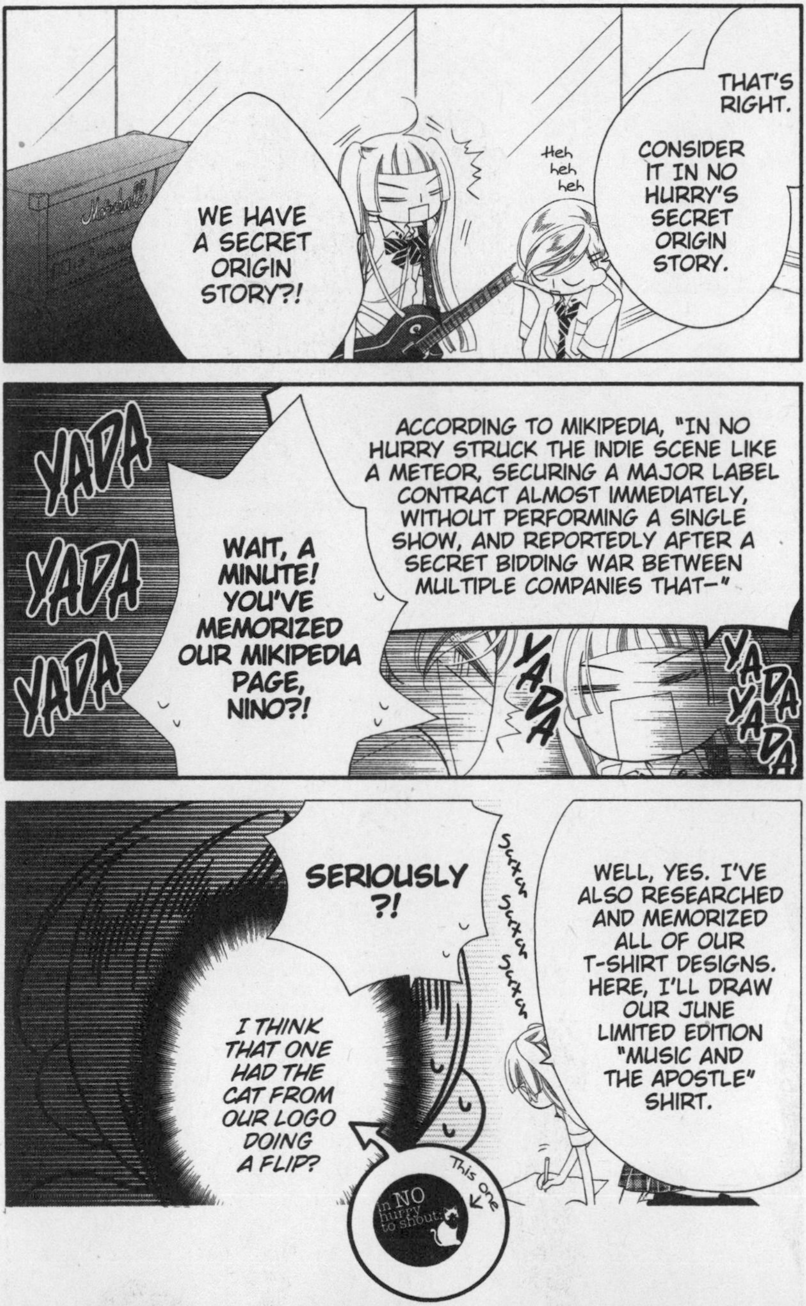
THAT'S RIGHT.
CONSIDER IT IN NO HURRY'S SECRET ORIGIN STORY.
Heh heh heh
WE HAVE A SECRET ORIGIN STORY?!
ACCORDING TO MIKIPEDIA, "IN NO HURRY STRUCK THE INDIE SCENE LIKE A METEOR, SECURING A MAJOR LABEL CONTRACT ALMOST IMMEDIATELY, WITHOUT PERFORMING A SINGLE SHOW, AND REPORTEDLY AFTER A SECRET BIDDING WAR BETWEEN MULTIPLE COMPANIES THAT–"
YADA YADA YADA
YADA
WAIT, A MINUTE! YOU'VE MEMORIZED OUR MIKIPEDIA PAGE, NINO?!
YADA YADA YADA
WELL, YES. I'VE ALSO RESEARCHED AND MEMORIZED ALL OF OUR T-SHIRT DESIGNS. HERE, I'LL DRAW OUR JUNE LIMITED EDITION "MUSIC AND THE APOSTLE" SHIRT.
SERIOUSLY ?!
I THINK THAT ONE HAD THE CAT FROM OUR LOGO DOING A FLIP?
This one
in NO hurry to shout;

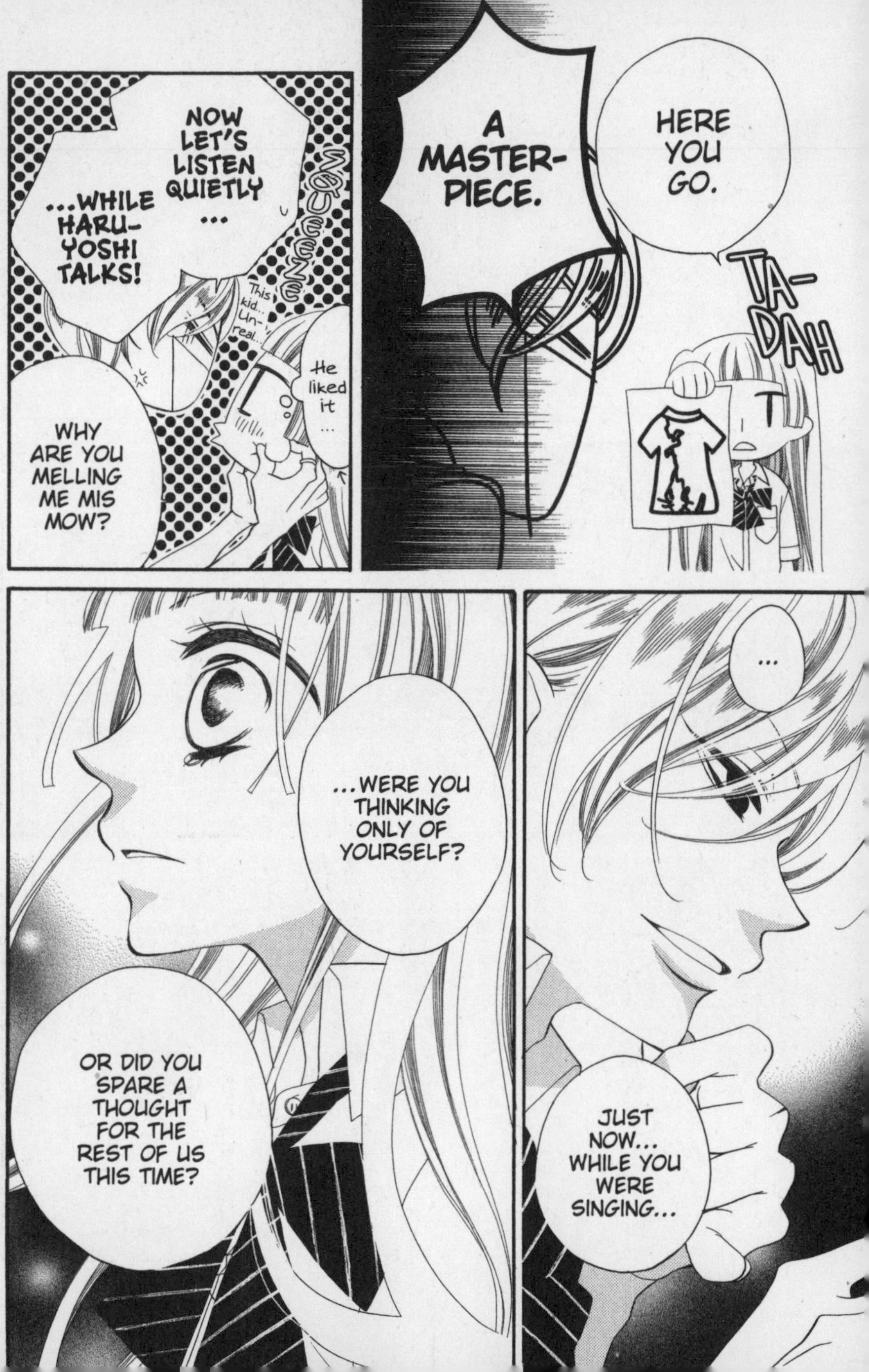
HERE YOU GO.
TA-DAH
A MASTER-PIECE.
SQUEEZE
NOW LET'S LISTEN QUIETLY...
...WHILE HARUYOSHI TALKS!
This kid... Unreal...
He liked it...
WHY ARE YOU MELLING ME MIS MOW?
...
JUST NOW... WHILE YOU WERE SINGING...
...WERE YOU THINKING ONLY OF YOURSELF?
OR DID YOU SPARE A THOUGHT FOR THE REST OF US THIS TIME?

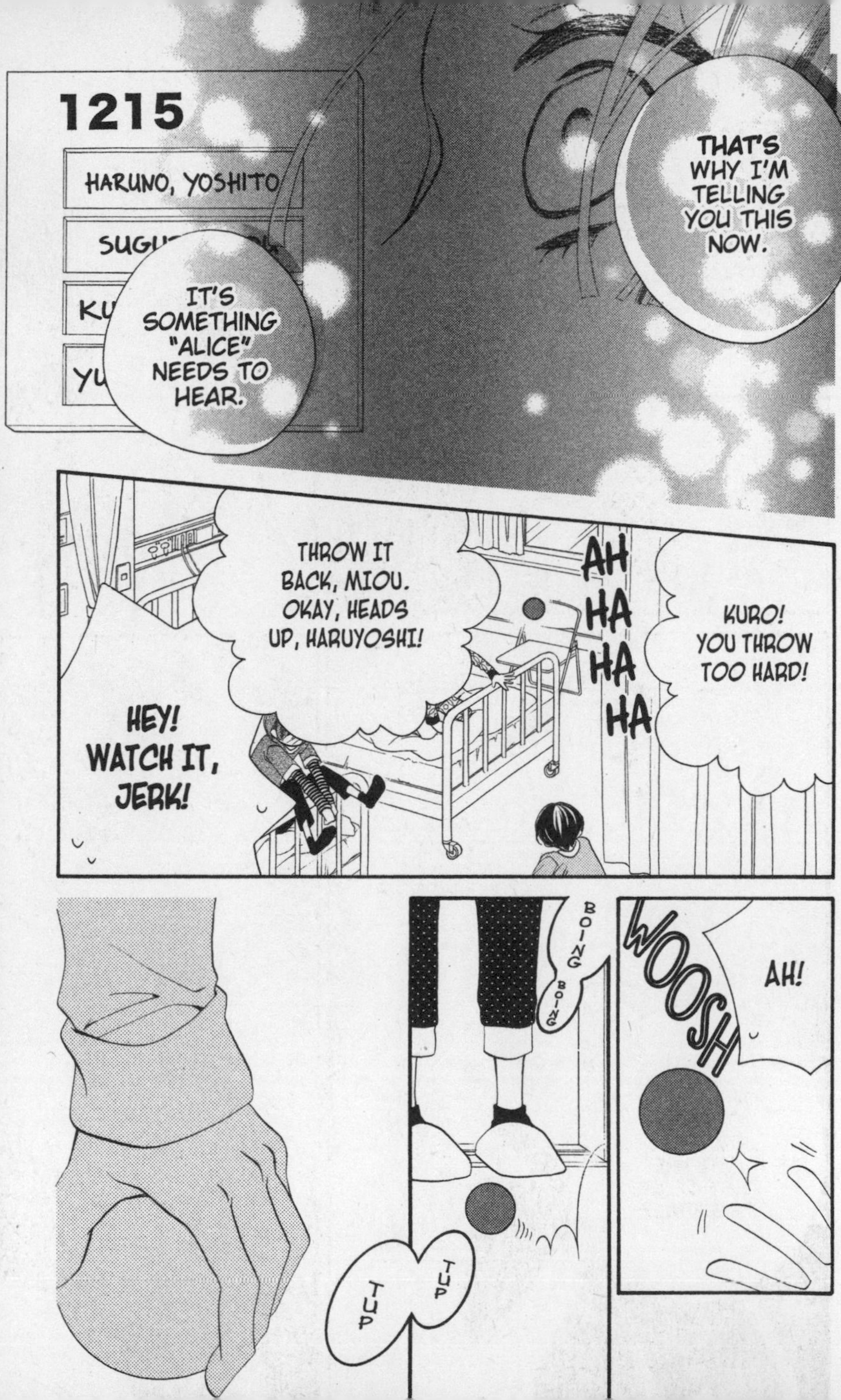
THAT'S WHY I'M TELLING YOU THIS NOW.
1215
HARUNO, YOSHITO
IT'S SOMETHING "ALICE" NEEDS TO HEAR.
KURO! YOU THROW TOO HARD!
AH HA HA HA
THROW IT BACK, MIOU. OKAY, HEADS UP, HARUYOSHI!
HEY! WATCH IT, JERK!
WOOSH
AH!
BOING BOING
TUP TUP

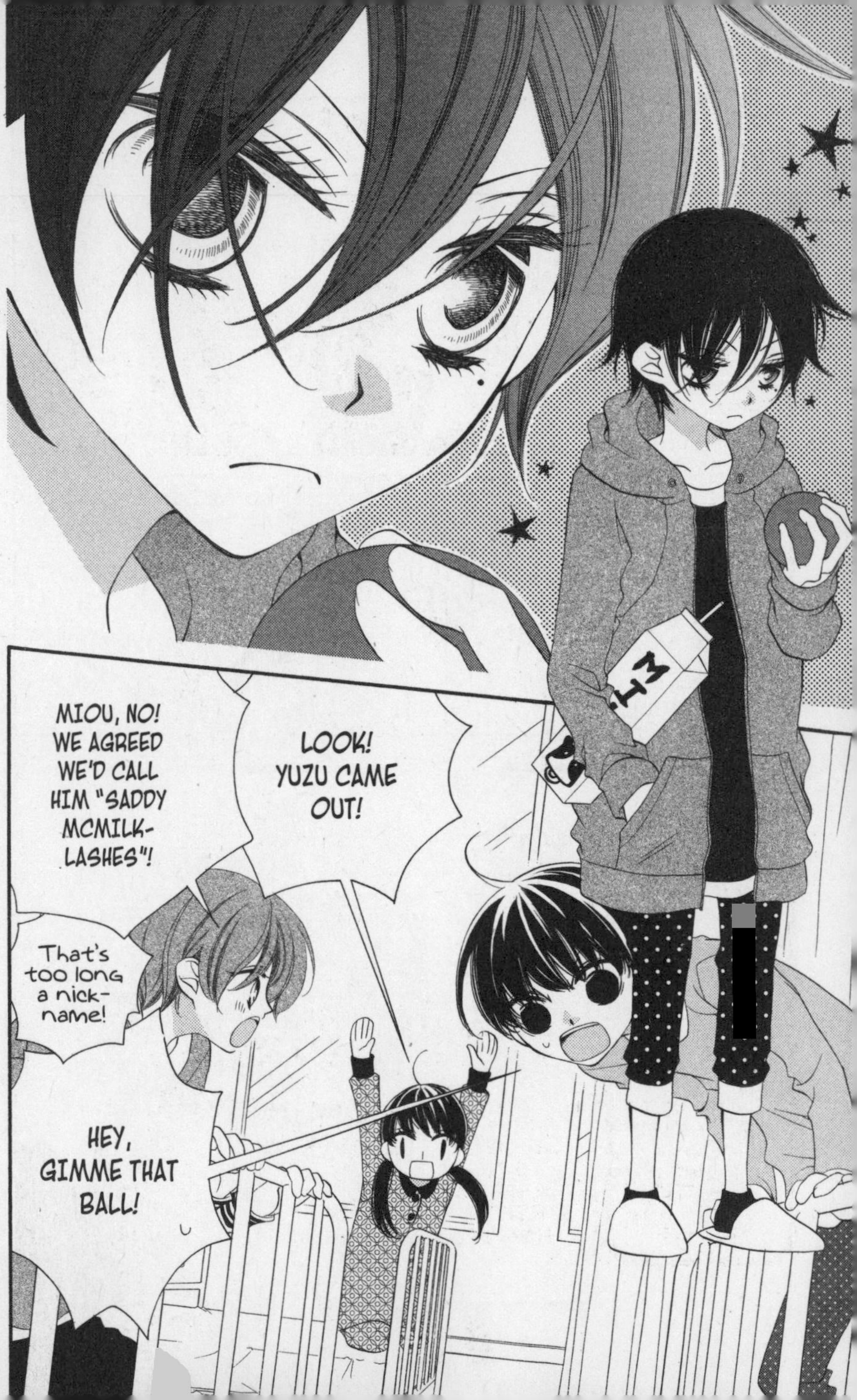
LOOK! YUZU CAME OUT!
MIOU, NO! WE AGREED WE'D CALL HIM "SADDY MCMILK-LASHES"!
That's too long a nick-name!
HEY, GIMME THAT BALL!

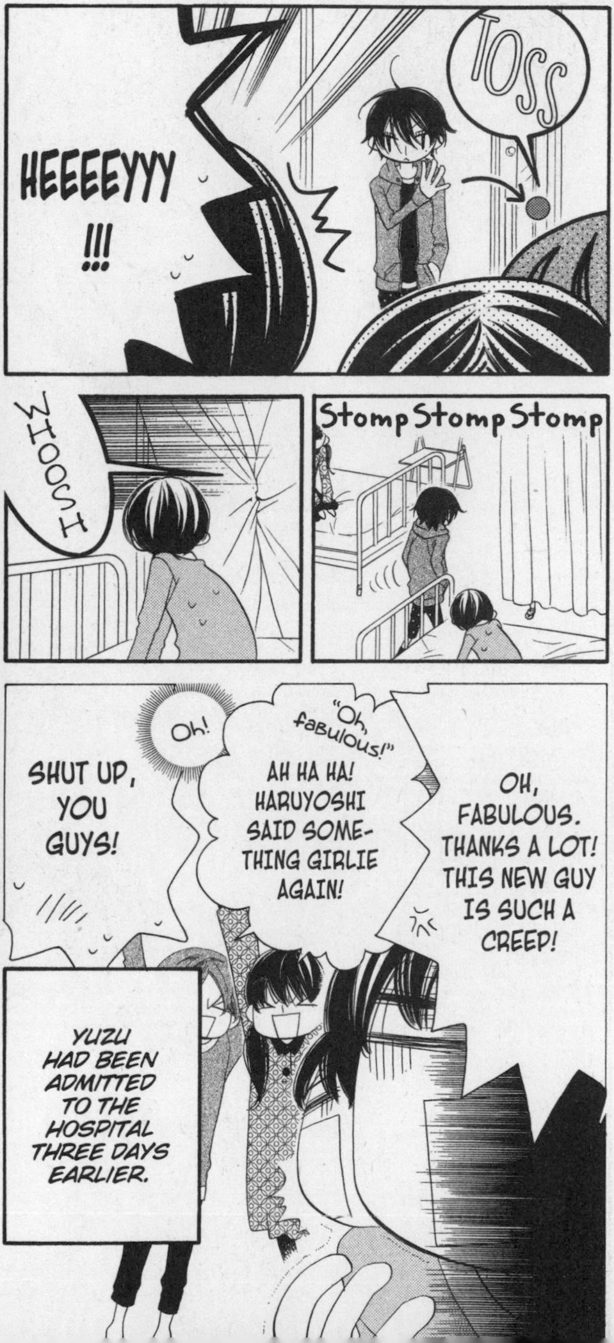
TOSS
HEEEEYYY!!!
Stomp Stomp Stomp
WHOOSH
OH, FABULOUS. THANKS A LOT! THIS NEW GUY IS SUCH A CREEP!
"Oh, fabulous!"
AH HA HA! HARUYOSHI SAID SOMETHING GIRLIE AGAIN!
Oh!
SHUT UP, YOU GUYS!
YUZU HAD BEEN ADMITTED TO THE HOSPITAL THREE DAYS EARLIER.

3

It'd been 10 years since I'd last gone to the Rock in Japan festival! I can't believe how fast time flies. This time our goal was to get reference photos, so my editor and I both brought cameras. We weren't sure how much we'd be allowed to photograph, but it turned out we could take photos during the first two songs of each artist, from the photography section.

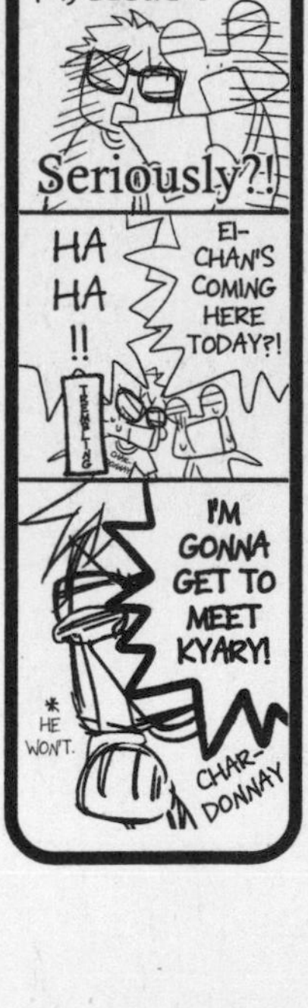
Seriously?!
HA HA!!
EI-CHAN'S COMING HERE TODAY?!
I'M GONNA GET TO MEET KYARY!
* HE WON'T.
CHAR-DONNAY

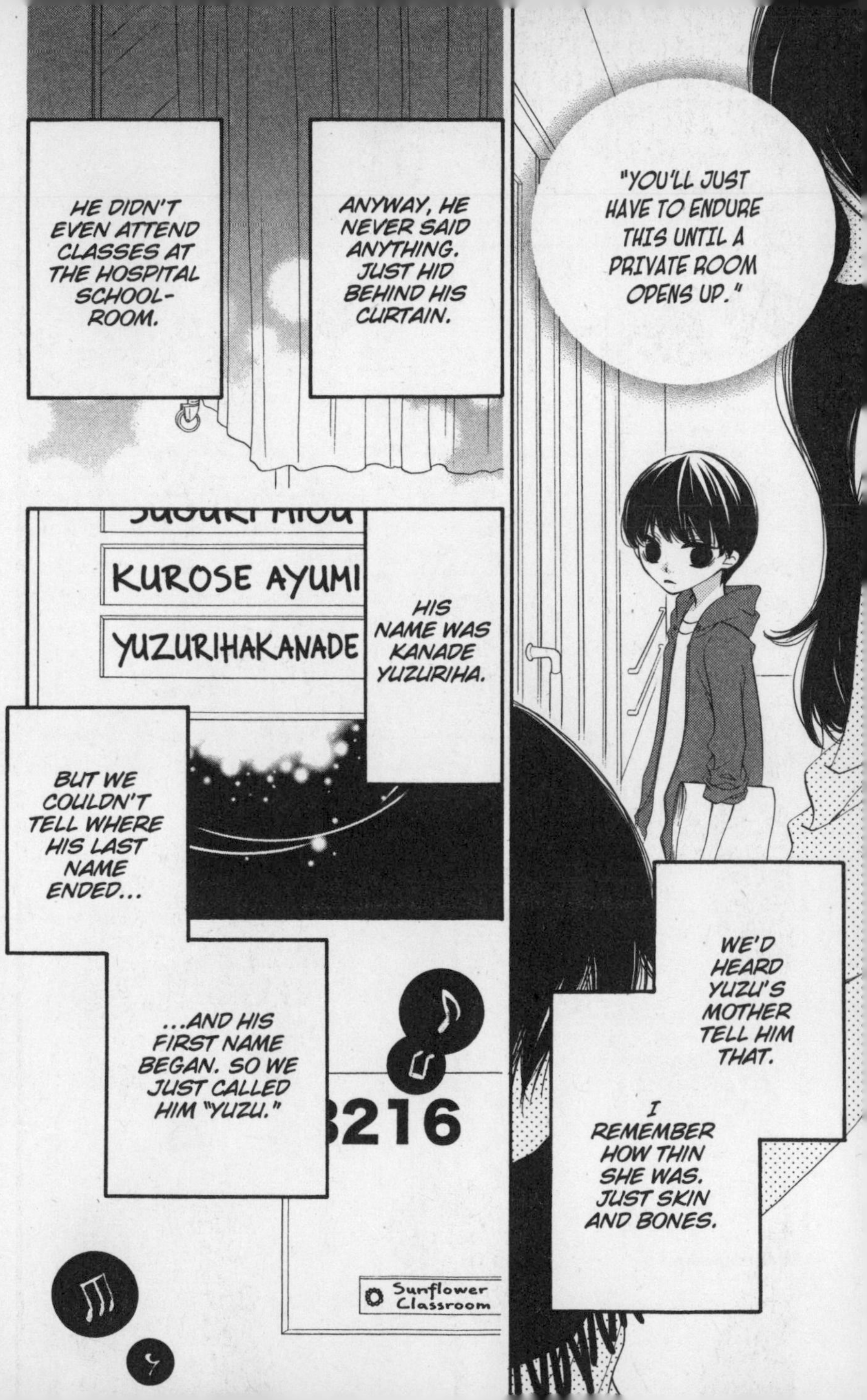
"YOU'LL JUST HAVE TO ENDURE THIS UNTIL A PRIVATE ROOM OPENS UP."
WE'D HEARD YUZU'S MOTHER TELL HIM THAT.
I REMEMBER HOW THIN SHE WAS. JUST SKIN AND BONES.
ANYWAY, HE NEVER SAID ANYTHING. JUST HID BEHIND HIS CURTAIN.
HE DIDN'T EVEN ATTEND CLASSES AT THE HOSPITAL SCHOOL-ROOM.
HIS NAME WAS KANADE YUZURIHA.
KUROSE AYUMI
YUZURIHAKANADE
BUT WE COULDN'T TELL WHERE HIS LAST NAME ENDED...
...AND HIS FIRST NAME BEGAN. SO WE JUST CALLED HIM "YUZU."
3216
Sunflower Classroom

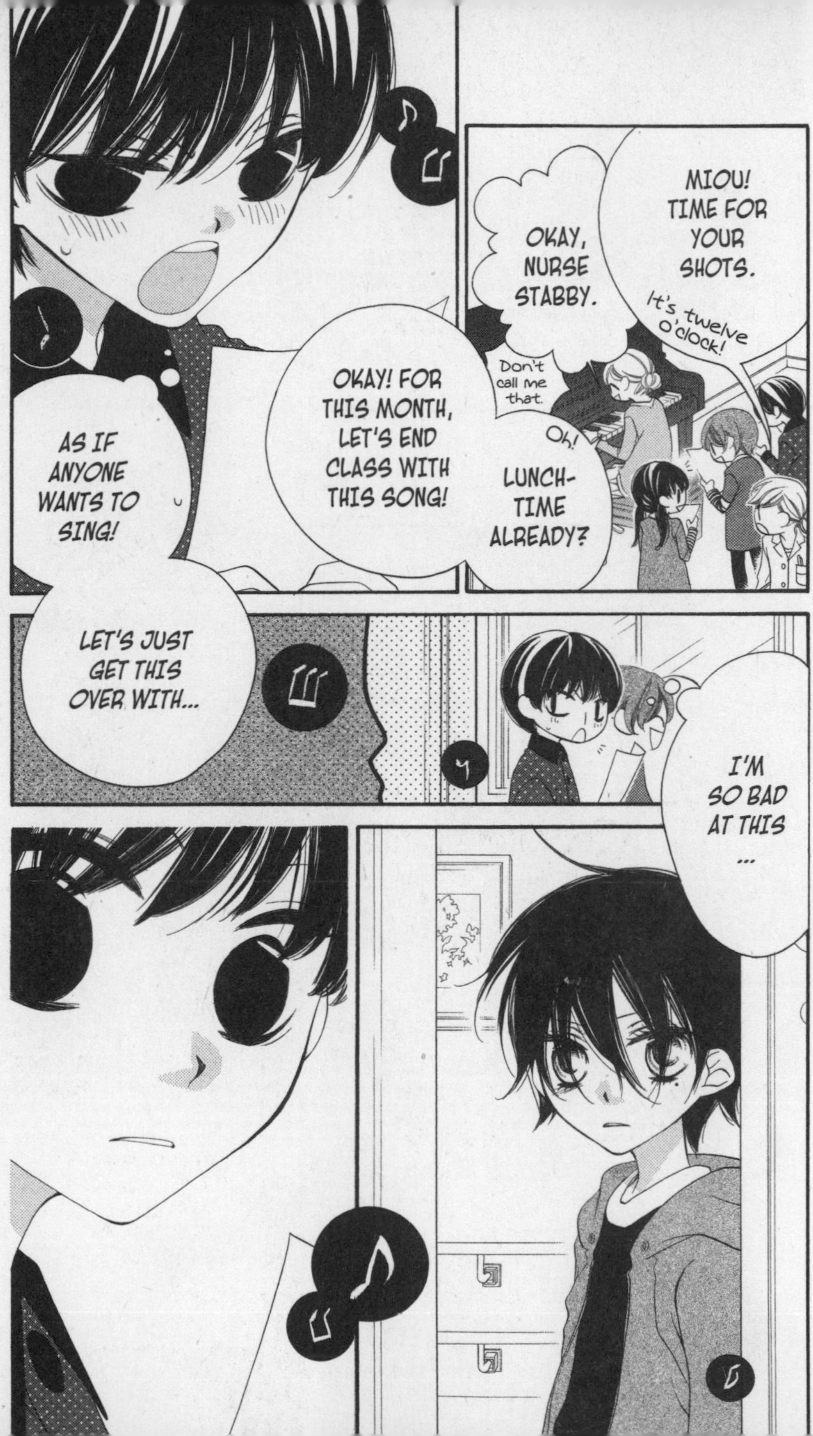
MIOU! TIME FOR YOUR SHOTS.
It's twelve o'clock!
OKAY, NURSE STABBY.
Don't call me that.
Oh!
LUNCH-TIME ALREADY?
OKAY! FOR THIS MONTH, LET'S END CLASS WITH THIS SONG!
AS IF ANYONE WANTS TO SING!
I'M SO BAD AT THIS ...
LET'S JUST GET THIS OVER WITH...

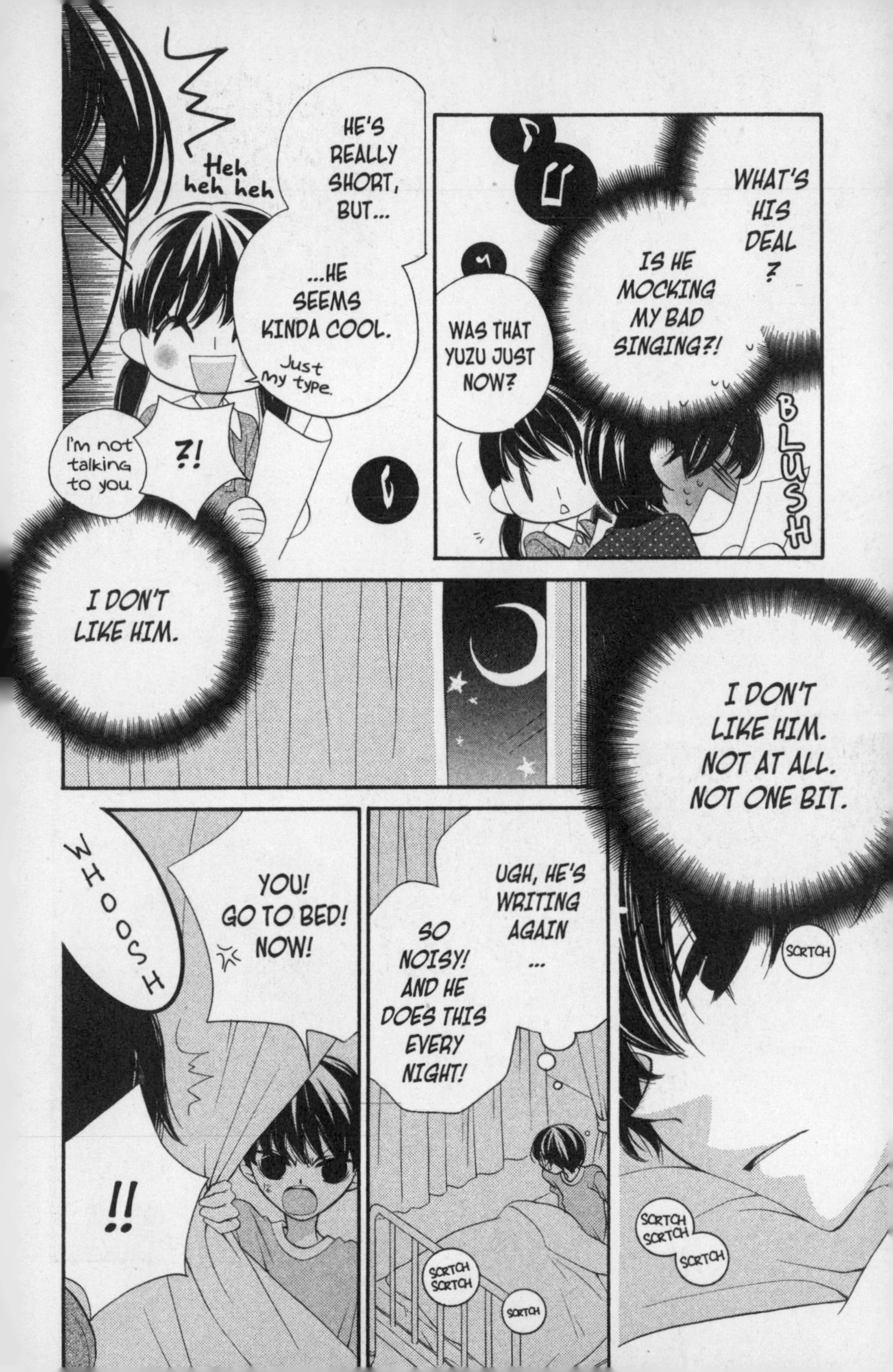
WHAT'S HIS DEAL ?
IS HE MOCKING MY BAD SINGING?!
WAS THAT YUZU JUST NOW?
BLUSH
Heh heh heh
HE'S REALLY SHORT, BUT...
...HE SEEMS KINDA COOL.
Just my type.
?!
I'm not talking to you.
I DON'T LIKE HIM.
I DON'T LIKE HIM. NOT AT ALL. NOT ONE BIT.
SCRTCH
SCRTCH SCRTCH
SCRTCH
UGH, HE'S WRITING AGAIN ...
SO NOISY! AND HE DOES THIS EVERY NIGHT!
SCRTCH SCRTCH
SCRTCH
WHOOSH
YOU! GO TO BED! NOW!
!!

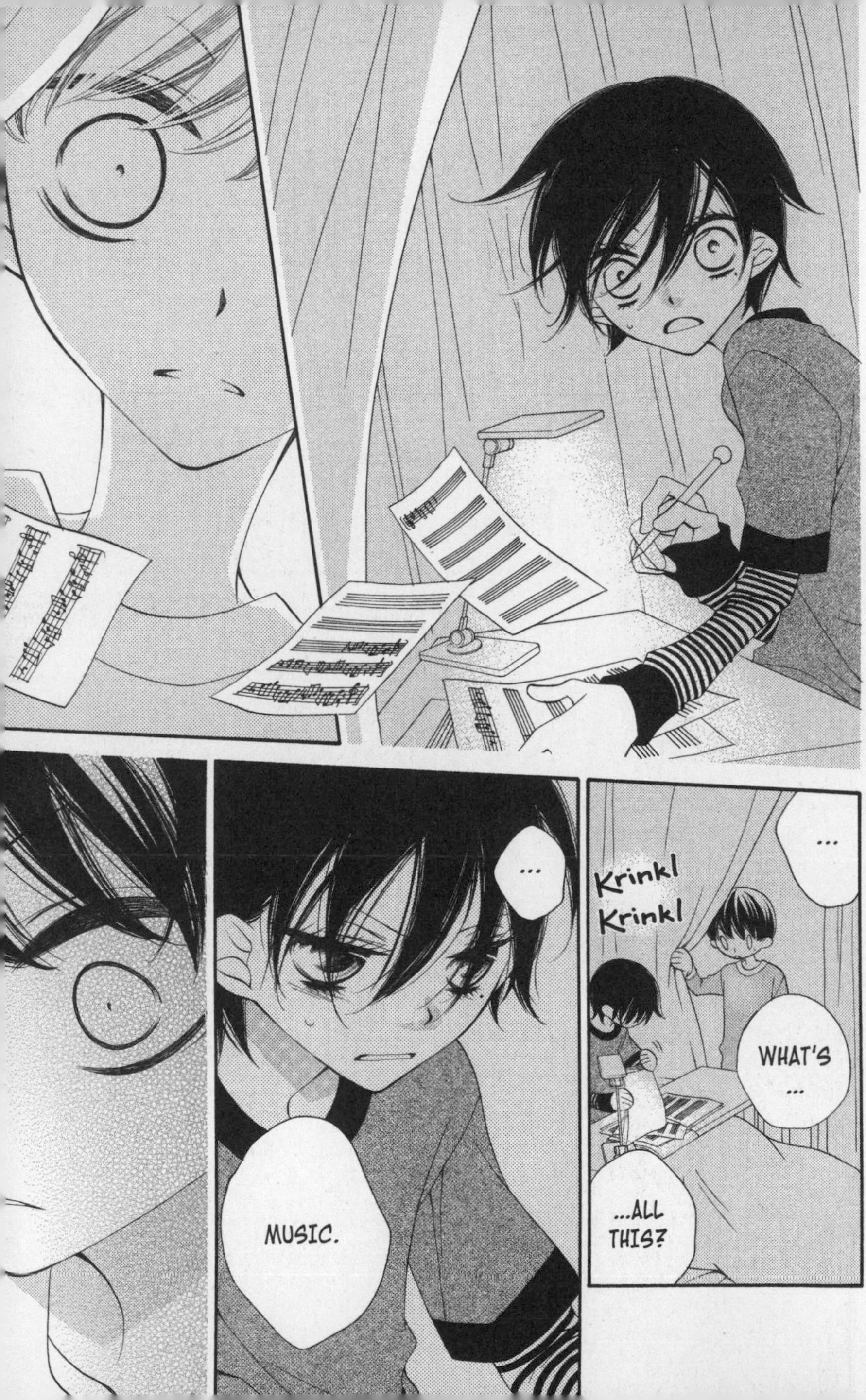
...
Krinkl
Krinkl
WHAT'S ...
...ALL THIS?
...
MUSIC.

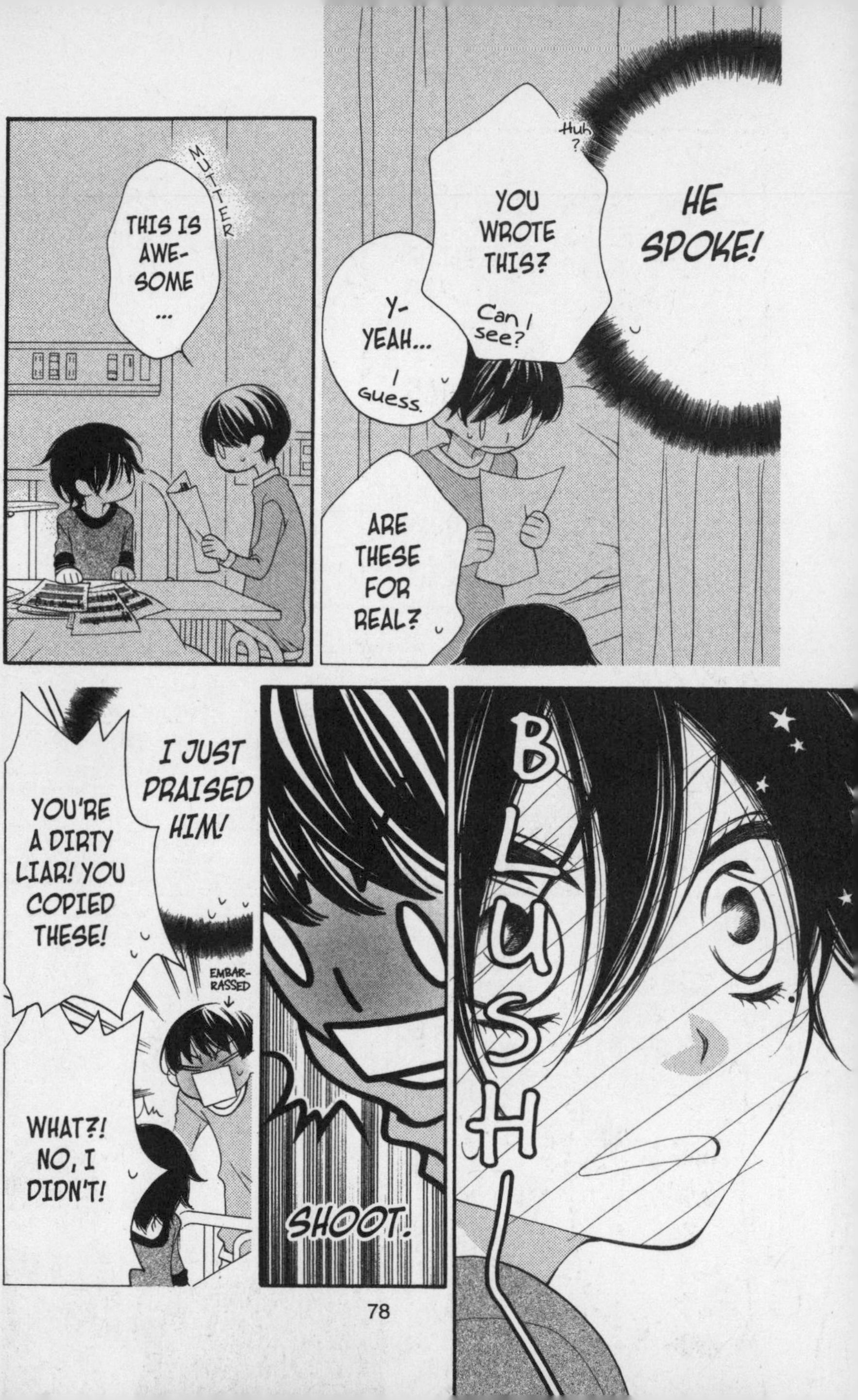

Huh?
HE SPOKE!
YOU WROTE THIS?
Can I see?
Y-YEAH... I Guess.
ARE THESE FOR REAL?
MUTTER
THIS IS AWE-SOME ...
BLUSH
SHOOT.
I JUST PRAISED HIM!
YOU'RE A DIRTY LIAR! YOU COPIED THESE!
EMBAR-RASSED
WHAT?! NO, I DIDN'T!

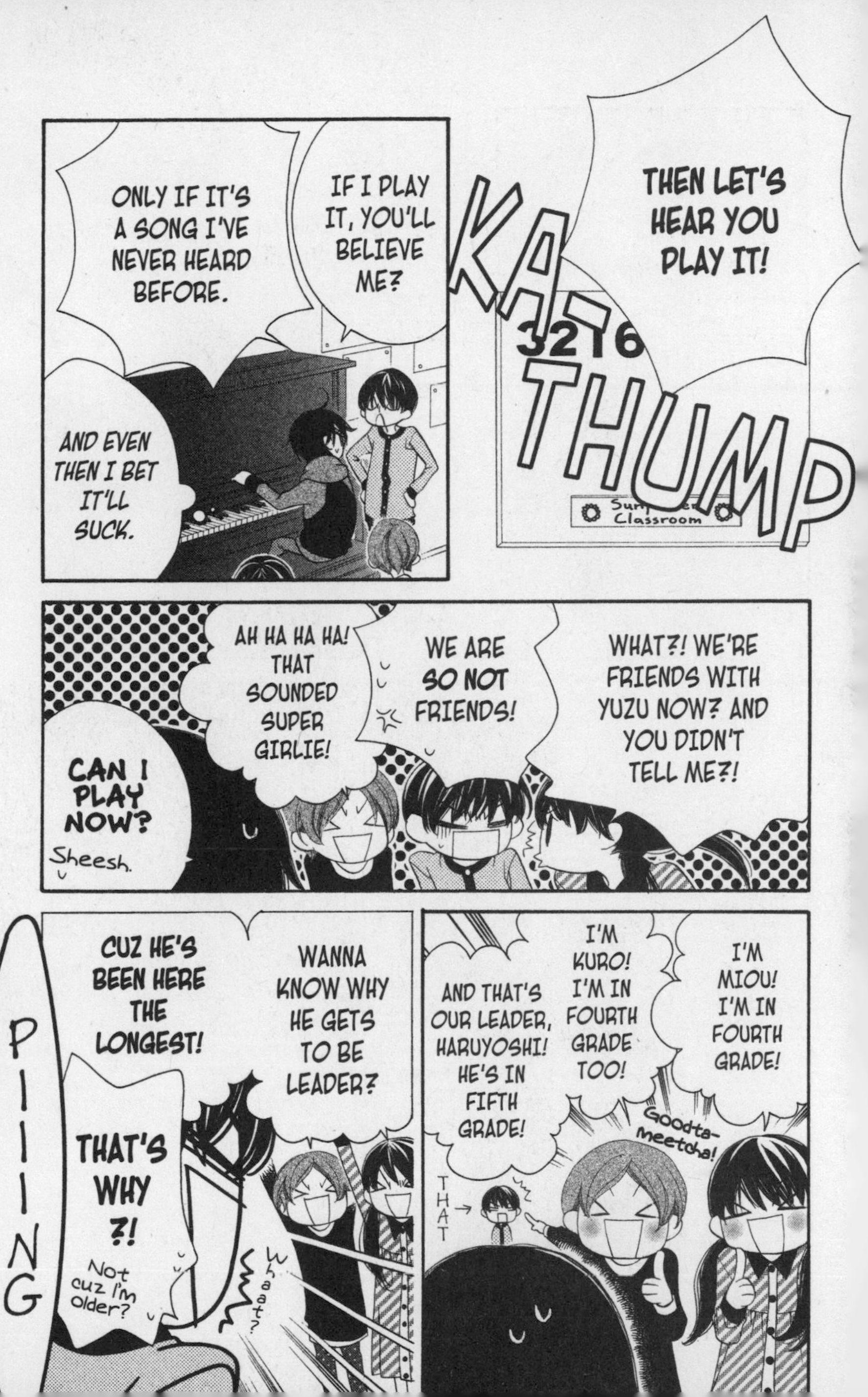
THEN LET'S HEAR YOU PLAY IT!
KA-THUMP
3216
Classroom
IF I PLAY IT, YOU'LL BELIEVE ME?
ONLY IF IT'S A SONG I'VE NEVER HEARD BEFORE.
AND EVEN THEN I BET IT'LL SUCK.
WHAT?! WE'RE FRIENDS WITH YUZU NOW? AND YOU DIDN'T TELL ME?!
WE ARE SO NOT FRIENDS!
AH HA HA HA! THAT SOUNDED SUPER GIRLIE!
CAN I PLAY NOW?
Sheesh.
I'M MIOU! I'M IN FOURTH GRADE!
I'M KURO! I'M IN FOURTH GRADE TOO!
AND THAT'S OUR LEADER, HARUYOSHI! HE'S IN FIFTH GRADE!
Goodta-meetcha!
THAT
WANNA KNOW WHY HE GETS TO BE LEADER?
CUZ HE'S BEEN HERE THE LONGEST!
PIIING
THAT'S WHY?!
Not cuz I'm older?
Whaat?

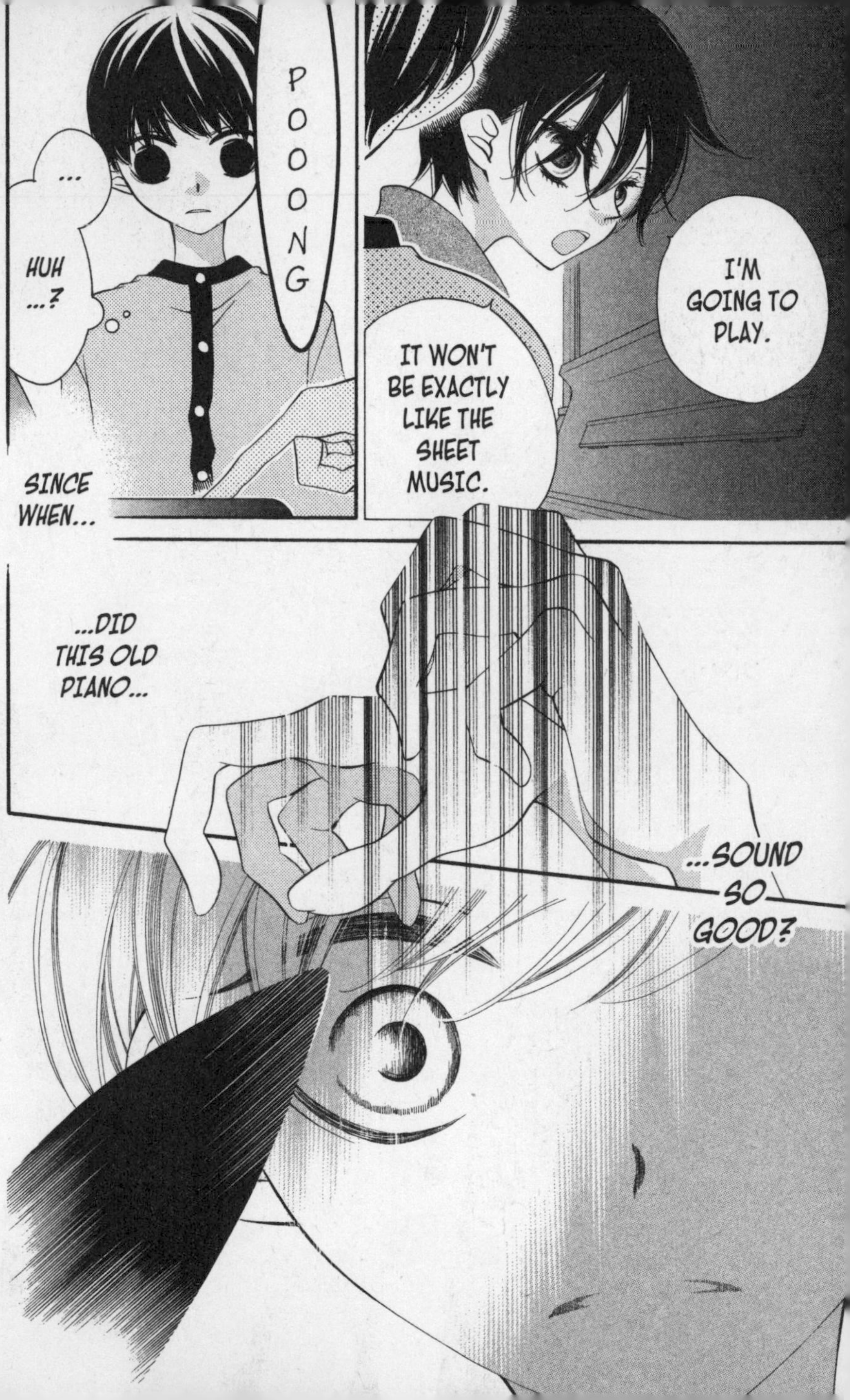
I'M GOING TO PLAY.
IT WON'T BE EXACTLY LIKE THE SHEET MUSIC.
POOOONG
...
HUH ...?
SINCE WHEN...
...DID THIS OLD PIANO...
...SOUND SO GOOD?

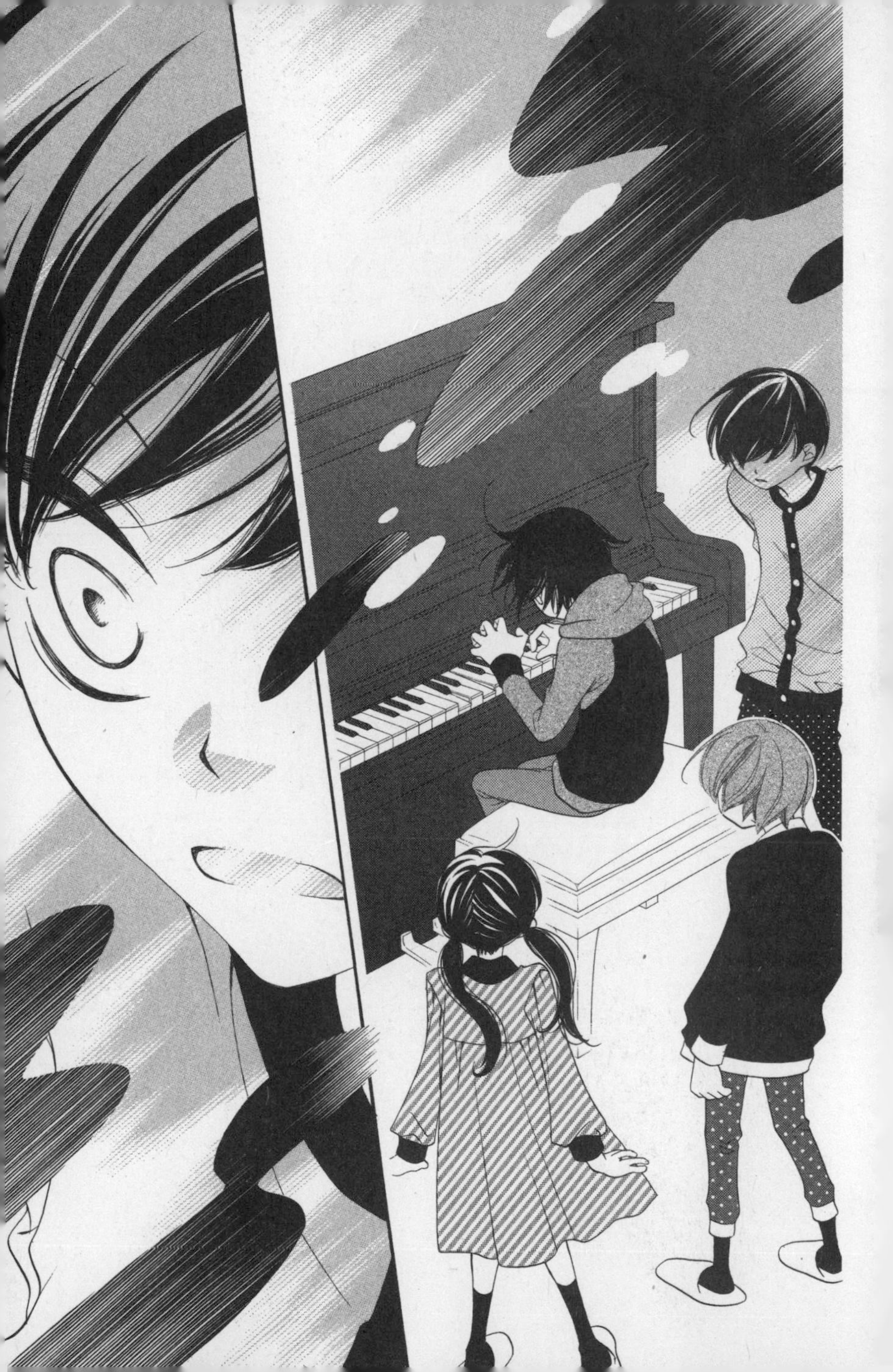

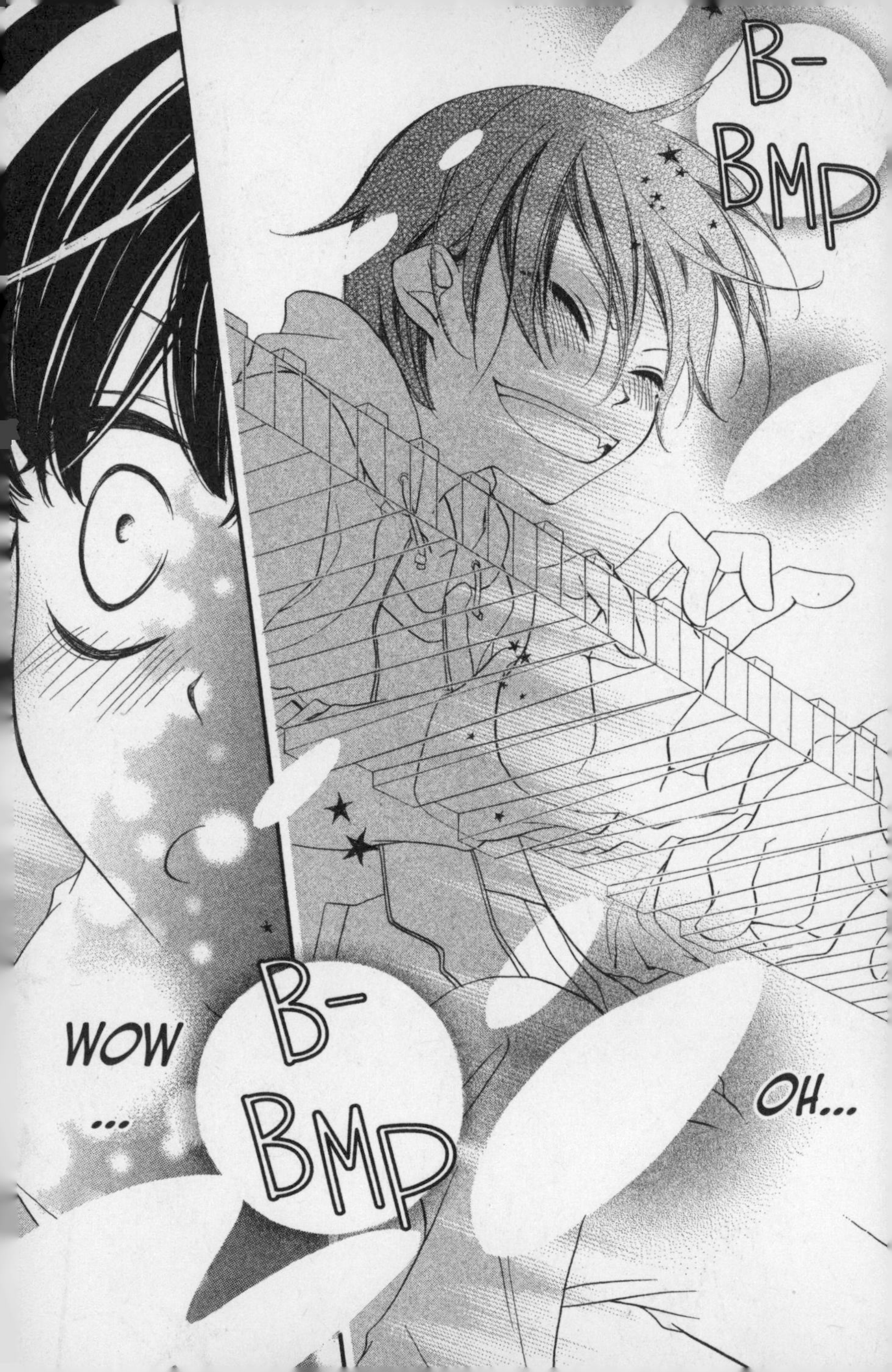
B-BMP
OH...
B-BMP
WOW ...

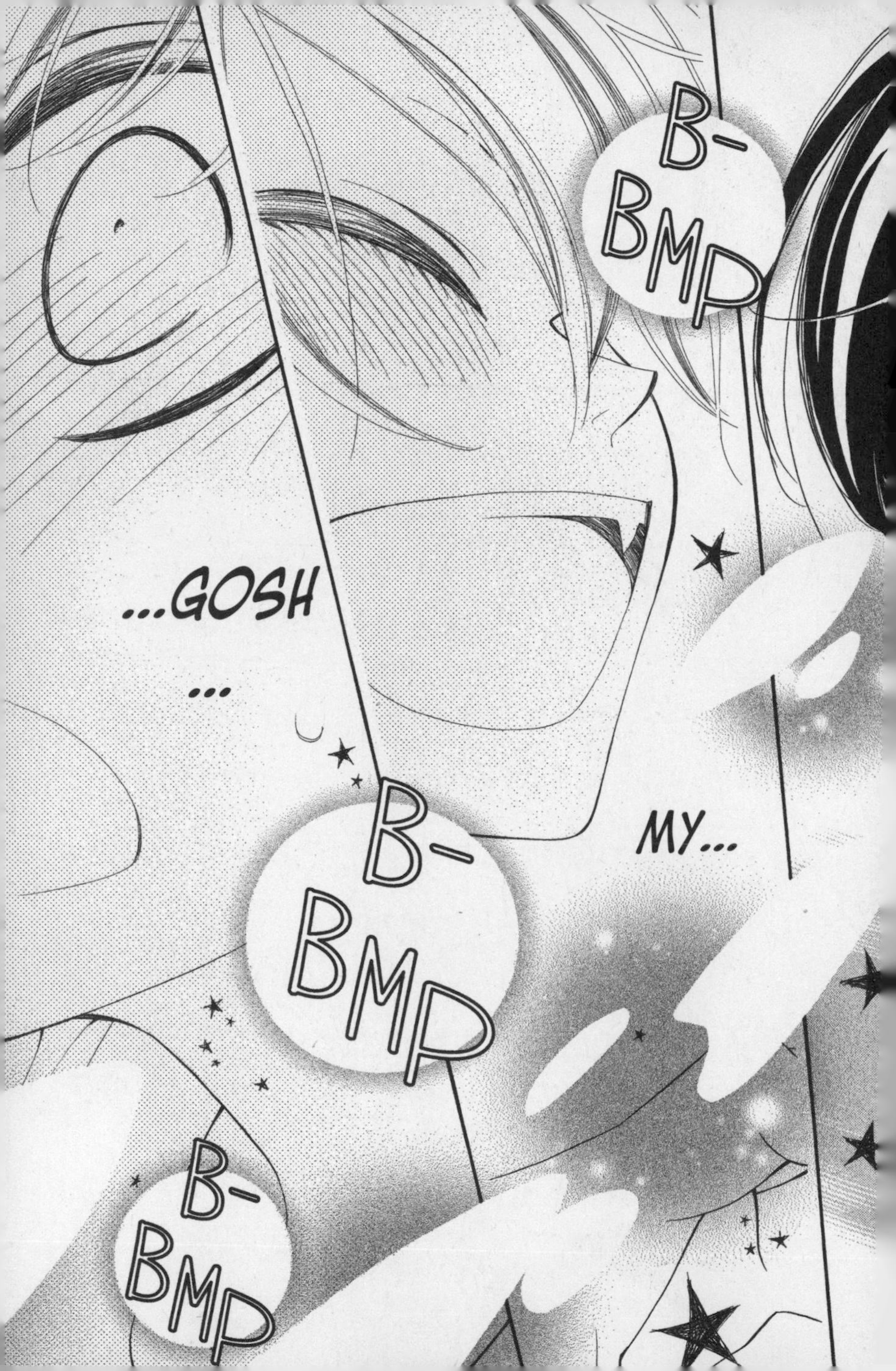
B-BMP
...GOSH
...
MY...
B-BMP
B-BMP

I TOLD YOU, NO MORE MUSIC!

...

I'M SORRY... I...

WHAT ARE YOU DOING, KANADE?

84

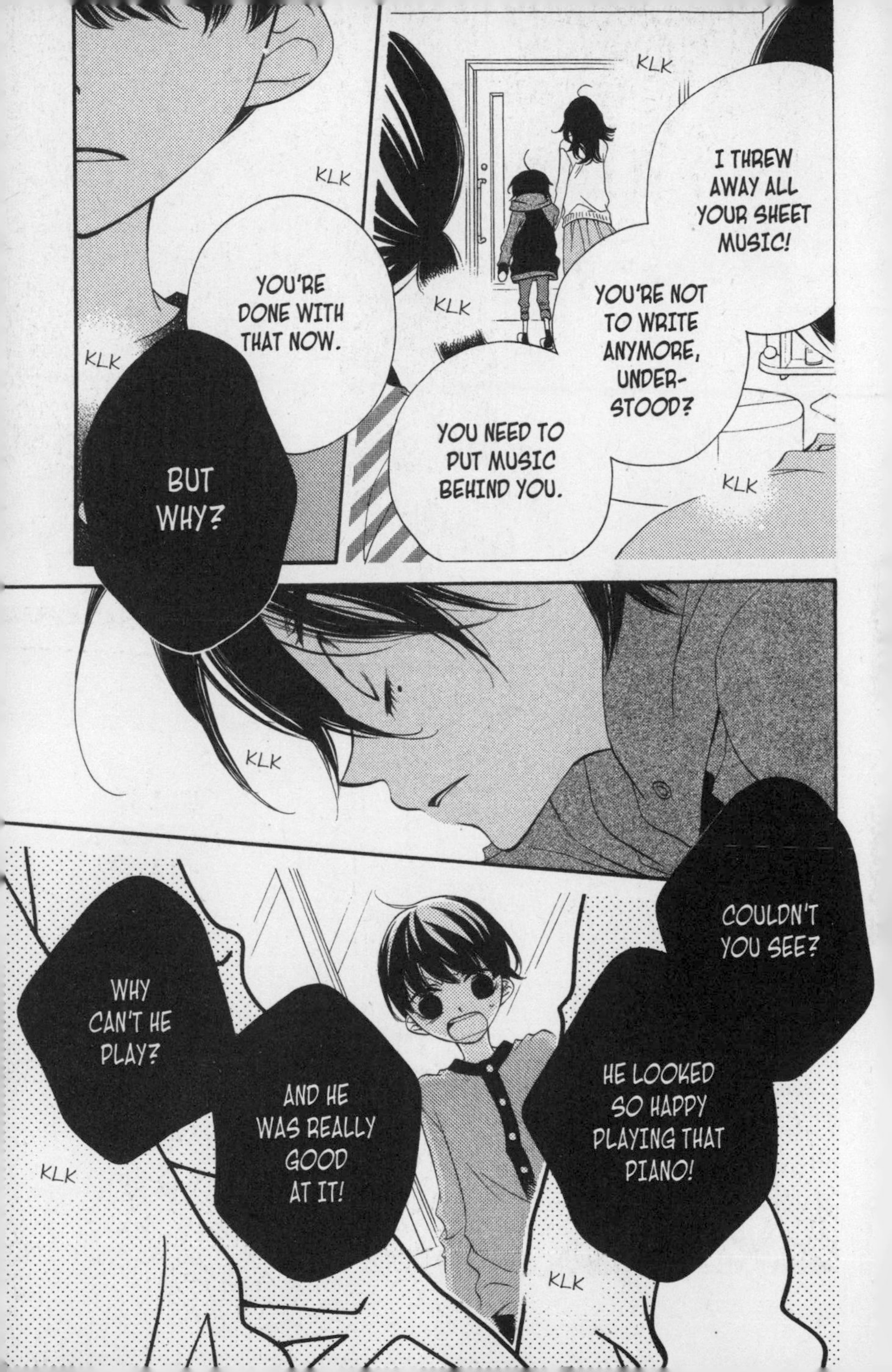
KLK
I THREW AWAY ALL YOUR SHEET MUSIC!
YOU'RE NOT TO WRITE ANYMORE, UNDER-STOOD?
KLK
YOU NEED TO PUT MUSIC BEHIND YOU.
KLK
YOU'RE DONE WITH THAT NOW.
KLK
KLK
BUT WHY?
KLK
COULDN'T YOU SEE?
HE LOOKED SO HAPPY PLAYING THAT PIANO!
AND HE WAS REALLY GOOD AT IT!
WHY CAN'T HE PLAY?
KLK
KLK

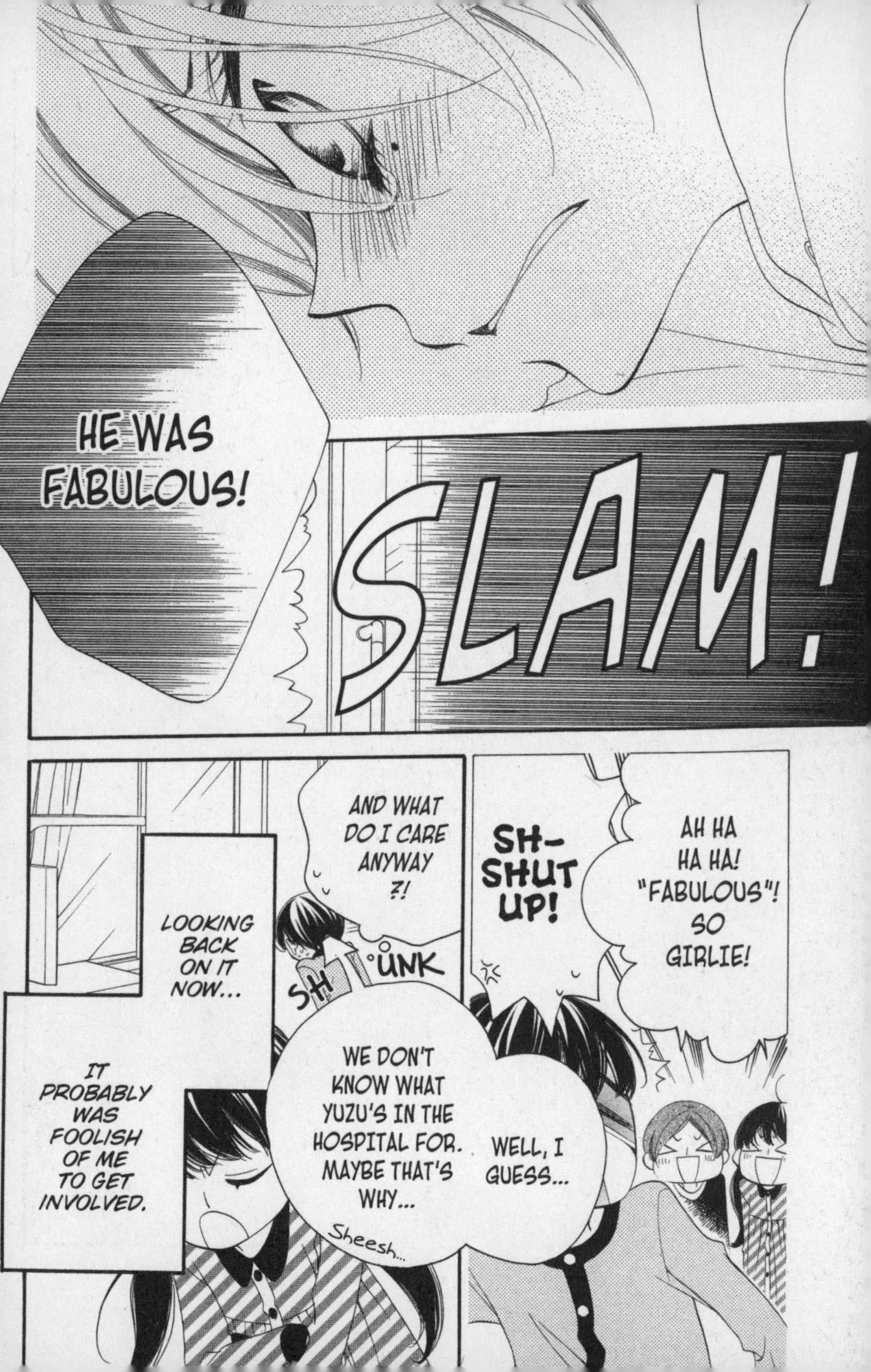
HE WAS FABULOUS!
SLAM!
AH HA HA HA! "FABULOUS"! SO GIRLIE!
SH-SHUT UP!
WELL, I GUESS...
WE DON'T KNOW WHAT YUZU'S IN THE HOSPITAL FOR. MAYBE THAT'S WHY...
Sheesh...
AND WHAT DO I CARE ANYWAY?!
SHUNK
LOOKING BACK ON IT NOW...
IT PROBABLY WAS FOOLISH OF ME TO GET INVOLVED.

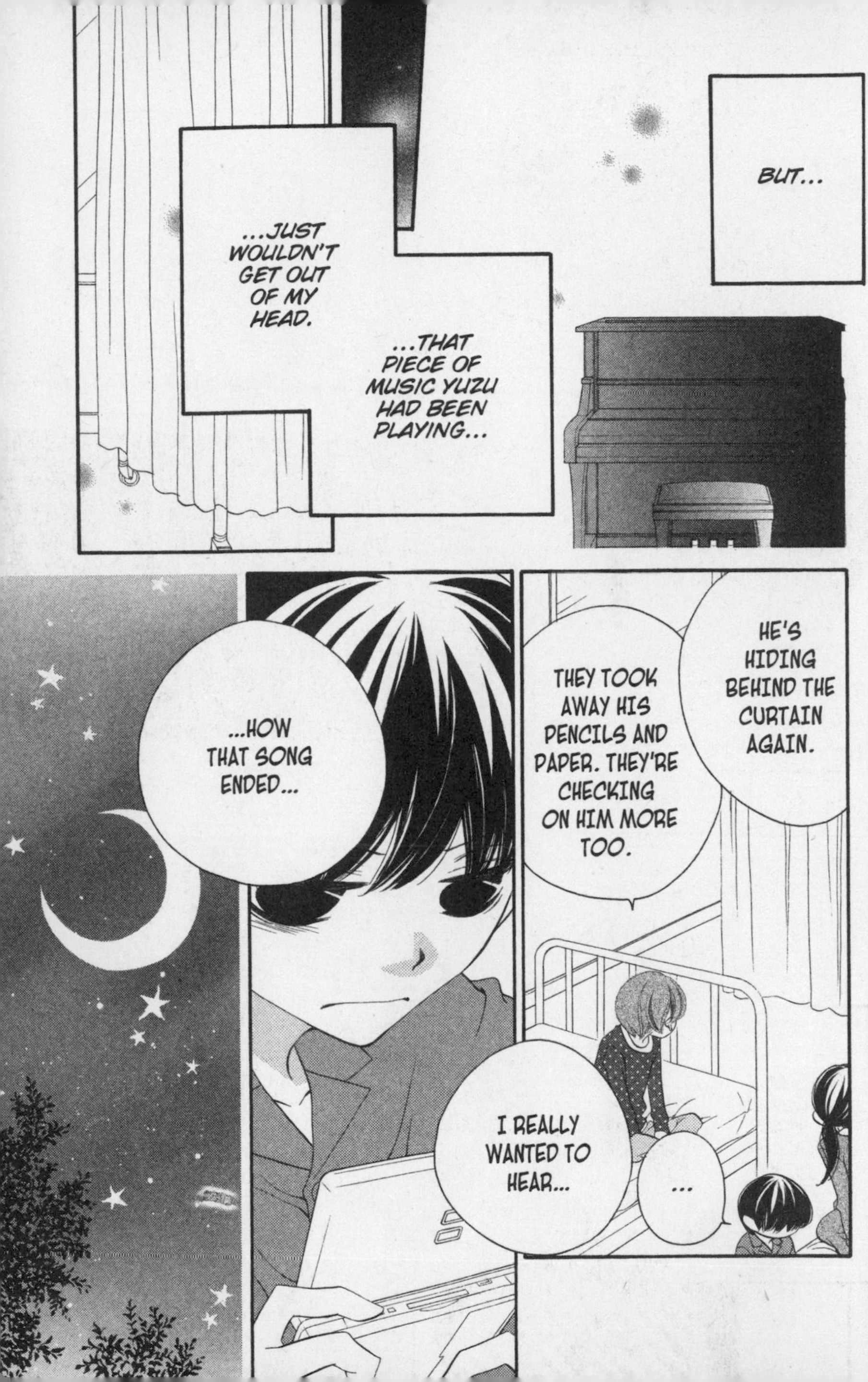
BUT...
...THAT PIECE OF MUSIC YUZU HAD BEEN PLAYING...
...JUST WOULDN'T GET OUT OF MY HEAD.
HE'S HIDING BEHIND THE CURTAIN AGAIN.
THEY TOOK AWAY HIS PENCILS AND PAPER. THEY'RE CHECKING ON HIM MORE TOO.
...
I REALLY WANTED TO HEAR...
...HOW THAT SONG ENDED...

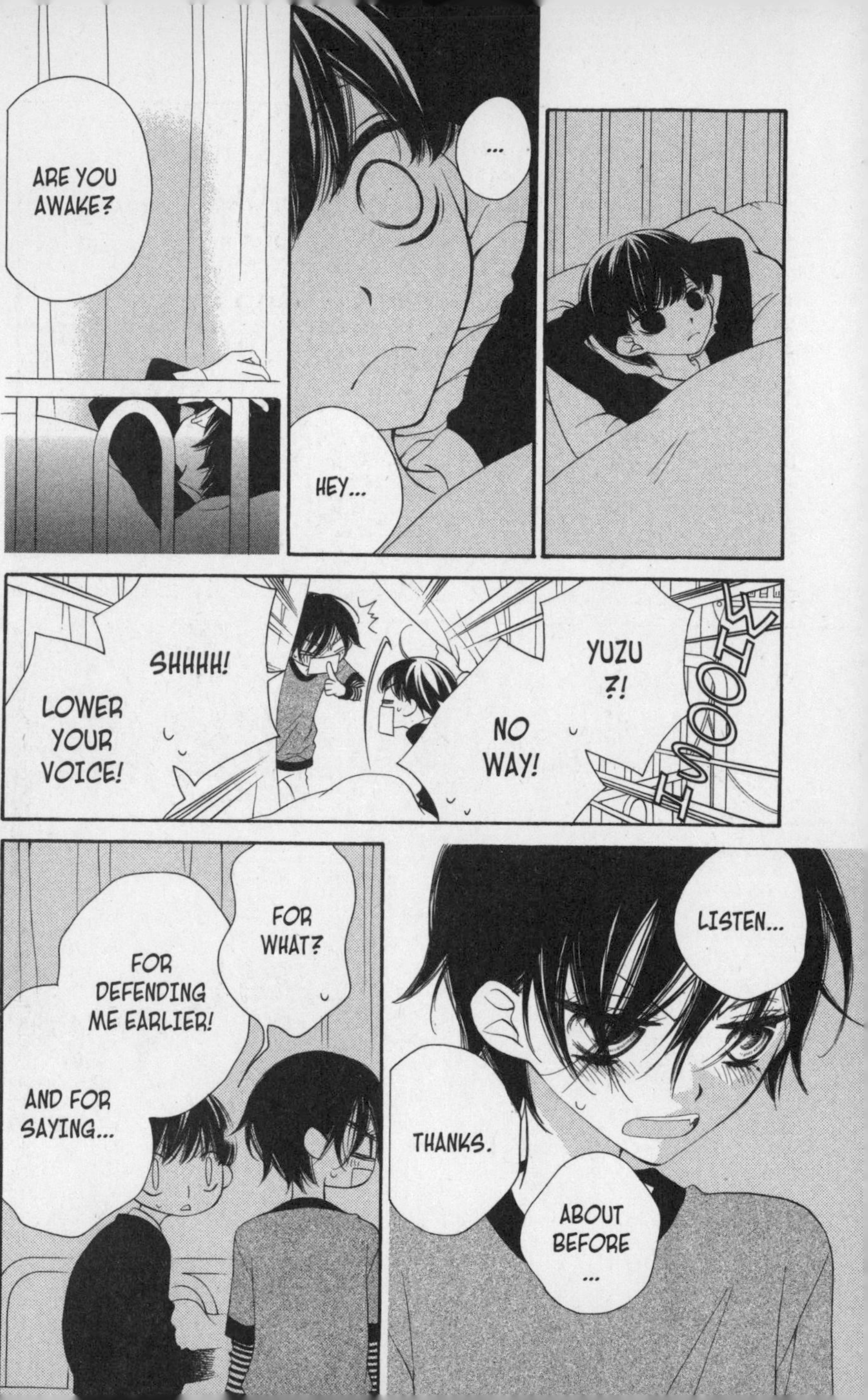
...
HEY...
ARE YOU AWAKE?
WHOOSH
YUZU ?!
NO WAY!
SHHHH!
LOWER YOUR VOICE!
LISTEN...
ABOUT BEFORE ...
THANKS.
FOR WHAT?
FOR DEFENDING ME EARLIER!
AND FOR SAYING...

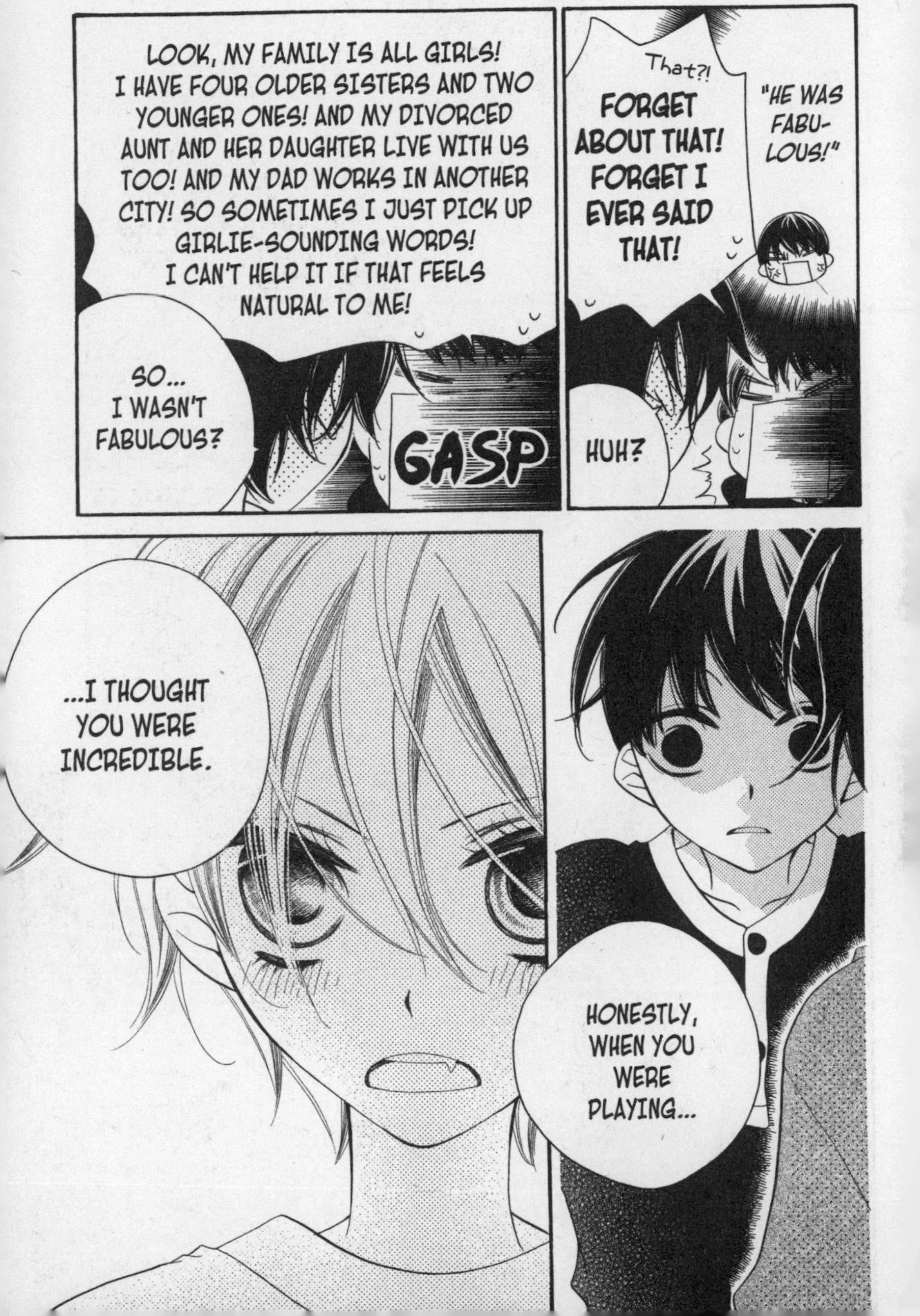

That?!
FORGET ABOUT THAT! FORGET I EVER SAID THAT!
"HE WAS FABULOUS!"
HUH?
LOOK, MY FAMILY IS ALL GIRLS! I HAVE FOUR OLDER SISTERS AND TWO YOUNGER ONES! AND MY DIVORCED AUNT AND HER DAUGHTER LIVE WITH US TOO! AND MY DAD WORKS IN ANOTHER CITY! SO SOMETIMES I JUST PICK UP GIRLIE-SOUNDING WORDS! I CAN'T HELP IT IF THAT FEELS NATURAL TO ME!
GASP
SO... I WASN'T FABULOUS?
HONESTLY, WHEN YOU WERE PLAYING...
...I THOUGHT YOU WERE INCREDIBLE.

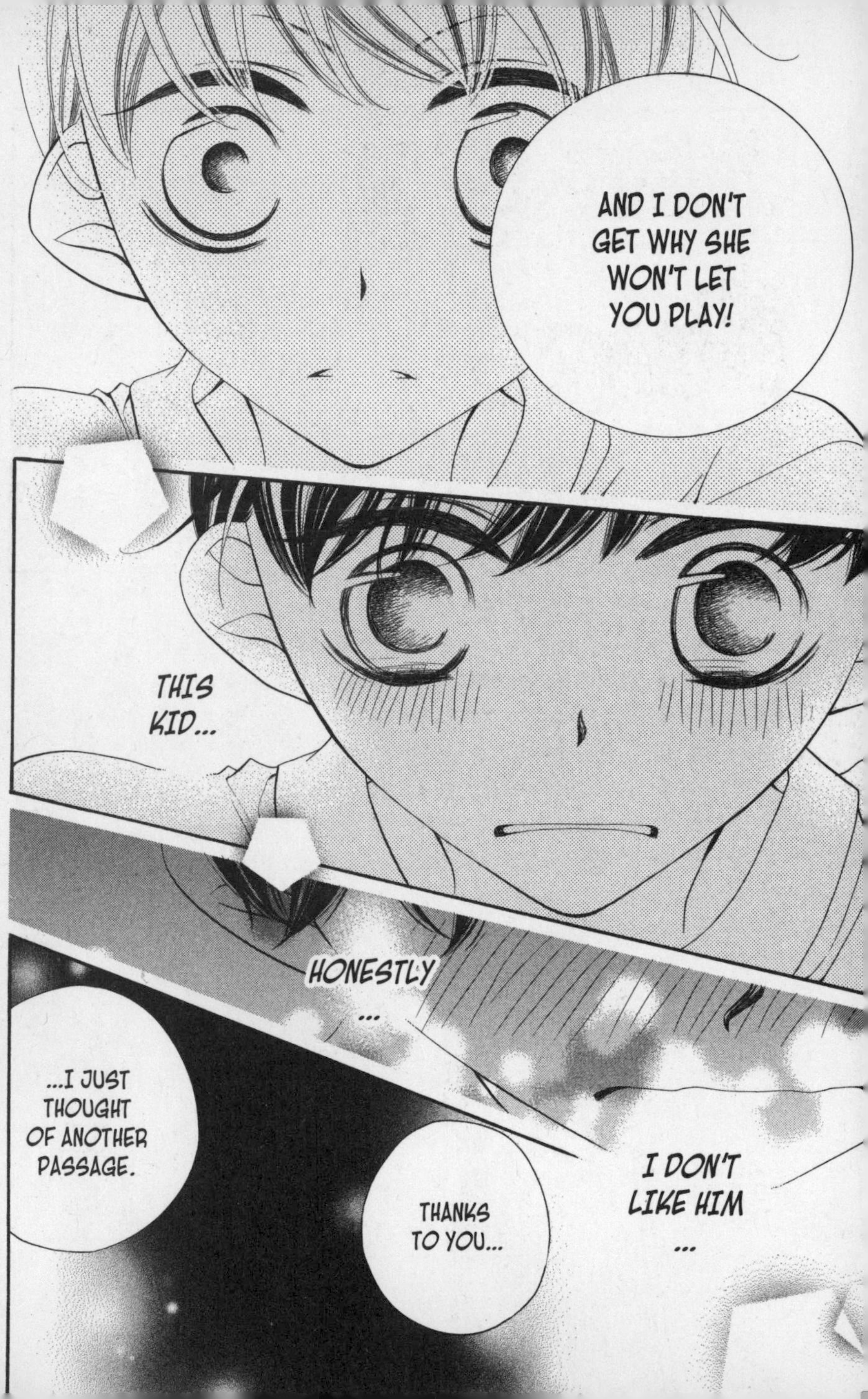
AND I DON'T GET WHY SHE WON'T LET YOU PLAY!
THIS KID...
HONESTLY ...
I DON'T LIKE HIM ...
THANKS TO YOU...
...I JUST THOUGHT OF ANOTHER PASSAGE.

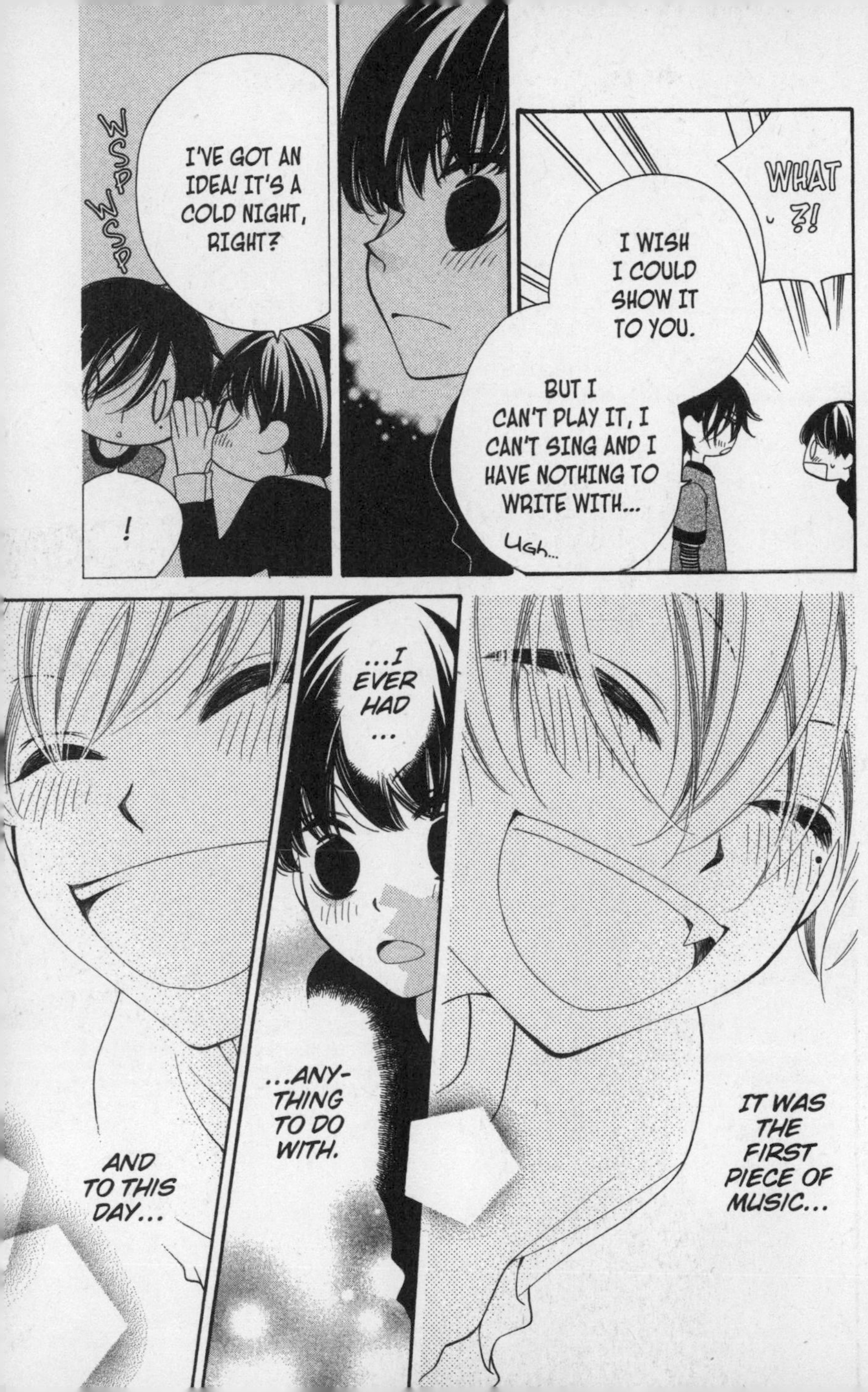
WHAT ?!
I WISH I COULD SHOW IT TO YOU.
BUT I CAN'T PLAY IT, I CAN'T SING AND I HAVE NOTHING TO WRITE WITH...
Ugh...
I'VE GOT AN IDEA! IT'S A COLD NIGHT, RIGHT?
WSP WSP WSP
!
IT WAS THE FIRST PIECE OF MUSIC...
...I EVER HAD...
...ANY-THING TO DO WITH.
AND TO THIS DAY...

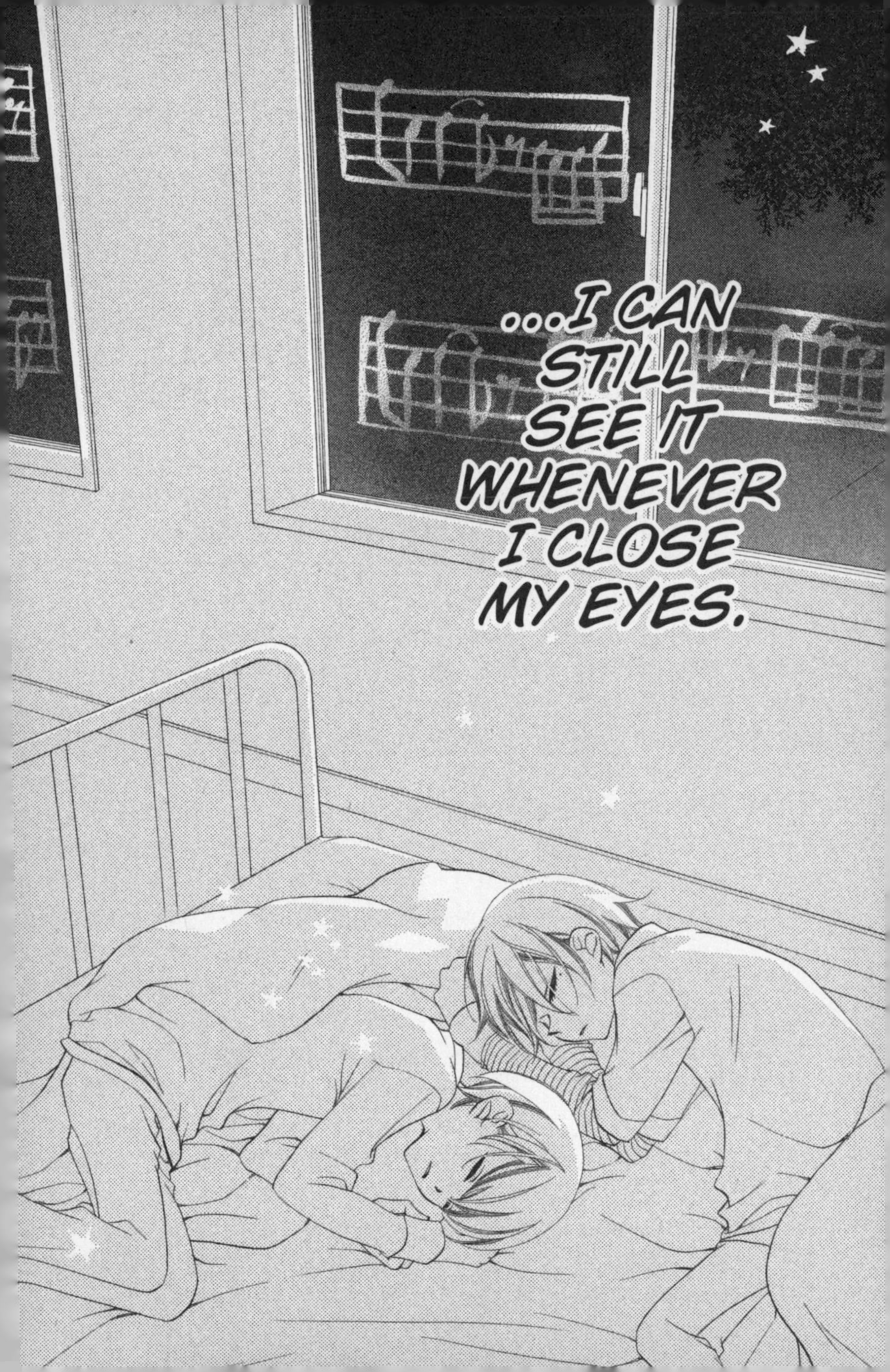
...I CAN STILL SEE IT WHENEVER I CLOSE MY EYES.

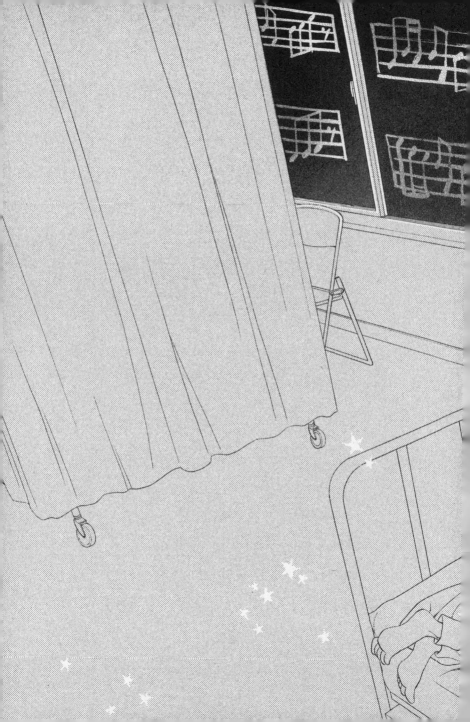

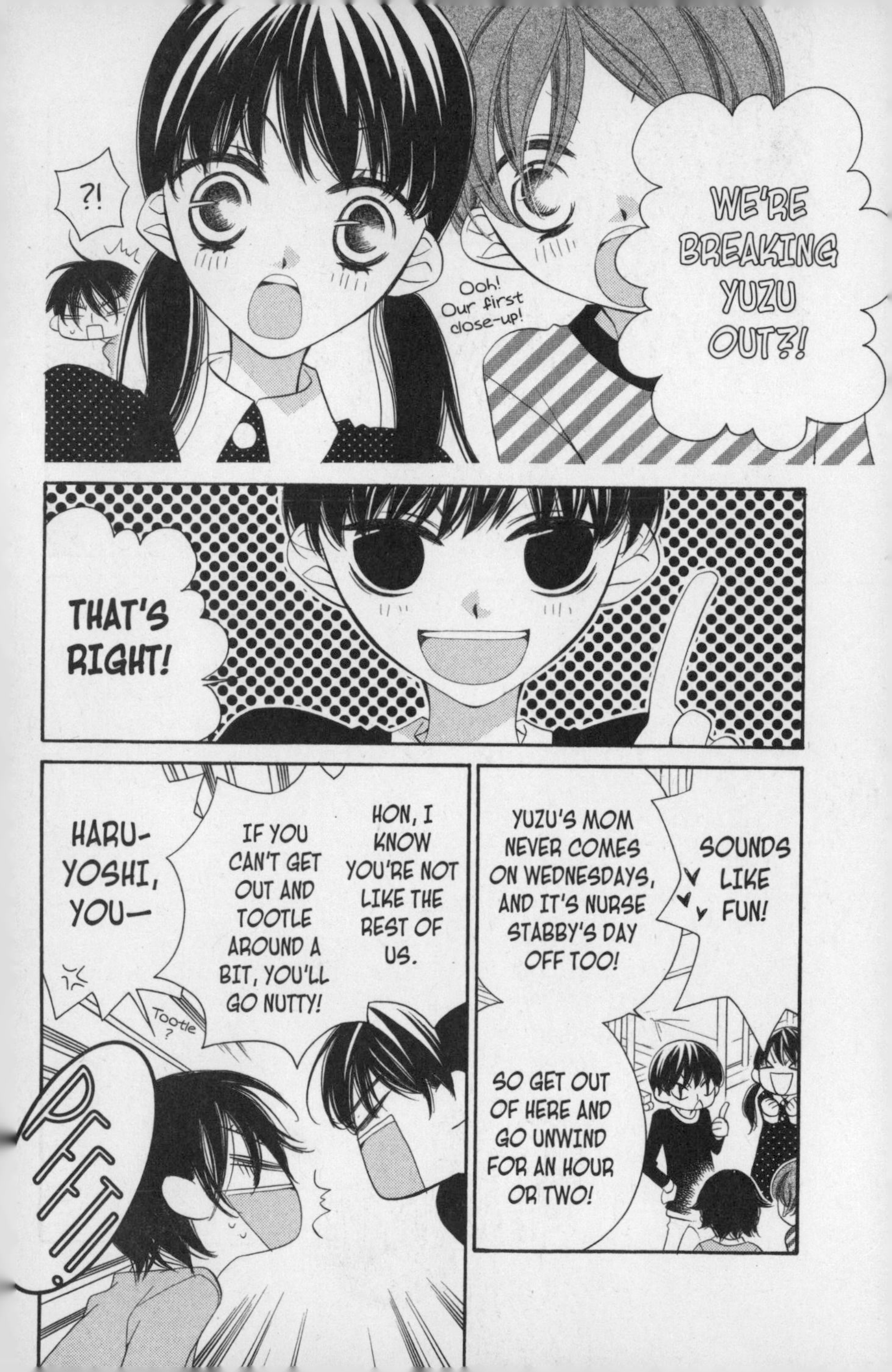

WE'RE BREAKING YUZU OUT?!
Ooh! Our first close-up!
?!
THAT'S RIGHT!
SOUNDS LIKE FUN!
YUZU'S MOM NEVER COMES ON WEDNESDAYS, AND IT'S NURSE STABBY'S DAY OFF TOO!
SO GET OUT OF HERE AND GO UNWIND FOR AN HOUR OR TWO!
HON, I KNOW YOU'RE NOT LIKE THE REST OF US.
IF YOU CAN'T GET OUT AND TOOTLE AROUND A BIT, YOU'LL GO NUTTY!
HARU-YOSHI, YOU—
Tootle?
PFFT!!

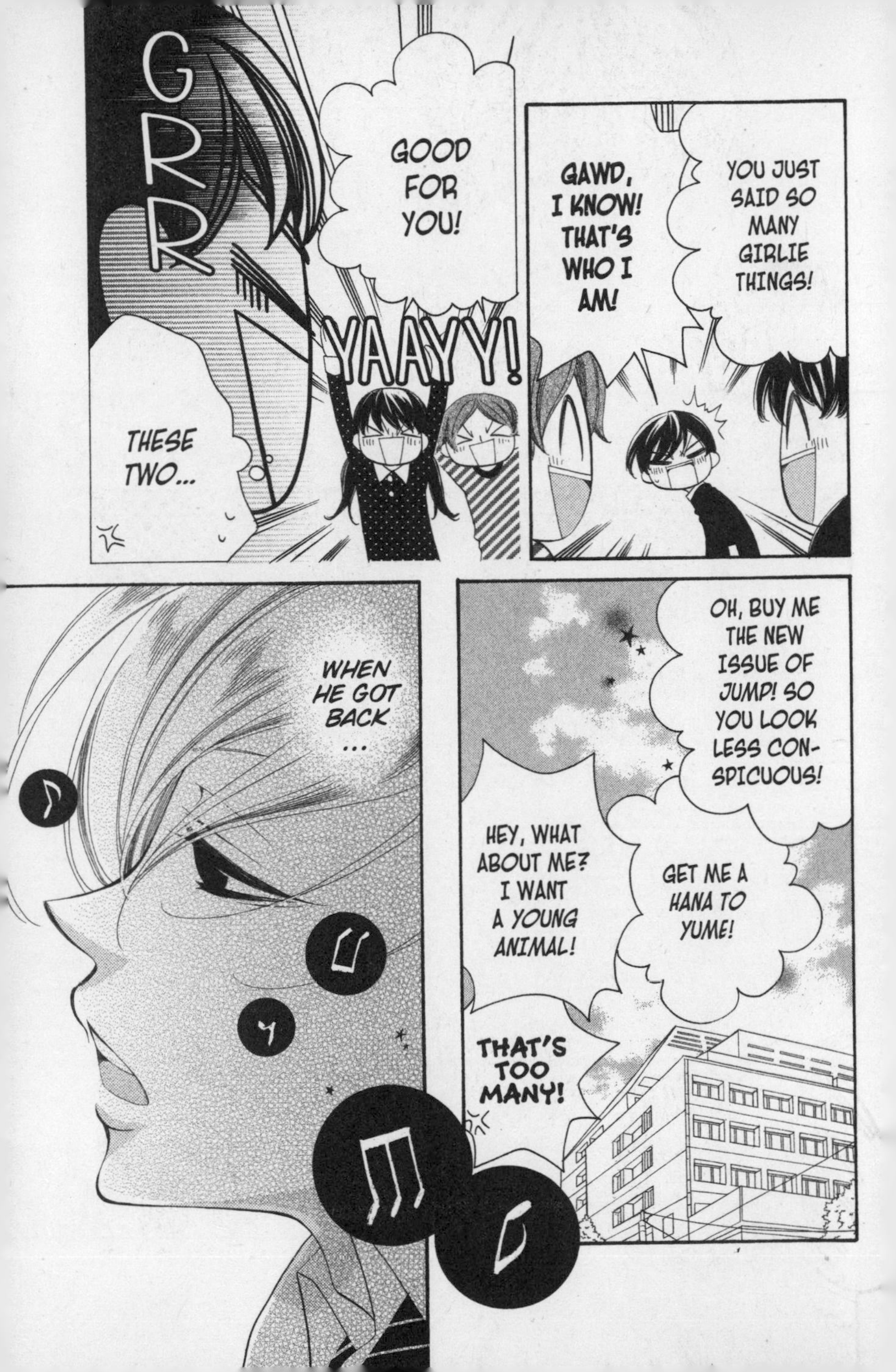
YOU JUST SAID SO MANY GIRLIE THINGS!
GAWD, I KNOW! THAT'S WHO I AM!
GOOD FOR YOU!
GRR
YAAYY!
THESE TWO...
OH, BUY ME THE NEW ISSUE OF JUMP! SO YOU LOOK LESS CON-SPICUOUS!
GET ME A HANA TO YUME!
HEY, WHAT ABOUT ME? I WANT A YOUNG ANIMAL!
THAT'S TOO MANY!
WHEN HE GOT BACK ...

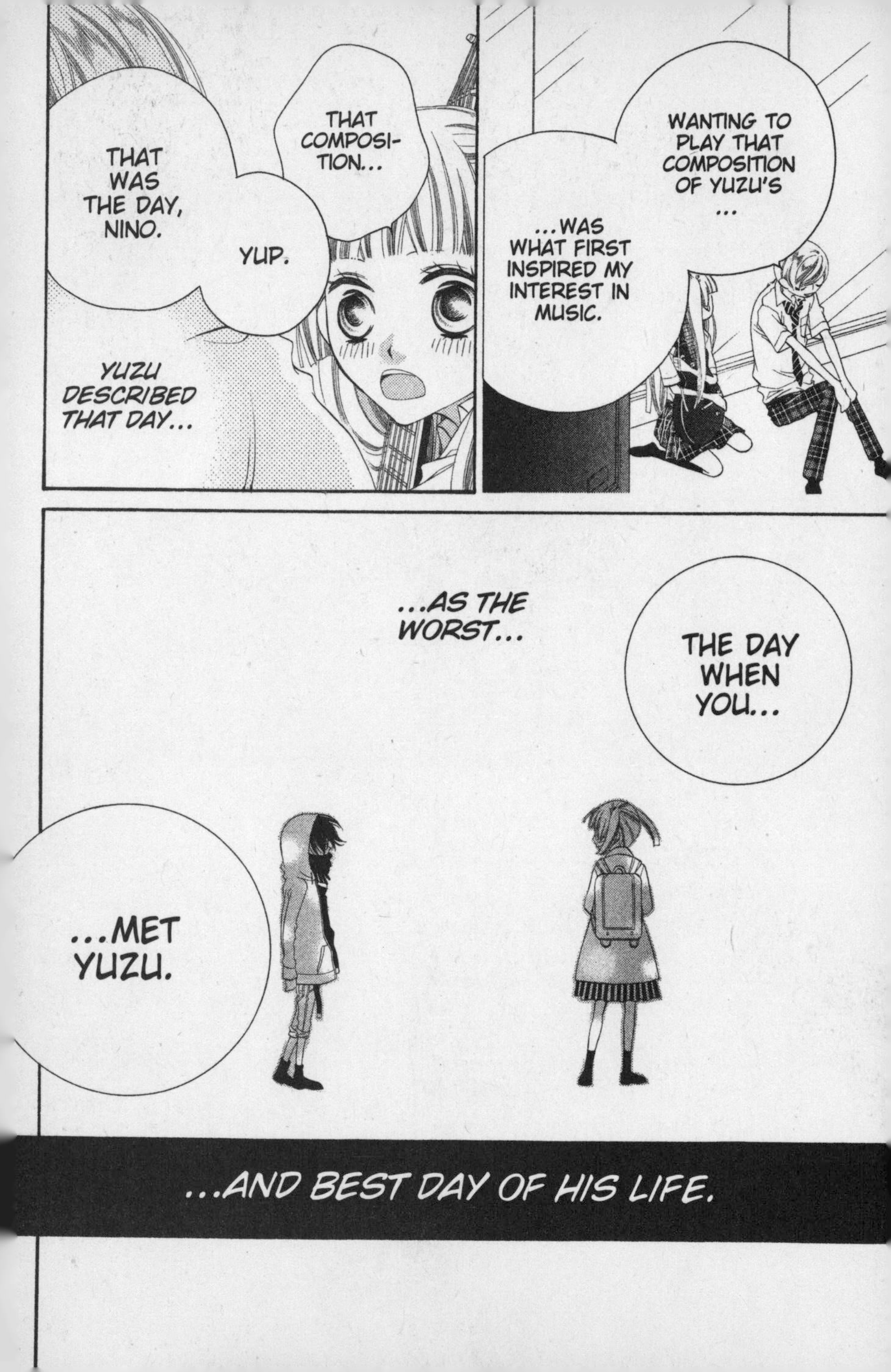
WANTING TO PLAY THAT COMPOSITION OF YUZU'S ...
...WAS WHAT FIRST INSPIRED MY INTEREST IN MUSIC.
THAT COMPOSITION...
THAT WAS THE DAY, NINO.
YUP.
YUZU DESCRIBED THAT DAY...
...AS THE WORST...
THE DAY WHEN YOU...
...MET YUZU.
...AND BEST DAY OF HIS LIFE.

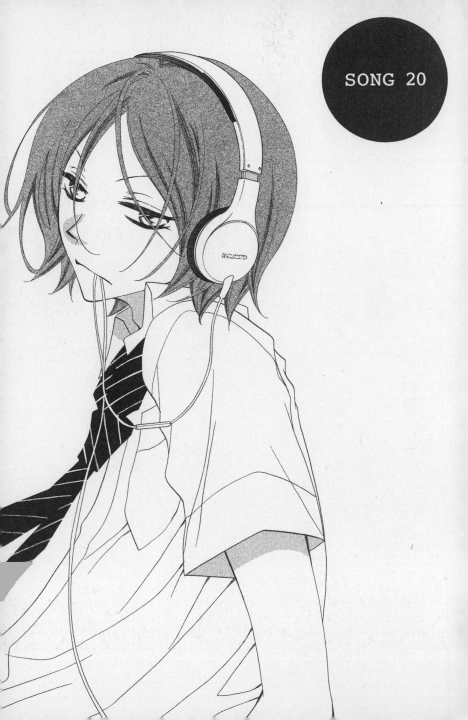

SONG 20

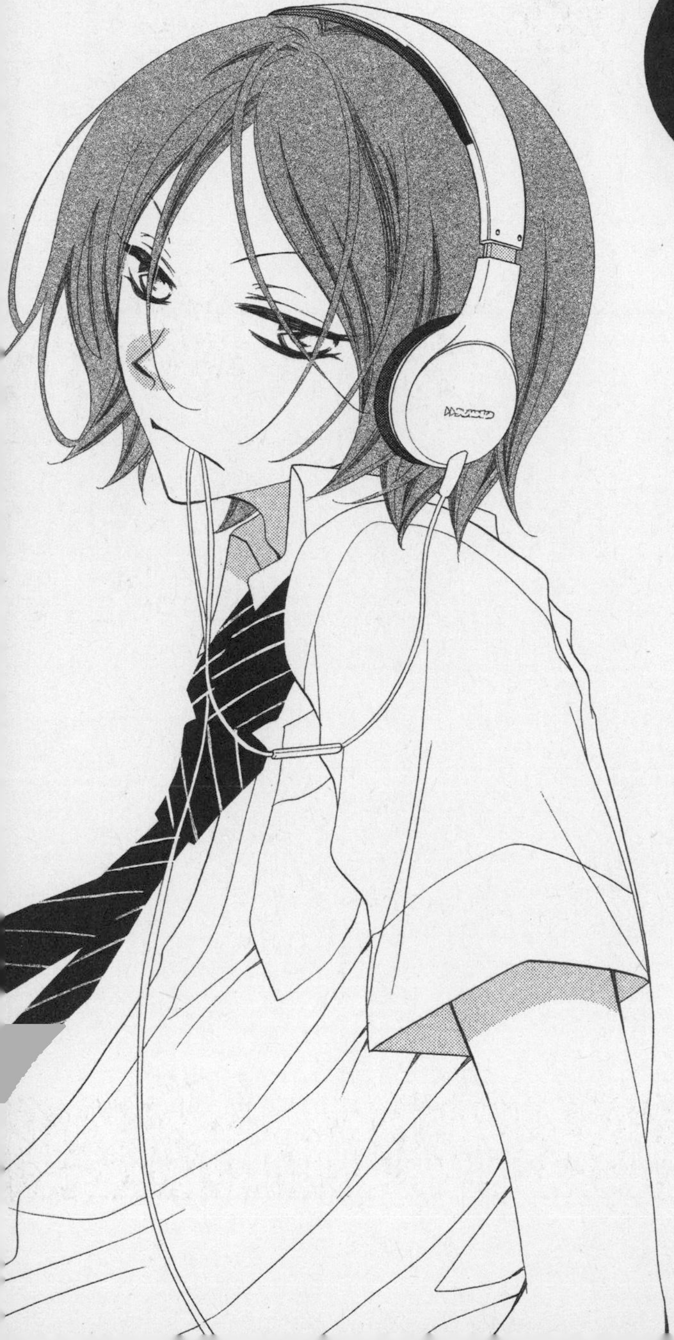

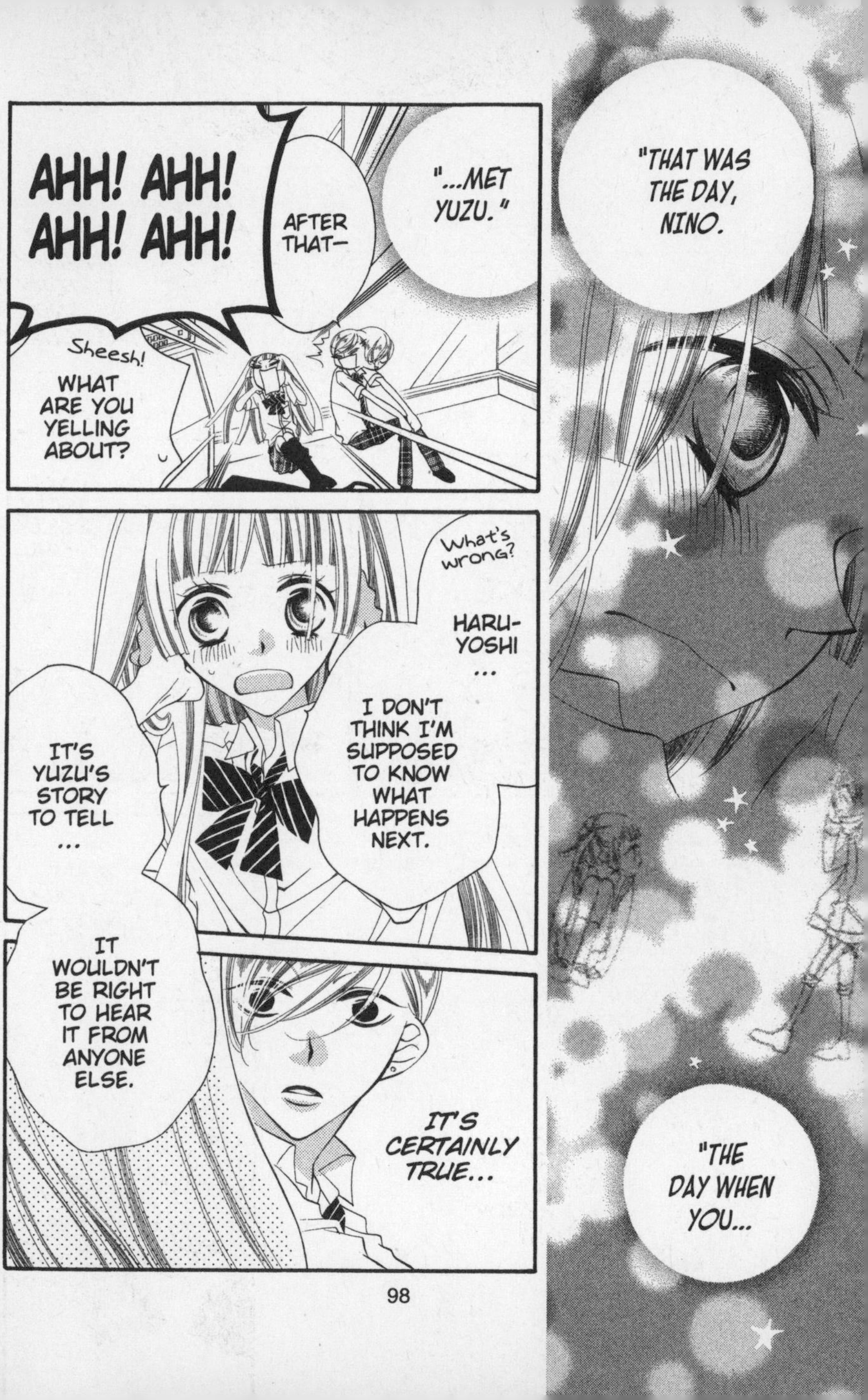
"THAT WAS THE DAY, NINO.
"THE DAY WHEN YOU...
"...MET YUZU."
AFTER THAT—
AHH! AHH! AHH! AHH!
Sheesh!
WHAT ARE YOU YELLING ABOUT?
What's wrong?
HARU-YOSHI...
I DON'T THINK I'M SUPPOSED TO KNOW WHAT HAPPENS NEXT.
IT'S YUZU'S STORY TO TELL...
IT WOULDN'T BE RIGHT TO HEAR IT FROM ANYONE ELSE.
IT'S CERTAINLY TRUE...

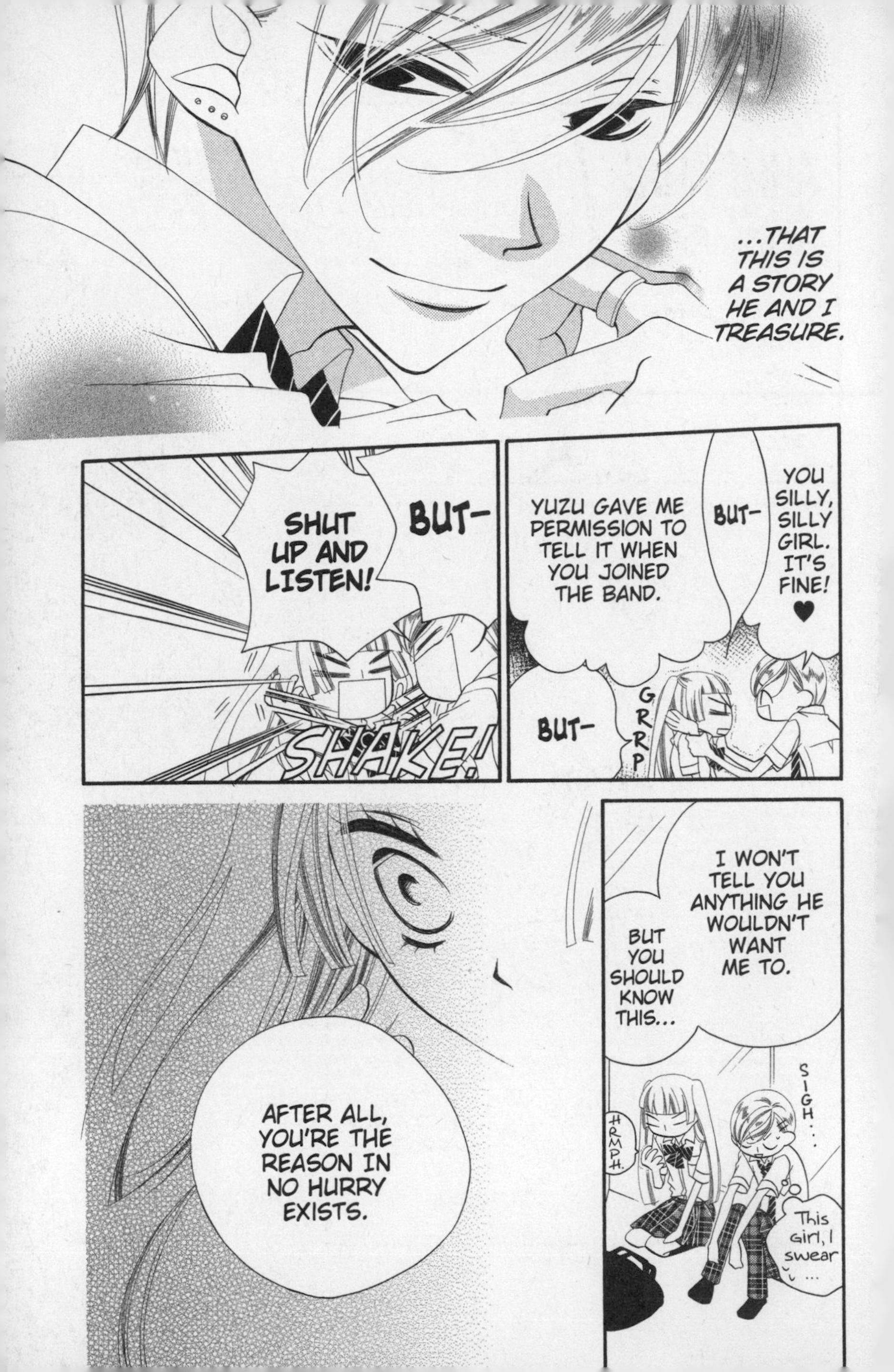
...THAT THIS IS A STORY HE AND I TREASURE.
YOU SILLY, SILLY GIRL. IT'S FINE! ♥
BUT-
YUZU GAVE ME PERMISSION TO TELL IT WHEN YOU JOINED THE BAND.
GRRP
BUT-
BUT-
SHUT UP AND LISTEN!
SHAKE!
I WON'T TELL YOU ANYTHING HE WOULDN'T WANT ME TO.
BUT YOU SHOULD KNOW THIS...
SIGH...
HRMPH.
This girl, I swear...
AFTER ALL, YOU'RE THE REASON IN NO HURRY EXISTS.

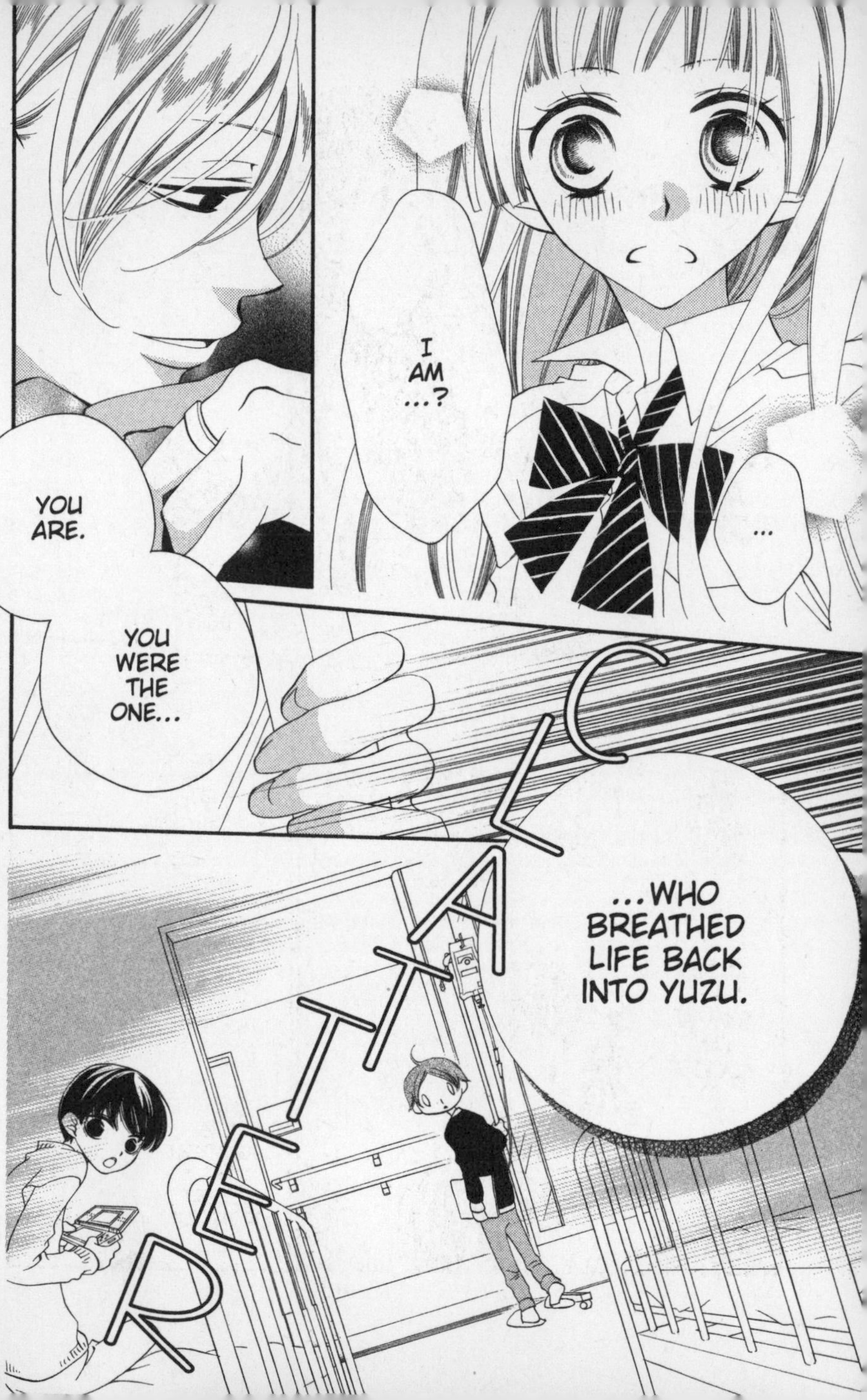
I AM ...?
...
YOU ARE.
YOU WERE THE ONE...
...WHO BREATHED LIFE BACK INTO YUZU.
CLATTER

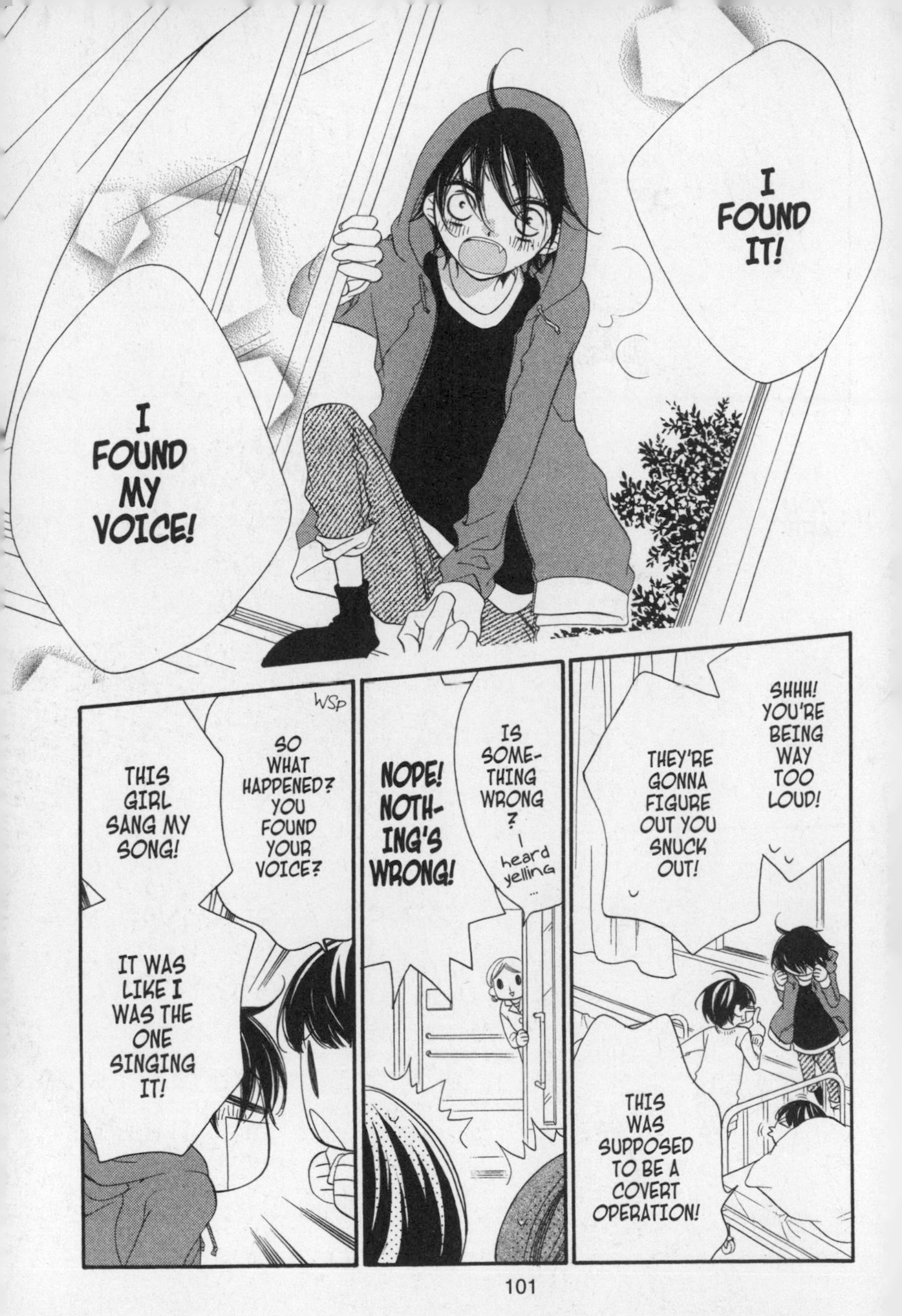

I FOUND IT!
I FOUND MY VOICE!
SHHH! YOU'RE BEING WAY TOO LOUD!
THEY'RE GONNA FIGURE OUT YOU SNUCK OUT!
THIS WAS SUPPOSED TO BE A COVERT OPERATION!
IS SOMETHING WRONG?
I heard yelling...
NOPE! NOTHING'S WRONG!
WSP
SO WHAT HAPPENED? YOU FOUND YOUR VOICE?
THIS GIRL SANG MY SONG!
IT WAS LIKE I WAS THE ONE SINGING IT!

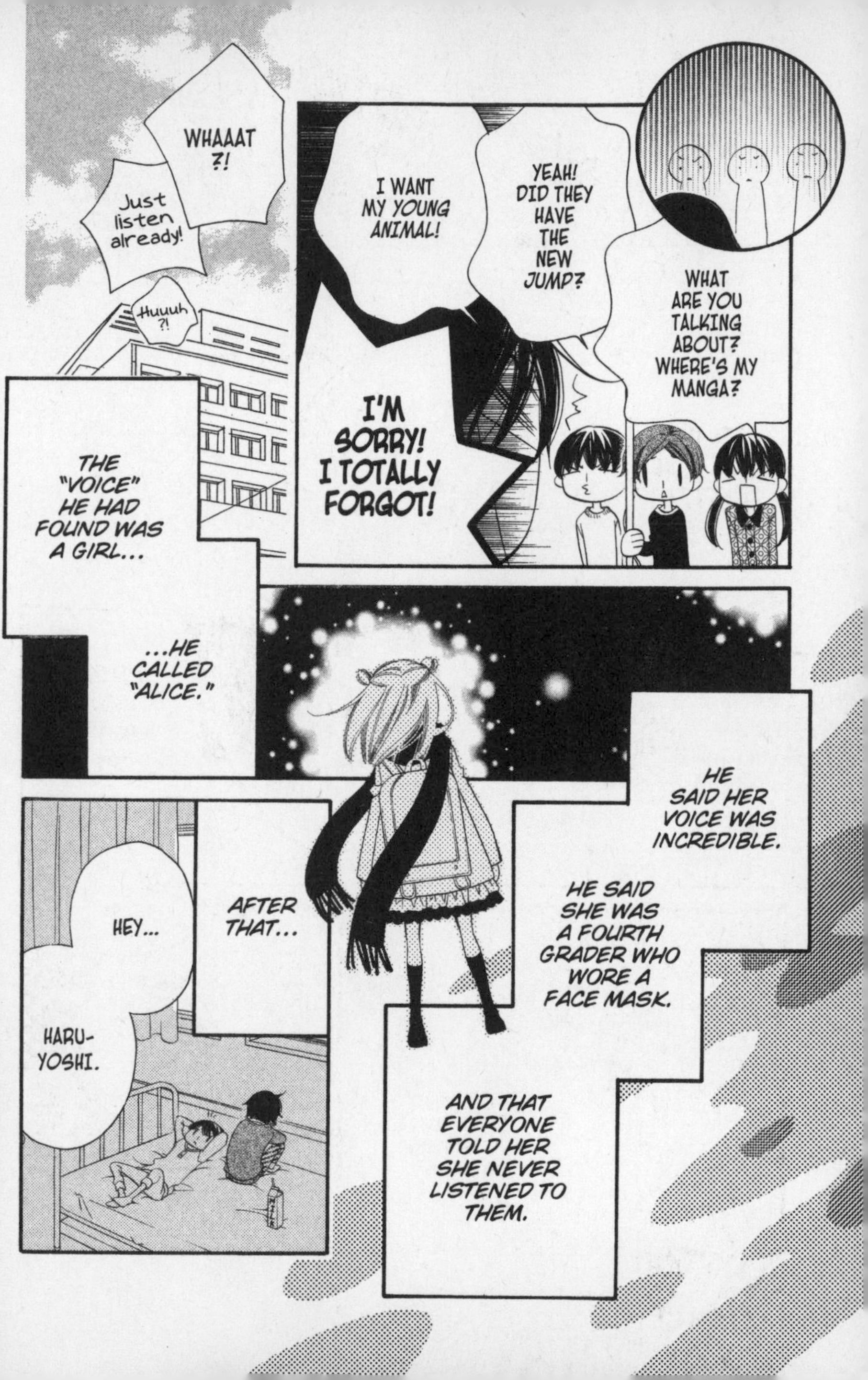
WHAT ARE YOU TALKING ABOUT? WHERE'S MY MANGA?
YEAH! DID THEY HAVE THE NEW JUMP?
I WANT MY YOUNG ANIMAL!
I'M SORRY! I TOTALLY FORGOT!
WHAAAT ?!
Just listen already!
Huuuh ?!
THE "VOICE" HE HAD FOUND WAS A GIRL...
...HE CALLED "ALICE."
HE SAID HER VOICE WAS INCREDIBLE.
HE SAID SHE WAS A FOURTH GRADER WHO WORE A FACE MASK.
AND THAT EVERYONE TOLD HER SHE NEVER LISTENED TO THEM.
AFTER THAT...
HEY...
HARU-YOSHI.

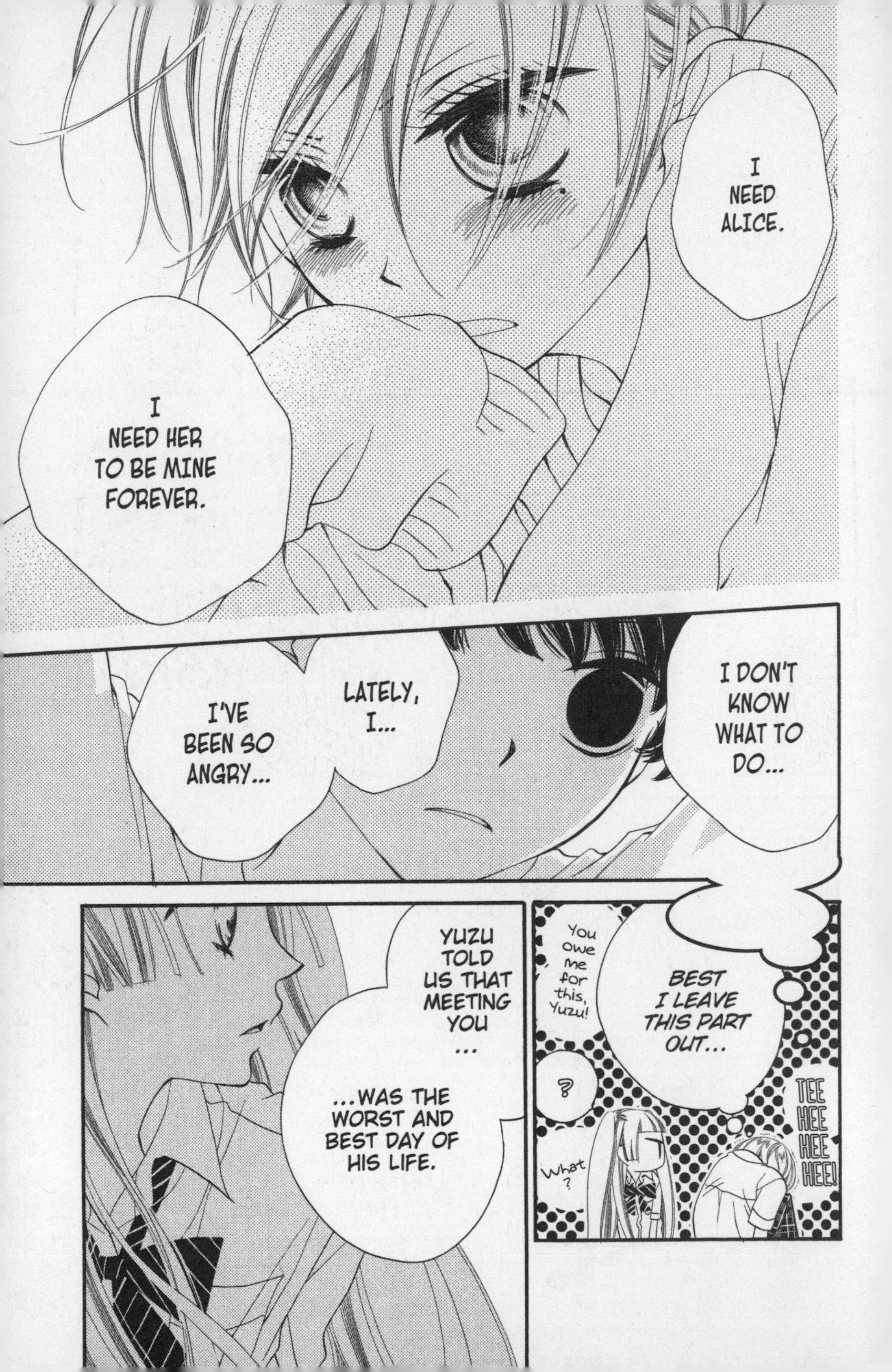
I NEED ALICE.
I NEED HER TO BE MINE FOREVER.
I DON'T KNOW WHAT TO DO...
LATELY, I...
I'VE BEEN SO ANGRY...
BEST I LEAVE THIS PART OUT...
You owe me for this, Yuzu!
TEE HEE HEE HEE!
?
What?
YUZU TOLD US THAT MEETING YOU ...
...WAS THE WORST AND BEST DAY OF HIS LIFE.

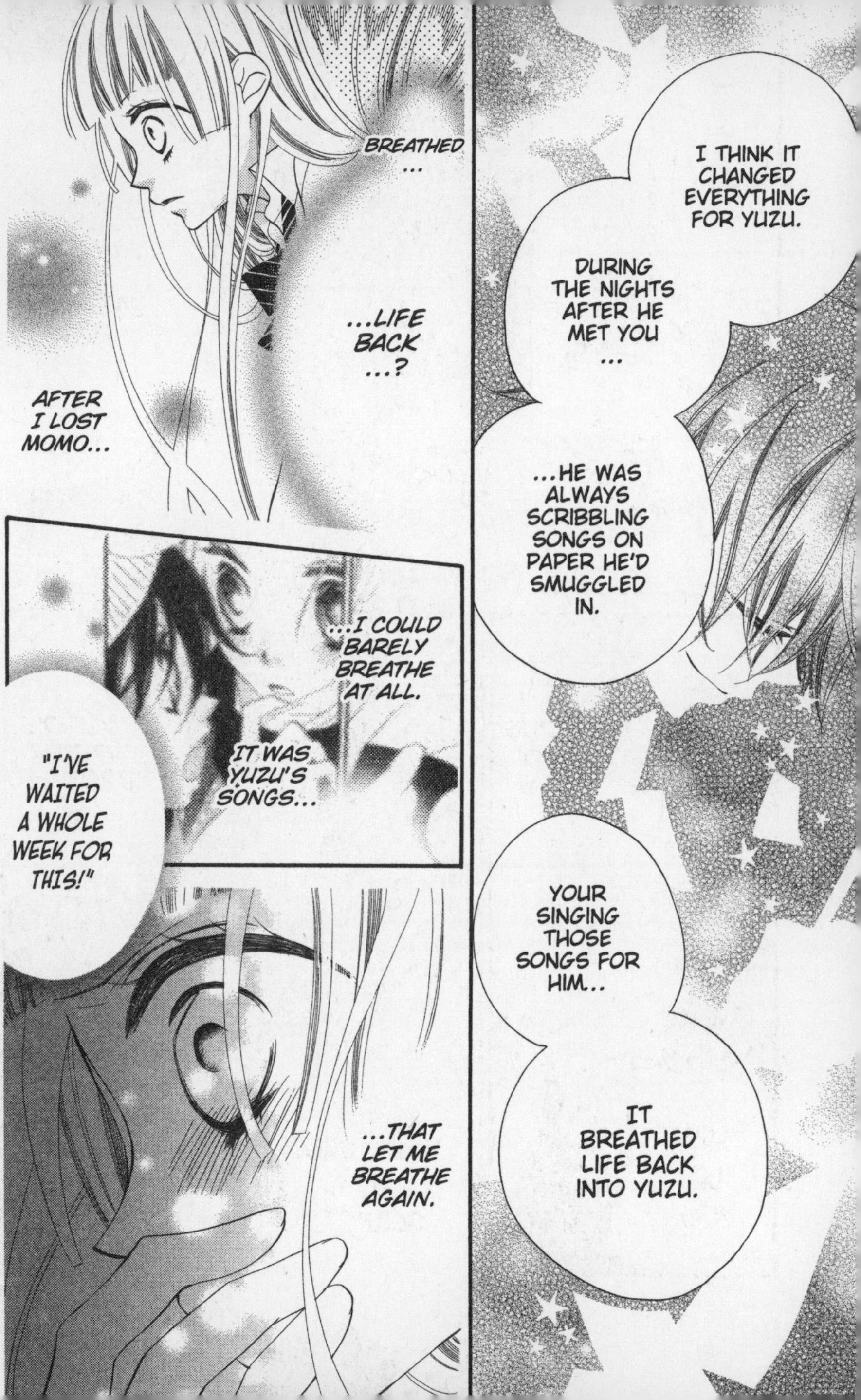
I THINK IT CHANGED EVERYTHING FOR YUZU.
DURING THE NIGHTS AFTER HE MET YOU ...
...HE WAS ALWAYS SCRIBBLING SONGS ON PAPER HE'D SMUGGLED IN.
YOUR SINGING THOSE SONGS FOR HIM...
IT BREATHED LIFE BACK INTO YUZU.
BREATHED ...
...LIFE BACK ...?
AFTER I LOST MOMO...
...I COULD BARELY BREATHE AT ALL.
IT WAS YUZU'S SONGS...
"I'VE WAITED A WHOLE WEEK FOR THIS!"
...THAT LET ME BREATHE AGAIN.

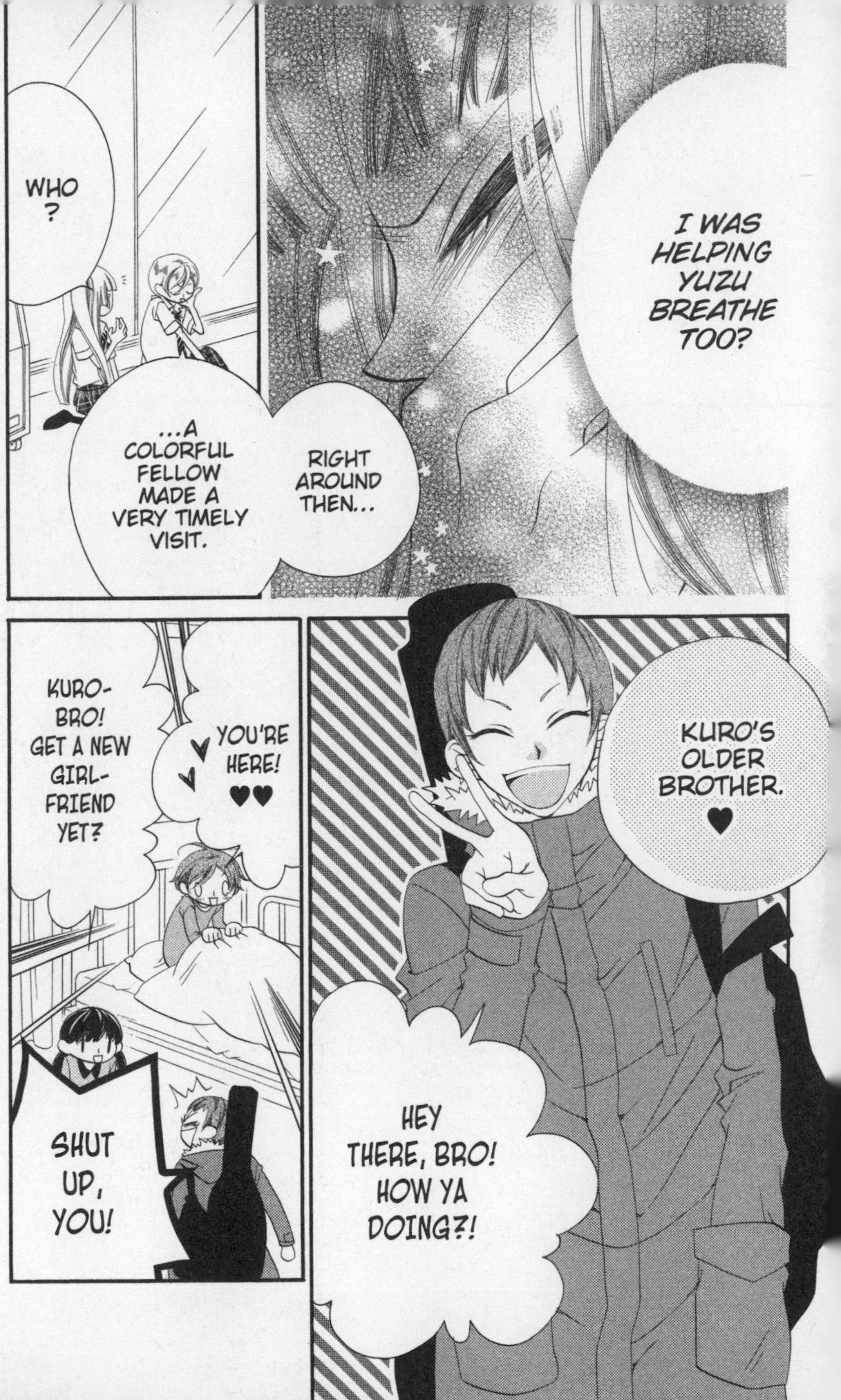
I WAS HELPING YUZU BREATHE TOO?
WHO?
RIGHT AROUND THEN...
...A COLORFUL FELLOW MADE A VERY TIMELY VISIT.
KURO'S OLDER BROTHER. ♥
HEY THERE, BRO! HOW YA DOING?!
YOU'RE HERE! ♥♥
KURO-BRO! GET A NEW GIRL-FRIEND YET?
SHUT UP, YOU!

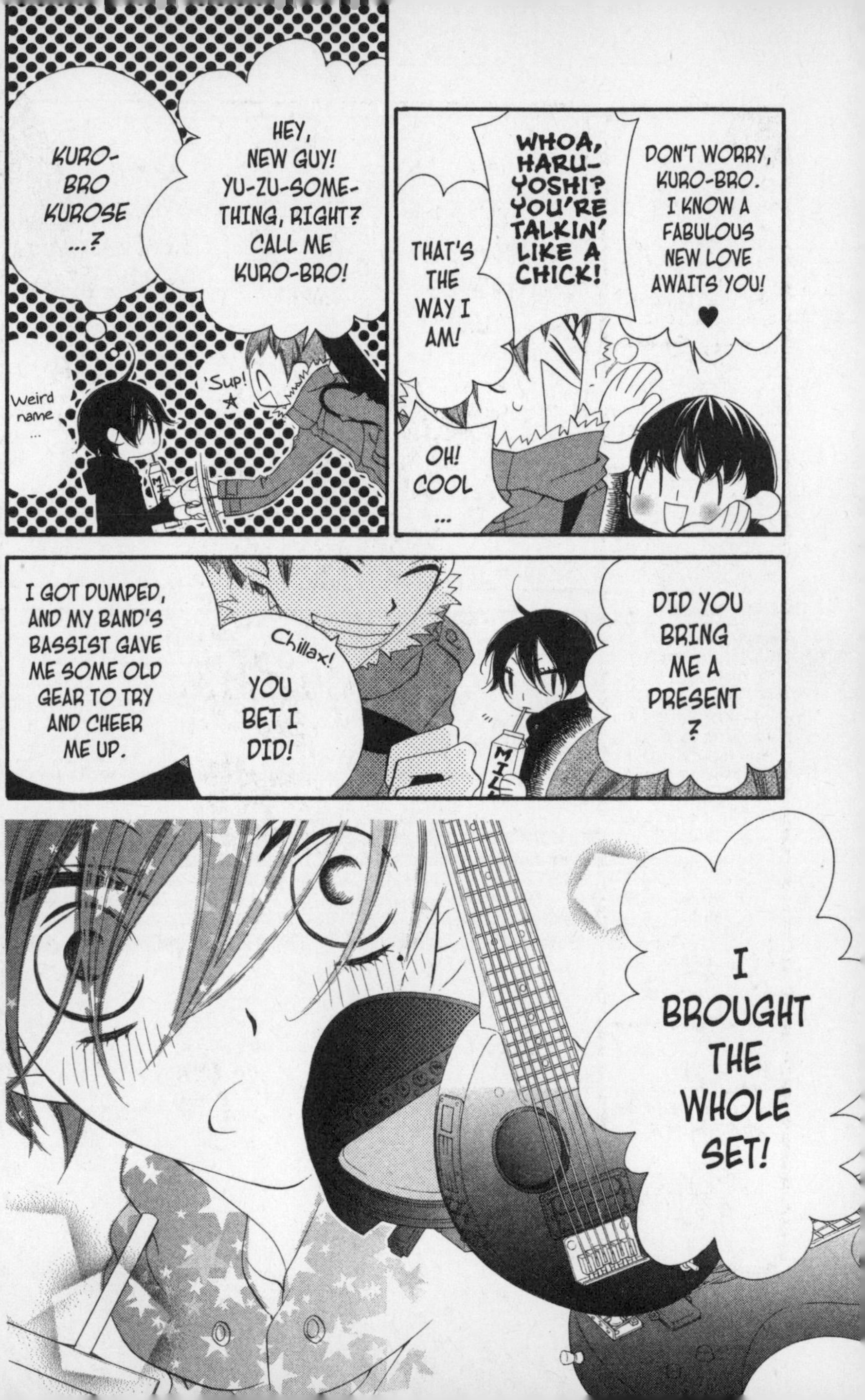
DON'T WORRY, KURO-BRO. I KNOW A FABULOUS NEW LOVE AWAITS YOU! ♥
WHOA, HARU-YOSHI? YOU'RE TALKIN' LIKE A CHICK!
THAT'S THE WAY I AM!
OH! COOL ...
HEY, NEW GUY! YU-ZU-SOME-THING, RIGHT? CALL ME KURO-BRO!
'Sup! ★
KURO-BRO KUROSE ...?
Weird name ...
DID YOU BRING ME A PRESENT?
YOU BET I DID!
Chillax!
I GOT DUMPED, AND MY BAND'S BASSIST GAVE ME SOME OLD GEAR TO TRY AND CHEER ME UP.
I BROUGHT THE WHOLE SET!

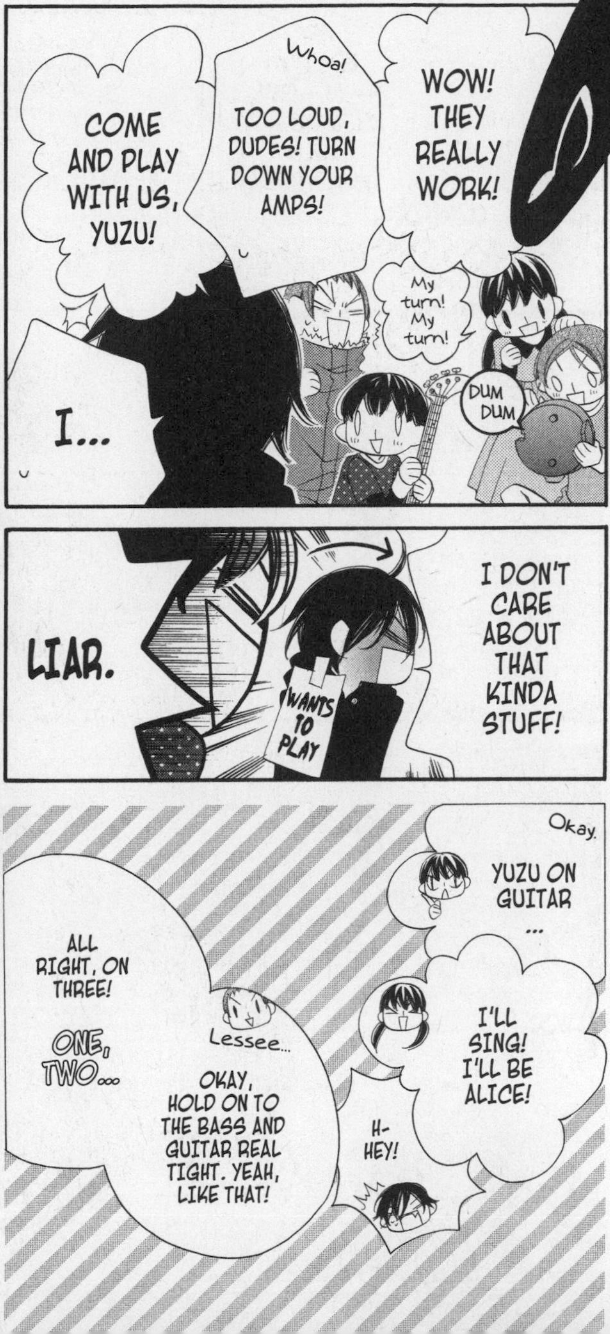
WOW! THEY REALLY WORK!
Whoa!
TOO LOUD, DUDES! TURN DOWN YOUR AMPS!
COME AND PLAY WITH US, YUZU!
My turn! My turn!
DUM DUM
I...
I DON'T CARE ABOUT THAT KINDA STUFF!
WANTS TO PLAY
LIAR.
Okay.
YUZU ON GUITAR...
I'LL SING! I'LL BE ALICE!
H-HEY!
Lessee...
OKAY, HOLD ON TO THE BASS AND GUITAR REAL TIGHT. YEAH, LIKE THAT!
ALL RIGHT, ON THREE!
ONE, TWO...

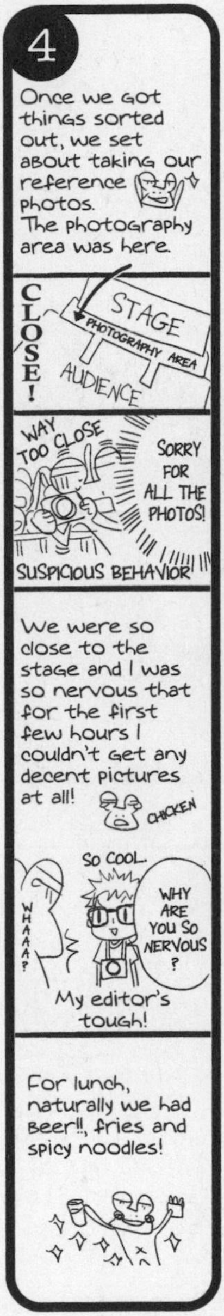
4
Once we got things sorted out, we set about taking our reference photos.
The photography area was here.
CLOSE!
STAGE
PHOTOGRAPHY AREA
AUDIENCE
WAY TOO CLOSE
SORRY FOR ALL THE PHOTOS!
SUSPICIOUS BEHAVIOR
We were so close to the stage and I was so nervous that for the first few hours I couldn't get any decent pictures at all!
CHICKEN
SO COOL.
WHAAAA?
WHY ARE YOU SO NERVOUS?
My editor's tough!
For lunch, naturally we had beer!!, fries and spicy noodles!

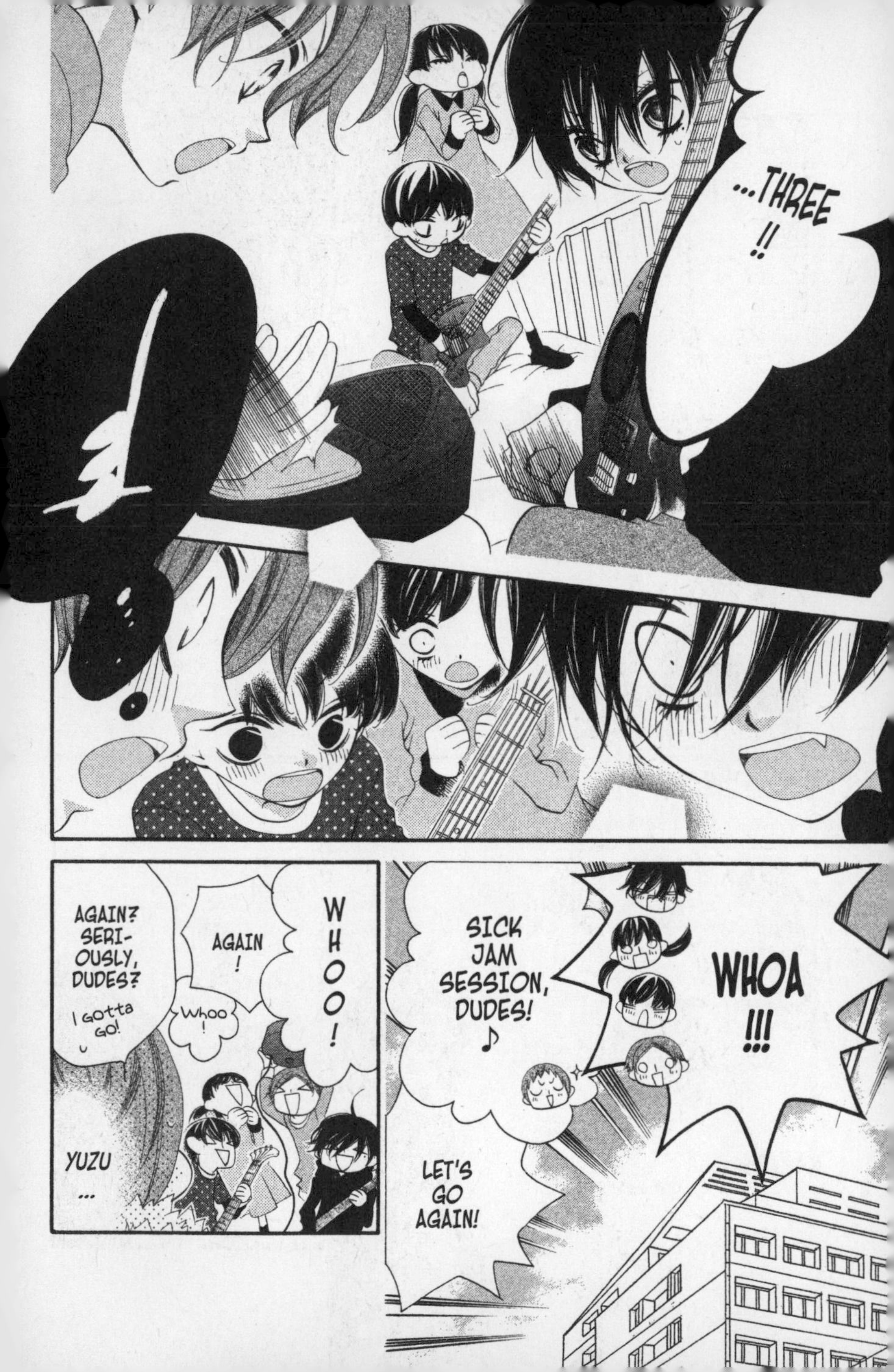
...THREE !!
WHOA !!!
SICK JAM SESSION, DUDES! ♪
LET'S GO AGAIN!
WHOOO!
AGAIN!
Whoo!
AGAIN? SERIOUSLY, DUDES?
I gotta go!
YUZU...

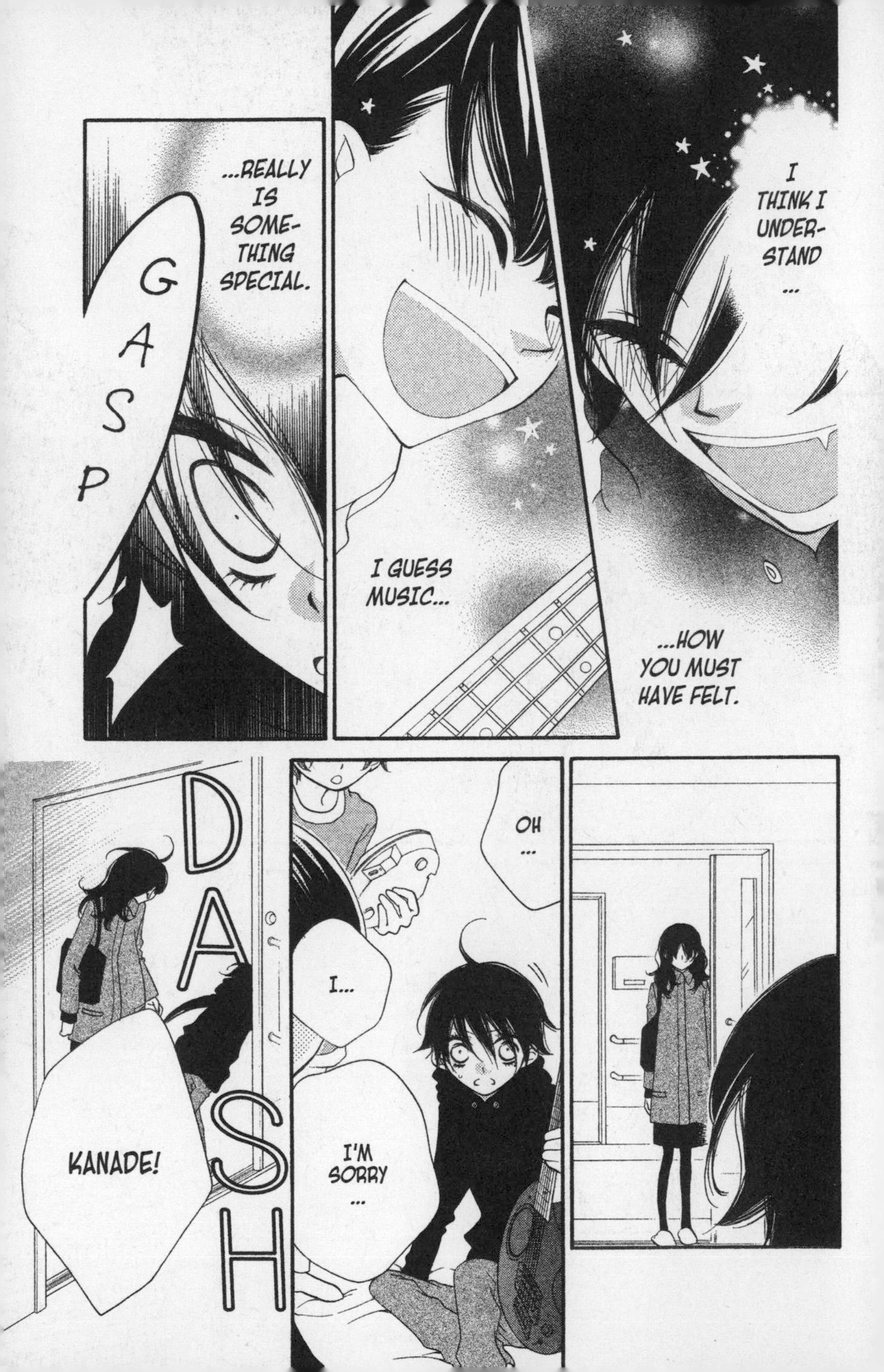
I THINK I UNDER-STAND...
...HOW YOU MUST HAVE FELT.
I GUESS MUSIC...
...REALLY IS SOME-THING SPECIAL.
GASP
OH...
I...
I'M SORRY...
DASH
KANADE!

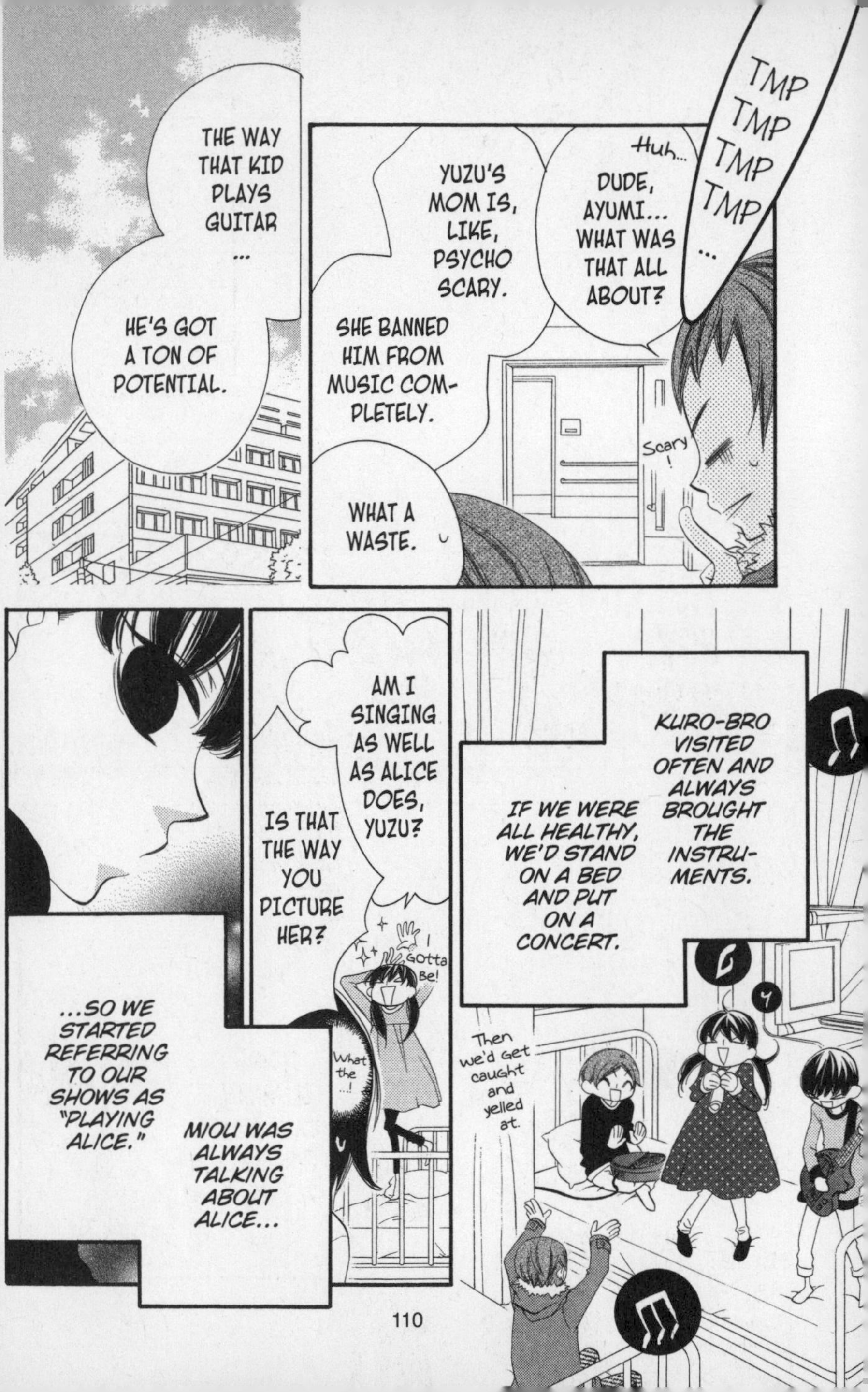
TMP TMP TMP TMP...
Huh...
DUDE, AYUMI... WHAT WAS THAT ALL ABOUT?
YUZU'S MOM IS, LIKE, PSYCHO SCARY.
SHE BANNED HIM FROM MUSIC COM-PLETELY.
Scary!
WHAT A WASTE.
THE WAY THAT KID PLAYS GUITAR ...
HE'S GOT A TON OF POTENTIAL.
KURO-BRO VISITED OFTEN AND ALWAYS BROUGHT THE INSTRU-MENTS.
IF WE WERE ALL HEALTHY, WE'D STAND ON A BED AND PUT ON A CONCERT.
Then we'd get caught and yelled at.
AM I SINGING AS WELL AS ALICE DOES, YUZU?
IS THAT THE WAY YOU PICTURE HER?
I gotta be!
What the...!
MIOU WAS ALWAYS TALKING ABOUT ALICE...
...SO WE STARTED REFERRING TO OUR SHOWS AS "PLAYING ALICE."

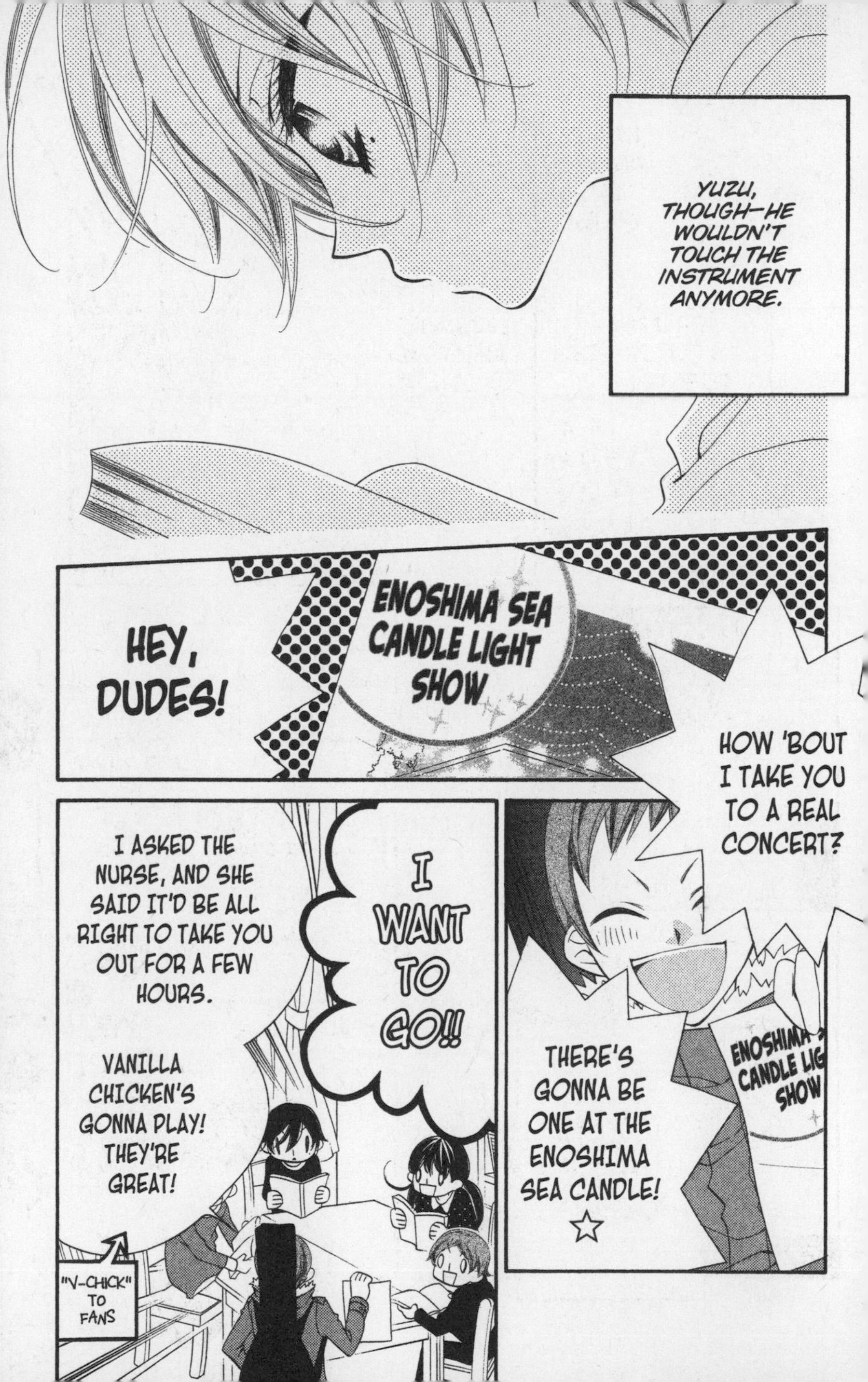
YUZU, THOUGH—HE WOULDN'T TOUCH THE INSTRUMENT ANYMORE.
ENOSHIMA SEA CANDLE LIGHT SHOW
HEY, DUDES!
HOW 'BOUT I TAKE YOU TO A REAL CONCERT?
THERE'S GONNA BE ONE AT THE ENOSHIMA SEA CANDLE! ☆
I WANT TO GO!!
I ASKED THE NURSE, AND SHE SAID IT'D BE ALL RIGHT TO TAKE YOU OUT FOR A FEW HOURS.
VANILLA CHICKEN'S GONNA PLAY! THEY'RE GREAT!
"V-CHICK" TO FANS

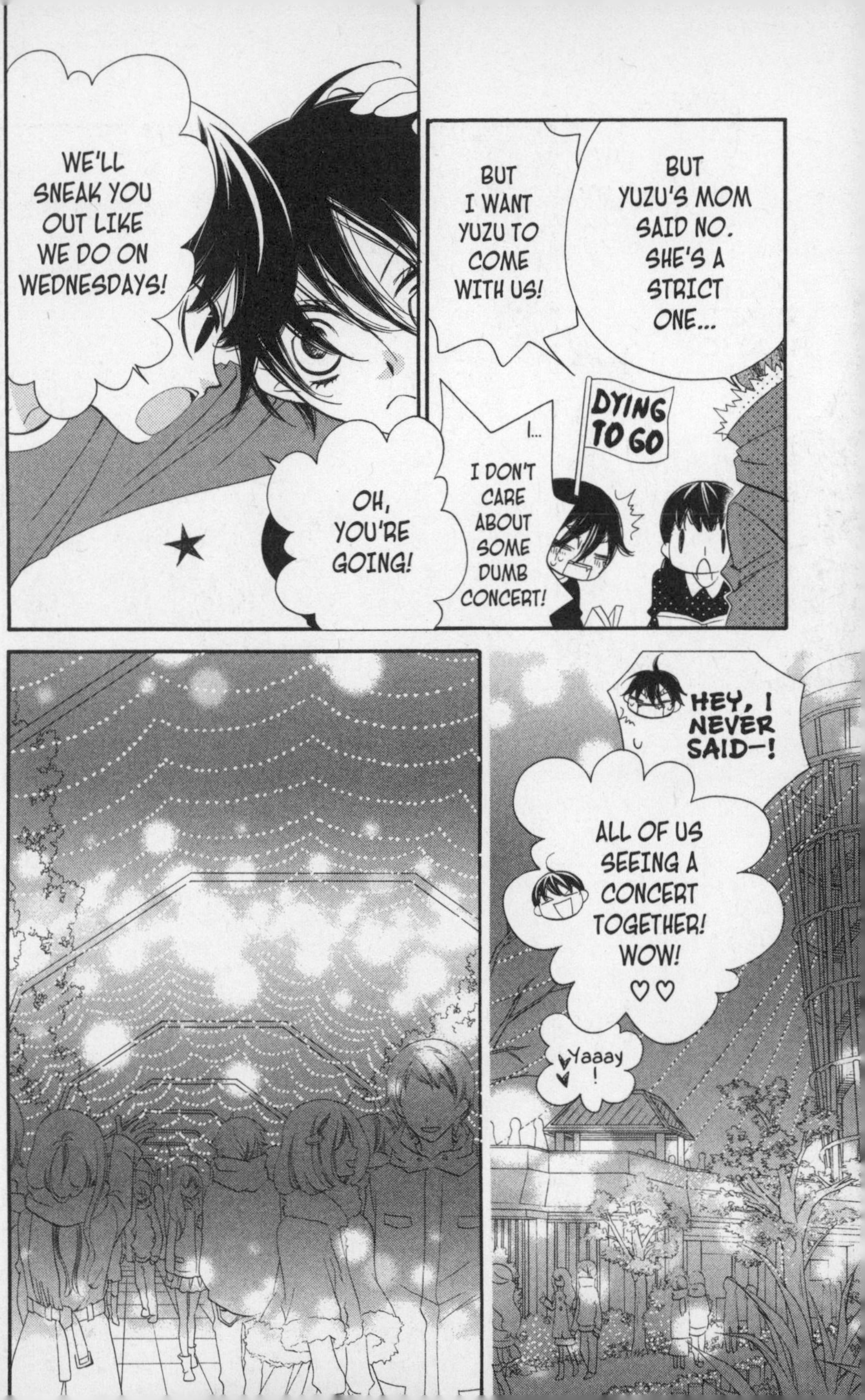
BUT YUZU'S MOM SAID NO. SHE'S A STRICT ONE...
BUT I WANT YUZU TO COME WITH US!
DYING TO GO
I...
I DON'T CARE ABOUT SOME DUMB CONCERT!
WE'LL SNEAK YOU OUT LIKE WE DO ON WEDNESDAYS!
OH, YOU'RE GOING!
HEY, I NEVER SAID—!
ALL OF US SEEING A CONCERT TOGETHER! WOW! ♡♡
Yaaay!

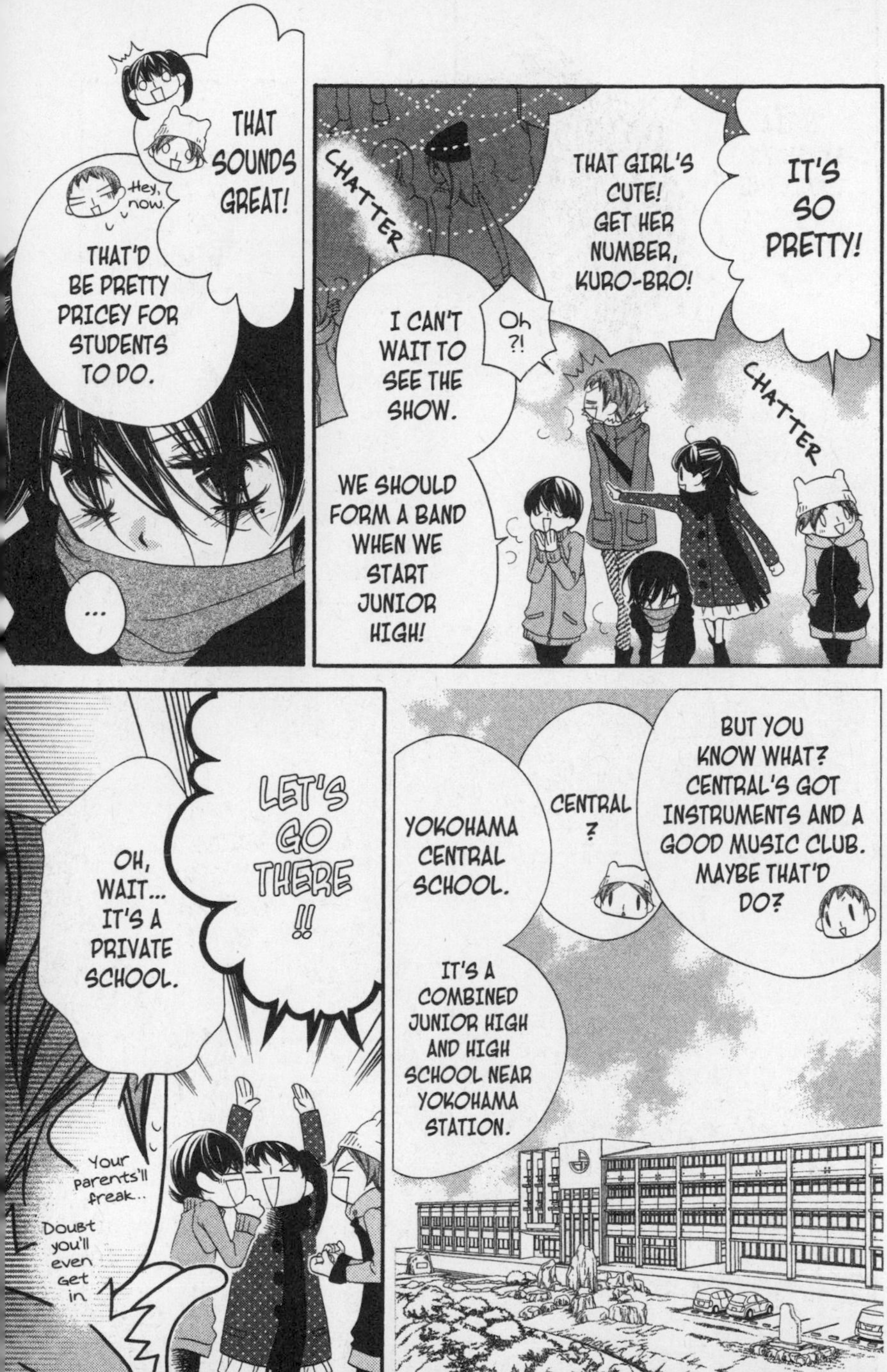
IT'S SO PRETTY!
THAT GIRL'S CUTE! GET HER NUMBER, KURO-BRO!
CHATTER
CHATTER
Oh ?!
I CAN'T WAIT TO SEE THE SHOW.
WE SHOULD FORM A BAND WHEN WE START JUNIOR HIGH!
THAT SOUNDS GREAT!
Hey, now.
THAT'D BE PRETTY PRICEY FOR STUDENTS TO DO.
...
BUT YOU KNOW WHAT? CENTRAL'S GOT INSTRUMENTS AND A GOOD MUSIC CLUB. MAYBE THAT'D DO?
CENTRAL?
YOKOHAMA CENTRAL SCHOOL.
IT'S A COMBINED JUNIOR HIGH AND HIGH SCHOOL NEAR YOKOHAMA STATION.
LET'S GO THERE!!
OH, WAIT... IT'S A PRIVATE SCHOOL.
Your parents'll freak...
Doubt you'll even get in.

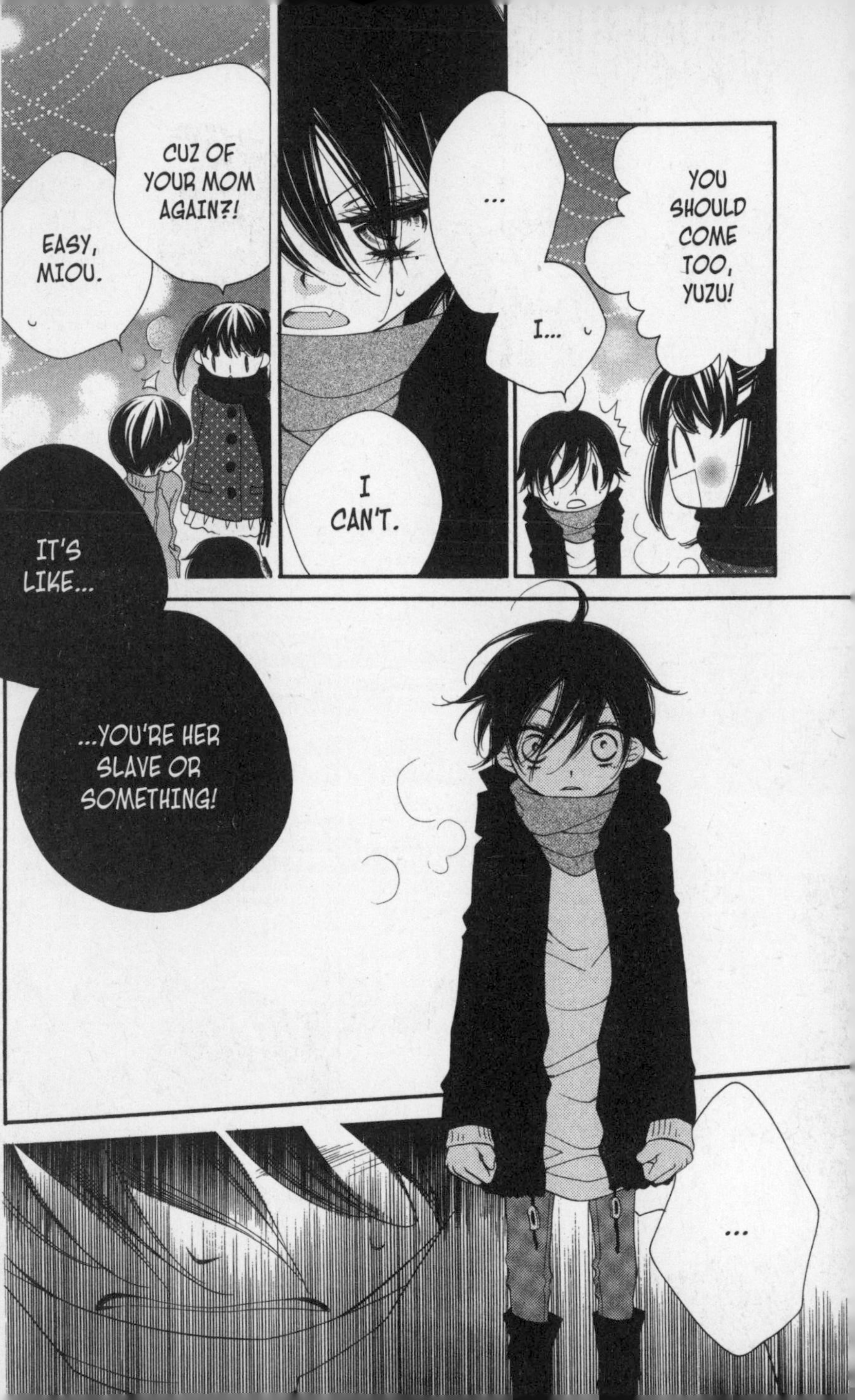
YOU SHOULD COME TOO, YUZU!
...
I...
I CAN'T.
CUZ OF YOUR MOM AGAIN?!
EASY, MIOU.
IT'S LIKE...
...YOU'RE HER SLAVE OR SOMETHING!
...

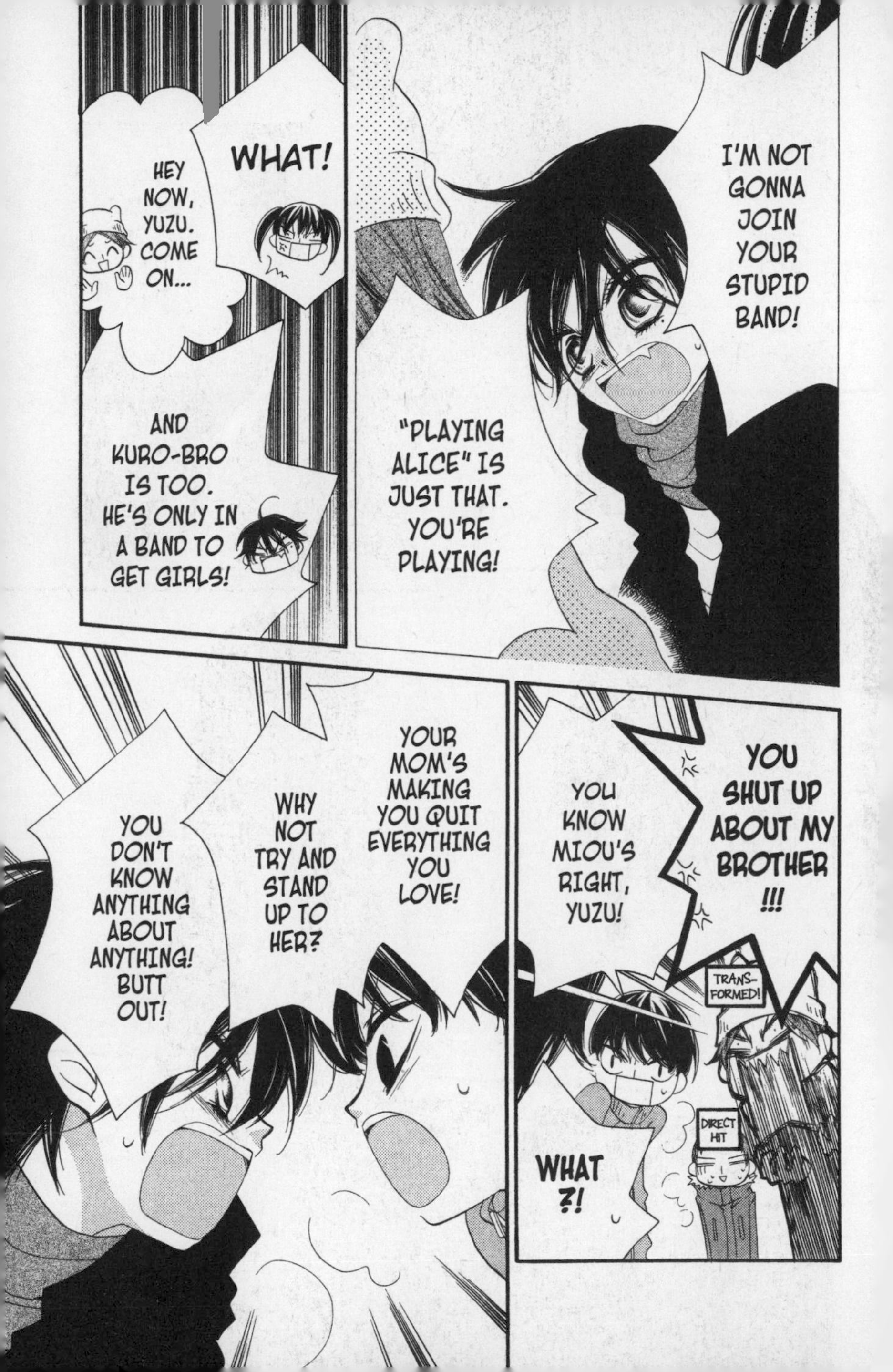
I'M NOT GONNA JOIN YOUR STUPID BAND!
"PLAYING ALICE" IS JUST THAT. YOU'RE PLAYING!
WHAT!
HEY NOW, YUZU. COME ON...
AND KURO-BRO IS TOO. HE'S ONLY IN A BAND TO GET GIRLS!
YOU SHUT UP ABOUT MY BROTHER!!!
YOU KNOW MIOU'S RIGHT, YUZU!
TRANS-FORMED!
DIRECT HIT
WHAT?!
YOUR MOM'S MAKING YOU QUIT EVERYTHING YOU LOVE!
WHY NOT TRY AND STAND UP TO HER?
YOU DON'T KNOW ANYTHING ABOUT ANYTHING! BUTT OUT!

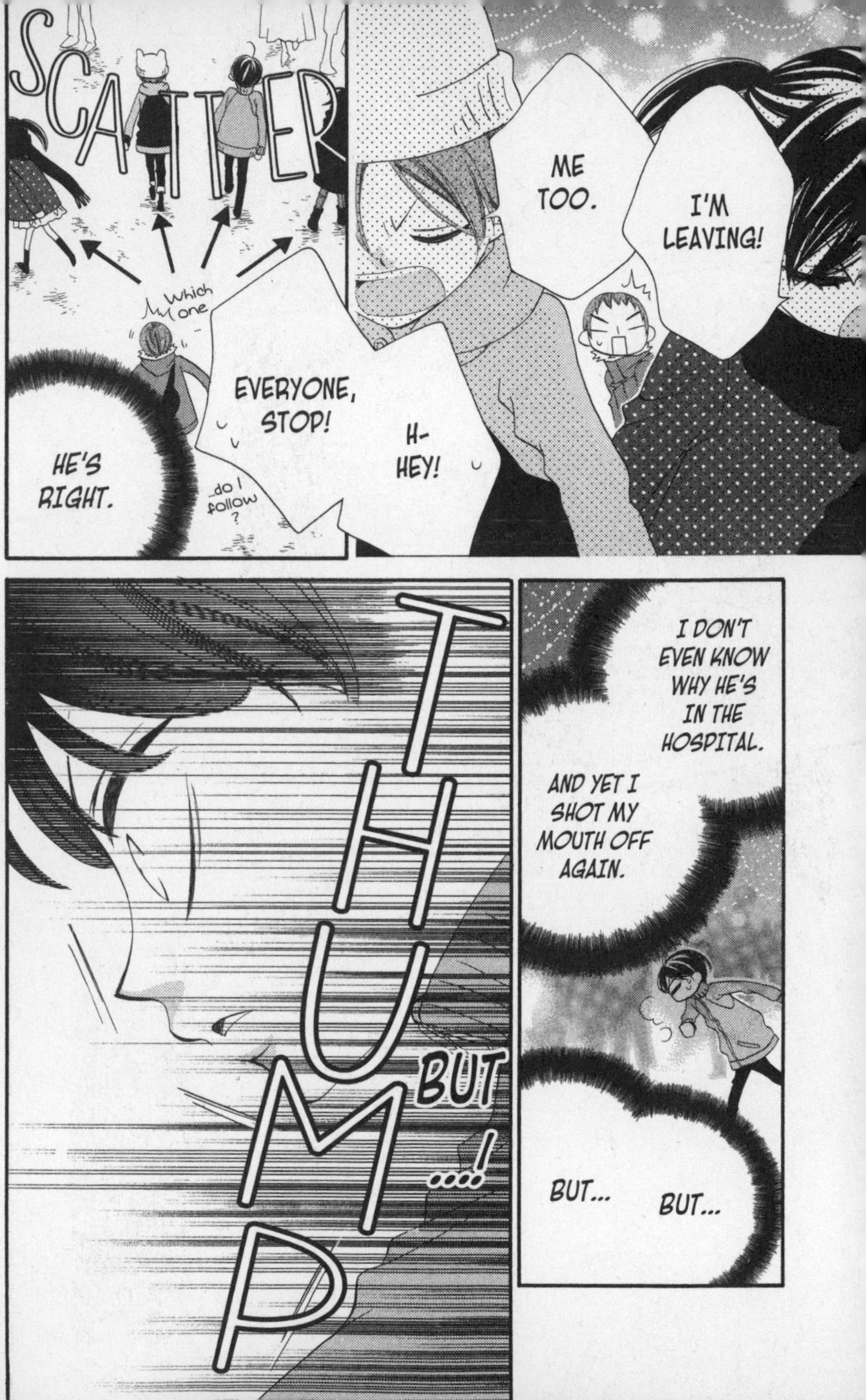
I'M LEAVING!
ME TOO.
H-HEY!
SCATTER
Which one
...do I follow?
EVERYONE, STOP!
HE'S RIGHT.
I DON'T EVEN KNOW WHY HE'S IN THE HOSPITAL.
AND YET I SHOT MY MOUTH OFF AGAIN.
BUT...
BUT...
THUMP
BUT...!

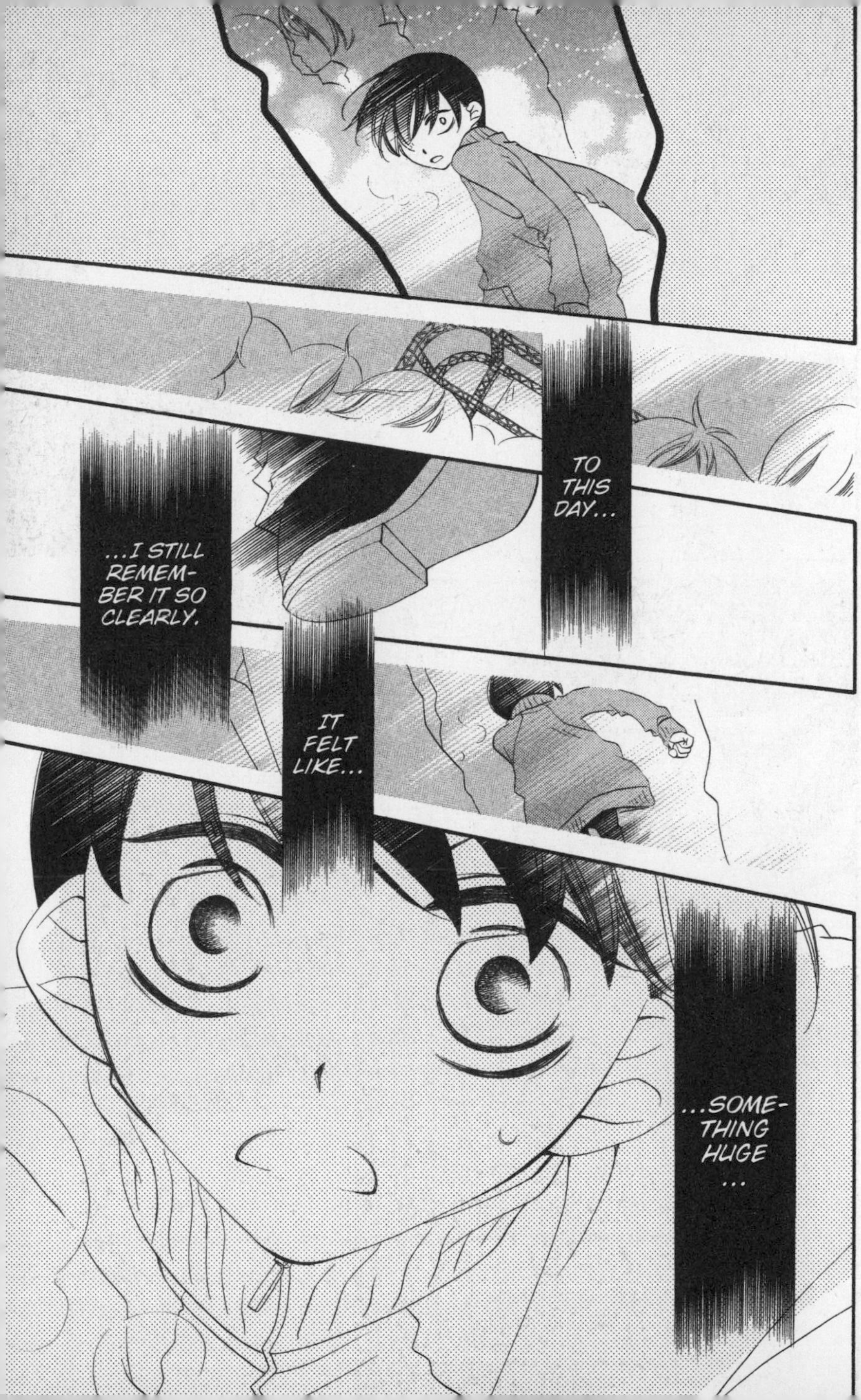
TO THIS DAY...
...I STILL REMEMBER IT SO CLEARLY.
IT FELT LIKE...
...SOMETHING HUGE...

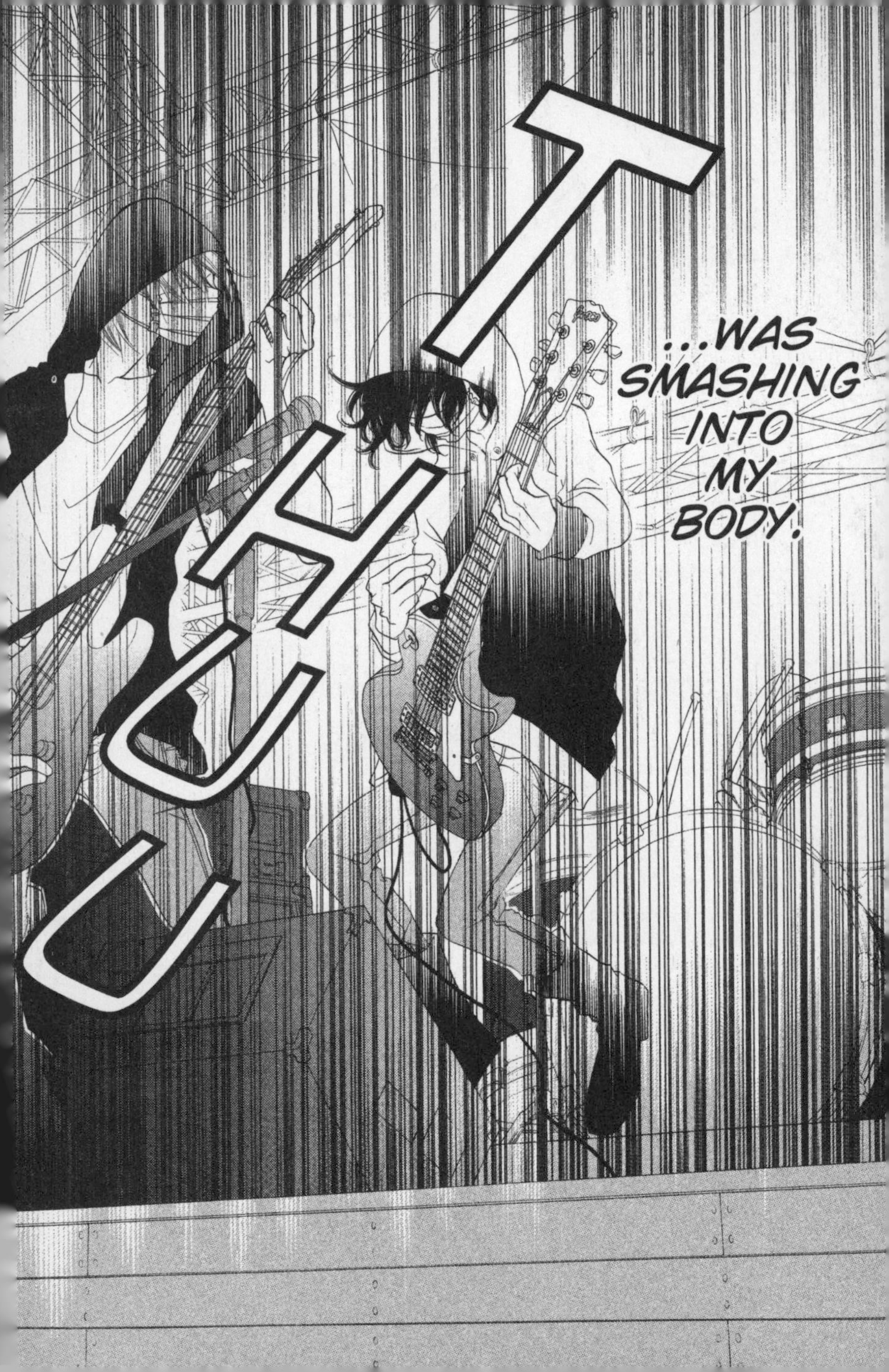
...WAS SMASHING INTO MY BODY.

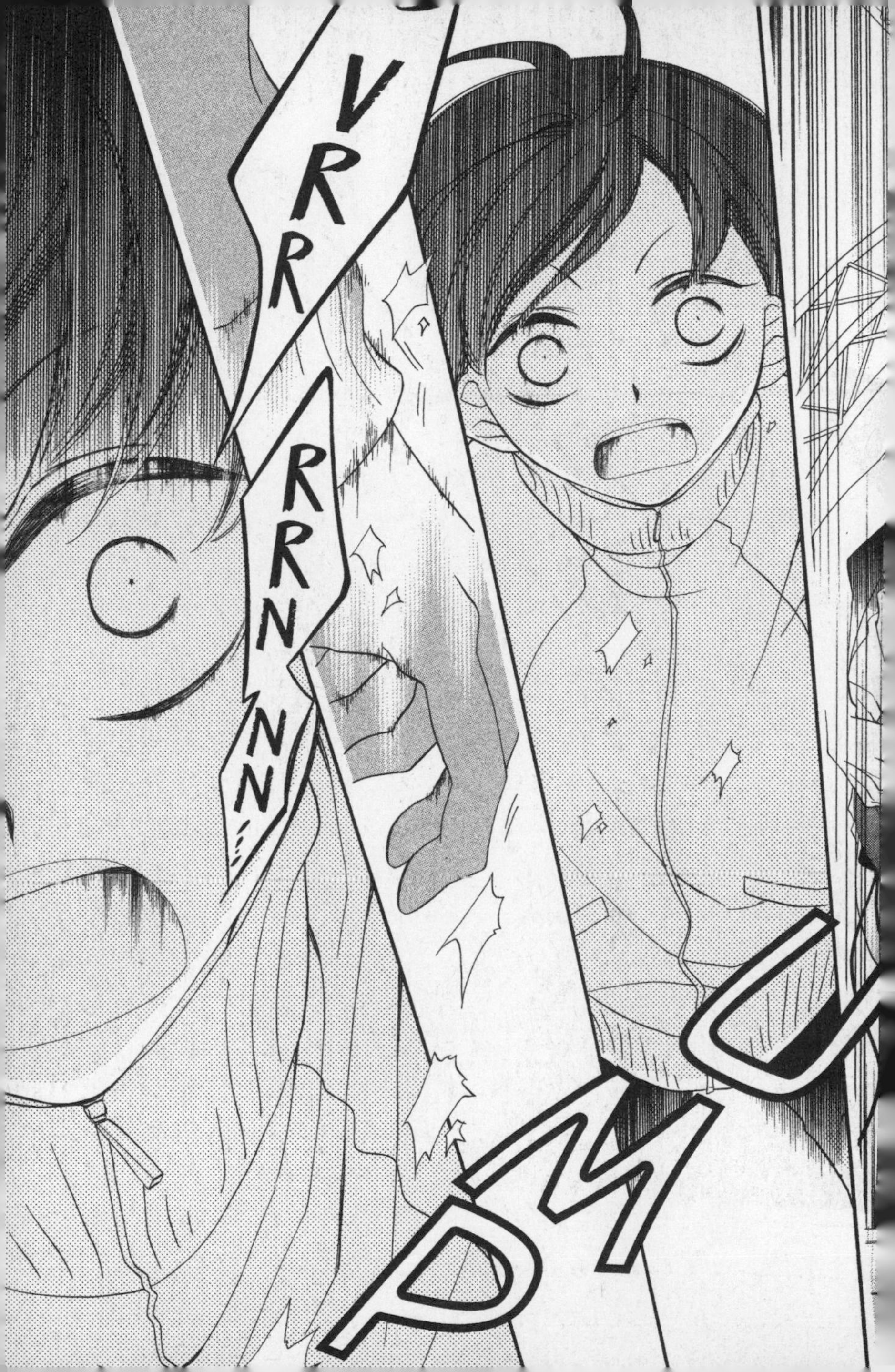
VRRR
RRRNNN...
UMP

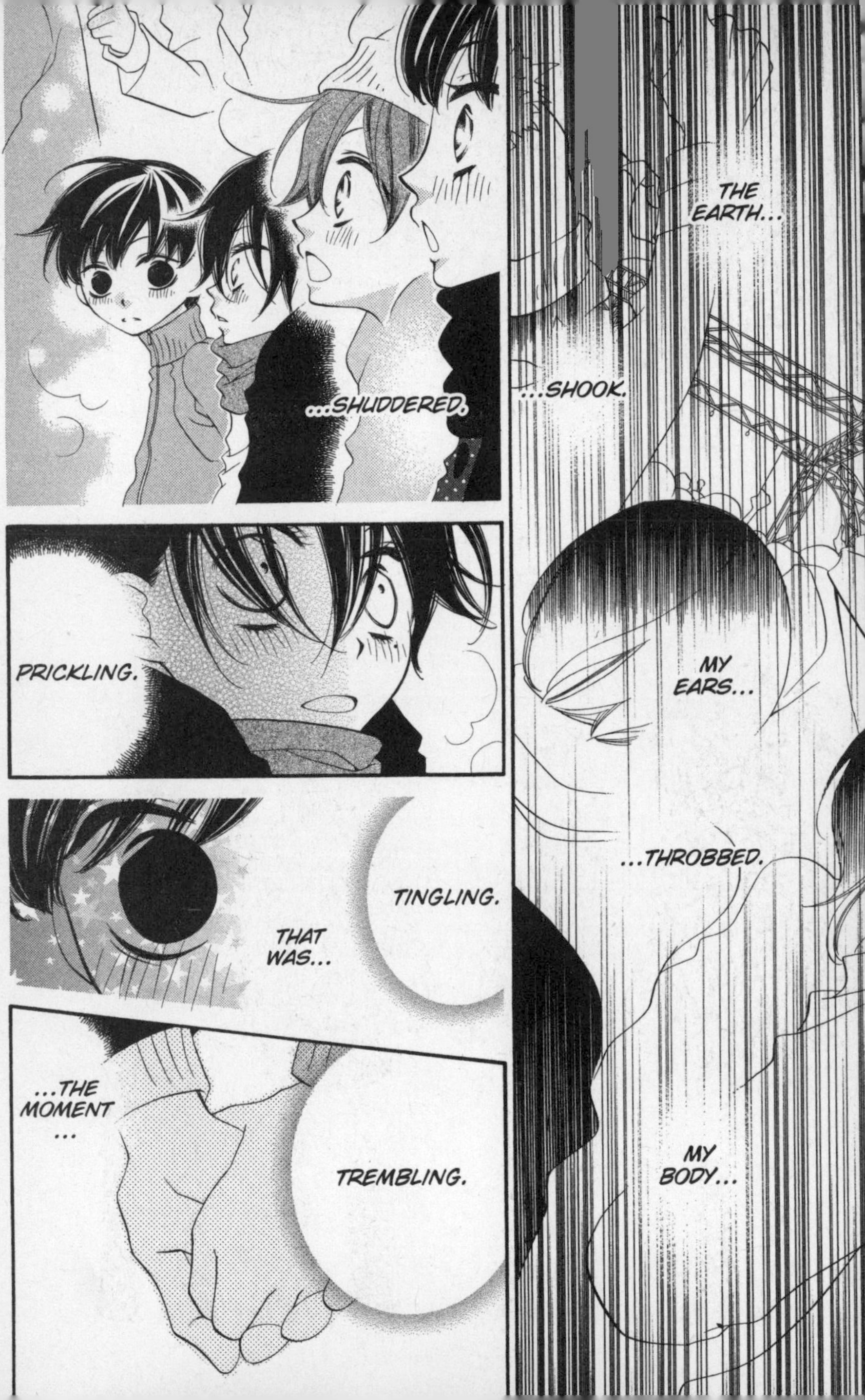
THE EARTH...
...SHOOK.
MY EARS...
...THROBBED.
MY BODY...
...SHUDDERED.
PRICKLING.
TINGLING.
THAT WAS...
...THE MOMENT ...
TREMBLING.

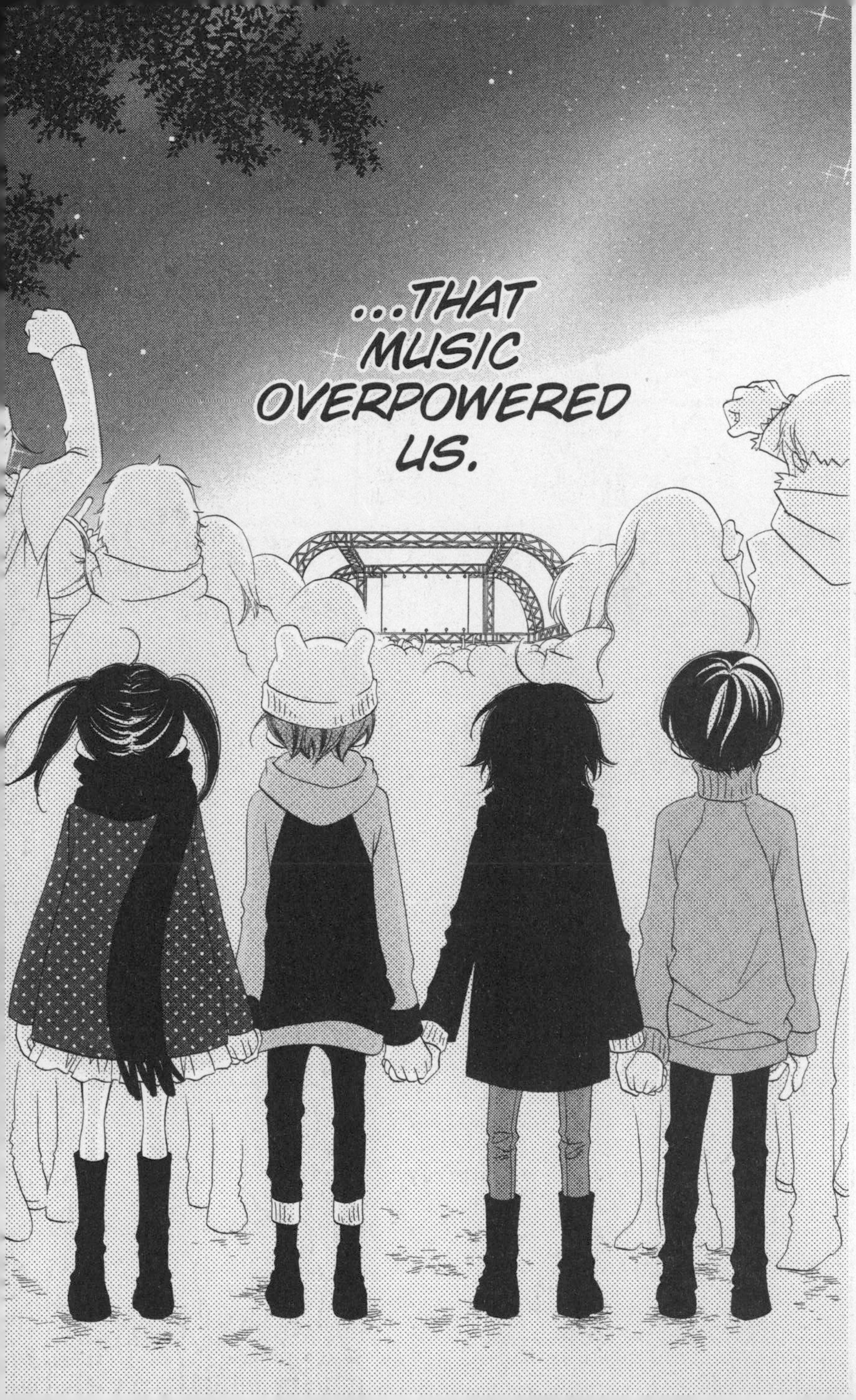
...THAT MUSIC OVERPOWERED US.

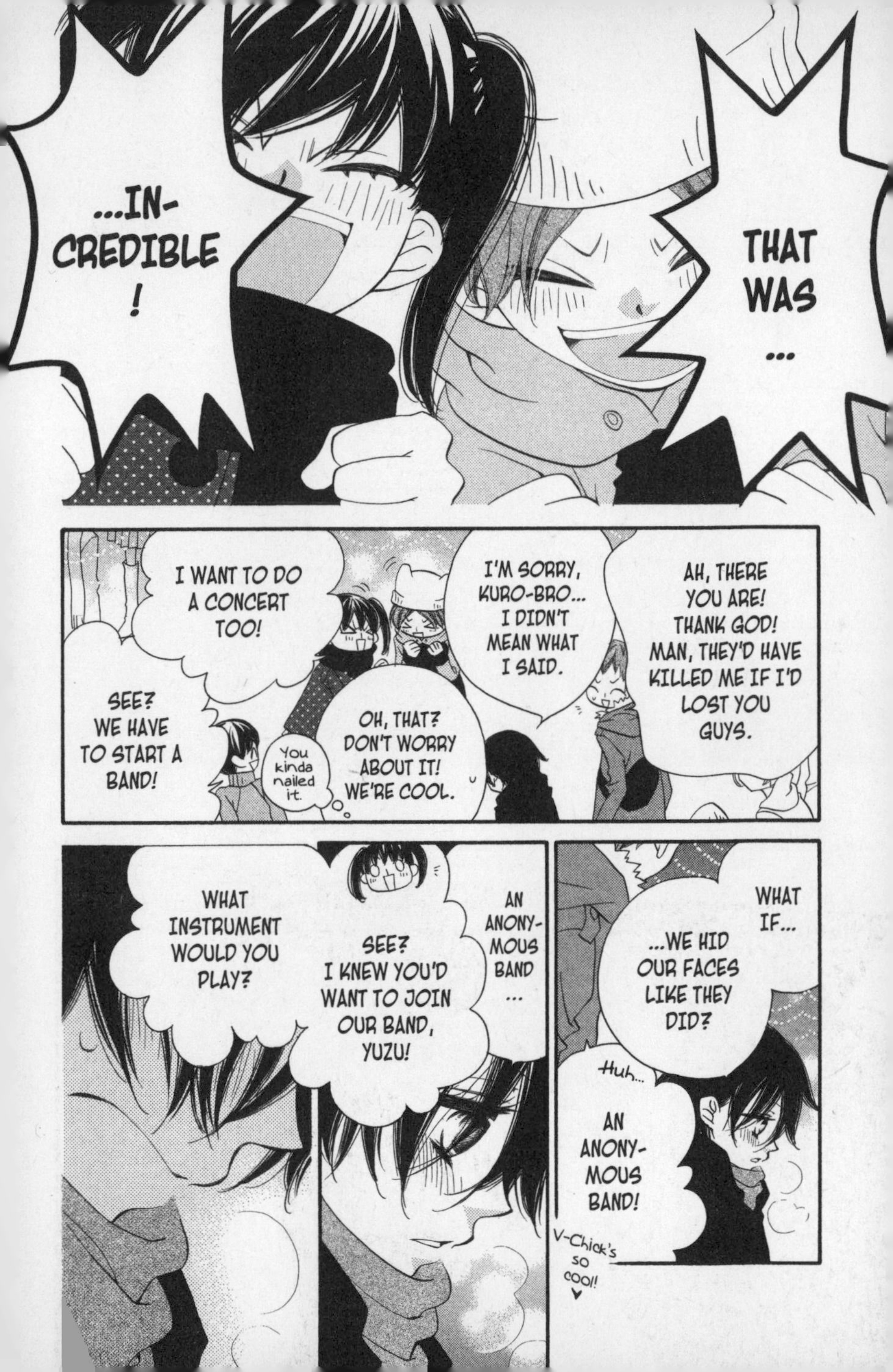
THAT WAS...
...IN-CREDIBLE!
AH, THERE YOU ARE! THANK GOD! MAN, THEY'D HAVE KILLED ME IF I'D LOST YOU GUYS.
I'M SORRY, KURO-BRO... I DIDN'T MEAN WHAT I SAID.
OH, THAT? DON'T WORRY ABOUT IT! WE'RE COOL.
You kinda nailed it.
I WANT TO DO A CONCERT TOO!
SEE? WE HAVE TO START A BAND!
WHAT IF...
...WE HID OUR FACES LIKE THEY DID?
Huh...
AN ANONY-MOUS BAND!
V-Chick's so cool! ♥
AN ANONY-MOUS BAND...
SEE? I KNEW YOU'D WANT TO JOIN OUR BAND, YUZU!
WHAT INSTRUMENT WOULD YOU PLAY?

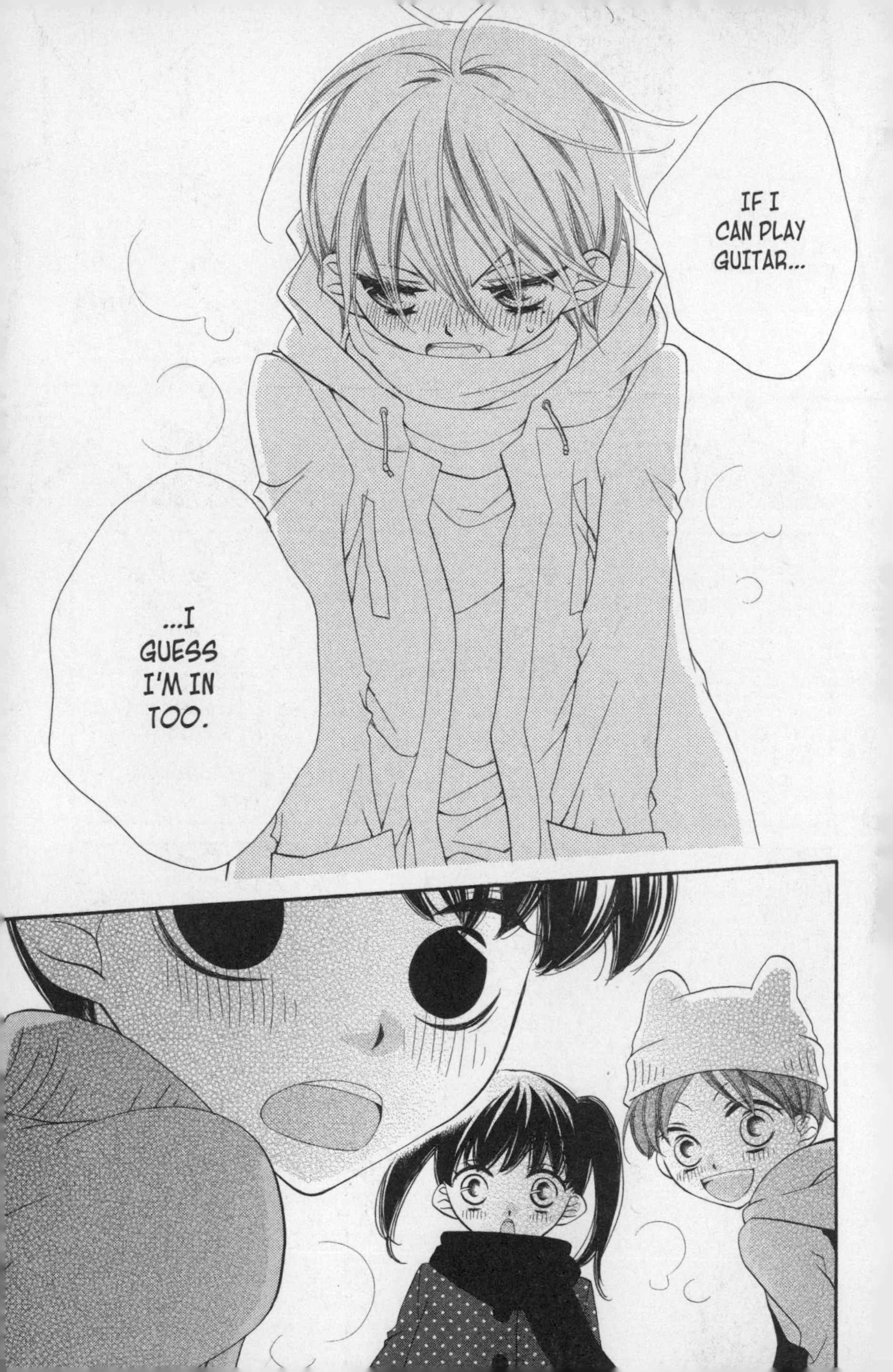
IF I CAN PLAY GUITAR...
...I GUESS I'M IN TOO.

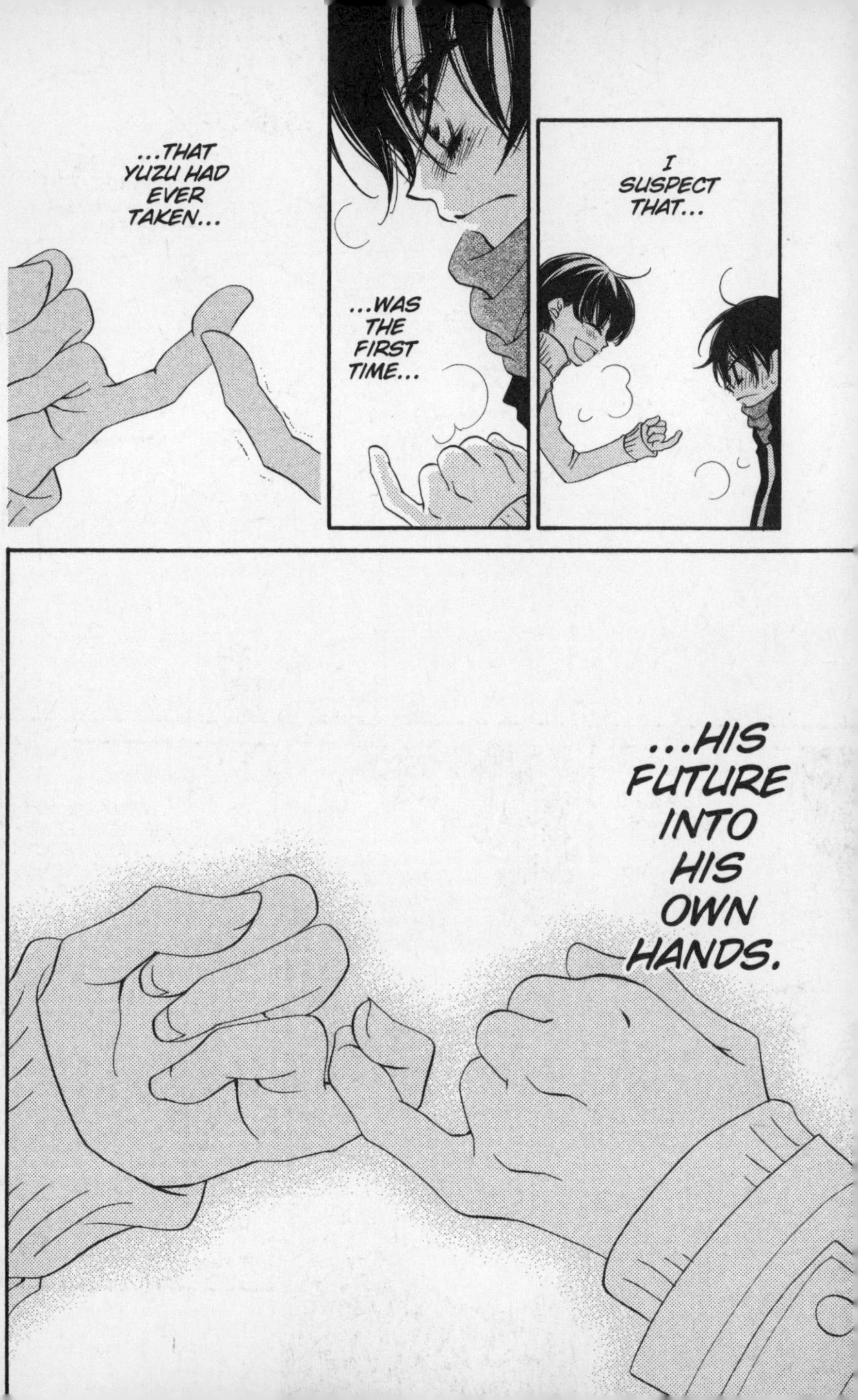
I SUSPECT THAT...
...WAS THE FIRST TIME...
...THAT YUZU HAD EVER TAKEN...
...HIS FUTURE INTO HIS OWN HANDS.

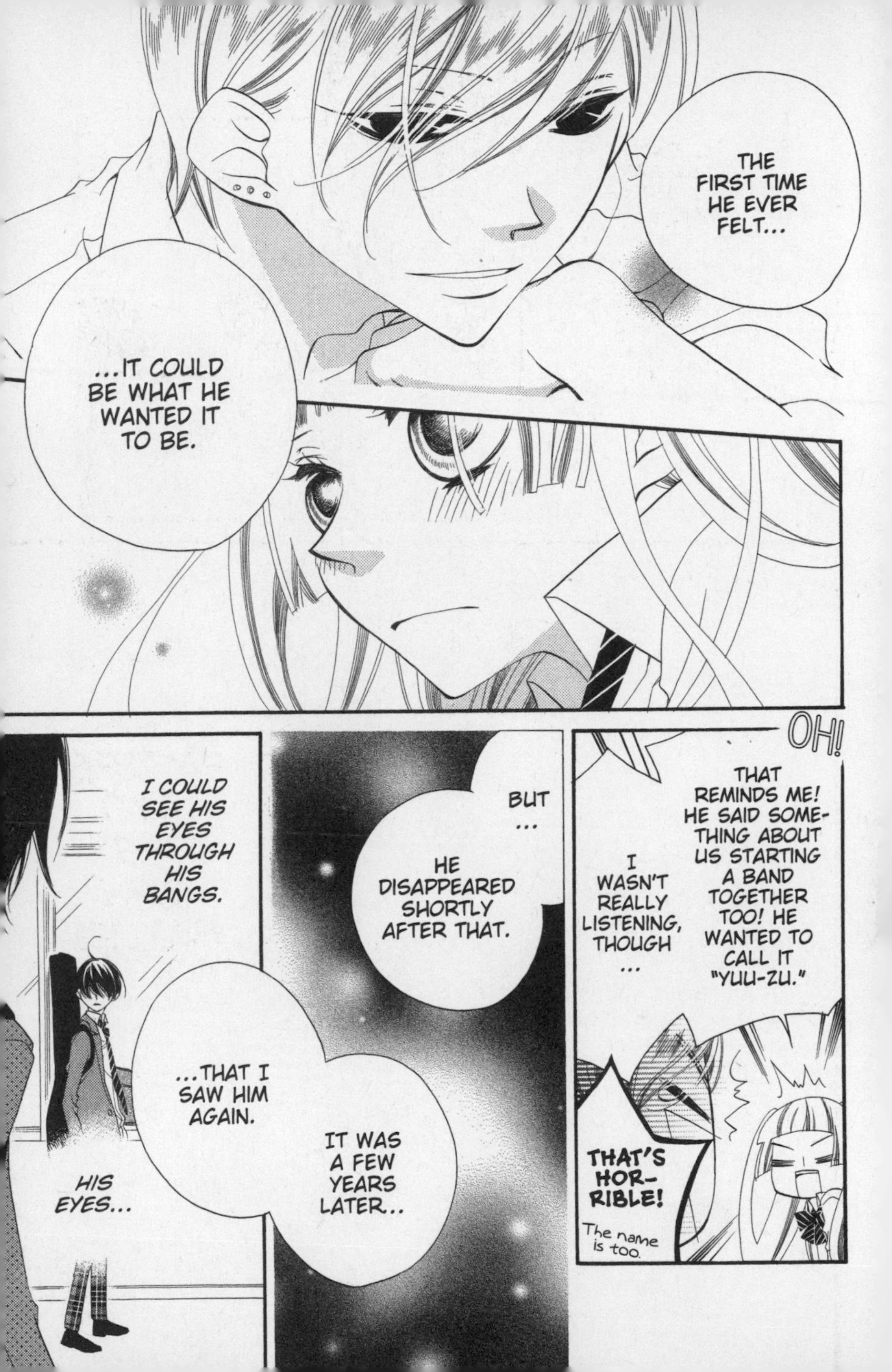
THE FIRST TIME HE EVER FELT...
...IT COULD BE WHAT HE WANTED IT TO BE.
OH!
THAT REMINDS ME! HE SAID SOME-THING ABOUT US STARTING A BAND TOGETHER TOO! HE WANTED TO CALL IT "YUU-ZU."
I WASN'T REALLY LISTENING, THOUGH...
THAT'S HOR-RIBLE!
The name is too.
BUT...
HE DISAPPEARED SHORTLY AFTER THAT.
IT WAS A FEW YEARS LATER...
...THAT I SAW HIM AGAIN.
I COULD SEE HIS EYES THROUGH HIS BANGS.
HIS EYES...

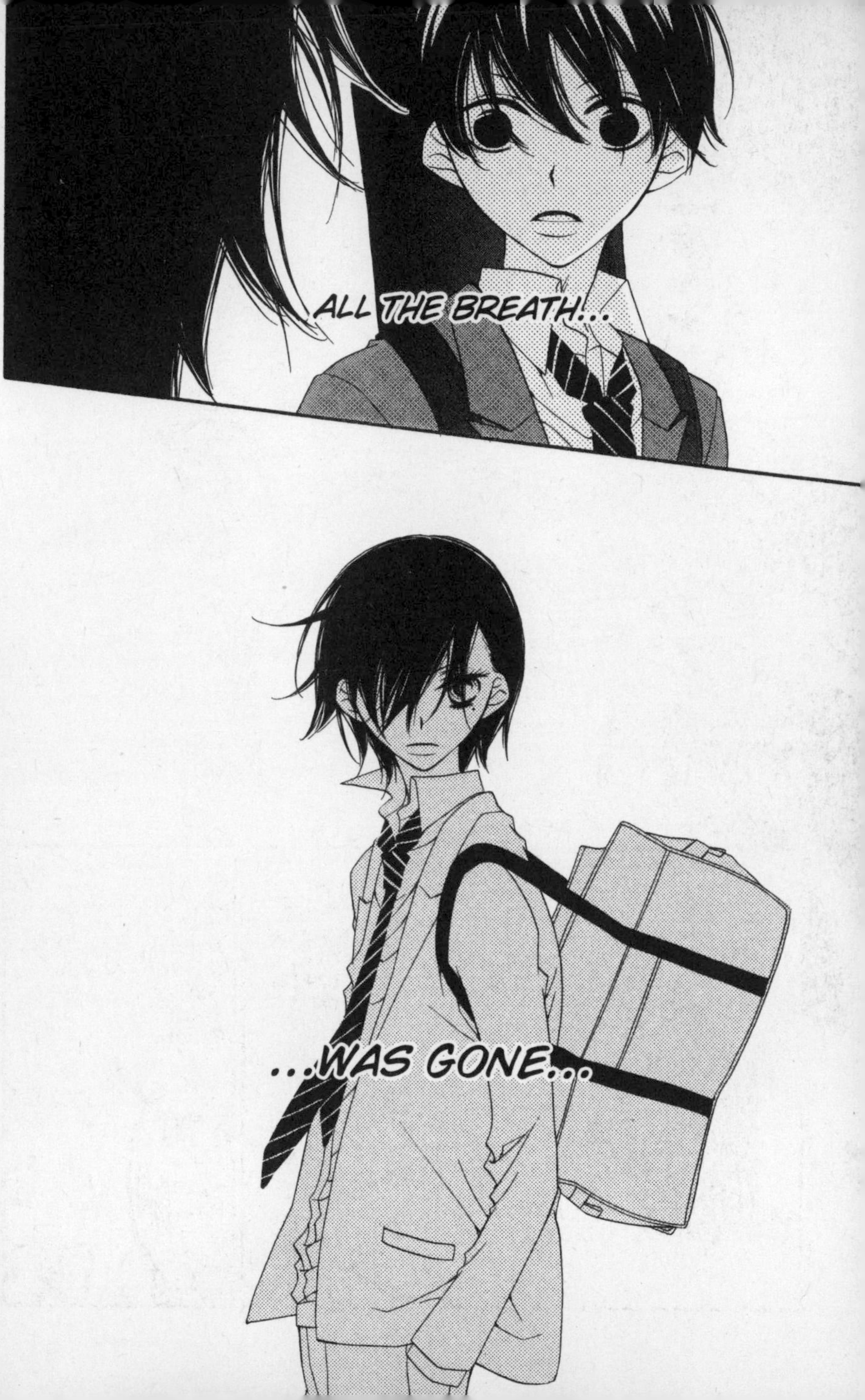
ALL THE BREATH...
...WAS GONE...

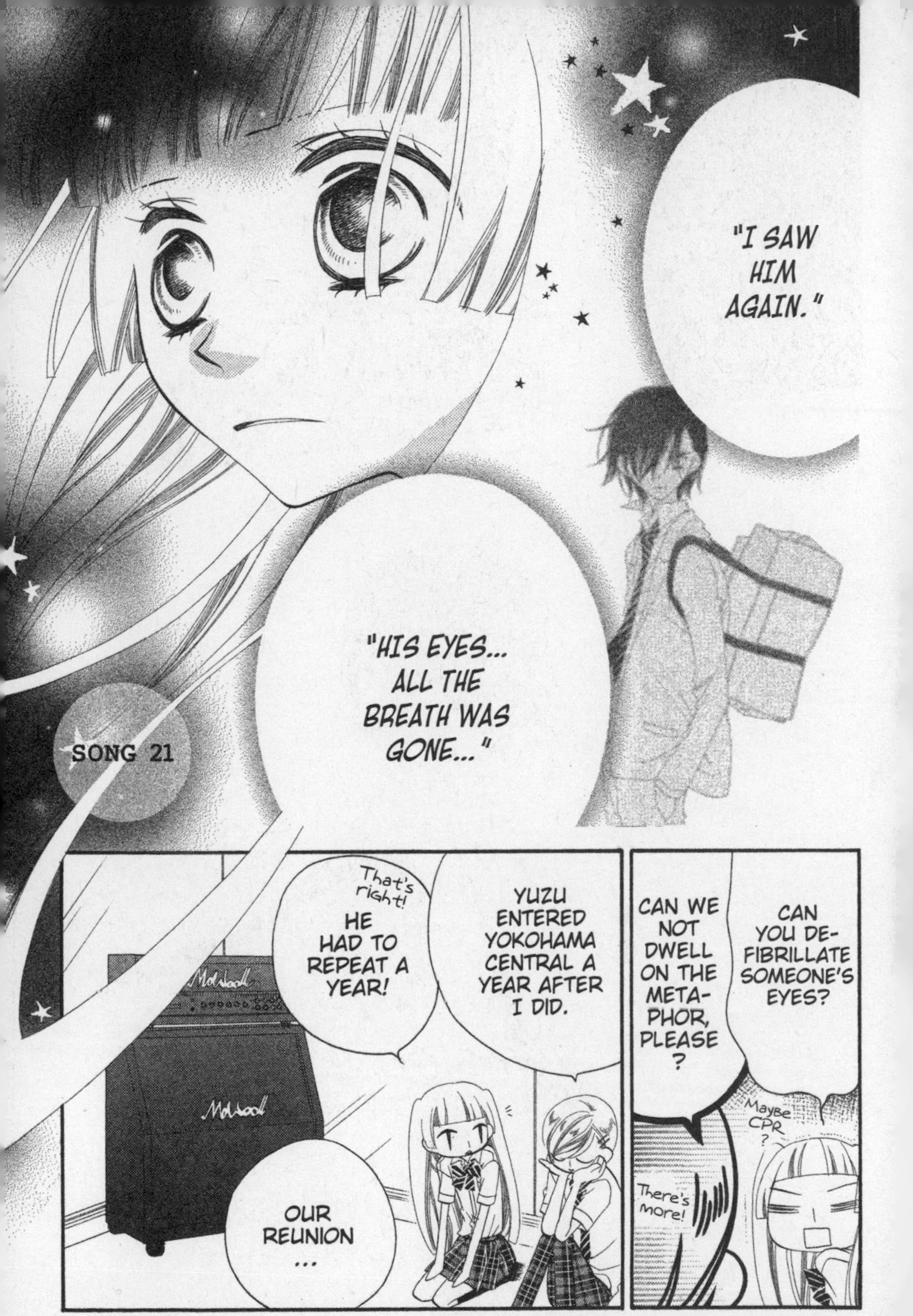
"I SAW HIM AGAIN."
"HIS EYES... ALL THE BREATH WAS GONE..."
SONG 21
CAN YOU DE-FIBRILLATE SOMEONE'S EYES?
CAN WE NOT DWELL ON THE META-PHOR, PLEASE?
Maybe CPR?
There's more!
YUZU ENTERED YOKOHAMA CENTRAL A YEAR AFTER I DID.
That's right!
HE HAD TO REPEAT A YEAR!
OUR REUNION ...

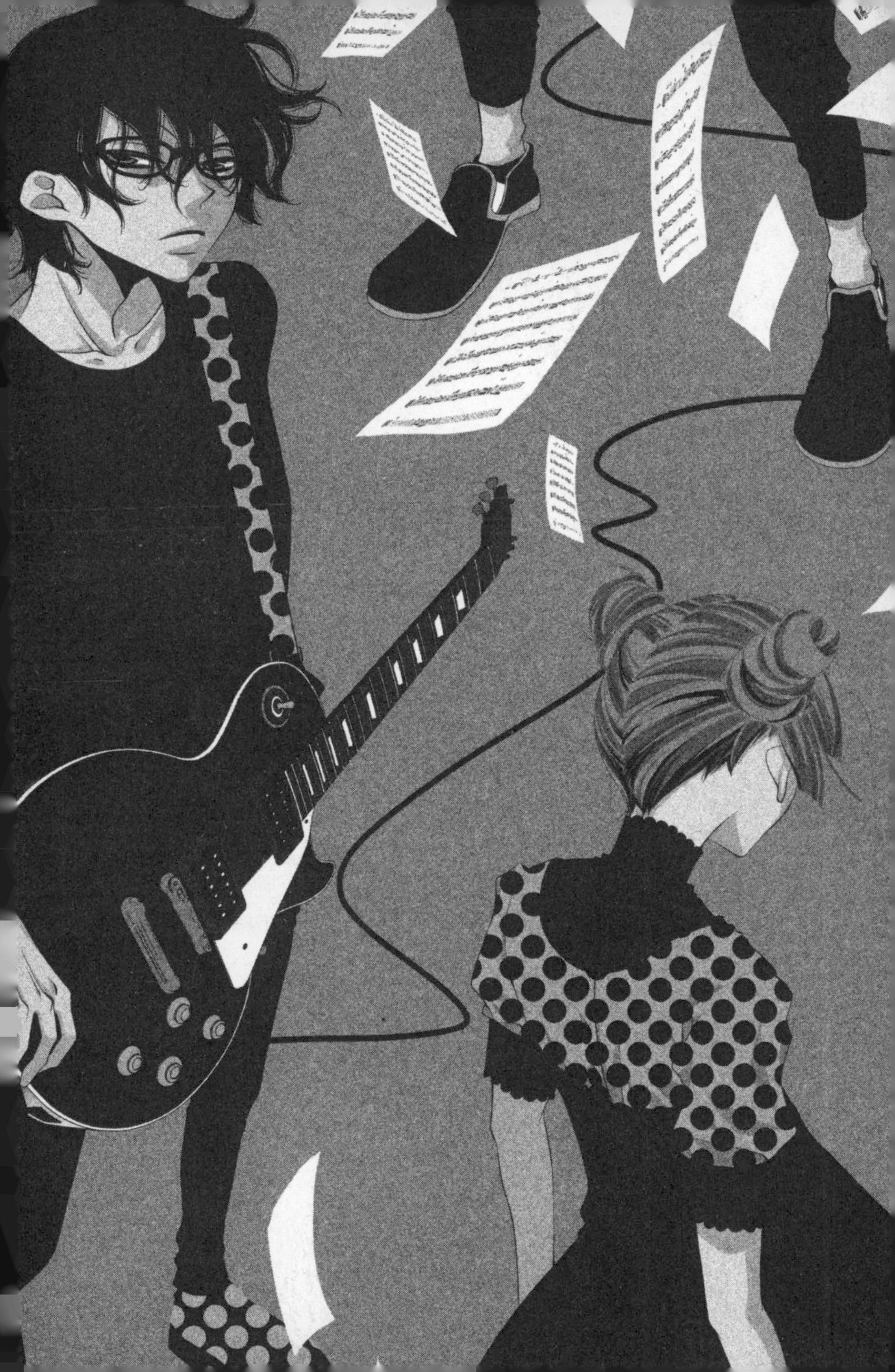

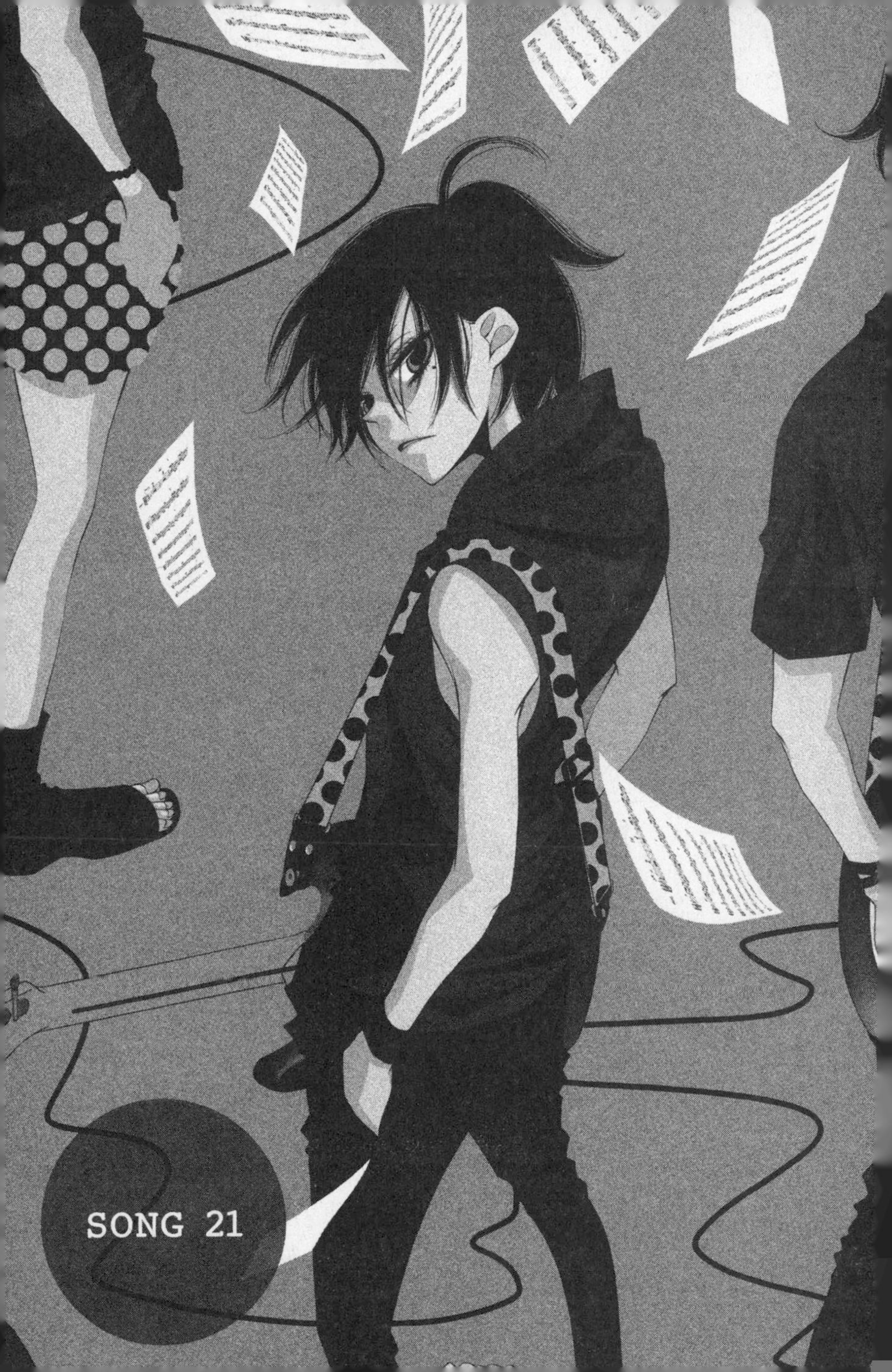
SONG 21

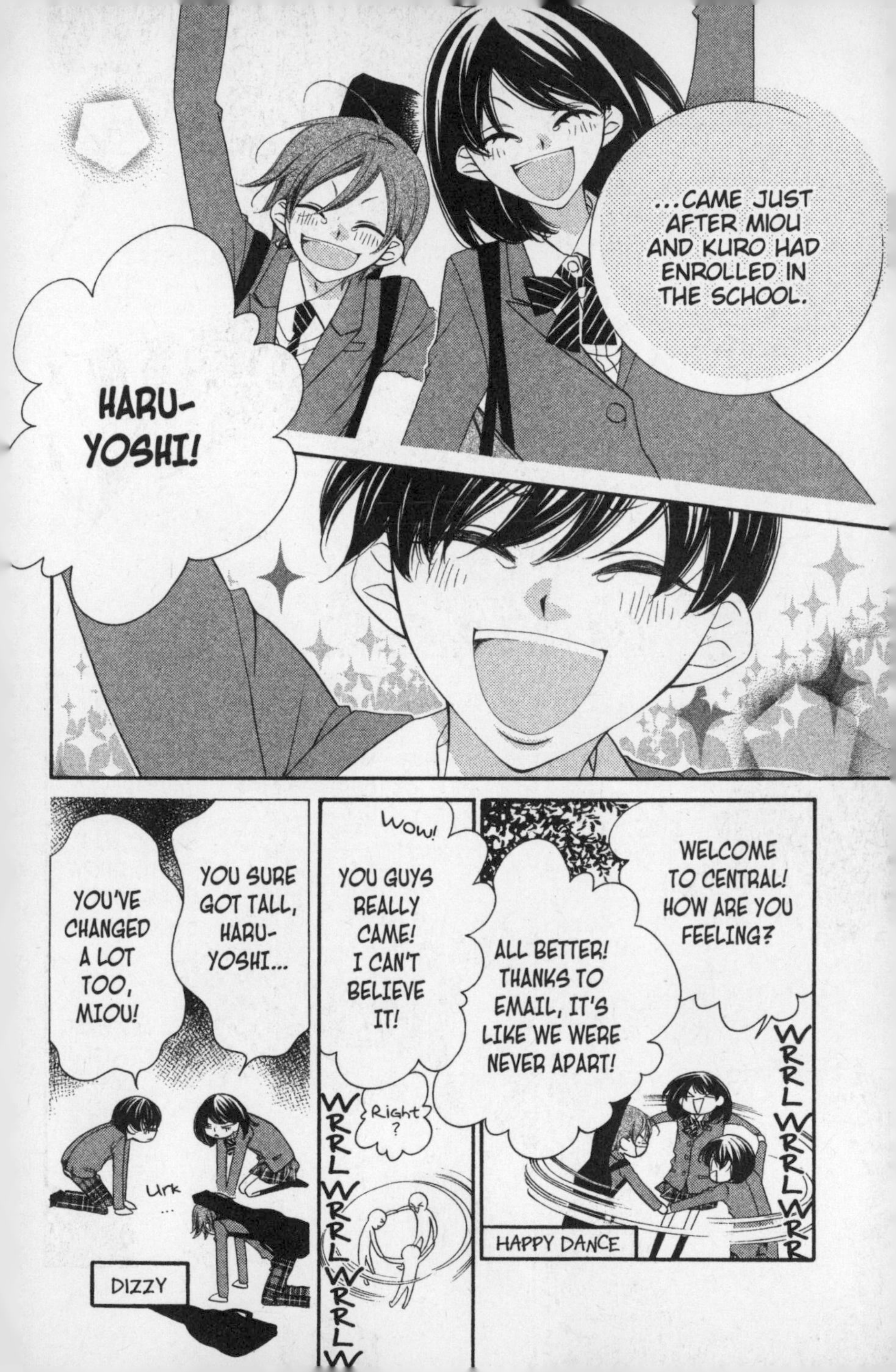
...CAME JUST AFTER MIOU AND KURO HAD ENROLLED IN THE SCHOOL.
HARU-YOSHI!
WELCOME TO CENTRAL! HOW ARE YOU FEELING?
ALL BETTER! THANKS TO EMAIL, IT'S LIKE WE WERE NEVER APART!
WRRL WRRL WRRL WRR
HAPPY DANCE
WOW!
YOU GUYS REALLY CAME! I CAN'T BELIEVE IT!
Right?
WRRL WRRL WRRL WRRL W
YOU SURE GOT TALL, HARU-YOSHI...
YOU'VE CHANGED A LOT TOO, MIOU!
Urk ...
DIZZY

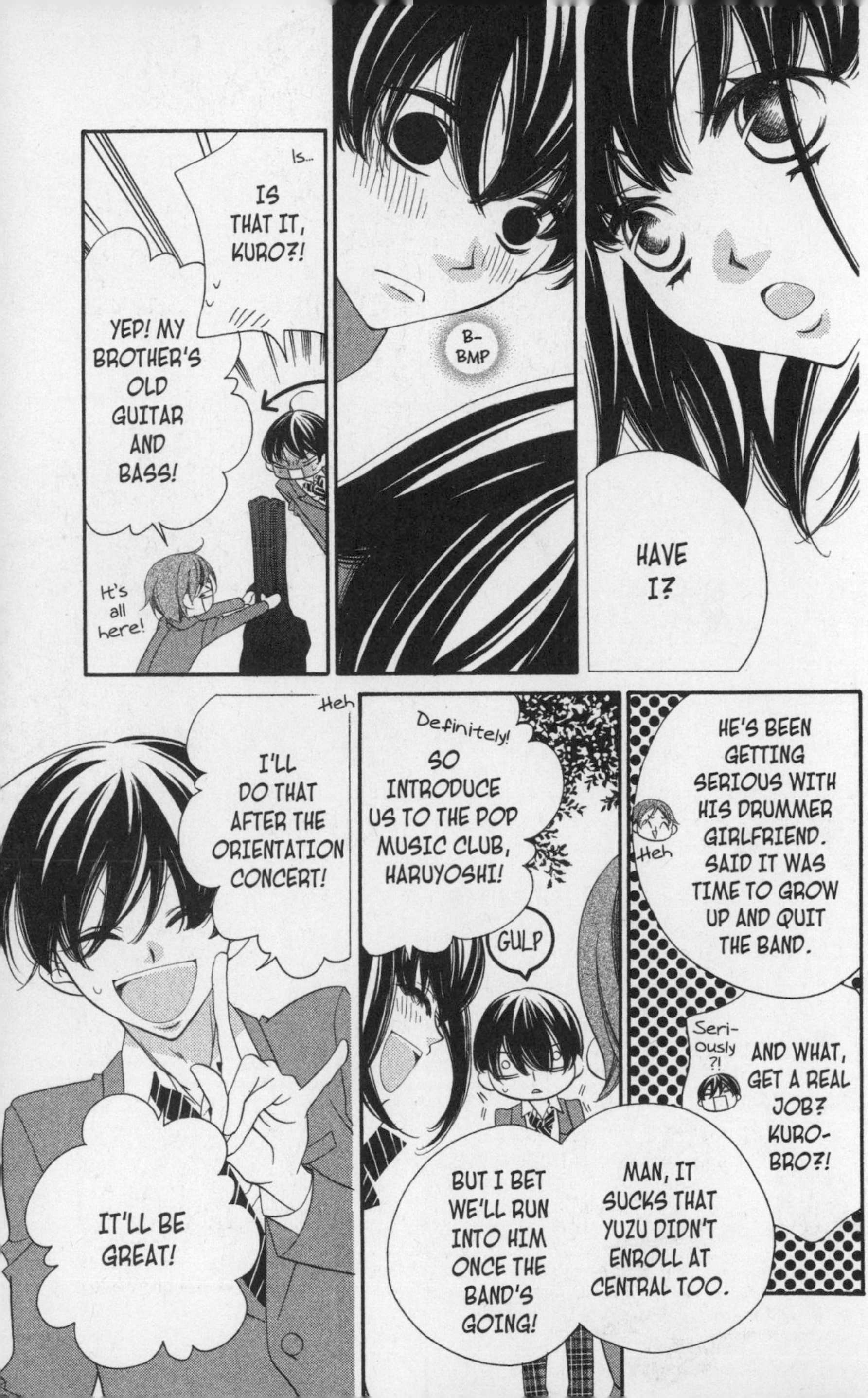
HAVE I?
B-BMP
Is...
IS THAT IT, KURO?!
YEP! MY BROTHER'S OLD GUITAR AND BASS!
It's all here!
HE'S BEEN GETTING SERIOUS WITH HIS DRUMMER GIRLFRIEND. SAID IT WAS TIME TO GROW UP AND QUIT THE BAND.
Heh
Seri-ously?!
AND WHAT, GET A REAL JOB? KURO-BRO?!
MAN, IT SUCKS THAT YUZU DIDN'T ENROLL AT CENTRAL TOO.
BUT I BET WE'LL RUN INTO HIM ONCE THE BAND'S GOING!
Definitely!
SO INTRODUCE US TO THE POP MUSIC CLUB, HARUYOSHI!
GULP
Heh
I'LL DO THAT AFTER THE ORIENTATION CONCERT!
IT'LL BE GREAT!

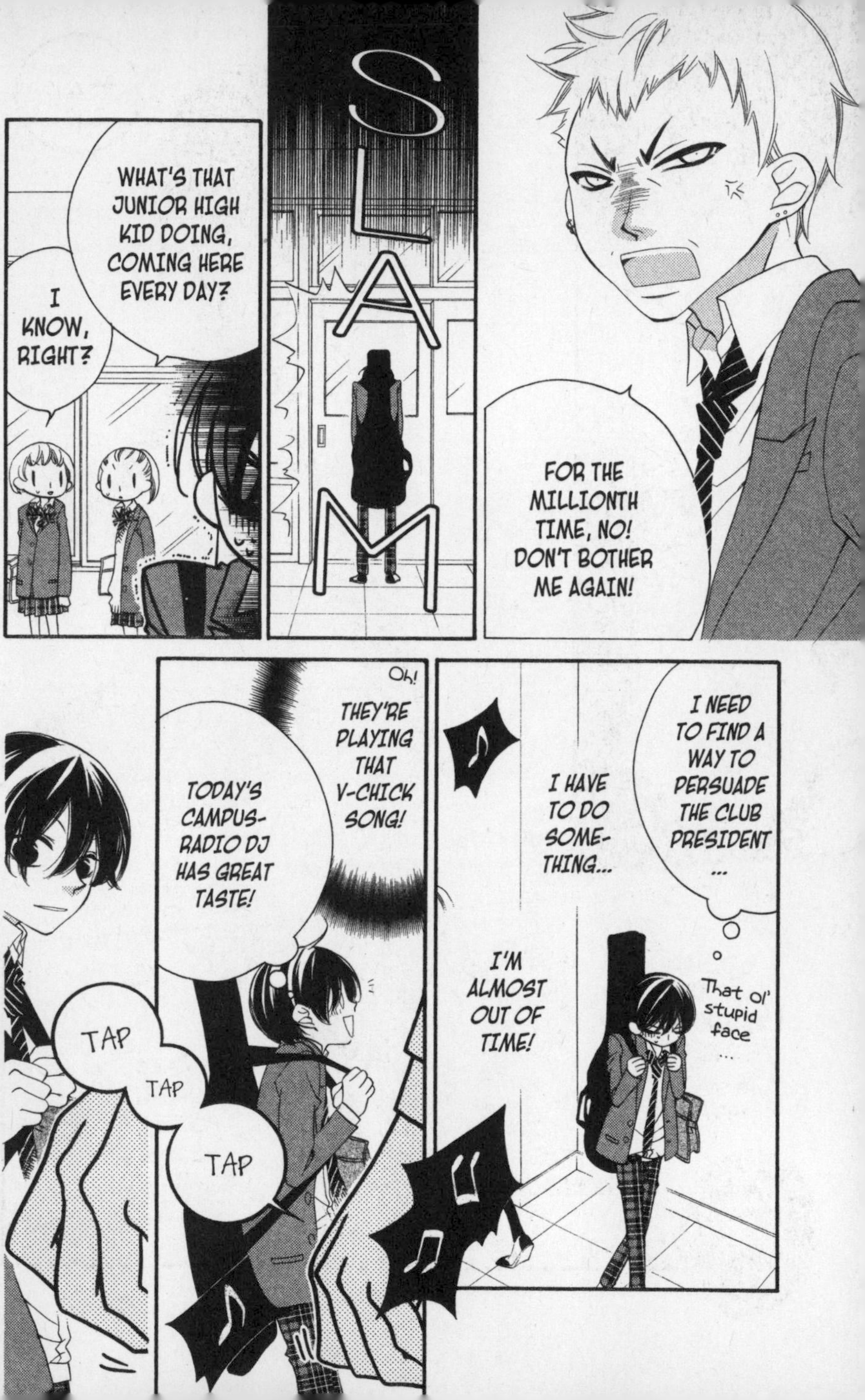
FOR THE MILLIONTH TIME, NO! DON'T BOTHER ME AGAIN!
SLAM
WHAT'S THAT JUNIOR HIGH KID DOING, COMING HERE EVERY DAY?
I KNOW, RIGHT?
I NEED TO FIND A WAY TO PERSUADE THE CLUB PRESIDENT ...
That ol' stupid face ...
I HAVE TO DO SOME-THING...
I'M ALMOST OUT OF TIME!
Oh!
THEY'RE PLAYING THAT V-CHICK SONG!
TODAY'S CAMPUS-RADIO DJ HAS GREAT TASTE!
TAP
TAP
TAP

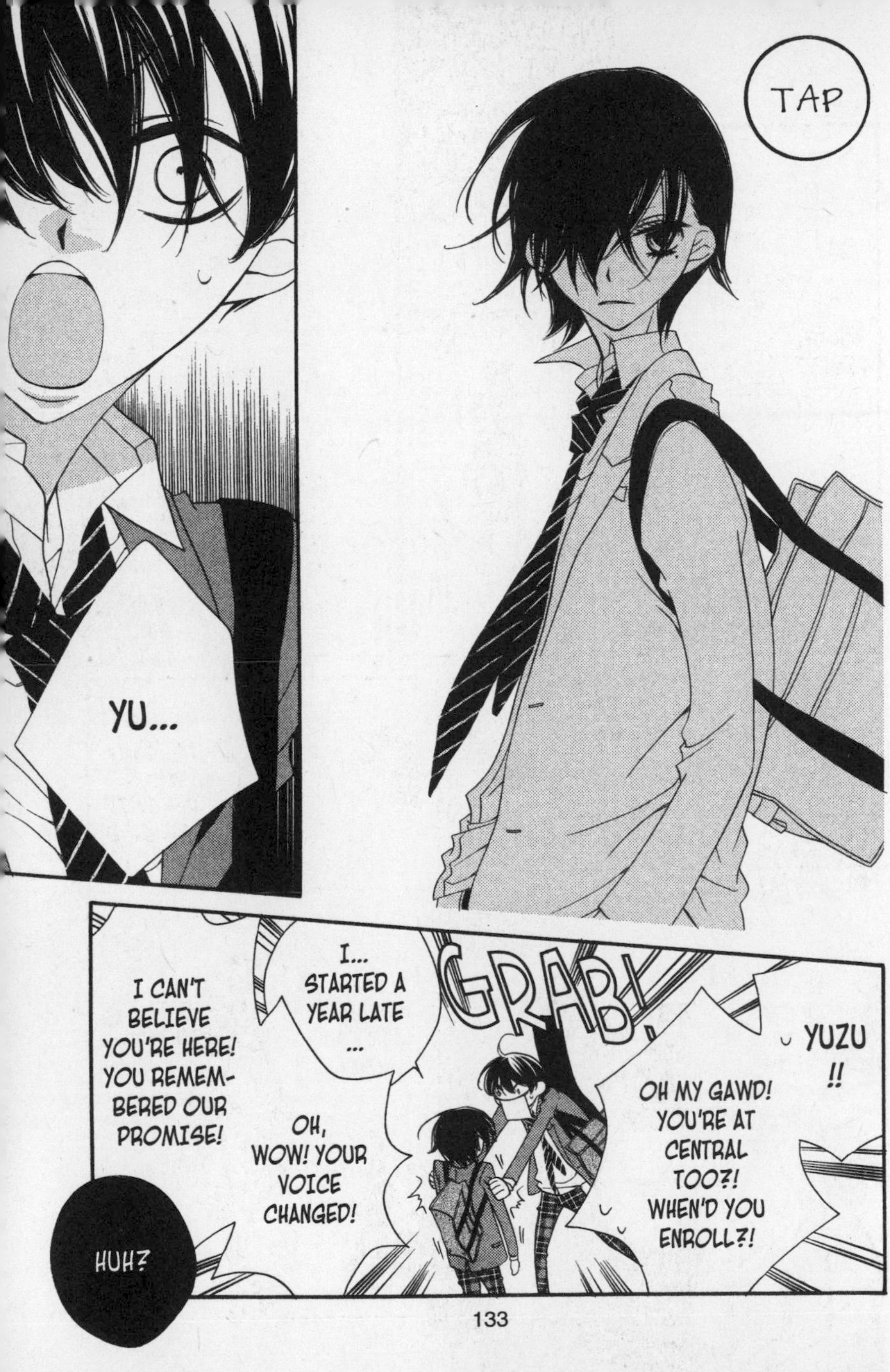
TAP
YU...
YUZU !!
GRAB!
OH MY GAWD! YOU'RE AT CENTRAL TOO?! WHEN'D YOU ENROLL?!
I... STARTED A YEAR LATE ...
OH, WOW! YOUR VOICE CHANGED!
I CAN'T BELIEVE YOU'RE HERE! YOU REMEMBERED OUR PROMISE!
HUH?

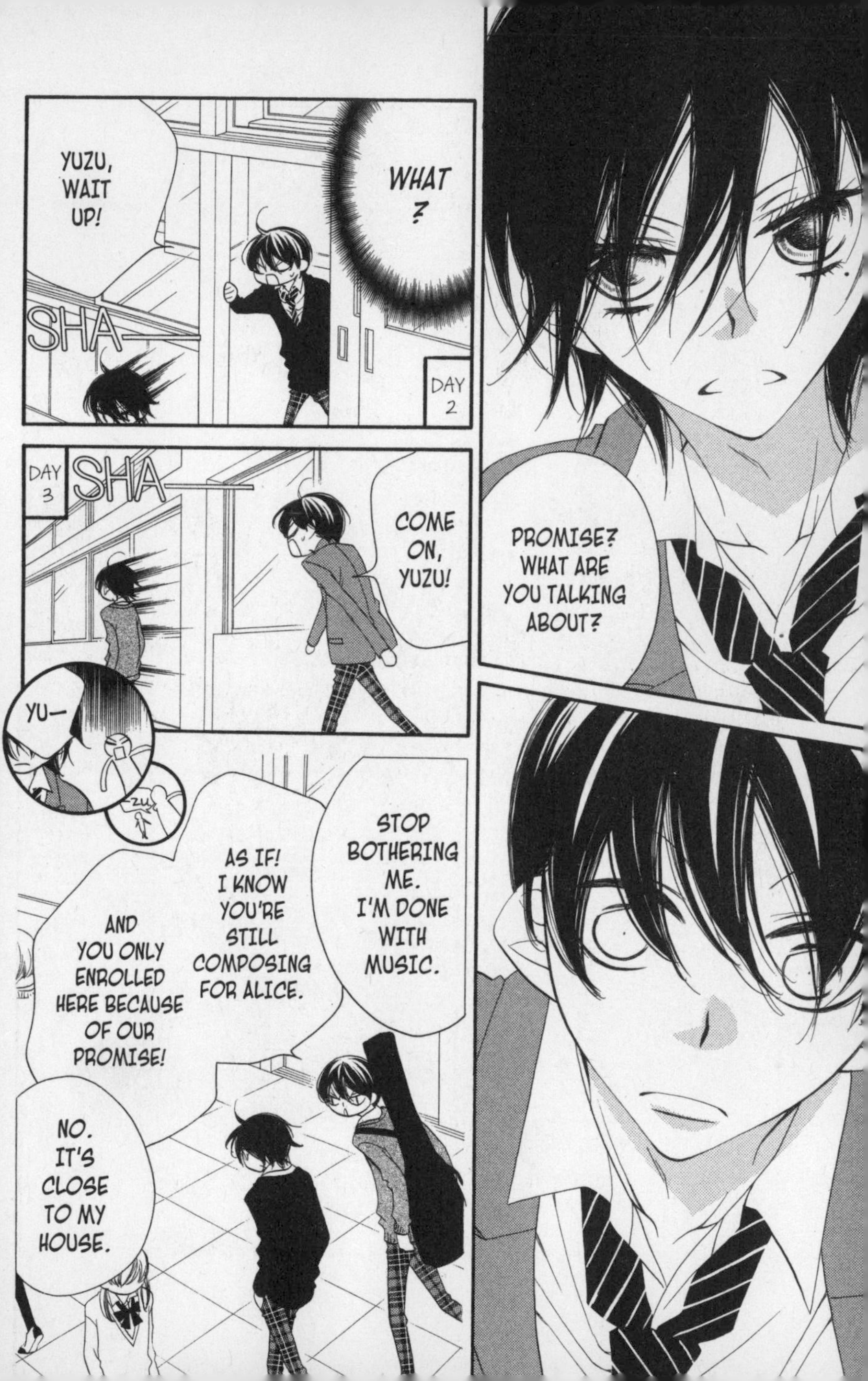

DAY 2
WHAT ?
YUZU, WAIT UP!
SHA—
DAY 3
COME ON, YUZU!
SHA—
YU—
-ZU
STOP BOTHERING ME. I'M DONE WITH MUSIC.
AS IF! I KNOW YOU'RE STILL COMPOSING FOR ALICE.
AND YOU ONLY ENROLLED HERE BECAUSE OF OUR PROMISE!
NO. IT'S CLOSE TO MY HOUSE.
PROMISE? WHAT ARE YOU TALKING ABOUT?

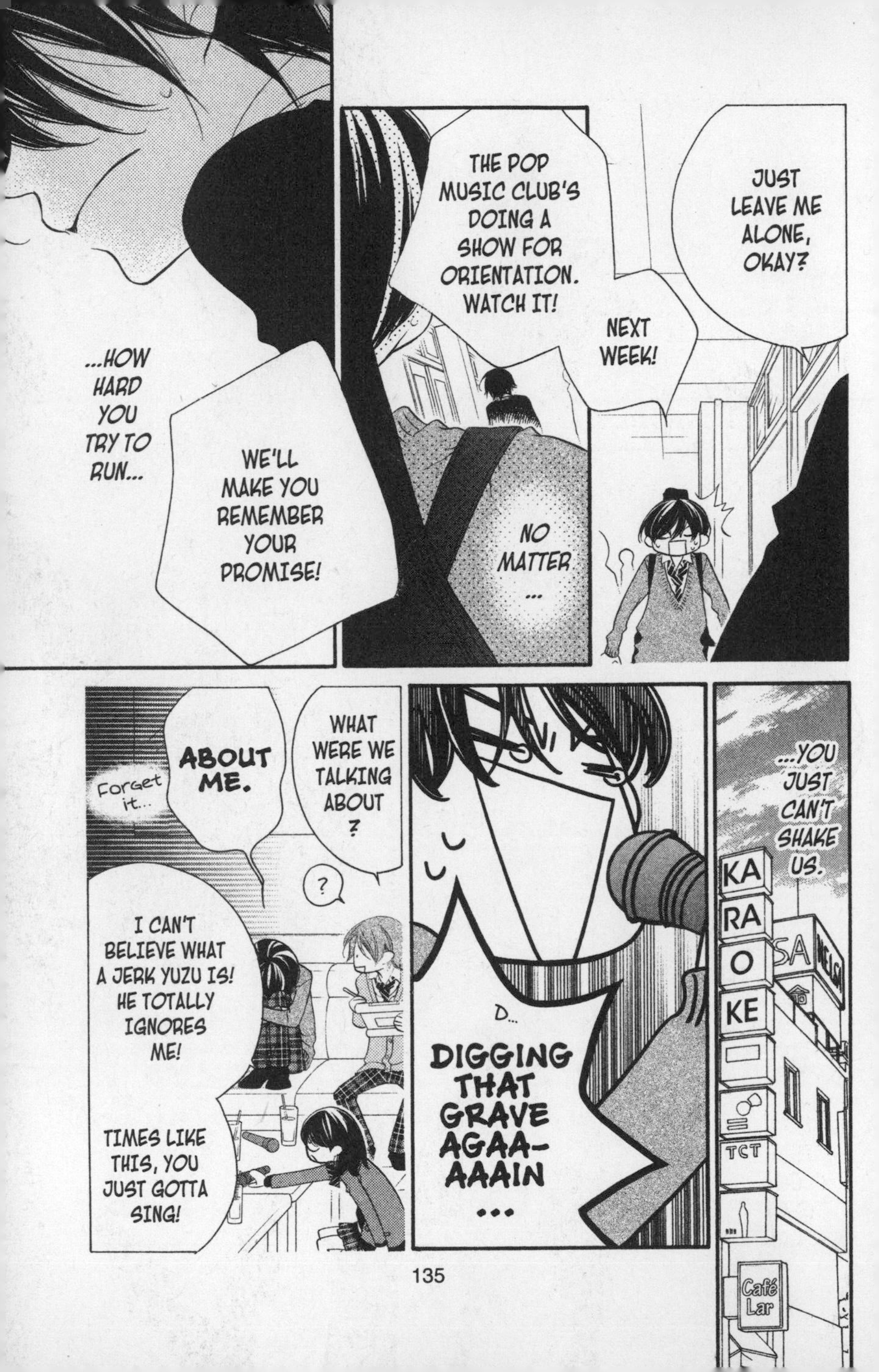
JUST LEAVE ME ALONE, OKAY?
NEXT WEEK!
THE POP MUSIC CLUB'S DOING A SHOW FOR ORIENTATION. WATCH IT!
NO MATTER...
...HOW HARD YOU TRY TO RUN...
WE'LL MAKE YOU REMEMBER YOUR PROMISE!
...YOU JUST CAN'T SHAKE US.
KARAOKE
SA
TCT
Café Lar
D...
DIGGING THAT GRAVE AGAA-AAAIN...
WHAT WERE WE TALKING ABOUT?
ABOUT ME.
Forget it...
?
I CAN'T BELIEVE WHAT A JERK YUZU IS! HE TOTALLY IGNORES ME!
TIMES LIKE THIS, YOU JUST GOTTA SING!

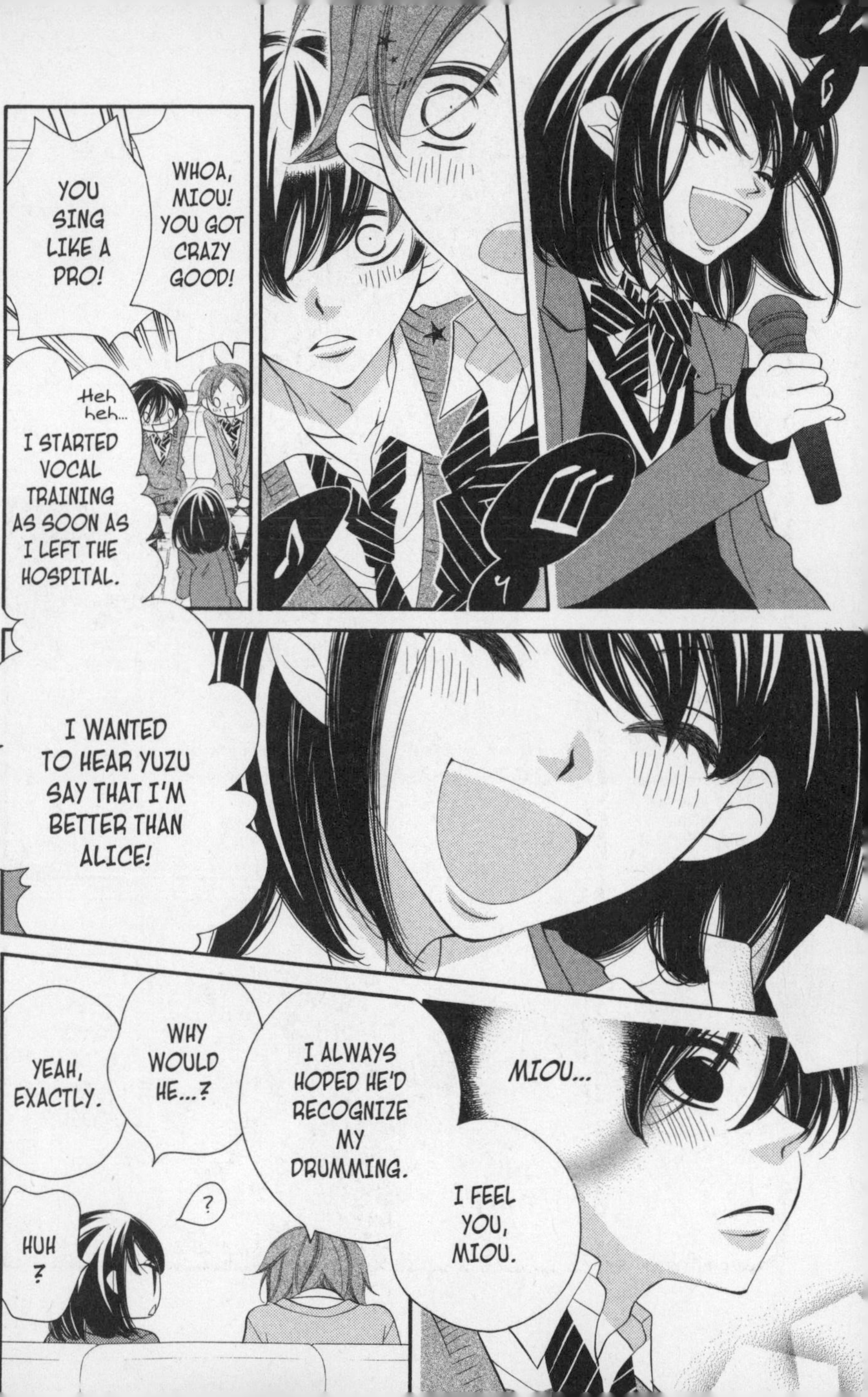
WHOA, MIOU! YOU GOT CRAZY GOOD!
YOU SING LIKE A PRO!
Heh heh...
I STARTED VOCAL TRAINING AS SOON AS I LEFT THE HOSPITAL.
I WANTED TO HEAR YUZU SAY THAT I'M BETTER THAN ALICE!
MIOU...
I FEEL YOU, MIOU.
I ALWAYS HOPED HE'D RECOGNIZE MY DRUMMING.
WHY WOULD HE...?
YEAH, EXACTLY.
?
HUH?

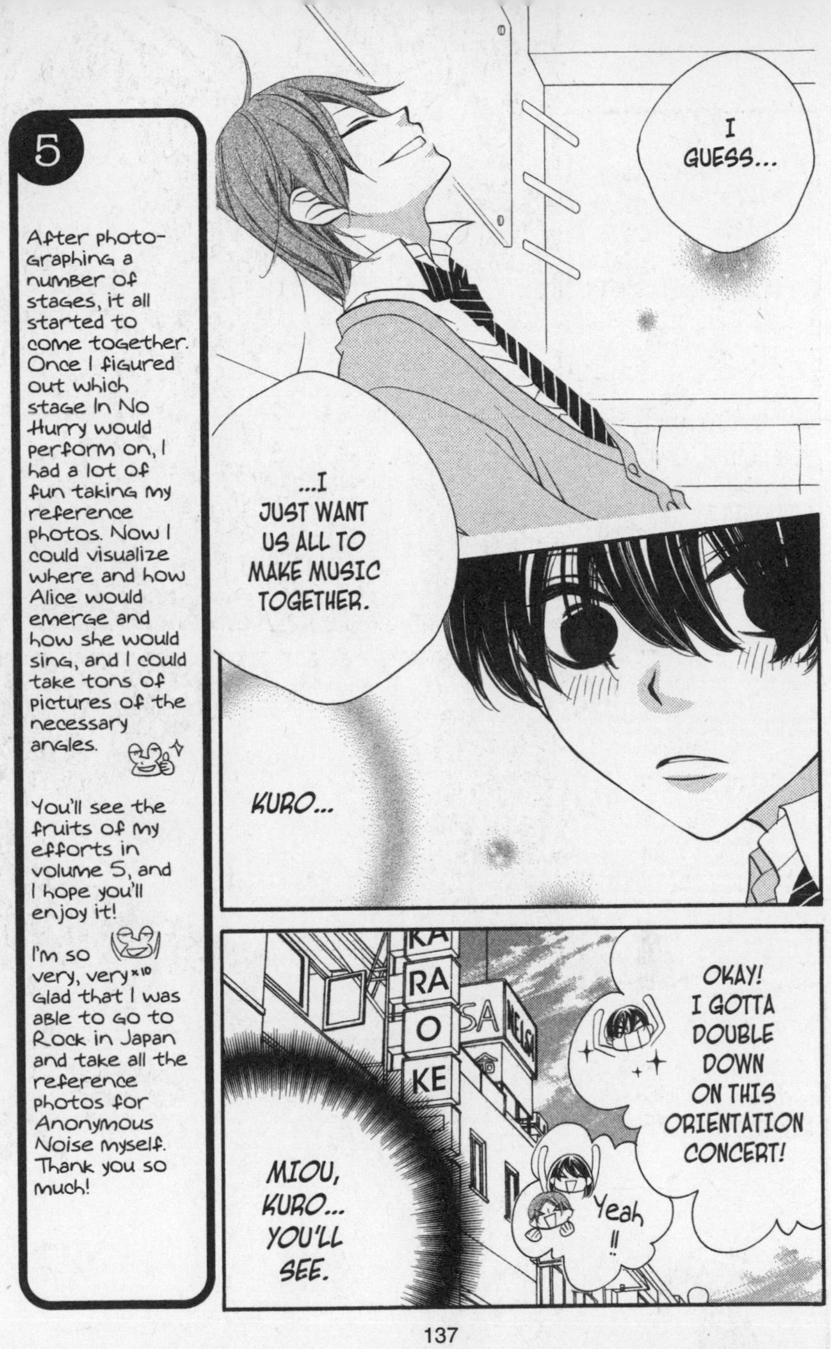
I GUESS...
...I JUST WANT US ALL TO MAKE MUSIC TOGETHER.
KURO...
KA RA O KE
OKAY! I GOTTA DOUBLE DOWN ON THIS ORIENTATION CONCERT!
Yeah!!
MIOU, KURO... YOU'LL SEE.

5

After photographing a number of stages, it all started to come together. Once I figured out which stage In No Hurry would perform on, I had a lot of fun taking my reference photos. Now I could visualize where and how Alice would emerge and how she would sing, and I could take tons of pictures of the necessary angles.

You'll see the fruits of my efforts in volume 5, and I hope you'll enjoy it!

I'm so very, very×10 glad that I was able to go to Rock in Japan and take all the reference photos for Anonymous Noise myself. Thank you so much!

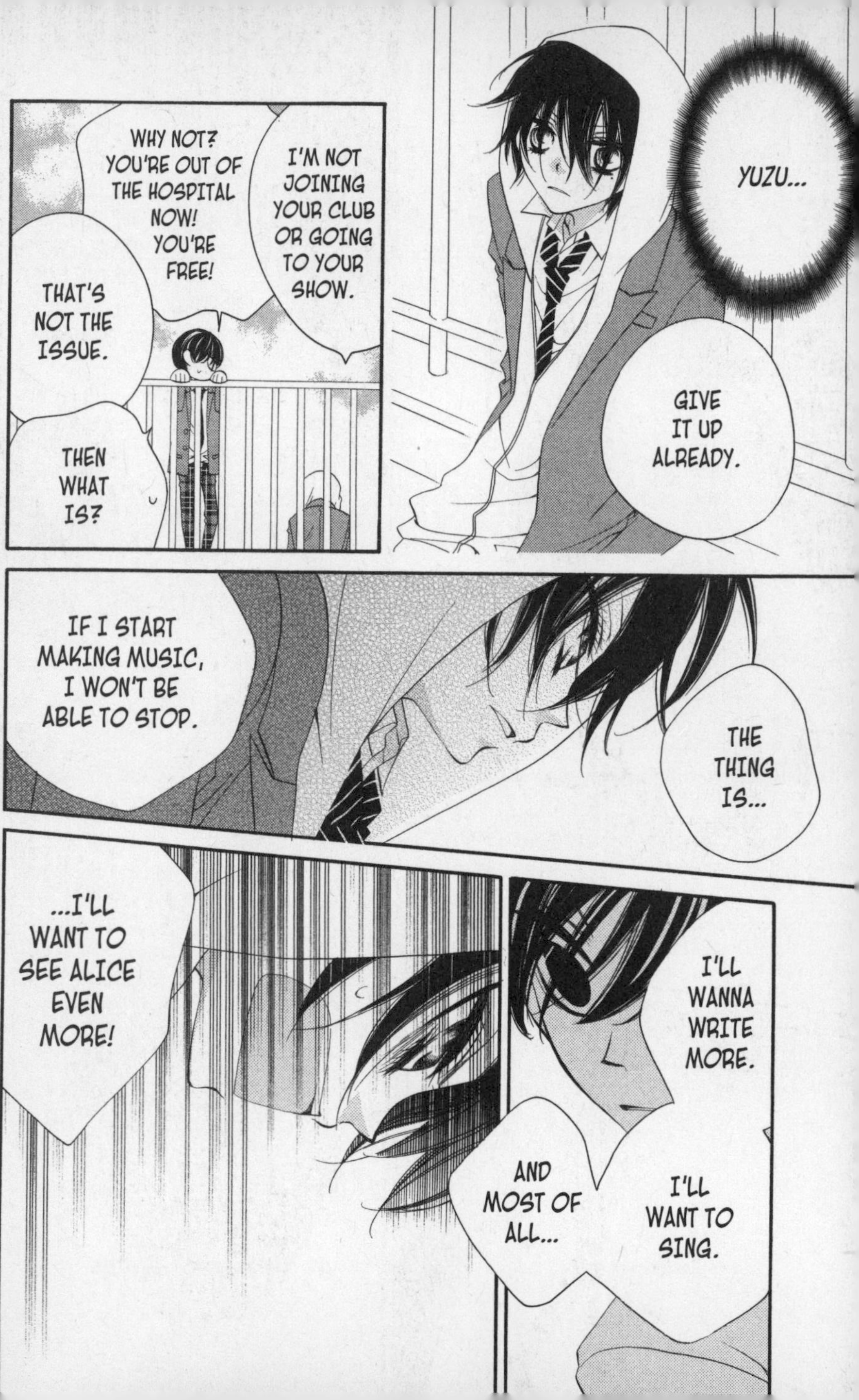
YUZU...
GIVE IT UP ALREADY.
I'M NOT JOINING YOUR CLUB OR GOING TO YOUR SHOW.
WHY NOT? YOU'RE OUT OF THE HOSPITAL NOW! YOU'RE FREE!
THAT'S NOT THE ISSUE.
THEN WHAT IS?
THE THING IS...
IF I START MAKING MUSIC, I WON'T BE ABLE TO STOP.
I'LL WANNA WRITE MORE.
I'LL WANT TO SING.
AND MOST OF ALL...
...I'LL WANT TO SEE ALICE EVEN MORE!

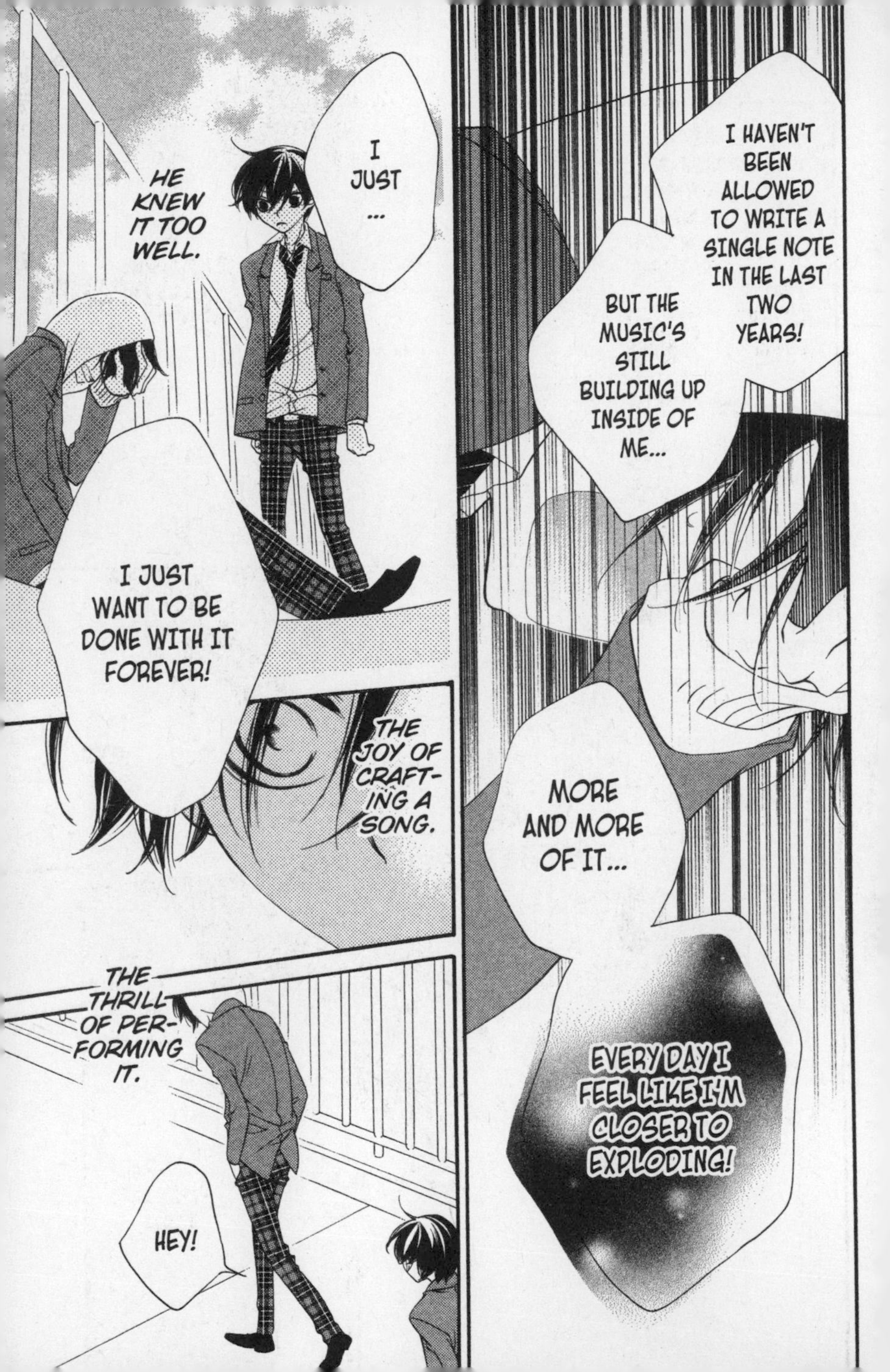
I HAVEN'T BEEN ALLOWED TO WRITE A SINGLE NOTE IN THE LAST TWO YEARS!
BUT THE MUSIC'S STILL BUILDING UP INSIDE OF ME...
MORE AND MORE OF IT...
EVERY DAY I FEEL LIKE I'M CLOSER TO EXPLODING!
I JUST ...
HE KNEW IT TOO WELL.
I JUST WANT TO BE DONE WITH IT FOREVER!
THE JOY OF CRAFT-ING A SONG.
THE THRILL OF PER-FORMING IT.
HEY!

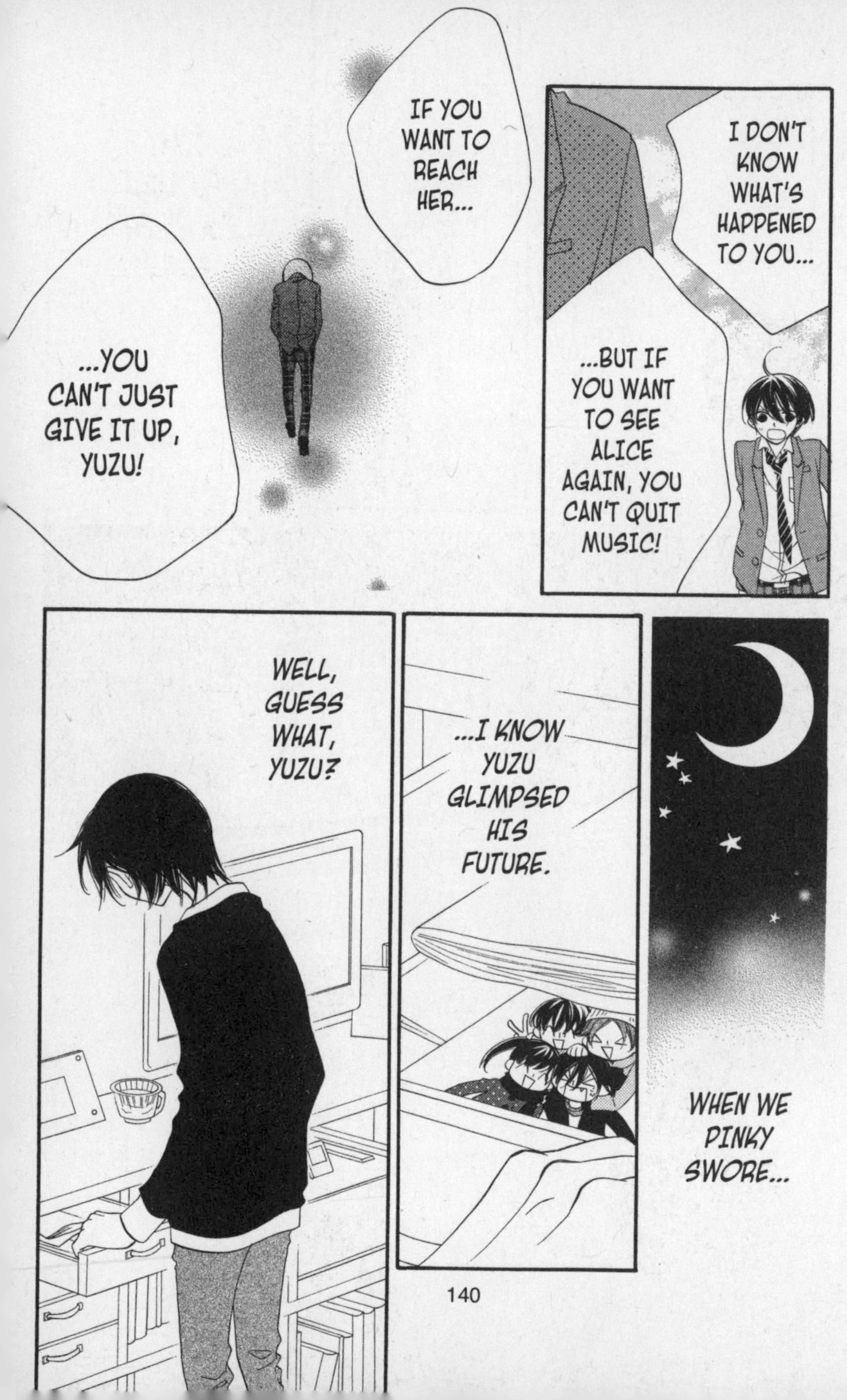
I DON'T KNOW WHAT'S HAPPENED TO YOU...
...BUT IF YOU WANT TO SEE ALICE AGAIN, YOU CAN'T QUIT MUSIC!
IF YOU WANT TO REACH HER...
...YOU CAN'T JUST GIVE IT UP, YUZU!
WHEN WE PINKY SWORE...
...I KNOW YUZU GLIMPSED HIS FUTURE.
WELL, GUESS WHAT, YUZU?

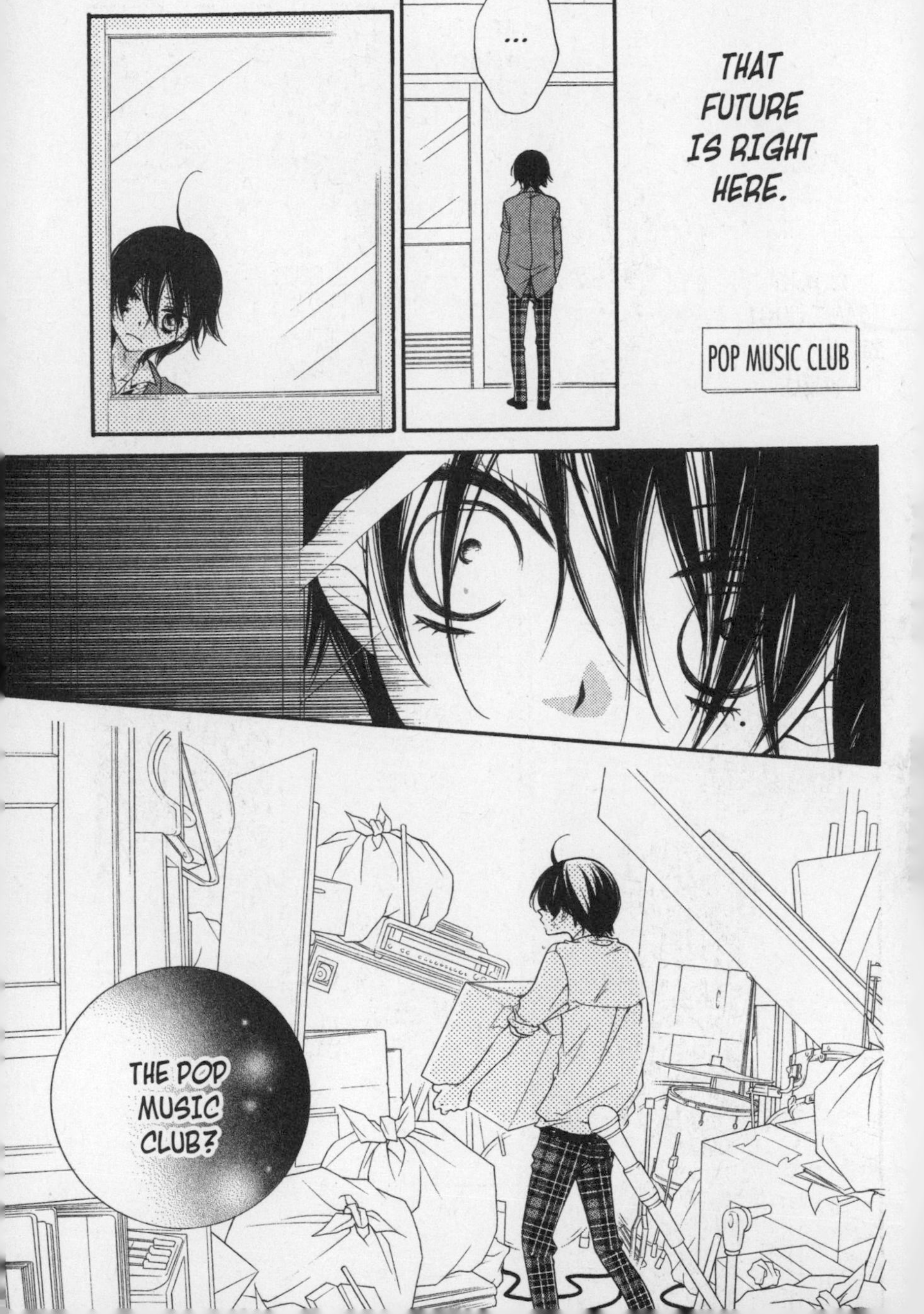
THAT FUTURE IS RIGHT HERE.
POP MUSIC CLUB
...
THE POP MUSIC CLUB?

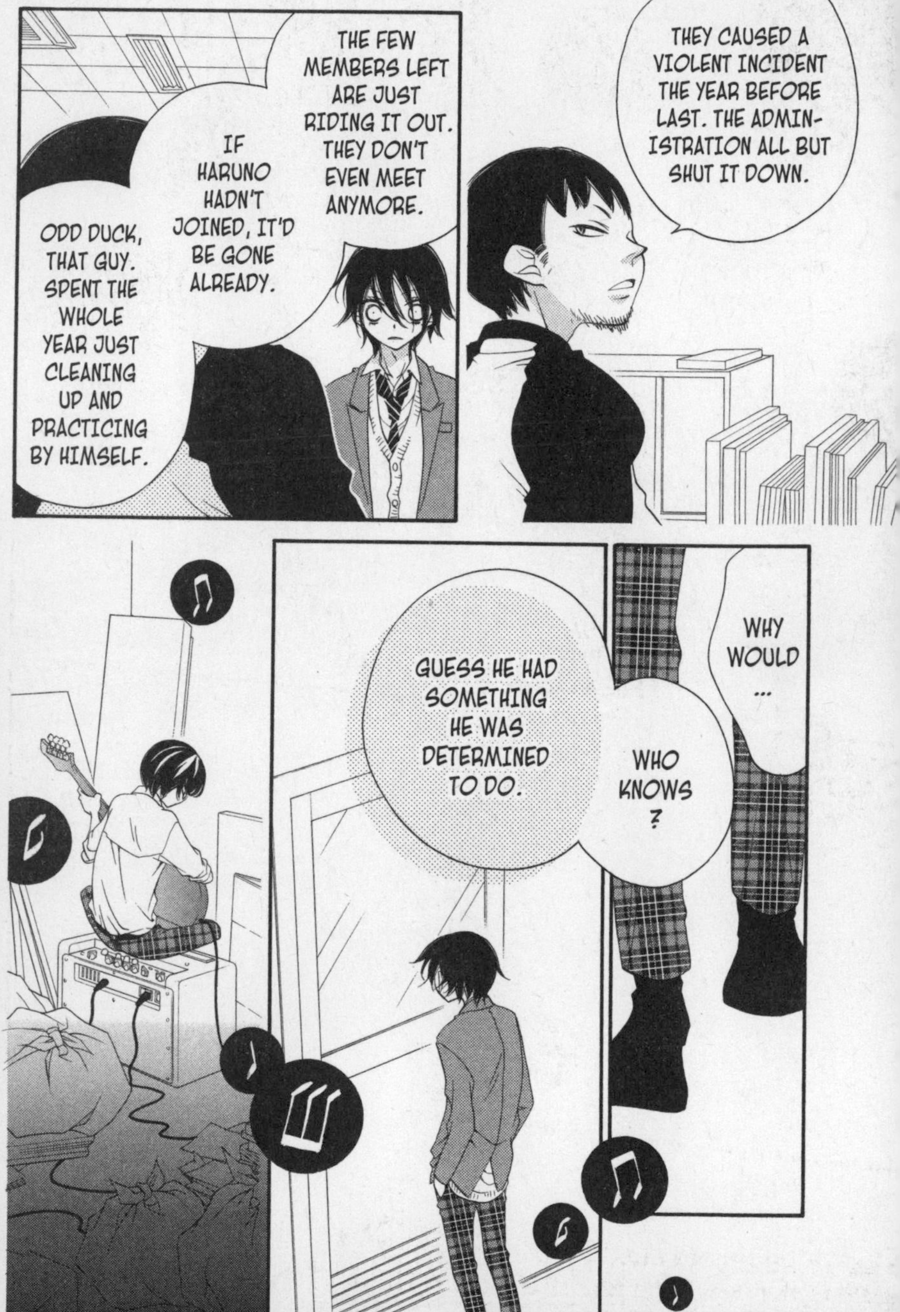
THEY CAUSED A VIOLENT INCIDENT THE YEAR BEFORE LAST. THE ADMIN-ISTRATION ALL BUT SHUT IT DOWN.
THE FEW MEMBERS LEFT ARE JUST RIDING IT OUT. THEY DON'T EVEN MEET ANYMORE.
IF HARUNO HADN'T JOINED, IT'D BE GONE ALREADY.
ODD DUCK, THAT GUY. SPENT THE WHOLE YEAR JUST CLEANING UP AND PRACTICING BY HIMSELF.
WHY WOULD ...
WHO KNOWS?
GUESS HE HAD SOMETHING HE WAS DETERMINED TO DO.

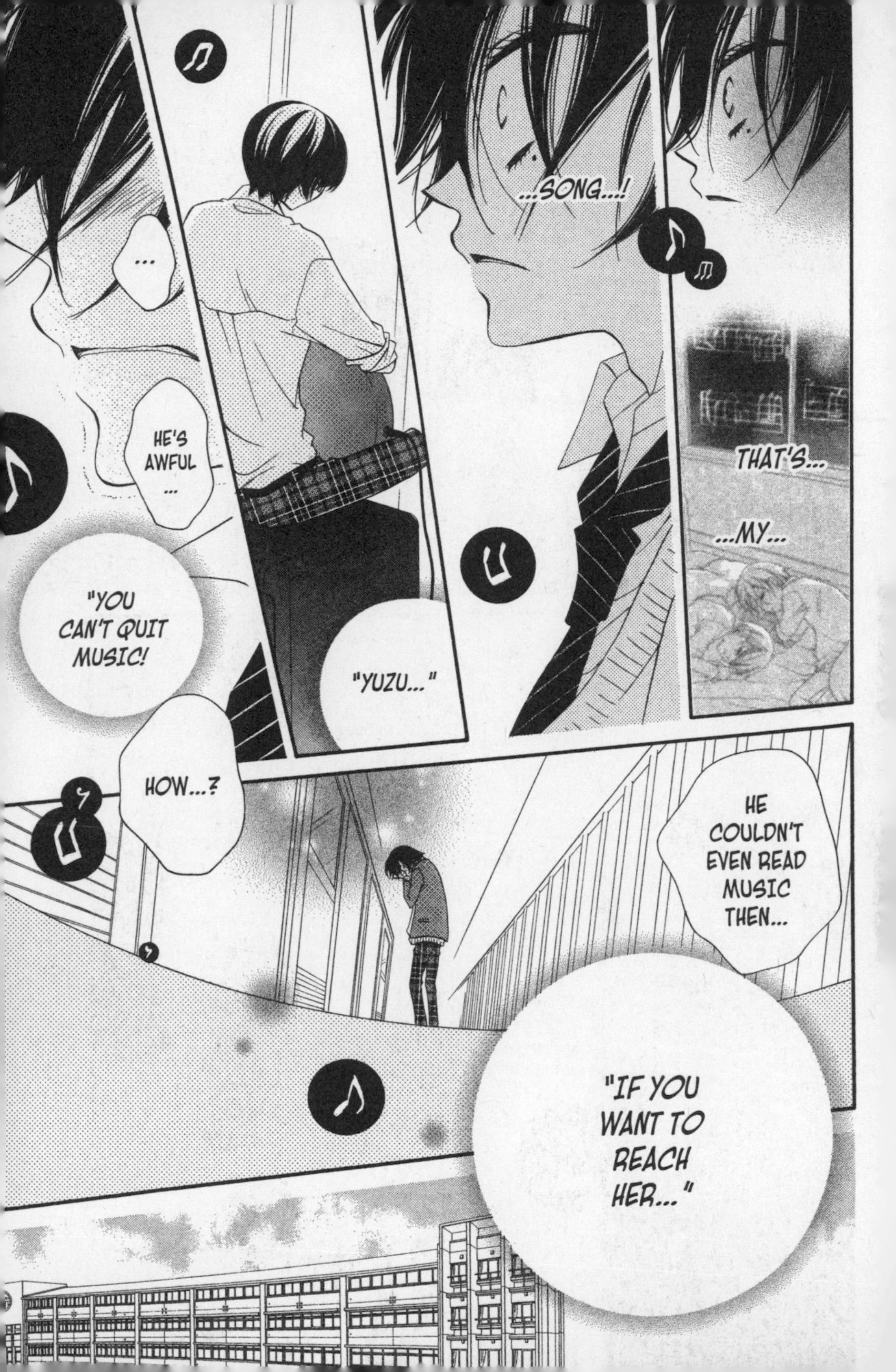
THAT'S...
...MY...
...SONG...!
"YUZU..."
...
HE'S AWFUL ...
"YOU CAN'T QUIT MUSIC!
HOW...?
HE COULDN'T EVEN READ MUSIC THEN...
"IF YOU WANT TO REACH HER..."

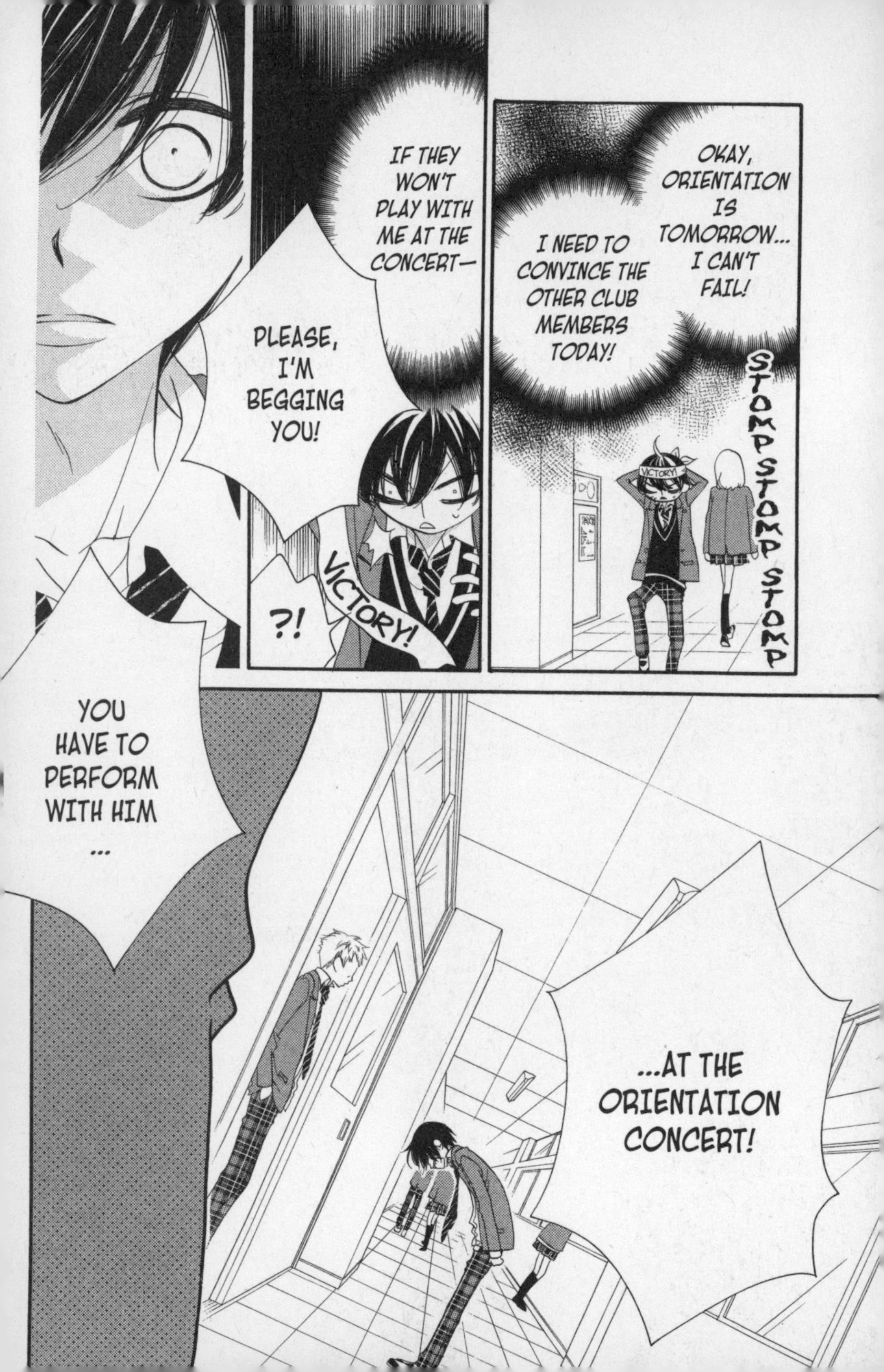
OKAY, ORIENTATION IS TOMORROW... I CAN'T FAIL!
I NEED TO CONVINCE THE OTHER CLUB MEMBERS TODAY!
VICTORY!
STOMP STOMP STOMP STOMP
IF THEY WON'T PLAY WITH ME AT THE CONCERT—
VICTORY!
?!
PLEASE, I'M BEGGING YOU!
YOU HAVE TO PERFORM WITH HIM ...
...AT THE ORIENTATION CONCERT!

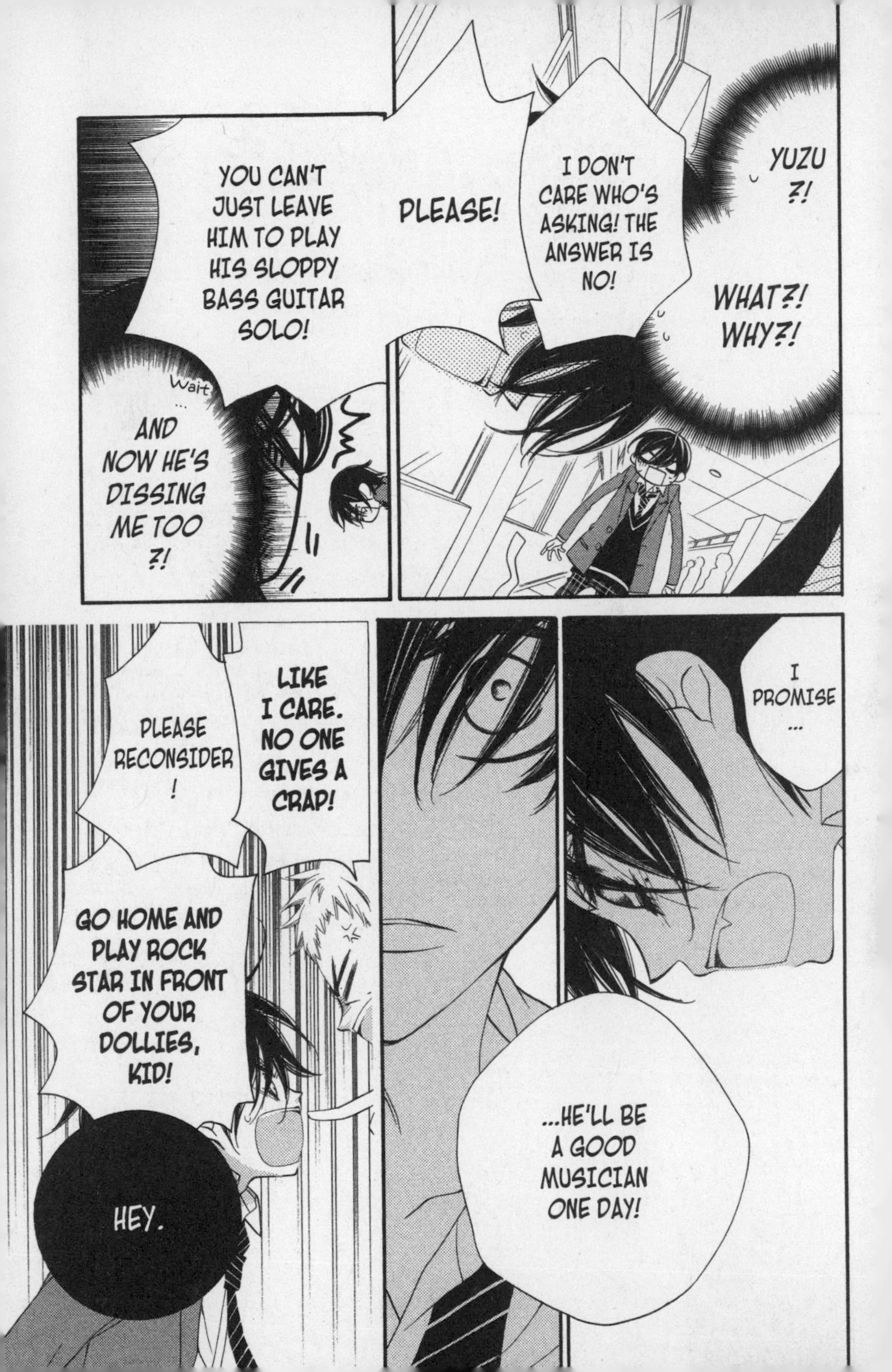
YUZU ?!
I DON'T CARE WHO'S ASKING! THE ANSWER IS NO!
PLEASE!
WHAT?! WHY?!
YOU CAN'T JUST LEAVE HIM TO PLAY HIS SLOPPY BASS GUITAR SOLO!
Wait...
AND NOW HE'S DISSING ME TOO ?!
I PROMISE ...
...HE'LL BE A GOOD MUSICIAN ONE DAY!
LIKE I CARE. NO ONE GIVES A CRAP!
PLEASE RECONSIDER !
GO HOME AND PLAY ROCK STAR IN FRONT OF YOUR DOLLIES, KID!
HEY.

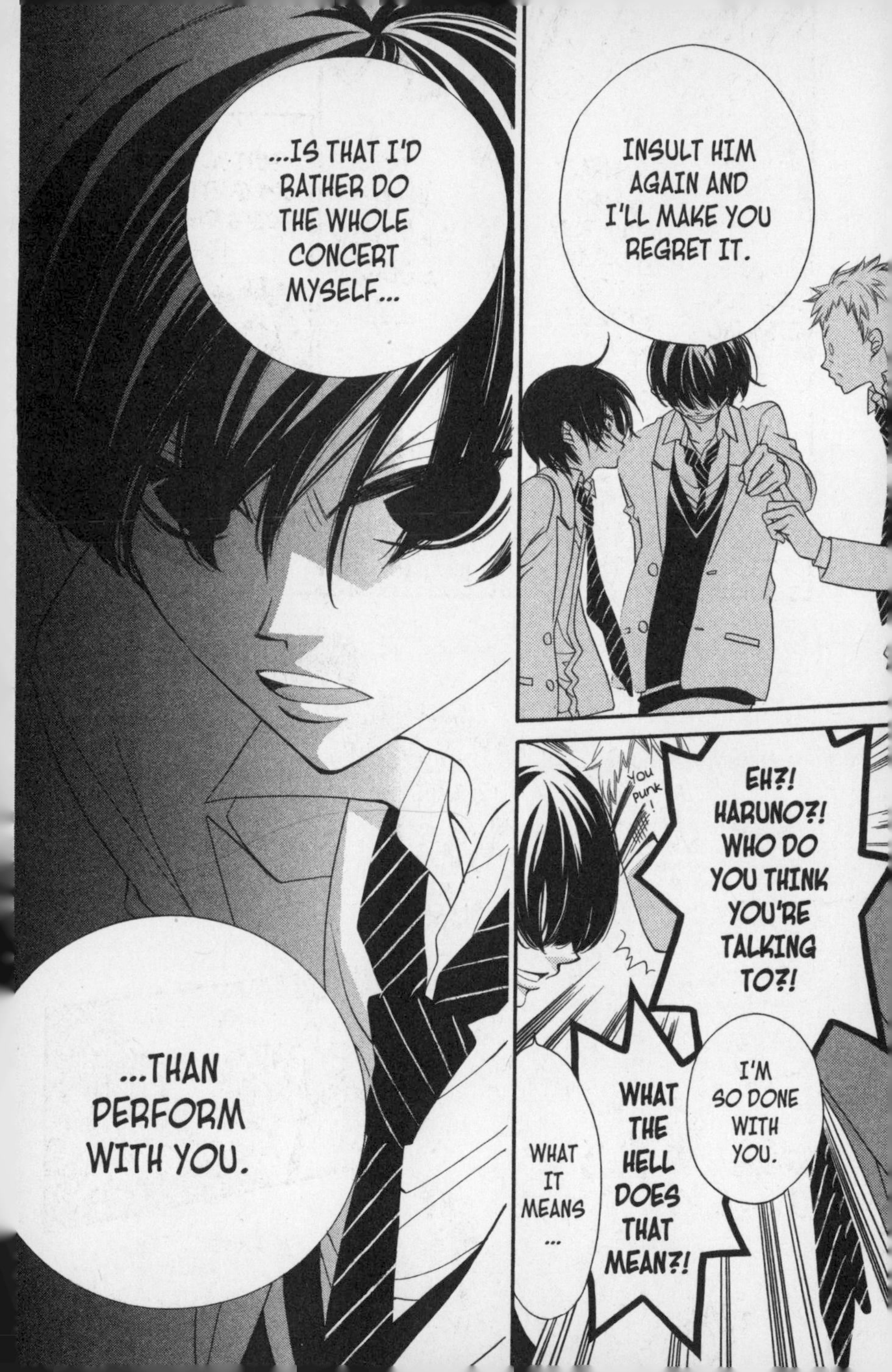
INSULT HIM AGAIN AND I'LL MAKE YOU REGRET IT.
EH?! HARUNO?! WHO DO YOU THINK YOU'RE TALKING TO?!
You punk!
I'M SO DONE WITH YOU.
WHAT THE HELL DOES THAT MEAN?!
WHAT IT MEANS...
...IS THAT I'D RATHER DO THE WHOLE CONCERT MYSELF...
...THAN PERFORM WITH YOU.

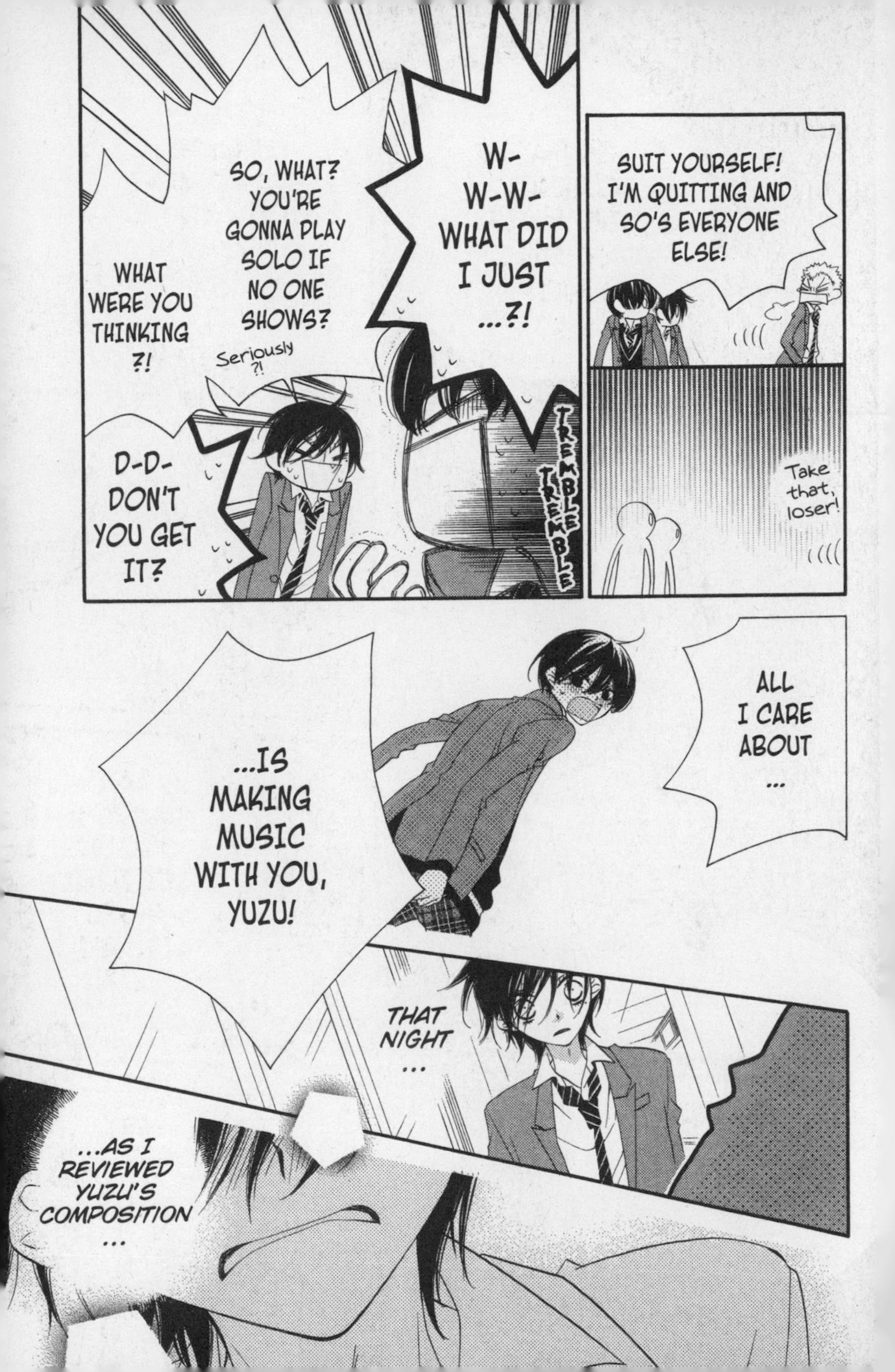
SUIT YOURSELF! I'M QUITTING AND SO'S EVERYONE ELSE!
Take that, loser!
W-W-W-WHAT DID I JUST ...?!
SO, WHAT? YOU'RE GONNA PLAY SOLO IF NO ONE SHOWS?
WHAT WERE YOU THINKING ?!
Seriously ?!
TREMBLE TREMBLE
D-D-DON'T YOU GET IT?
ALL I CARE ABOUT ...
...IS MAKING MUSIC WITH YOU, YUZU!
THAT NIGHT ...
...AS I REVIEWED YUZU'S COMPOSITION ...

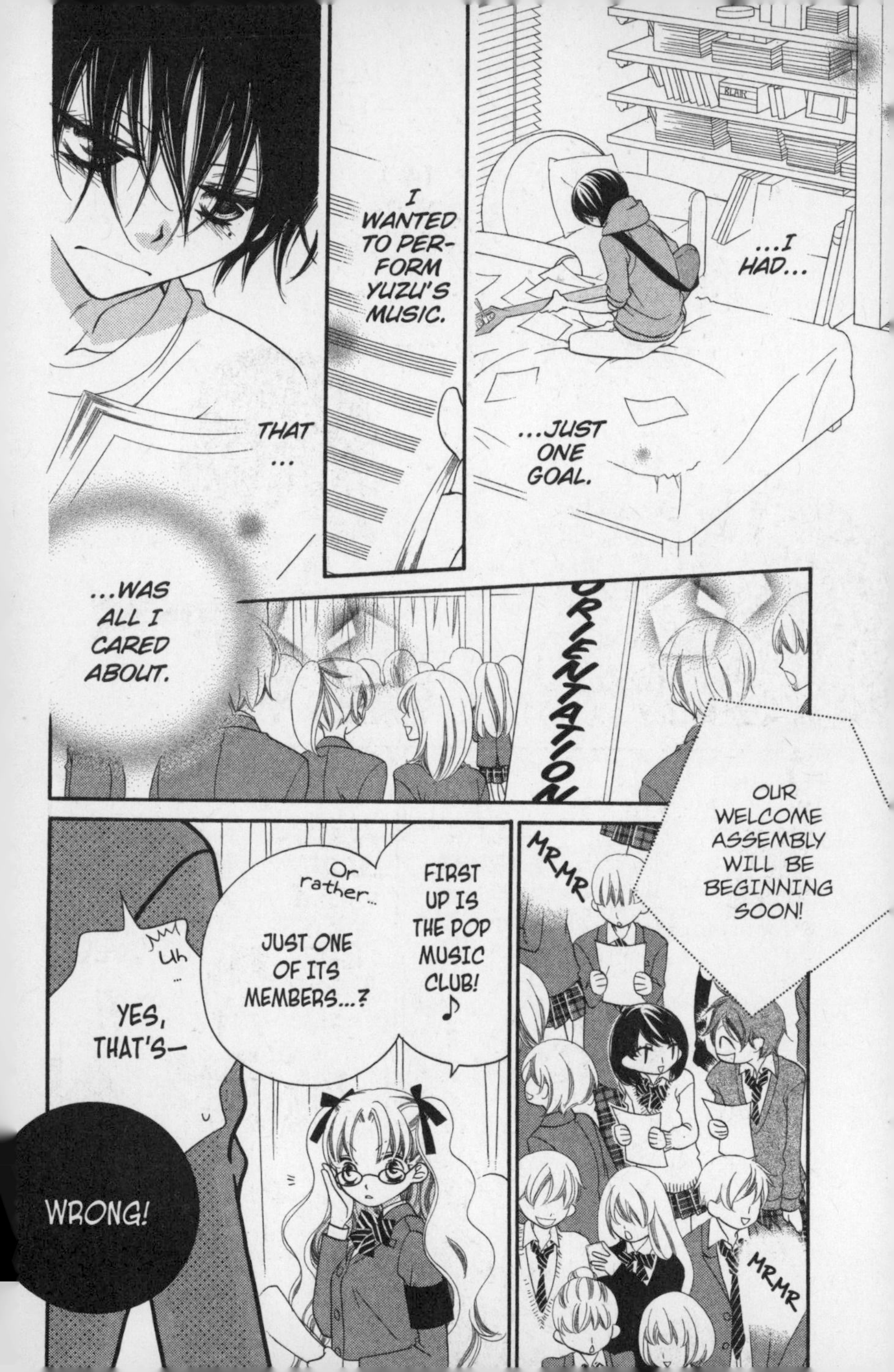
...I HAD...
...JUST ONE GOAL.
I WANTED TO PERFORM YUZU'S MUSIC.
THAT...
...WAS ALL I CARED ABOUT.
ORIENTATION
OUR WELCOME ASSEMBLY WILL BE BEGINNING SOON!
MRMR
MRMR
FIRST UP IS THE POP MUSIC CLUB! ♪
Or rather... JUST ONE OF ITS MEMBERS...?
Uh...
YES, THAT'S—
WRONG!

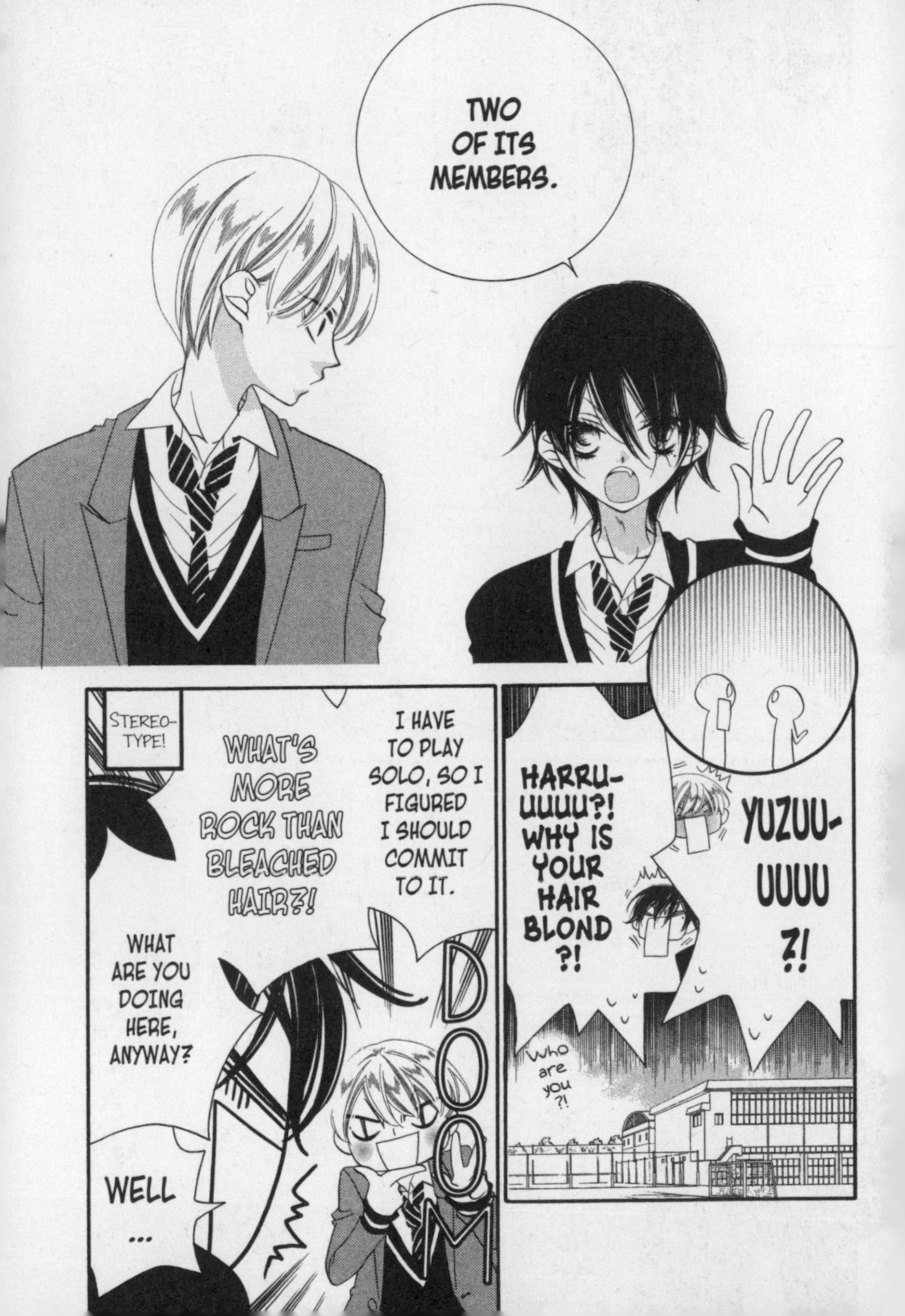
TWO OF ITS MEMBERS.
YUZUU-UUUU?!
HARRU-UUUU?! WHY IS YOUR HAIR BLOND?!
Who are you?!
I HAVE TO PLAY SOLO, SO I FIGURED I SHOULD COMMIT TO IT.
WHAT'S MORE ROCK THAN BLEACHED HAIR?!
STEREO-TYPE!
WHAT ARE YOU DOING HERE, ANYWAY?
DOOM
WELL ...

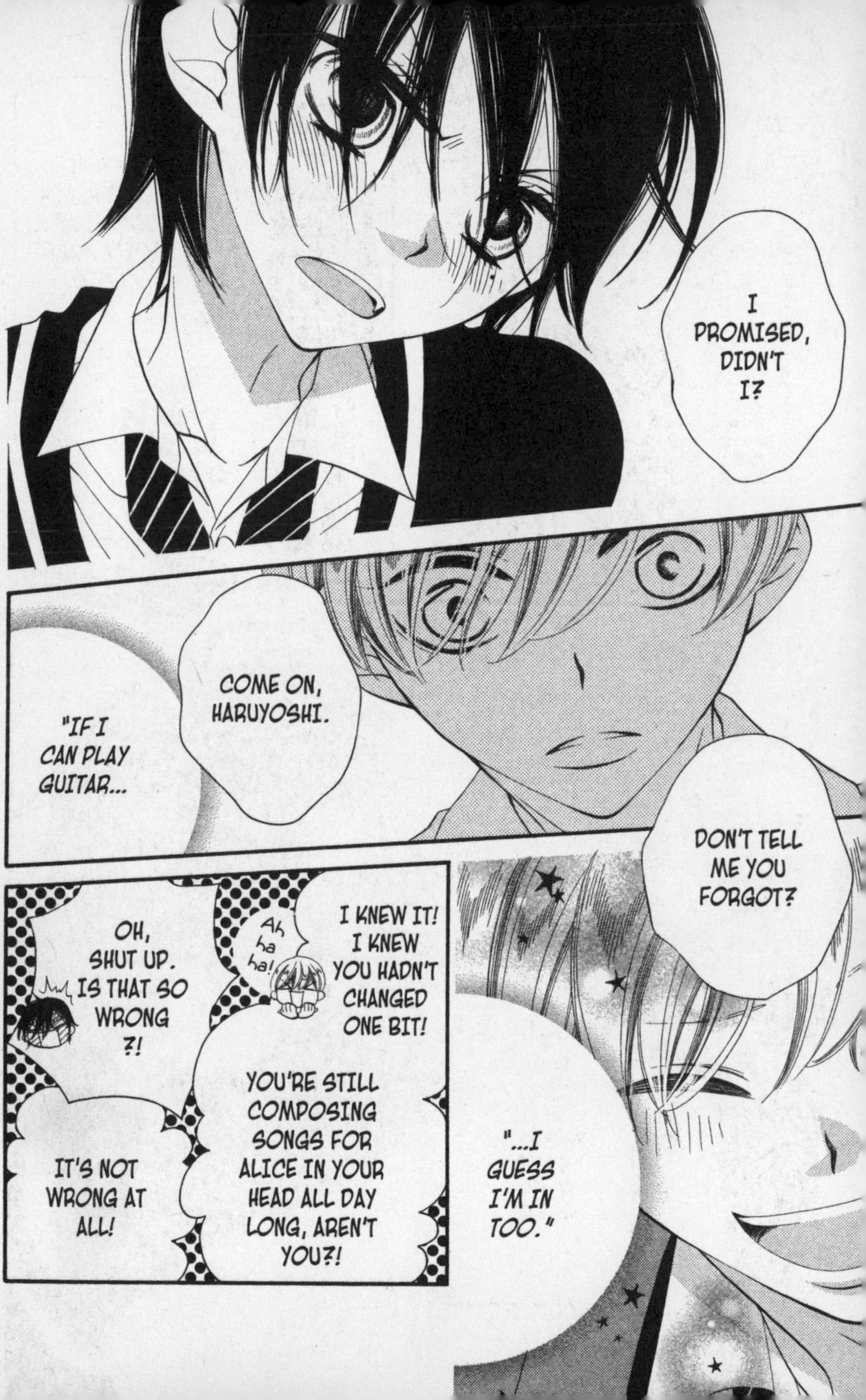
I PROMISED, DIDN'T I?
COME ON, HARUYOSHI.
"IF I CAN PLAY GUITAR...
DON'T TELL ME YOU FORGOT?
"...I GUESS I'M IN TOO."
I KNEW IT! I KNEW YOU HADN'T CHANGED ONE BIT!
Ah ha ha!
YOU'RE STILL COMPOSING SONGS FOR ALICE IN YOUR HEAD ALL DAY LONG, AREN'T YOU?!
OH, SHUT UP. IS THAT SO WRONG?!
IT'S NOT WRONG AT ALL!

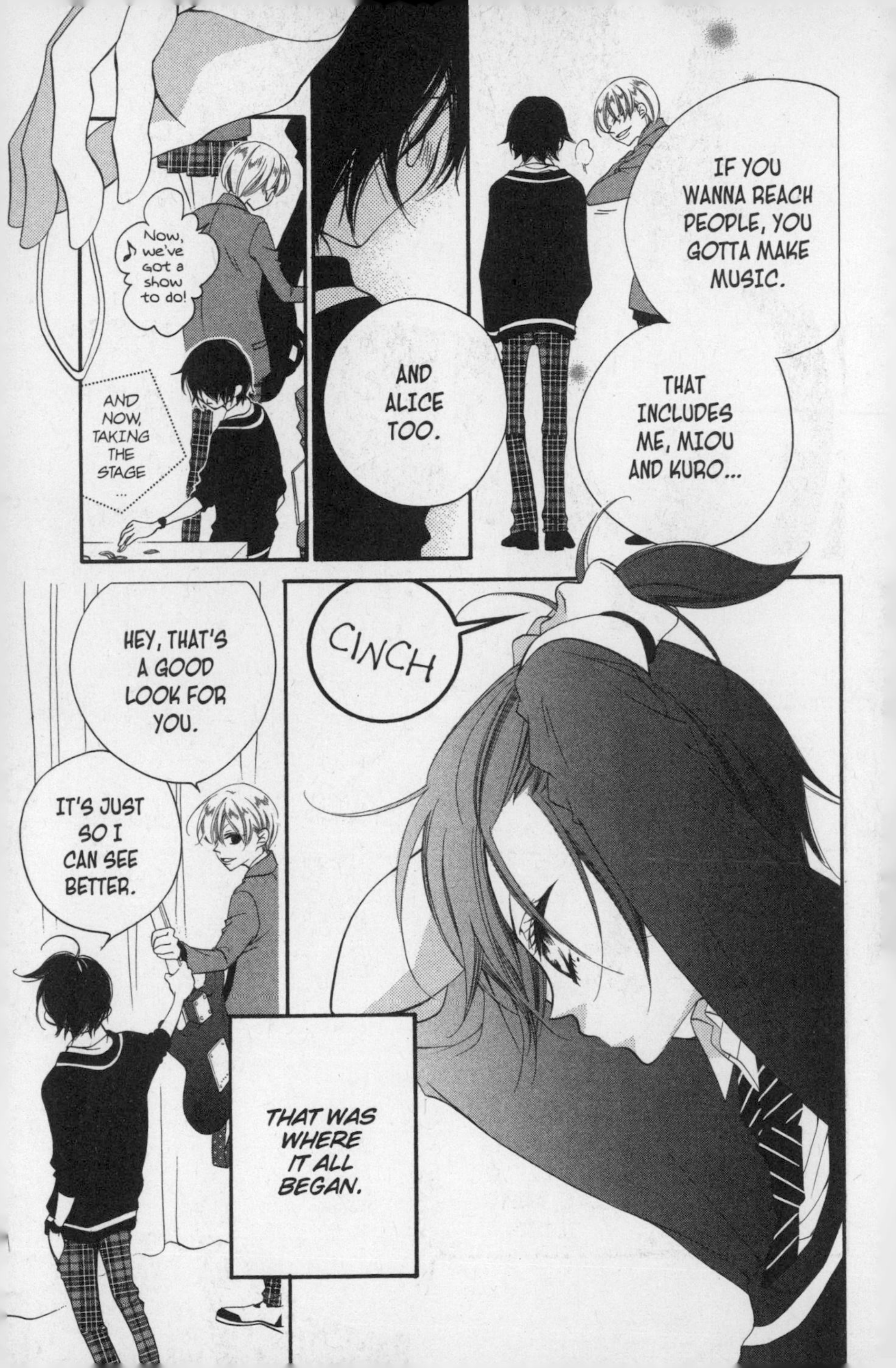
IF YOU WANNA REACH PEOPLE, YOU GOTTA MAKE MUSIC.
THAT INCLUDES ME, MIOU AND KURO...
AND ALICE TOO.
Now, we've got a show to do!
AND NOW, TAKING THE STAGE ...
CINCH
HEY, THAT'S A GOOD LOOK FOR YOU.
IT'S JUST SO I CAN SEE BETTER.
THAT WAS WHERE IT ALL BEGAN.

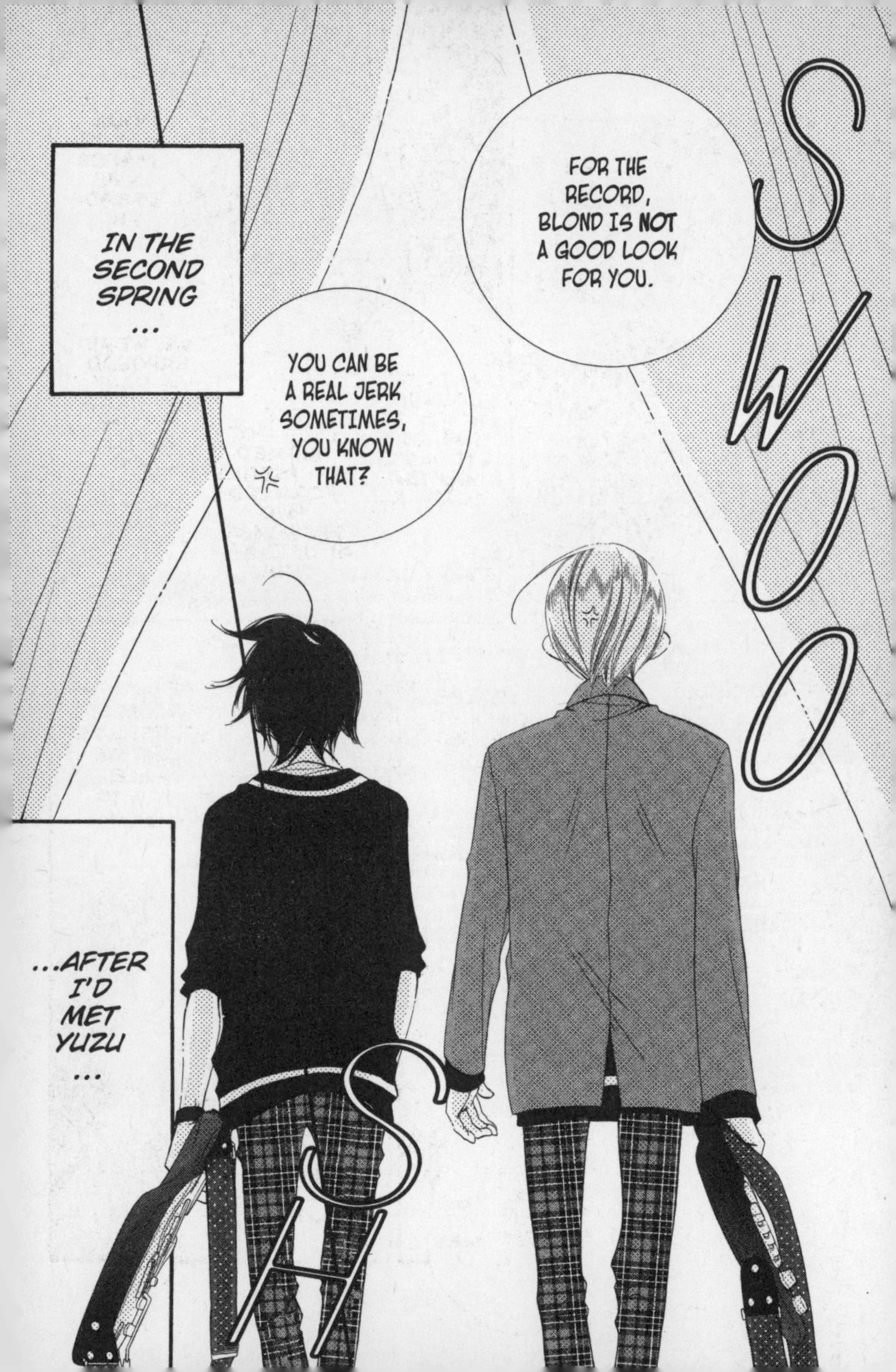
SWOOSH
FOR THE RECORD, BLOND IS NOT A GOOD LOOK FOR YOU.
YOU CAN BE A REAL JERK SOMETIMES, YOU KNOW THAT?
IN THE SECOND SPRING...
...AFTER I'D MET YUZU...

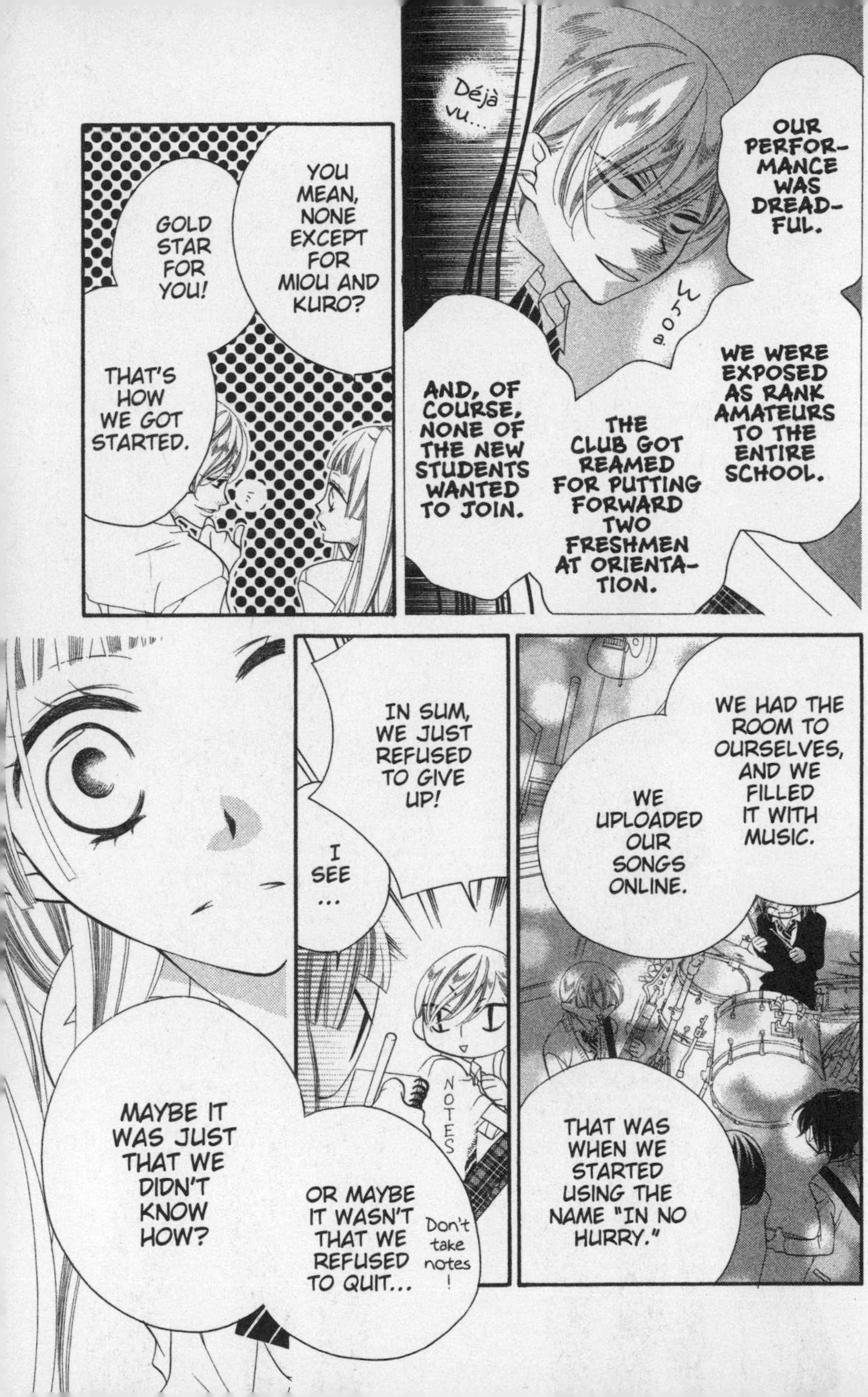
Déjà vu...
OUR PERFORMANCE WAS DREADFUL.
Whoa.
WE WERE EXPOSED AS RANK AMATEURS TO THE ENTIRE SCHOOL.
THE CLUB GOT REAMED FOR PUTTING FORWARD TWO FRESHMEN AT ORIENTATION.
AND, OF COURSE, NONE OF THE NEW STUDENTS WANTED TO JOIN.
YOU MEAN, NONE EXCEPT FOR MIOU AND KURO?
GOLD STAR FOR YOU!
THAT'S HOW WE GOT STARTED.
WE HAD THE ROOM TO OURSELVES, AND WE FILLED IT WITH MUSIC.
WE UPLOADED OUR SONGS ONLINE.
THAT WAS WHEN WE STARTED USING THE NAME "IN NO HURRY."
IN SUM, WE JUST REFUSED TO GIVE UP!
I SEE...
NOTES
Don't take notes!
OR MAYBE IT WASN'T THAT WE REFUSED TO QUIT...
MAYBE IT WAS JUST THAT WE DIDN'T KNOW HOW?

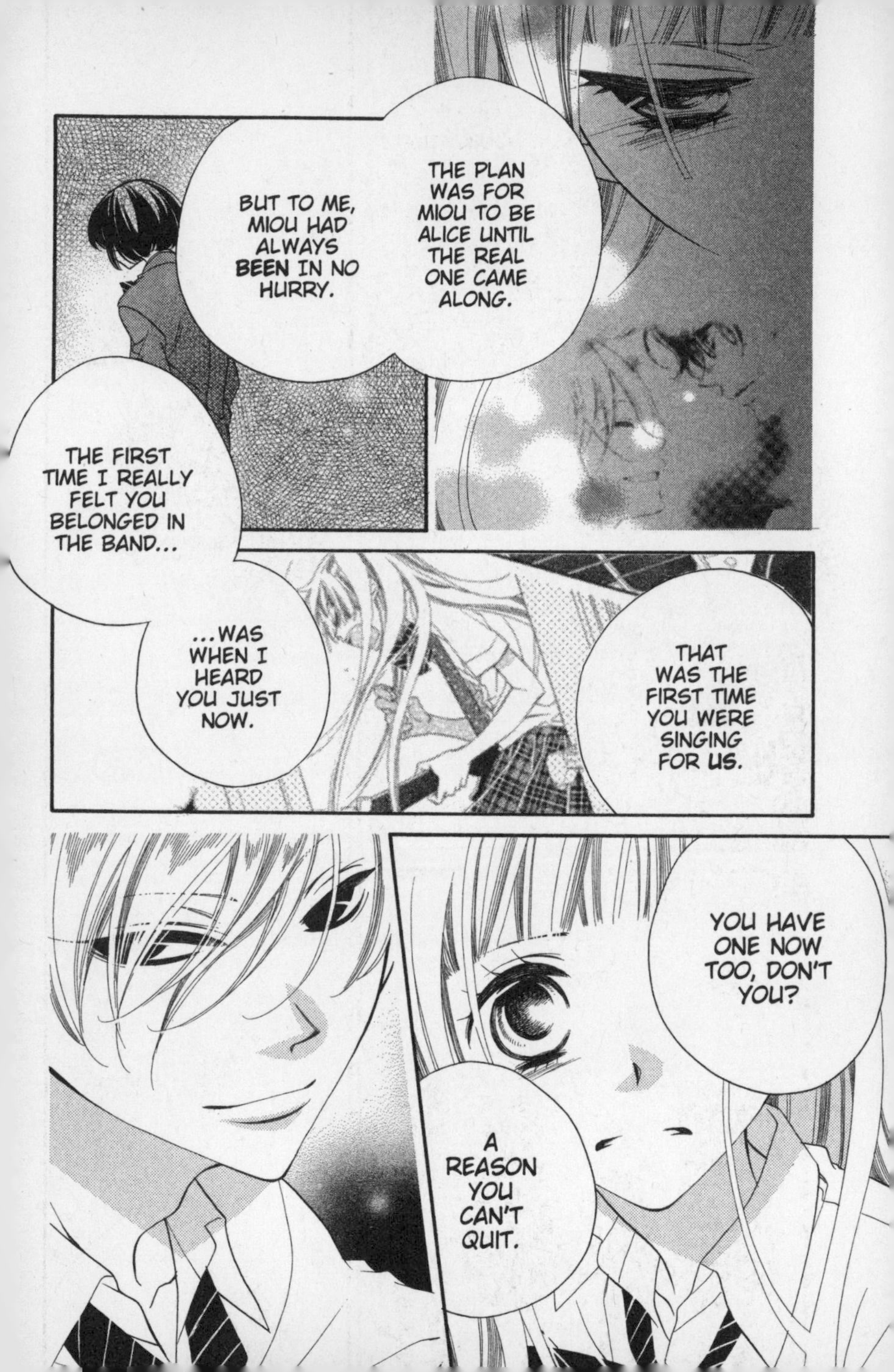
THE PLAN WAS FOR MIOU TO BE ALICE UNTIL THE REAL ONE CAME ALONG.
BUT TO ME, MIOU HAD ALWAYS BEEN IN NO HURRY.
THE FIRST TIME I REALLY FELT YOU BELONGED IN THE BAND...
...WAS WHEN I HEARD YOU JUST NOW.
THAT WAS THE FIRST TIME YOU WERE SINGING FOR US.
YOU HAVE ONE NOW TOO, DON'T YOU?
A REASON YOU CAN'T QUIT.

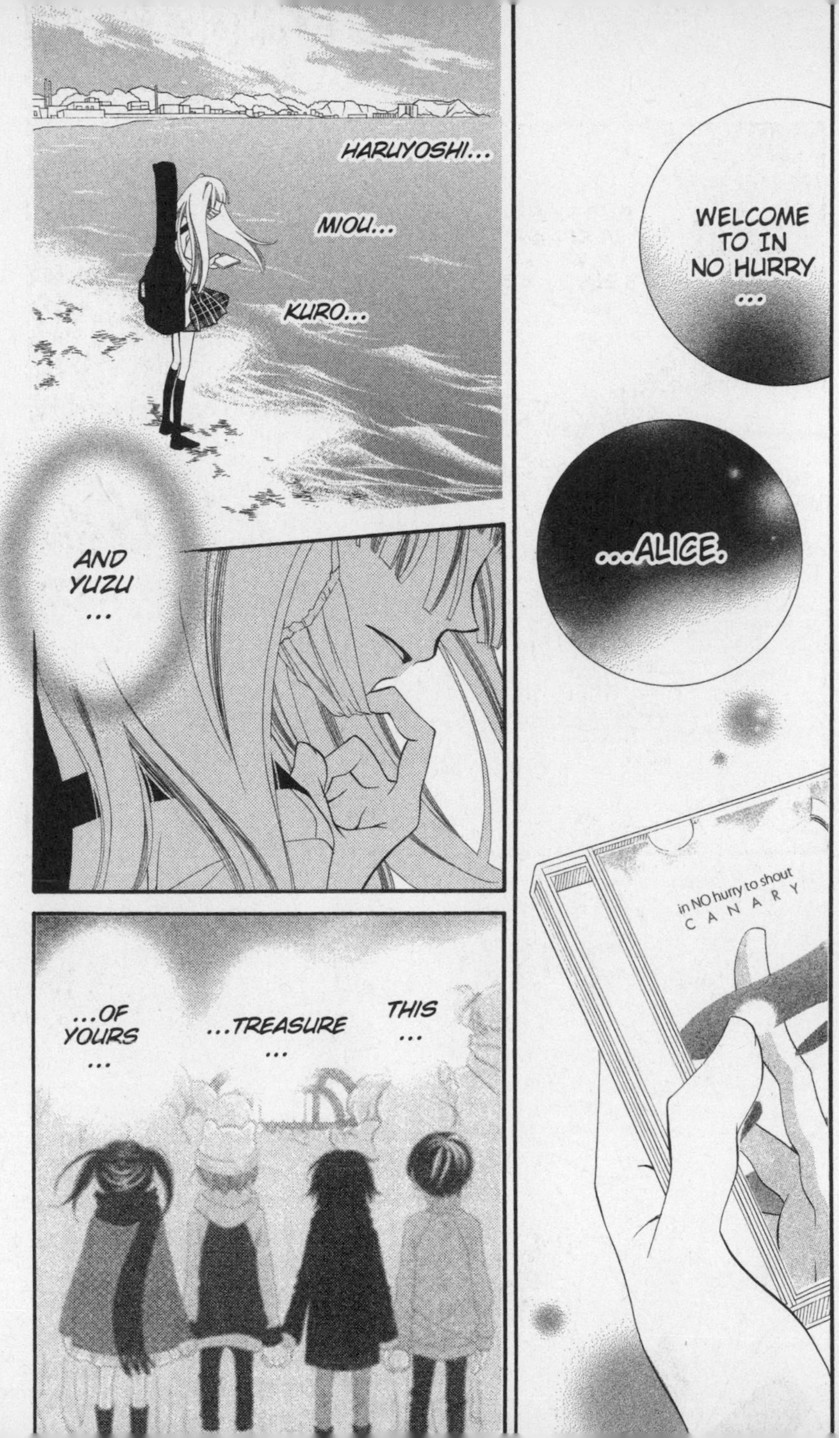
WELCOME TO IN NO HURRY ...
...ALICE.
in NO hurry to shout
CANARY
HARUYOSHI...
MIOU...
KURO...
AND YUZU ...
THIS ...
...TREASURE ...
...OF YOURS ...

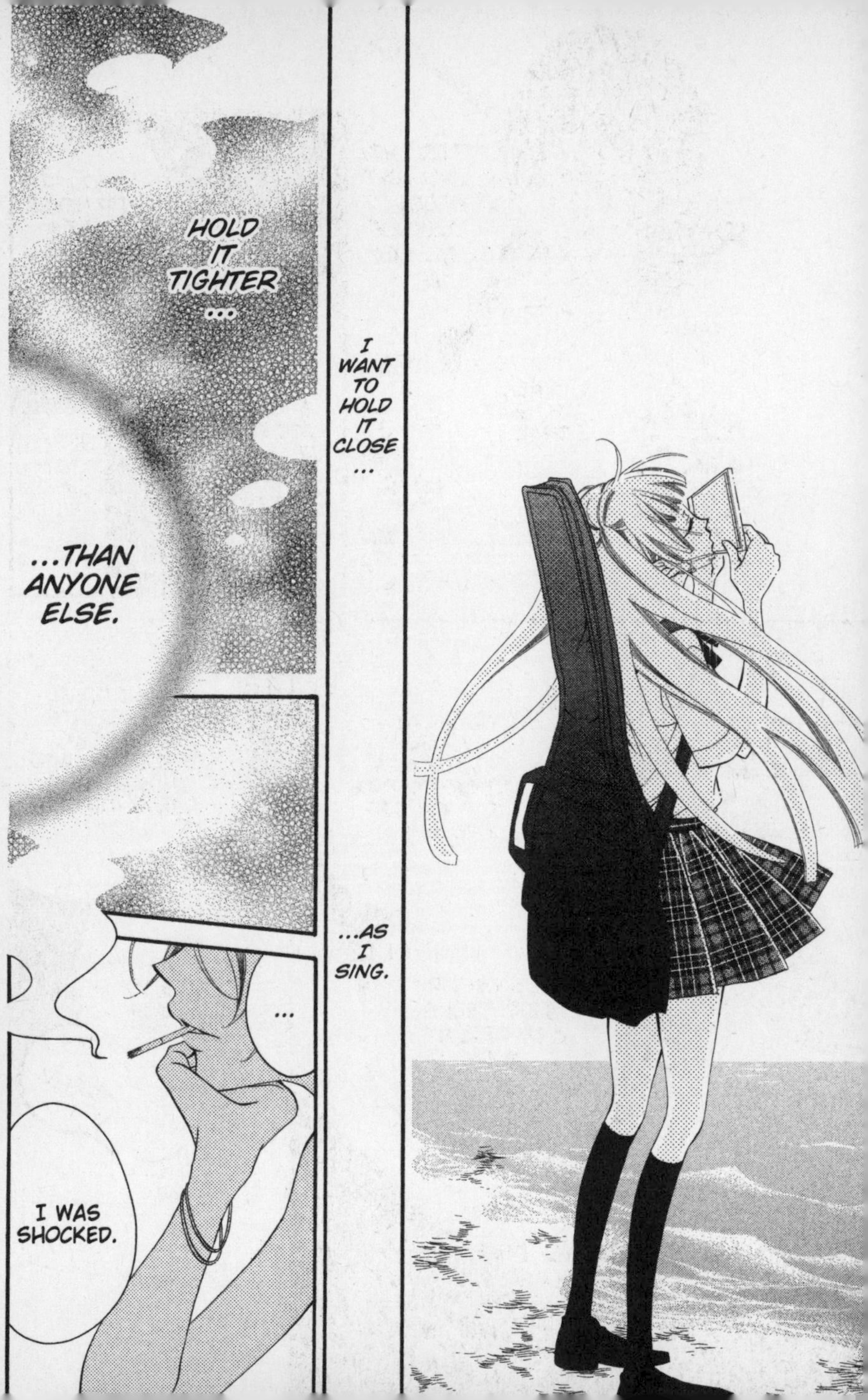
I WANT TO HOLD IT CLOSE ...
...AS I SING.
HOLD IT TIGHTER ...
...THAN ANYONE ELSE.
...
I WAS SHOCKED.

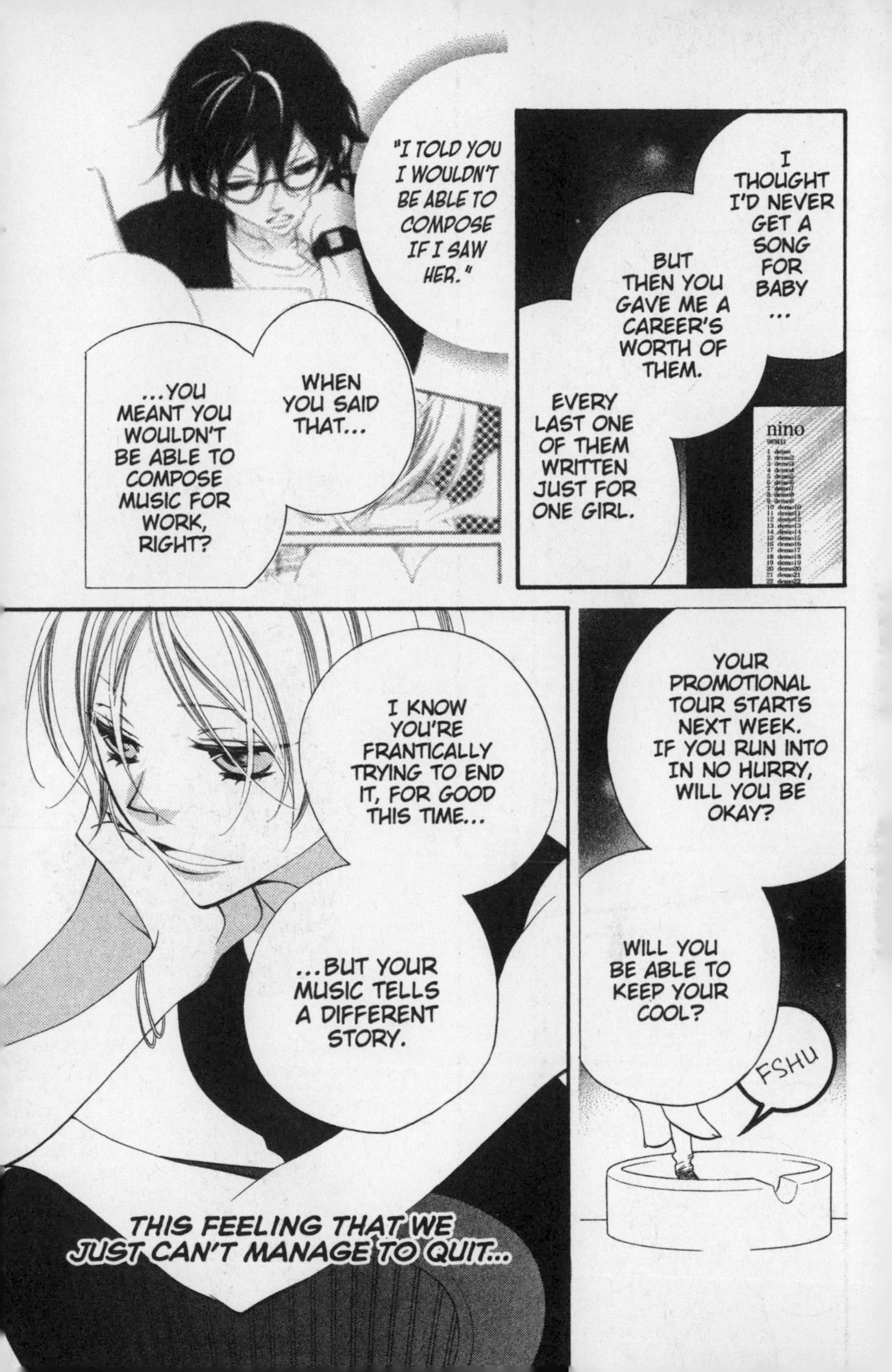
I THOUGHT I'D NEVER GET A SONG FOR BABY...
BUT THEN YOU GAVE ME A CAREER'S WORTH OF THEM.
EVERY LAST ONE OF THEM WRITTEN JUST FOR ONE GIRL.
nino
"I TOLD YOU I WOULDN'T BE ABLE TO COMPOSE IF I SAW HER."
WHEN YOU SAID THAT...
...YOU MEANT YOU WOULDN'T BE ABLE TO COMPOSE MUSIC FOR WORK, RIGHT?
YOUR PROMOTIONAL TOUR STARTS NEXT WEEK. IF YOU RUN INTO IN NO HURRY, WILL YOU BE OKAY?
WILL YOU BE ABLE TO KEEP YOUR COOL?
FSHU
I KNOW YOU'RE FRANTICALLY TRYING TO END IT, FOR GOOD THIS TIME...
...BUT YOUR MUSIC TELLS A DIFFERENT STORY.
THIS FEELING THAT WE JUST CAN'T MANAGE TO QUIT...

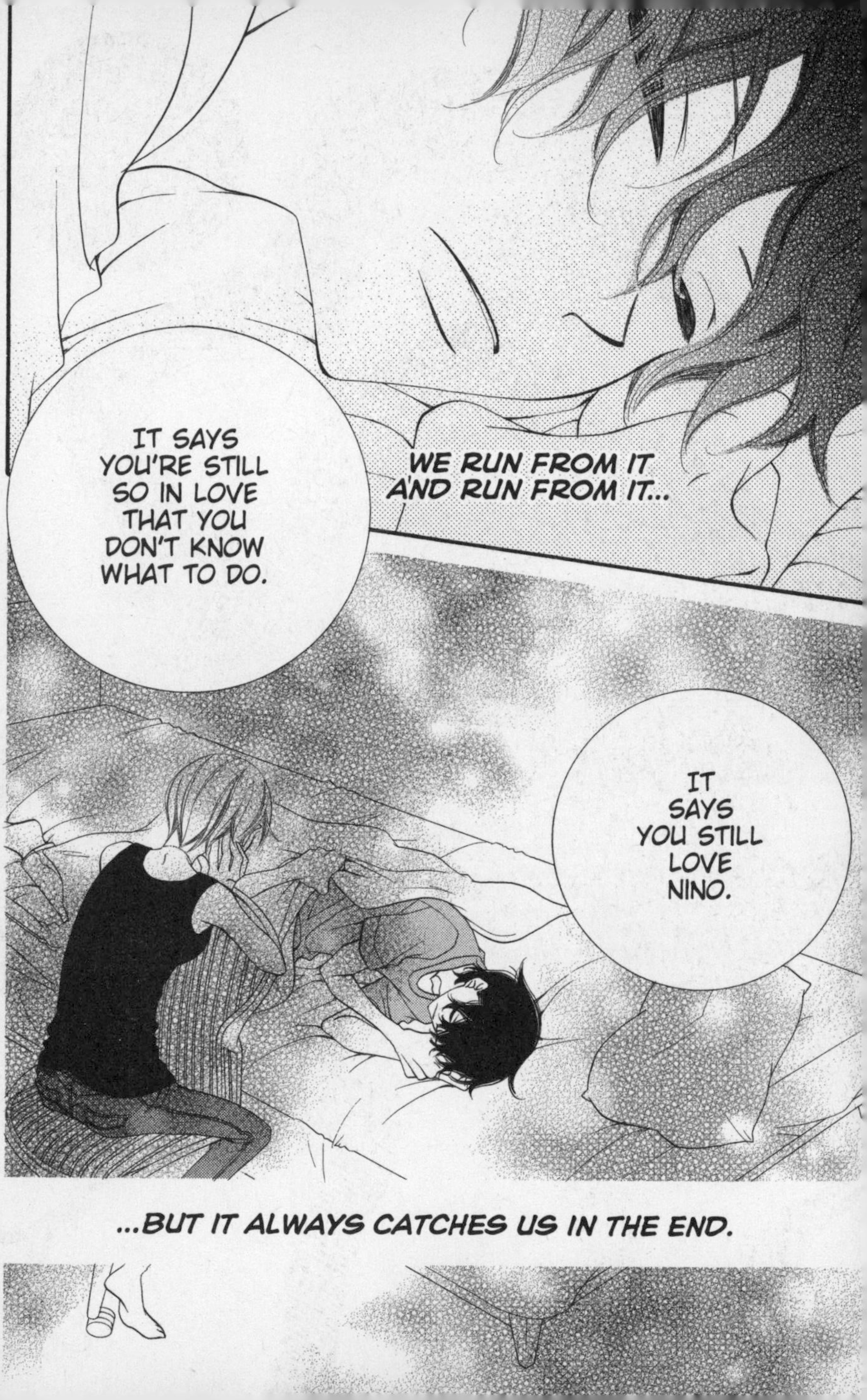
WE RUN FROM IT AND RUN FROM IT...
IT SAYS YOU'RE STILL SO IN LOVE THAT YOU DON'T KNOW WHAT TO DO.
IT SAYS YOU STILL LOVE NINO.
...BUT IT ALWAYS CATCHES US IN THE END.

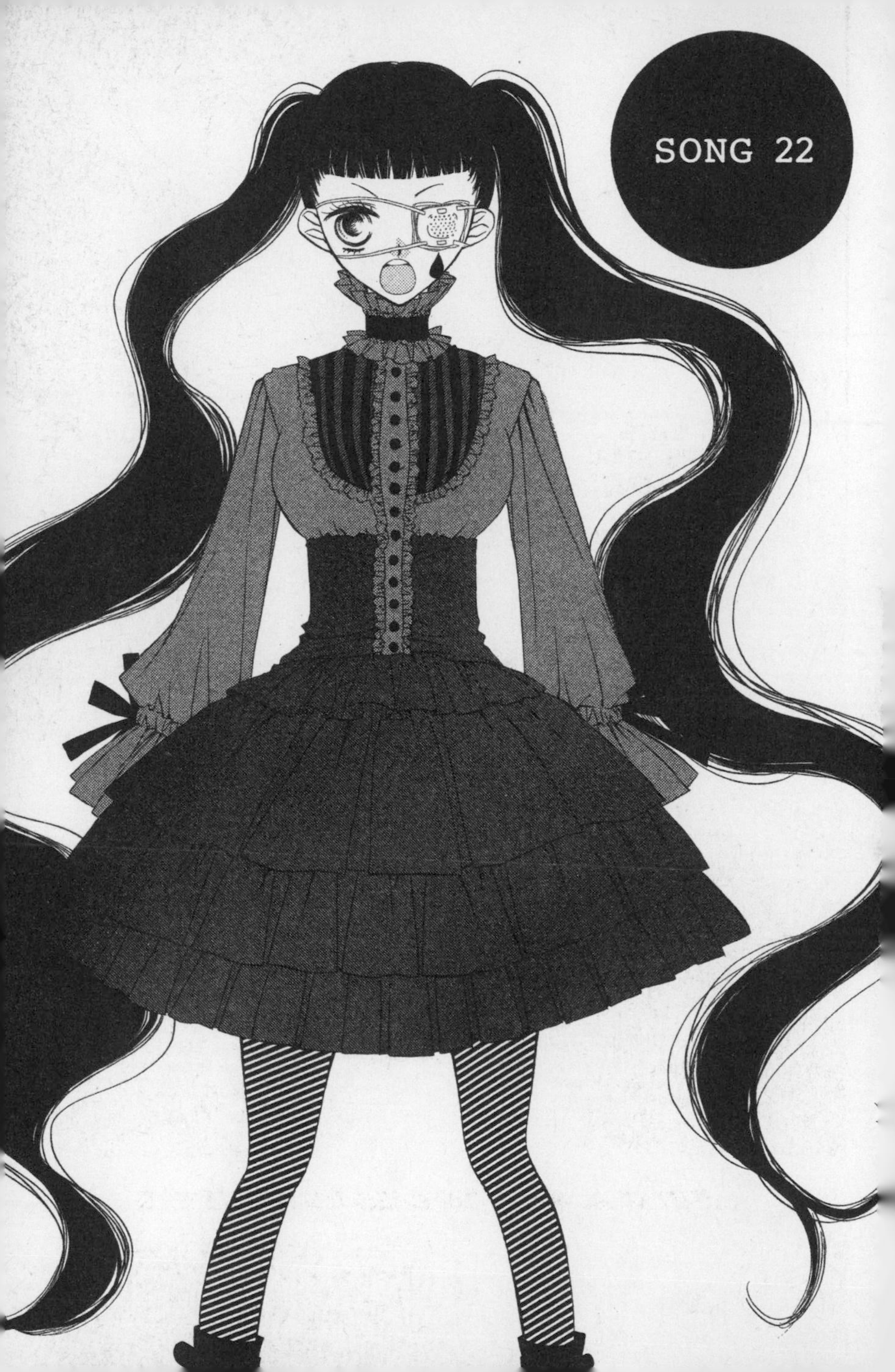
SONG 22

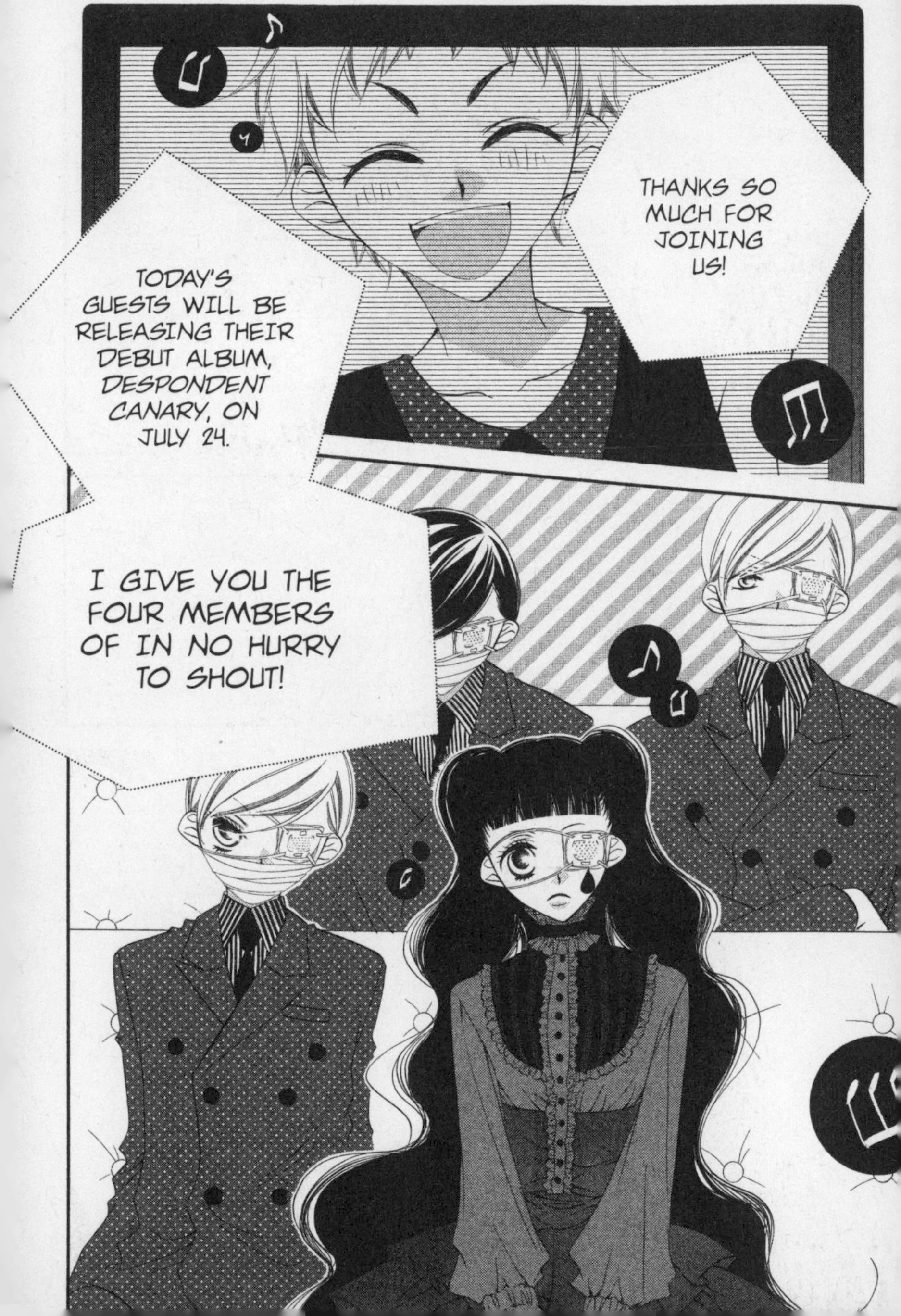
THANKS SO MUCH FOR JOINING US!
TODAY'S GUESTS WILL BE RELEASING THEIR DEBUT ALBUM, DESPONDENT CANARY, ON JULY 24.
I GIVE YOU THE FOUR MEMBERS OF IN NO HURRY TO SHOUT!

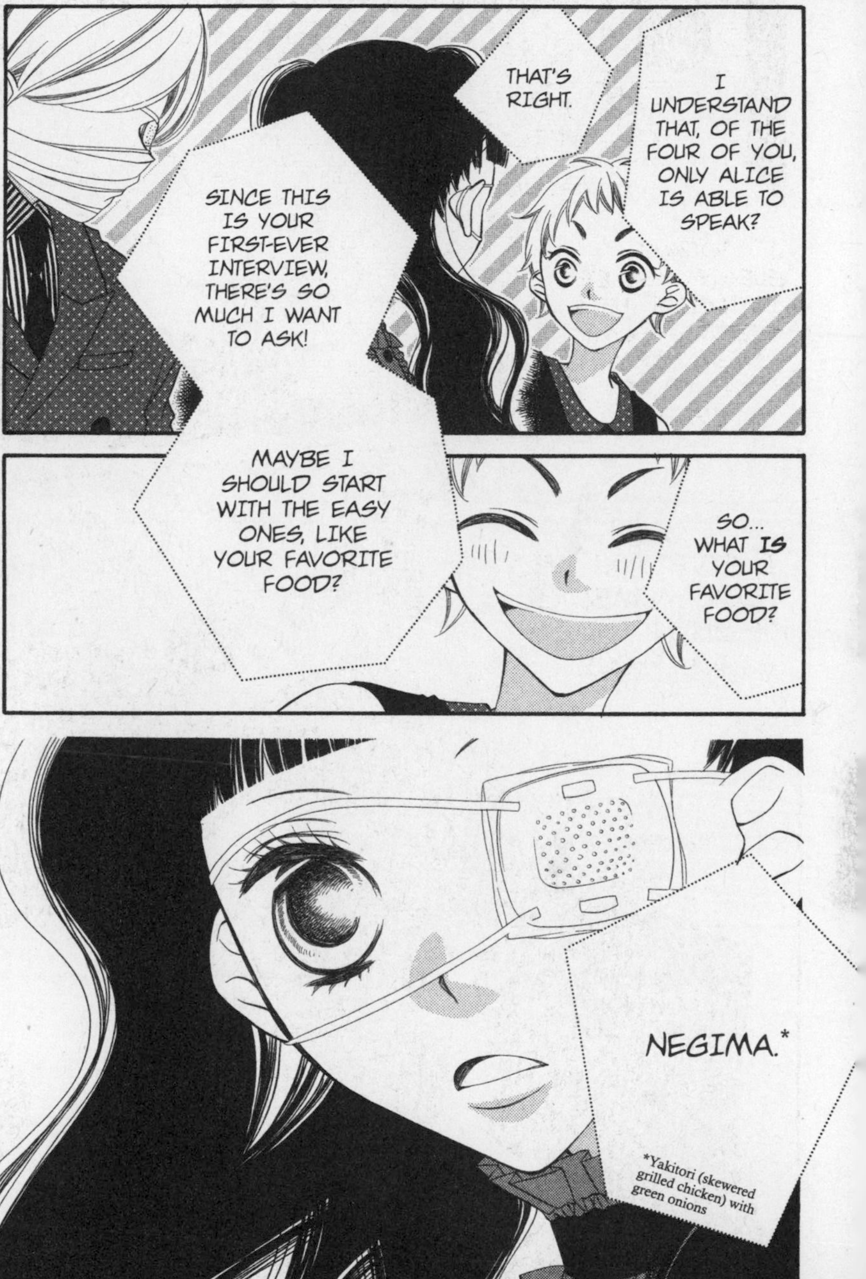
I UNDERSTAND THAT, OF THE FOUR OF YOU, ONLY ALICE IS ABLE TO SPEAK?
THAT'S RIGHT.
SINCE THIS IS YOUR FIRST-EVER INTERVIEW, THERE'S SO MUCH I WANT TO ASK!
MAYBE I SHOULD START WITH THE EASY ONES, LIKE YOUR FAVORITE FOOD?
SO... WHAT **IS** YOUR FAVORITE FOOD?
NEGIMA.*
*Yakitori (skewered grilled chicken) with green onions

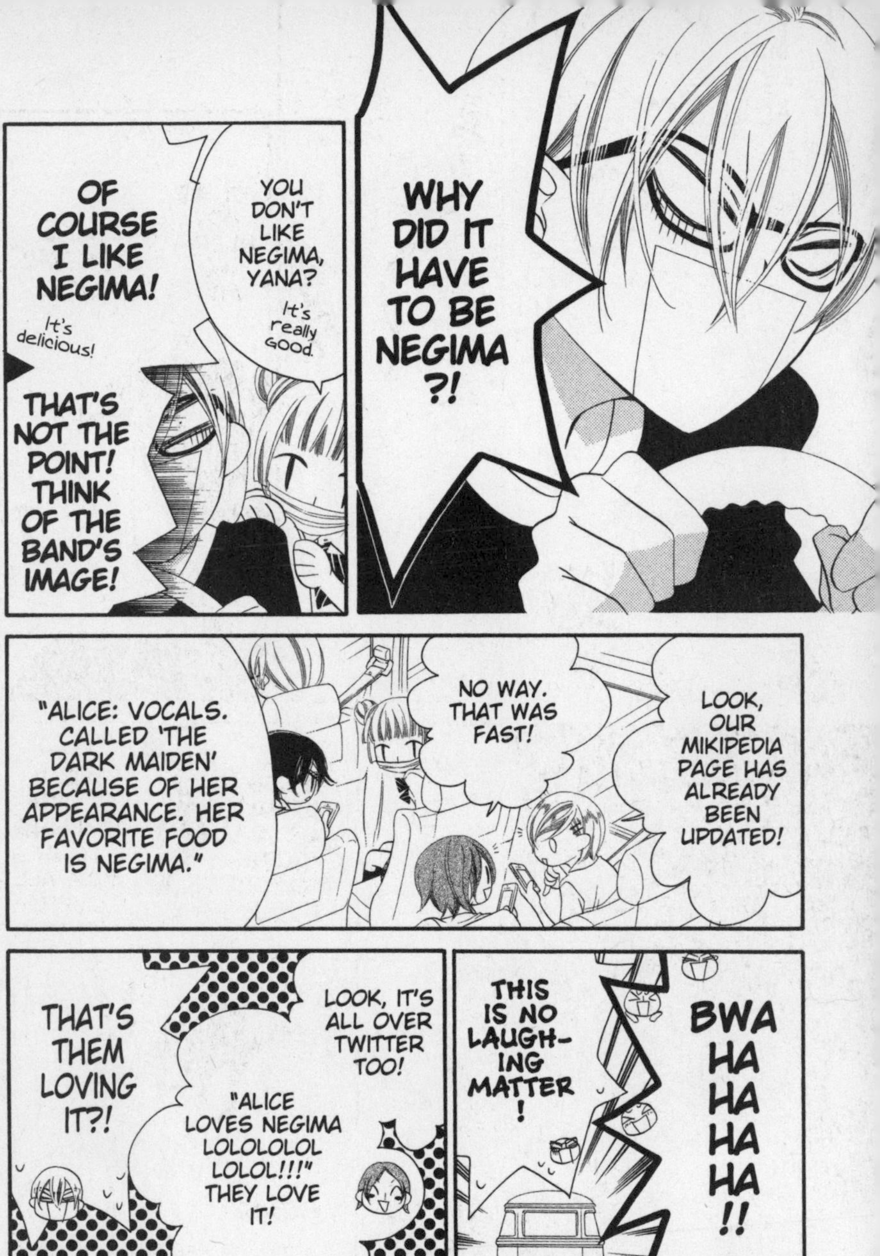
WHY DID IT HAVE TO BE NEGIMA?!
YOU DON'T LIKE NEGIMA, YANA?
It's really good.
OF COURSE I LIKE NEGIMA!
It's delicious!
THAT'S NOT THE POINT! THINK OF THE BAND'S IMAGE!
LOOK, OUR MIKIPEDIA PAGE HAS ALREADY BEEN UPDATED!
NO WAY. THAT WAS FAST!
"ALICE: VOCALS. CALLED 'THE DARK MAIDEN' BECAUSE OF HER APPEARANCE. HER FAVORITE FOOD IS NEGIMA."
BWA HA HA HA HA!!
THIS IS NO LAUGH-ING MATTER!
LOOK, IT'S ALL OVER TWITTER TOO!
"ALICE LOVES NEGIMA LOLOLOLOL LOLOL!!!" THEY LOVE IT!
THAT'S THEM LOVING IT?!

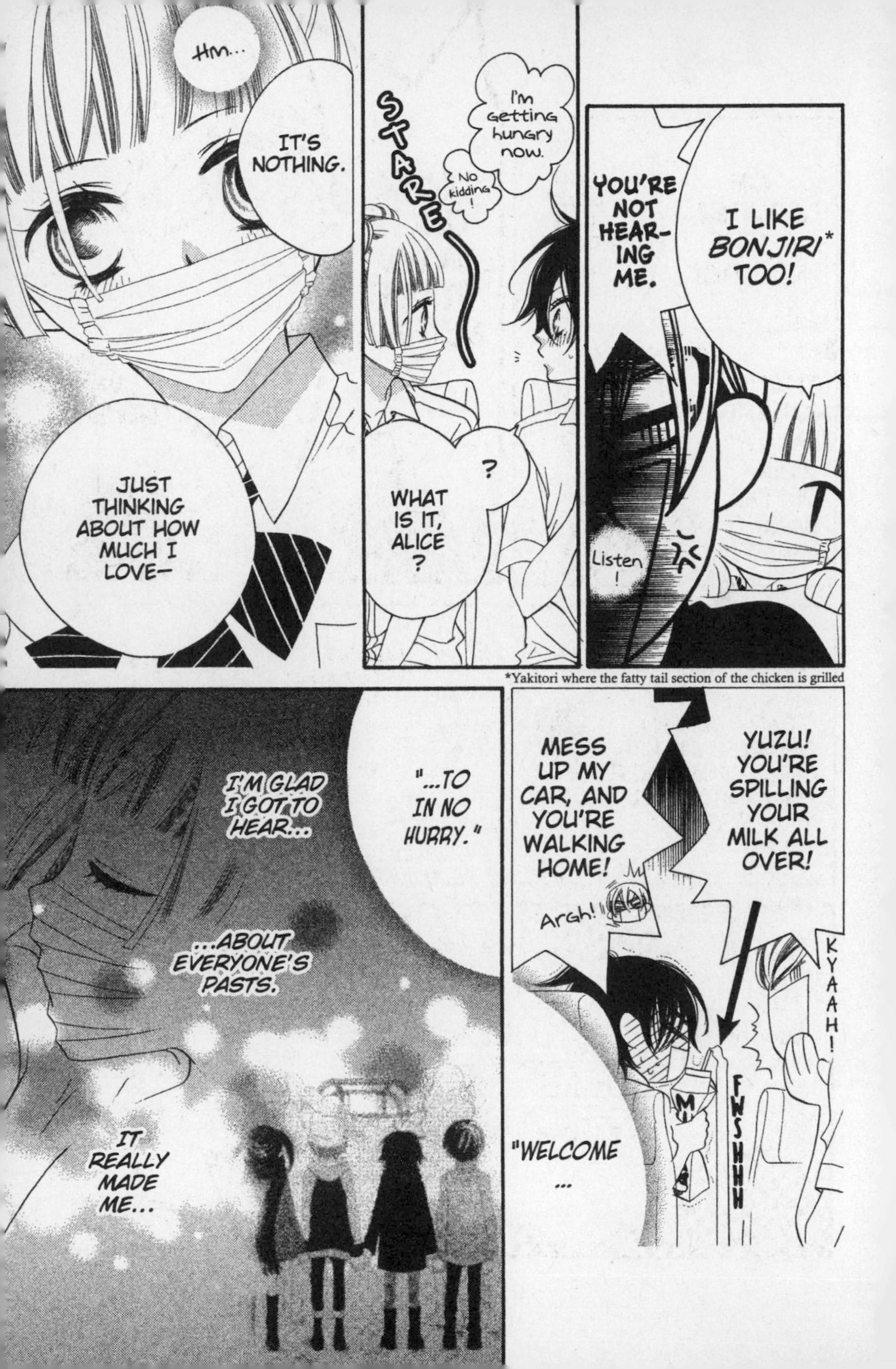
I LIKE BONJIRI* TOO!
YOU'RE NOT HEARING ME.
Listen!
STARE
I'm getting hungry now.
No kidding!
?
WHAT IS IT, ALICE?
Hm...
IT'S NOTHING.
JUST THINKING ABOUT HOW MUCH I LOVE—
*Yakitori where the fatty tail section of the chicken is grilled
YUZU! YOU'RE SPILLING YOUR MILK ALL OVER!
KYAAH!
MESS UP MY CAR, AND YOU'RE WALKING HOME!
Argh!
FWSHHH
"WELCOME ...
"...TO IN NO HURRY."
I'M GLAD I GOT TO HEAR...
...ABOUT EVERYONE'S PASTS.
IT REALLY MADE ME...

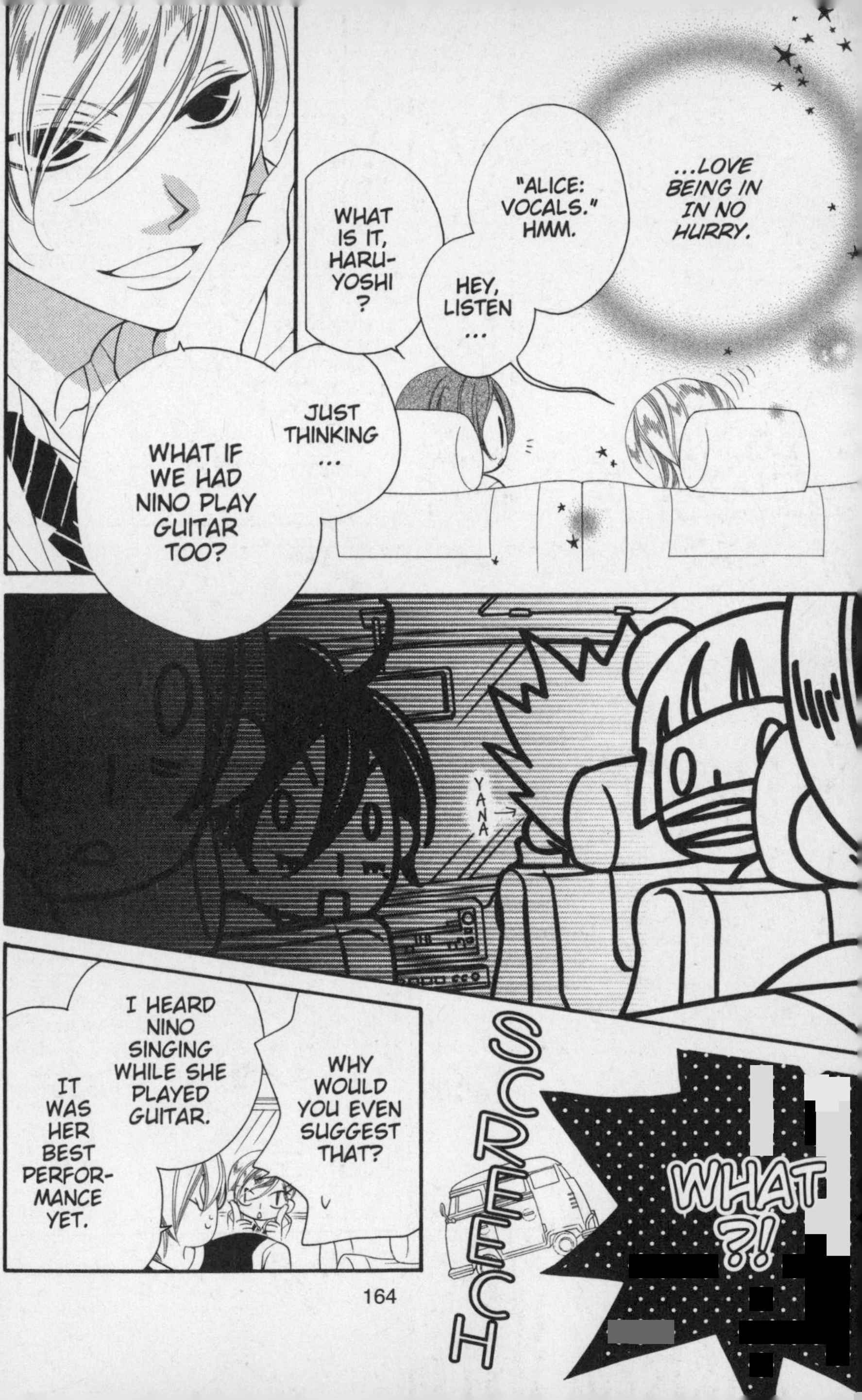
...LOVE BEING IN IN NO HURRY.
"ALICE: VOCALS." HMM.
HEY, LISTEN ...
WHAT IS IT, HARU-YOSHI ?
JUST THINKING ...
WHAT IF WE HAD NINO PLAY GUITAR TOO?
YANA
[redacted]
WHAT ?!
SCREECH
WHY WOULD YOU EVEN SUGGEST THAT?
I HEARD NINO SINGING WHILE SHE PLAYED GUITAR.
IT WAS HER BEST PERFORMANCE YET.

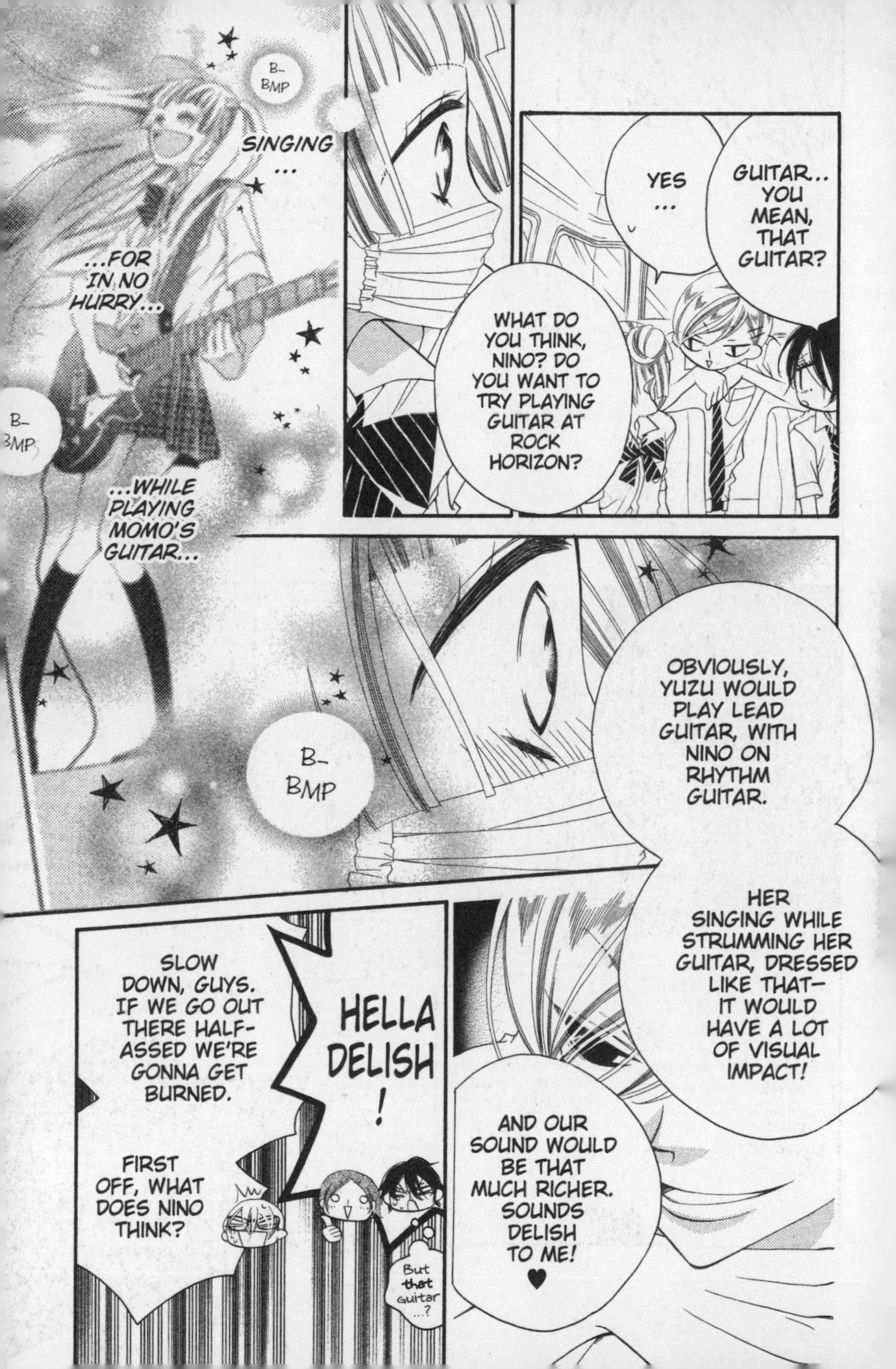
GUITAR... YOU MEAN, THAT GUITAR?
YES ...
WHAT DO YOU THINK, NINO? DO YOU WANT TO TRY PLAYING GUITAR AT ROCK HORIZON?
OBVIOUSLY, YUZU WOULD PLAY LEAD GUITAR, WITH NINO ON RHYTHM GUITAR.
HER SINGING WHILE STRUMMING HER GUITAR, DRESSED LIKE THAT— IT WOULD HAVE A LOT OF VISUAL IMPACT!
B-BMP
B-BMP
SINGING ...
...FOR IN NO HURRY...
B-BMP
...WHILE PLAYING MOMO'S GUITAR...
AND OUR SOUND WOULD BE THAT MUCH RICHER. SOUNDS DELISH TO ME! ♥
HELLA DELISH!
SLOW DOWN, GUYS. IF WE GO OUT THERE HALF-ASSED WE'RE GONNA GET BURNED.
FIRST OFF, WHAT DOES NINO THINK?
But that Guitar ...?

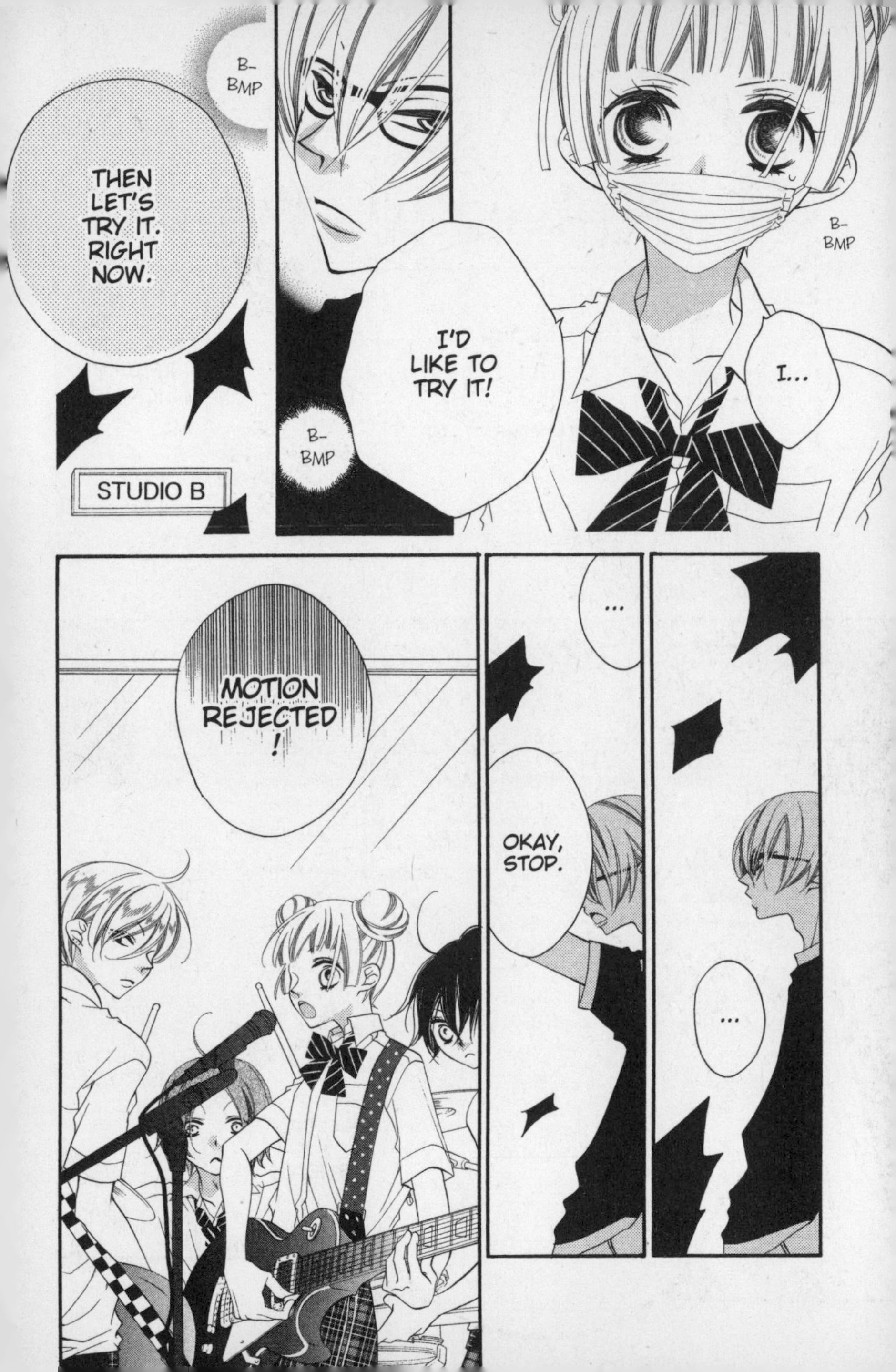
B-BMP
I...
I'D LIKE TO TRY IT!
B-BMP
B-BMP
THEN LET'S TRY IT. RIGHT NOW.
STUDIO B
...
...
OKAY, STOP.
MOTION REJECTED!

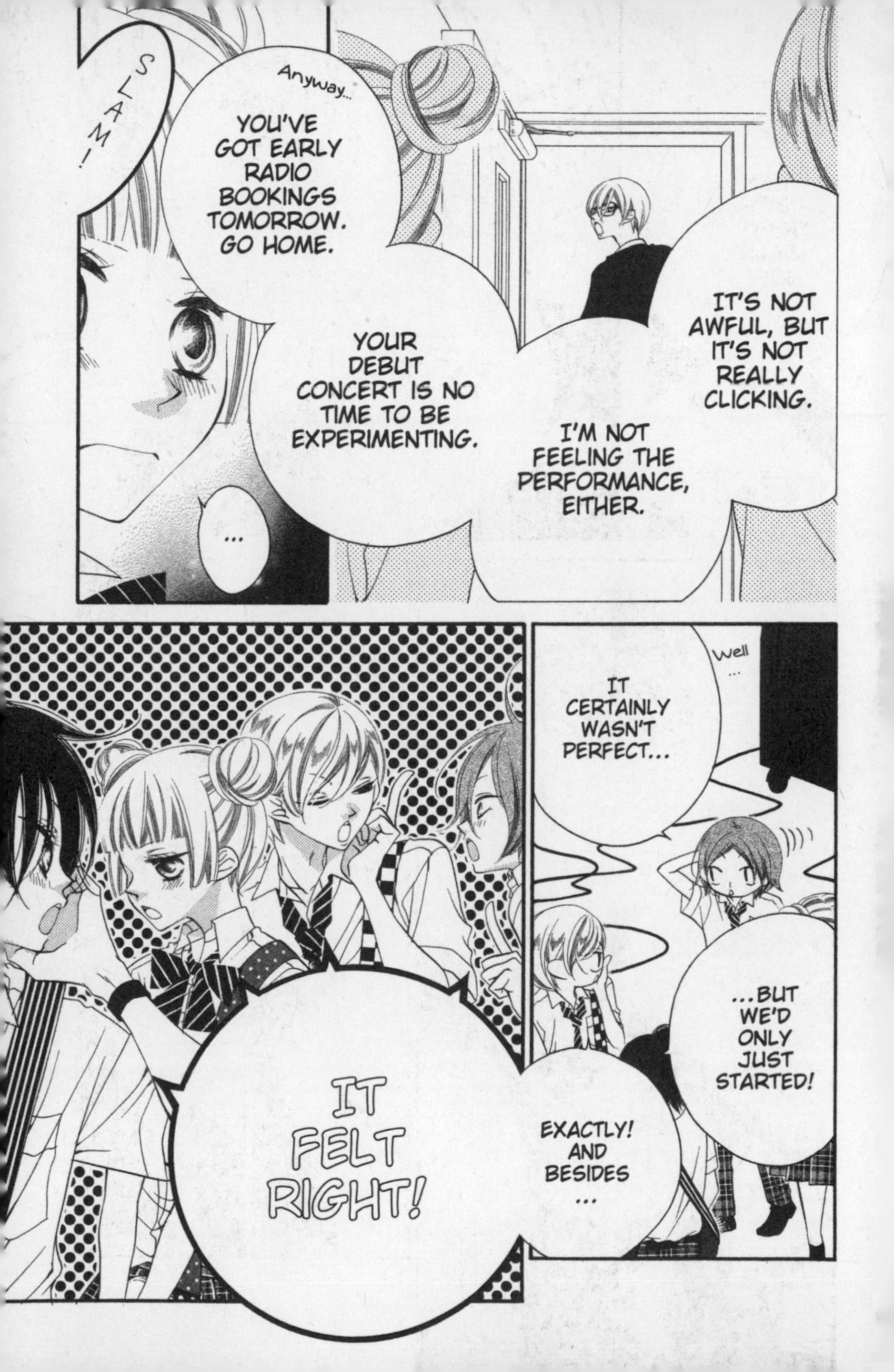
IT'S NOT AWFUL, BUT IT'S NOT REALLY CLICKING.
I'M NOT FEELING THE PERFORMANCE, EITHER.
YOUR DEBUT CONCERT IS NO TIME TO BE EXPERIMENTING.
Anyway... YOU'VE GOT EARLY RADIO BOOKINGS TOMORROW. GO HOME.
SLAM!
...
Well... IT CERTAINLY WASN'T PERFECT...
...BUT WE'D ONLY JUST STARTED!
EXACTLY! AND BESIDES ...
IT FELT RIGHT!

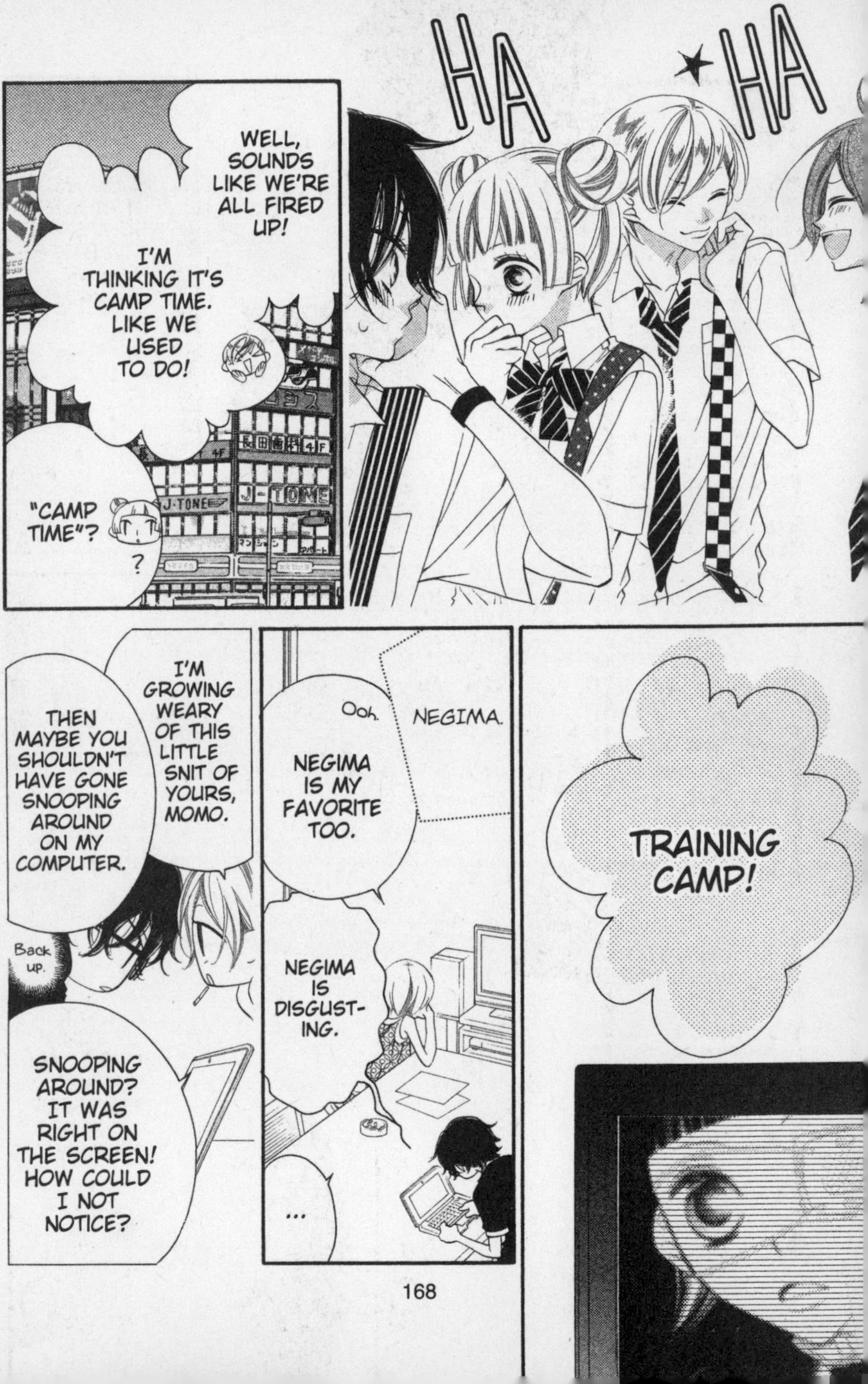
HA★HA
WELL, SOUNDS LIKE WE'RE ALL FIRED UP!
I'M THINKING IT'S CAMP TIME. LIKE WE USED TO DO!
J-TOME
J·TONE
"CAMP TIME"?
?
TRAINING CAMP!
NEGIMA.
Ooh.
NEGIMA IS MY FAVORITE TOO.
NEGIMA IS DISGUSTING.
...
I'M GROWING WEARY OF THIS LITTLE SNIT OF YOURS, MOMO.
THEN MAYBE YOU SHOULDN'T HAVE GONE SNOOPING AROUND ON MY COMPUTER.
Back up.
SNOOPING AROUND? IT WAS RIGHT ON THE SCREEN! HOW COULD I NOT NOTICE?

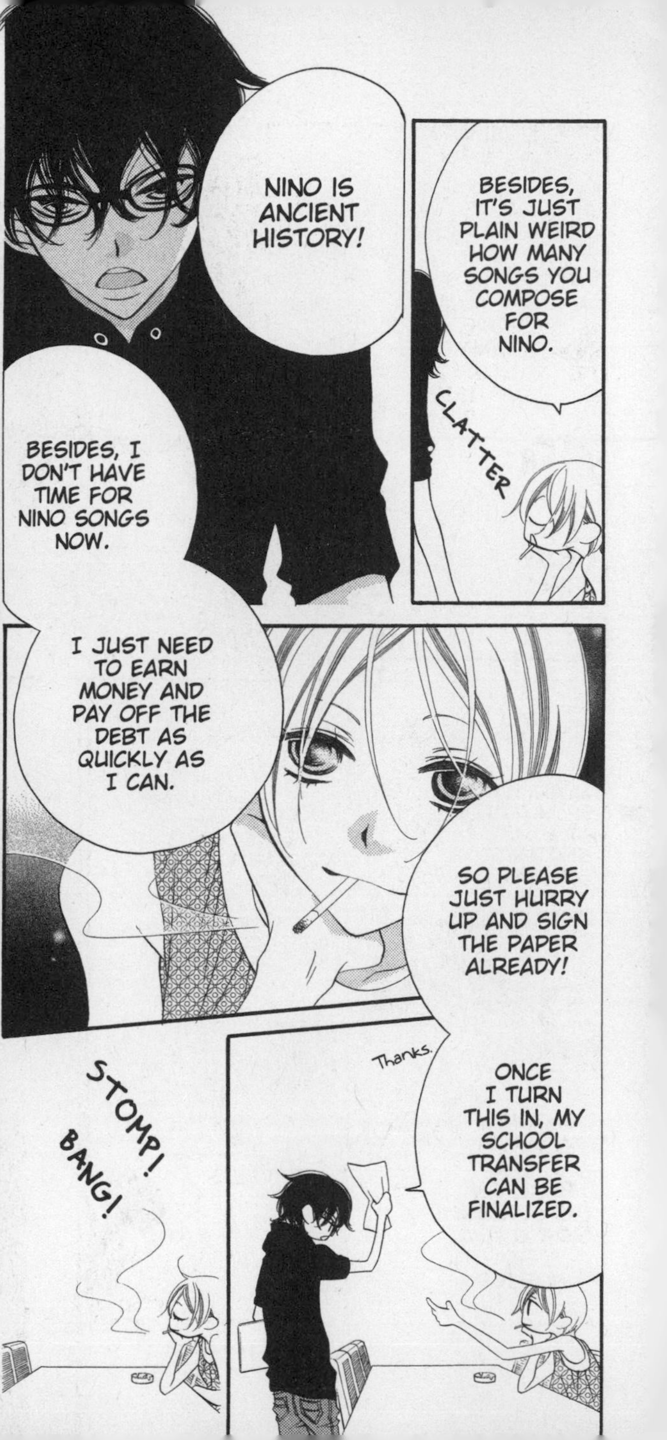
BESIDES, IT'S JUST PLAIN WEIRD HOW MANY SONGS YOU COMPOSE FOR NINO.
CLATTER
NINO IS ANCIENT HISTORY!
BESIDES, I DON'T HAVE TIME FOR NINO SONGS NOW.
I JUST NEED TO EARN MONEY AND PAY OFF THE DEBT AS QUICKLY AS I CAN.
SO PLEASE JUST HURRY UP AND SIGN THE PAPER ALREADY!
ONCE I TURN THIS IN, MY SCHOOL TRANSFER CAN BE FINALIZED.
Thanks.
STOMP!
BANG!

6

So, how did you all enjoy Anonymous Noise volume 4?

In the next volume, we finally experience Rock Horizon! I'm drawing it now and having a blast! When volume 5 is ready, I hope I'll see you there. Thank you so much for reading this!

-Ryoko Fukuyama

[SPECIAL THANKS]
IZUMI HIOU
MINI KOMATSU
TAKAYUKI NAGASHIMA
KENJU NORO
MY FAMILY
MY FRIENDS
AND YOU!!

Ryoko Fukuyama
c/o Anonymous Noise Editor
VIZ Media
P.O. Box 77010
San Francisco, CA

http://ryoconet.tumblr.com/

@ryocoryocoryoco

http://facebook.com/ryocoryocoryoco/

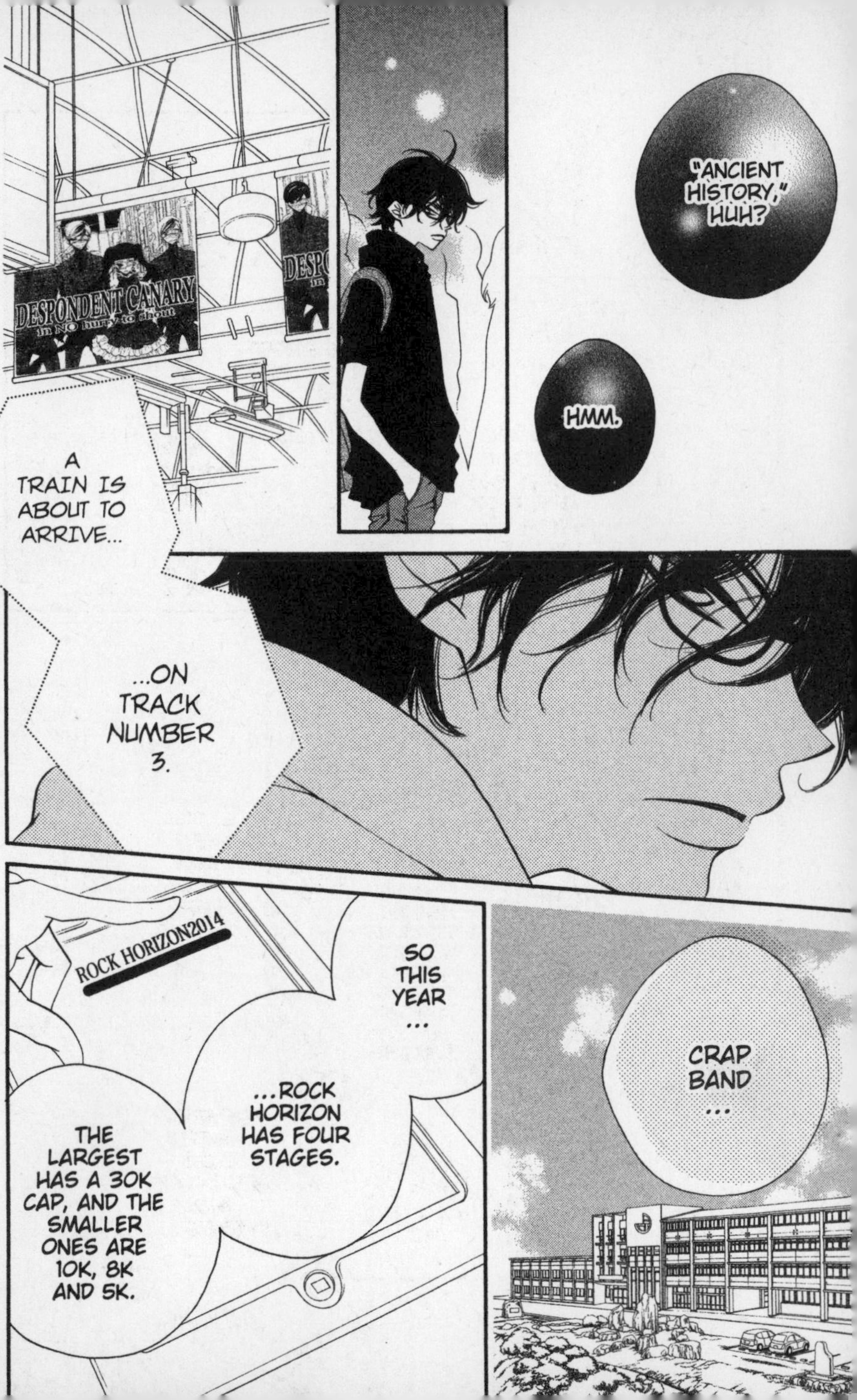
"ANCIENT HISTORY," HUH?
HMM.
DESPONDENT CANARY
in NO hurry to shout
A TRAIN IS ABOUT TO ARRIVE...
...ON TRACK NUMBER 3.
CRAP BAND...
ROCK HORIZON2014
SO THIS YEAR...
...ROCK HORIZON HAS FOUR STAGES.
THE LARGEST HAS A 30K CAP, AND THE SMALLER ONES ARE 10K, 8K AND 5K.

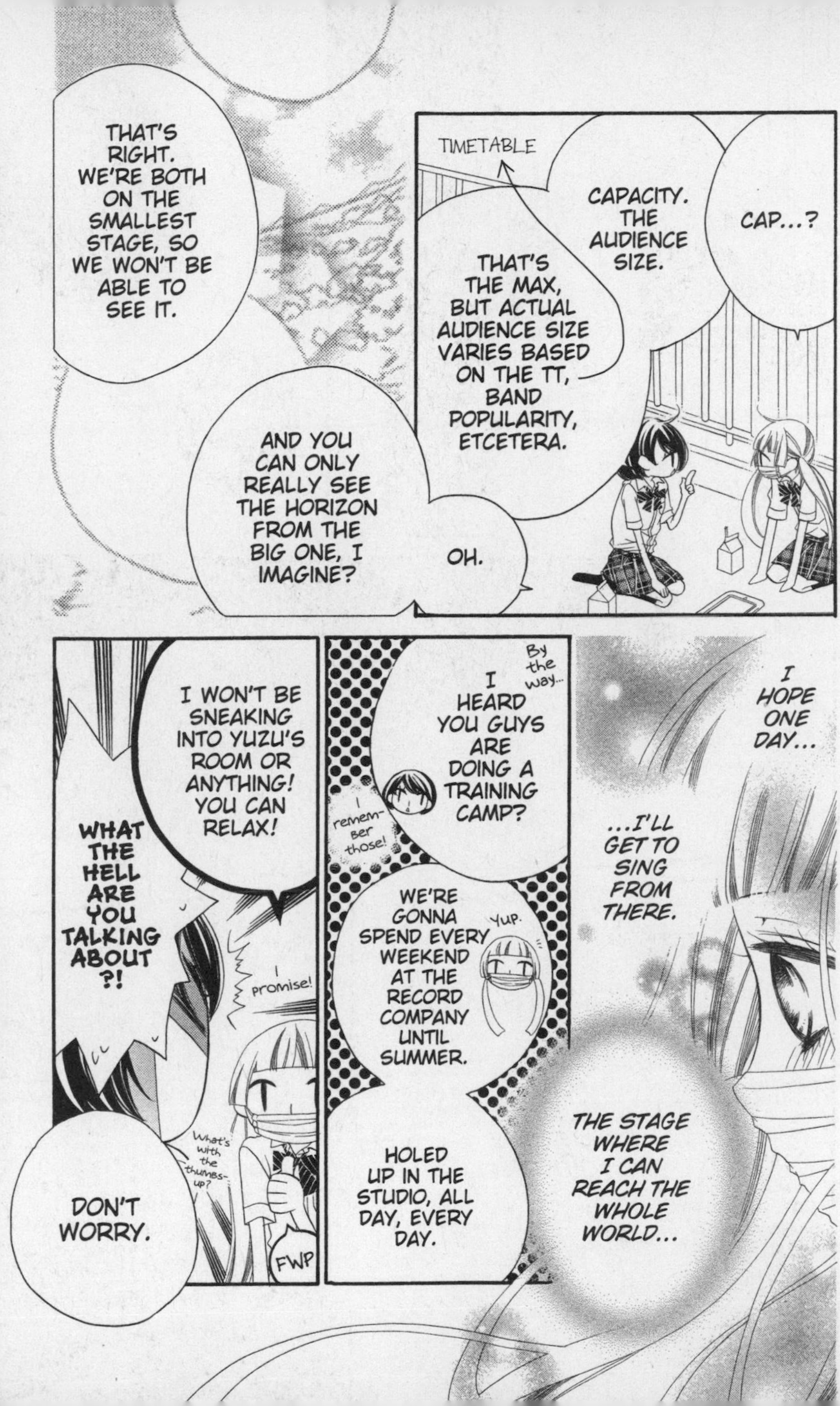
CAP...?
CAPACITY. THE AUDIENCE SIZE.
TIMETABLE
THAT'S THE MAX, BUT ACTUAL AUDIENCE SIZE VARIES BASED ON THE TT, BAND POPULARITY, ETCETERA.
OH.
THAT'S RIGHT. WE'RE BOTH ON THE SMALLEST STAGE, SO WE WON'T BE ABLE TO SEE IT.
AND YOU CAN ONLY REALLY SEE THE HORIZON FROM THE BIG ONE, I IMAGINE?
I HOPE ONE DAY...
...I'LL GET TO SING FROM THERE.
THE STAGE WHERE I CAN REACH THE WHOLE WORLD...
By the way...
I HEARD YOU GUYS ARE DOING A TRAINING CAMP?
I remember those!
WE'RE GONNA SPEND EVERY WEEKEND AT THE RECORD COMPANY UNTIL SUMMER.
Yup.
HOLED UP IN THE STUDIO, ALL DAY, EVERY DAY.
I WON'T BE SNEAKING INTO YUZU'S ROOM OR ANYTHING! YOU CAN RELAX!
WHAT THE HELL ARE YOU TALKING ABOUT?!
I promise!
What's with the thumbs-up?
DON'T WORRY.
FWP

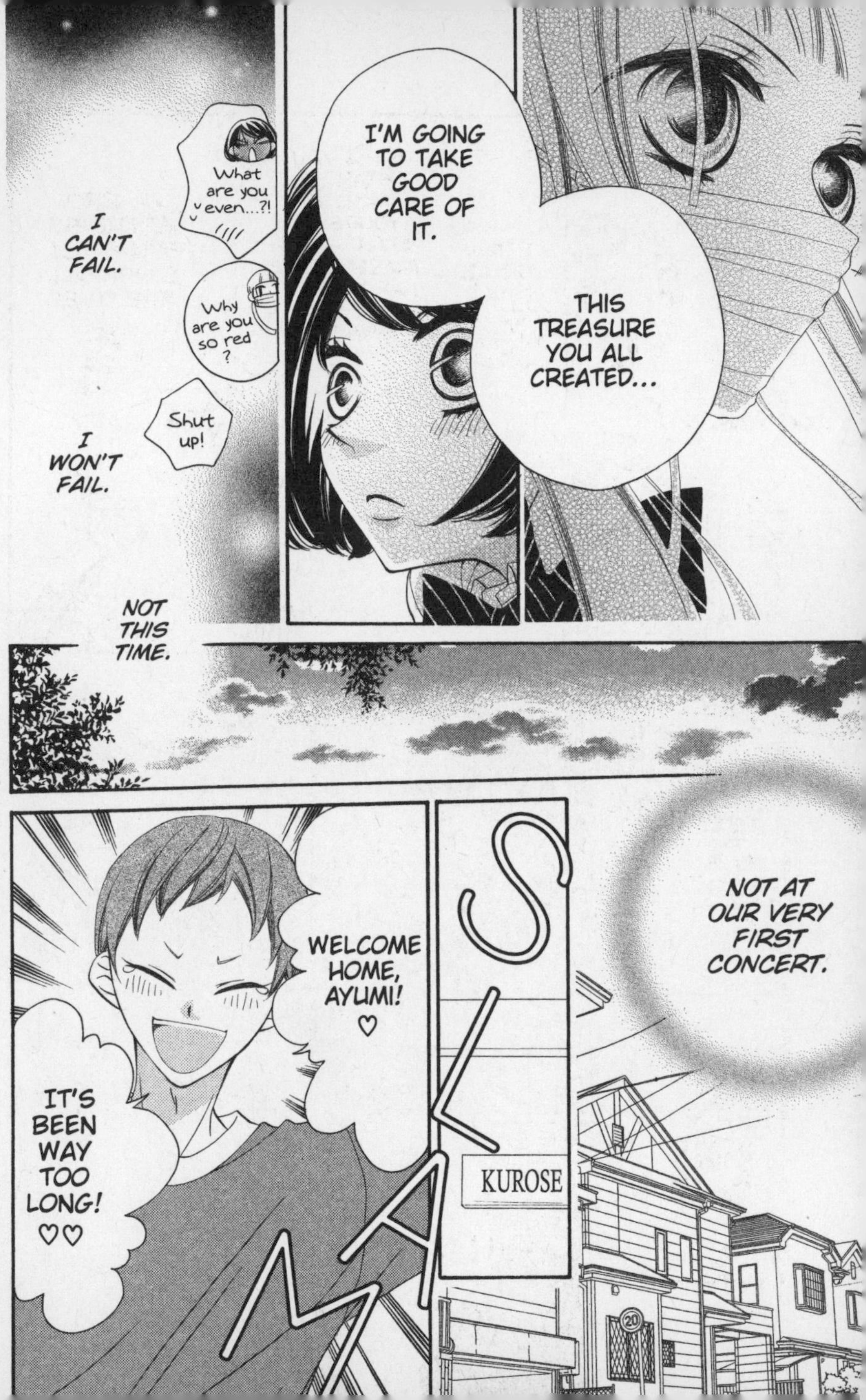
THIS TREASURE YOU ALL CREATED...
I'M GOING TO TAKE GOOD CARE OF IT.
What are you even...?!
Why are you so red?
Shut up!
I CAN'T FAIL.
I WON'T FAIL.
NOT THIS TIME.
NOT AT OUR VERY FIRST CONCERT.
SLAM
KUROSE
WELCOME HOME, AYUMI! ♡
IT'S BEEN WAY TOO LONG! ♡♡

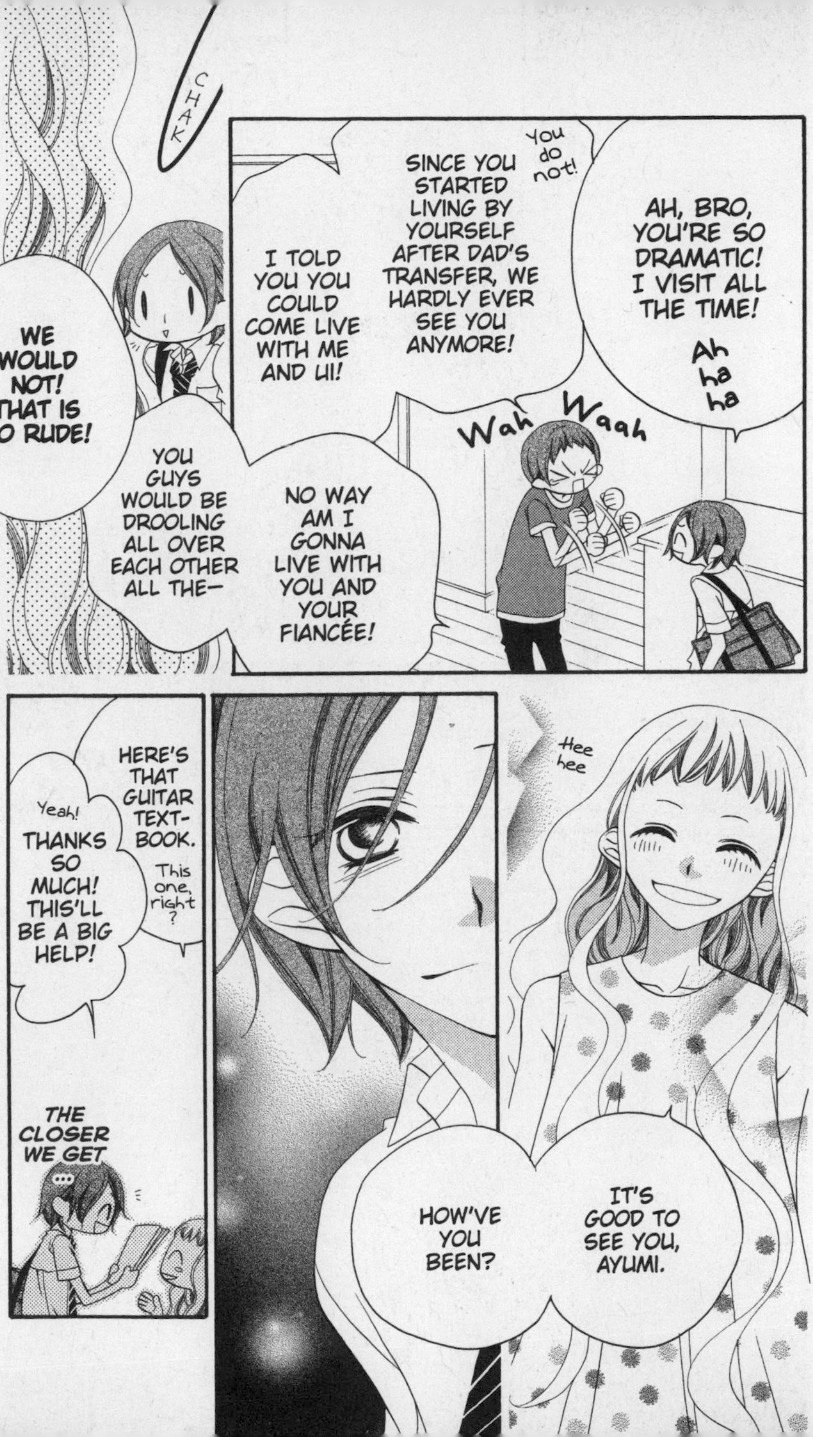
AH, BRO, YOU'RE SO DRAMATIC! I VISIT ALL THE TIME!
Ah ha ha
You do not!
SINCE YOU STARTED LIVING BY YOURSELF AFTER DAD'S TRANSFER, WE HARDLY EVER SEE YOU ANYMORE!
I TOLD YOU YOU COULD COME LIVE WITH ME AND UI!
Wah Waah
NO WAY AM I GONNA LIVE WITH YOU AND YOUR FIANCÉE!
YOU GUYS WOULD BE DROOLING ALL OVER EACH OTHER ALL THE—
CHAK
WE WOULD NOT! THAT IS SO RUDE!
Hee hee
IT'S GOOD TO SEE YOU, AYUMI.
HOW'VE YOU BEEN?
HERE'S THAT GUITAR TEXT-BOOK.
This one, right?
Yeah!
THANKS SO MUCH! THIS'LL BE A BIG HELP!
THE CLOSER WE GET

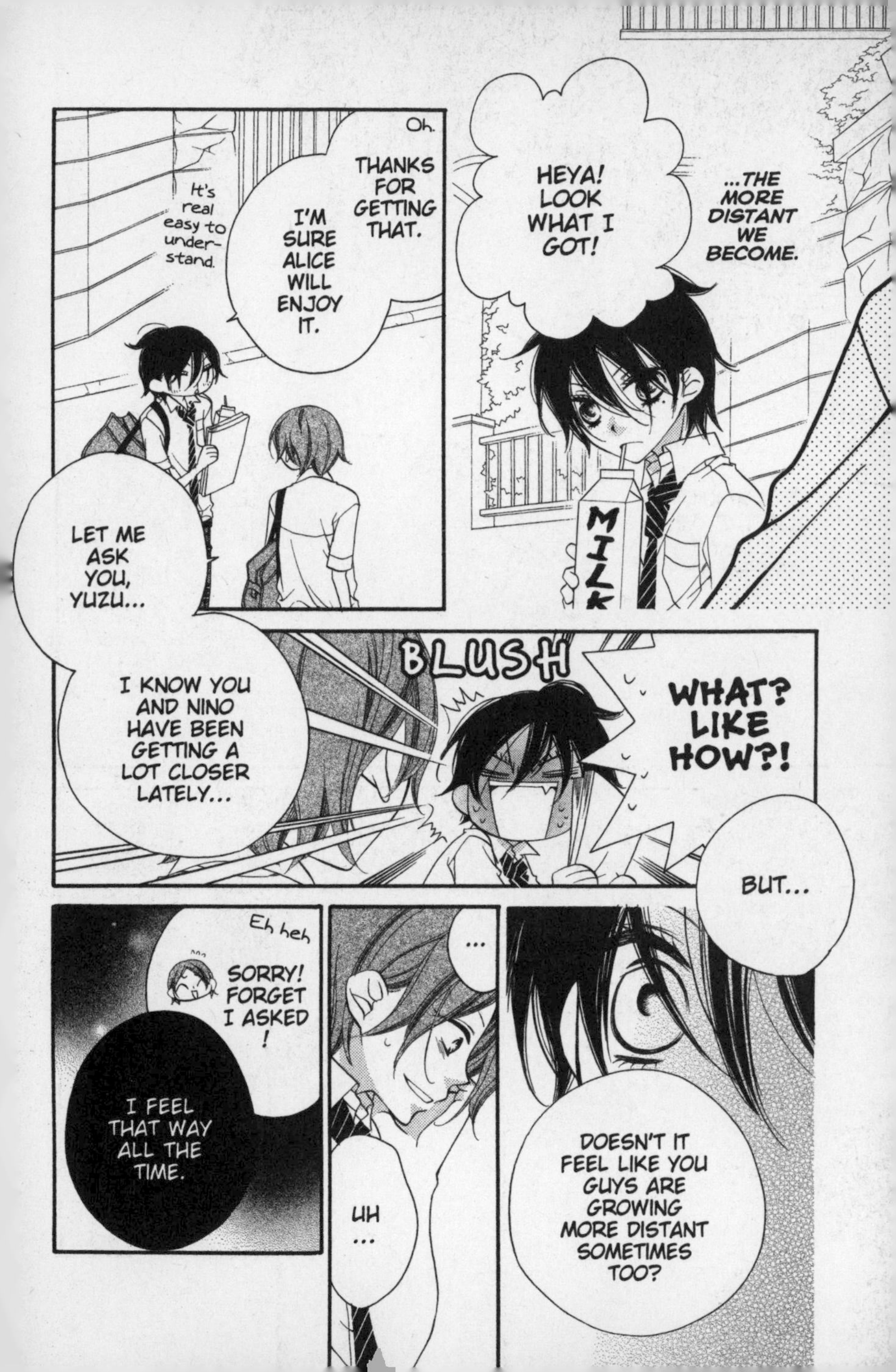
...THE MORE DISTANT WE BECOME.
HEYA! LOOK WHAT I GOT!
MILK
Oh.
THANKS FOR GETTING THAT.
I'M SURE ALICE WILL ENJOY IT.
It's real easy to under-stand.
LET ME ASK YOU, YUZU...
I KNOW YOU AND NINO HAVE BEEN GETTING A LOT CLOSER LATELY...
BLUSH
WHAT? LIKE HOW?!
BUT...
DOESN'T IT FEEL LIKE YOU GUYS ARE GROWING MORE DISTANT SOMETIMES TOO?
...
UH ...
Eh heh
SORRY! FORGET I ASKED!
I FEEL THAT WAY ALL THE TIME.

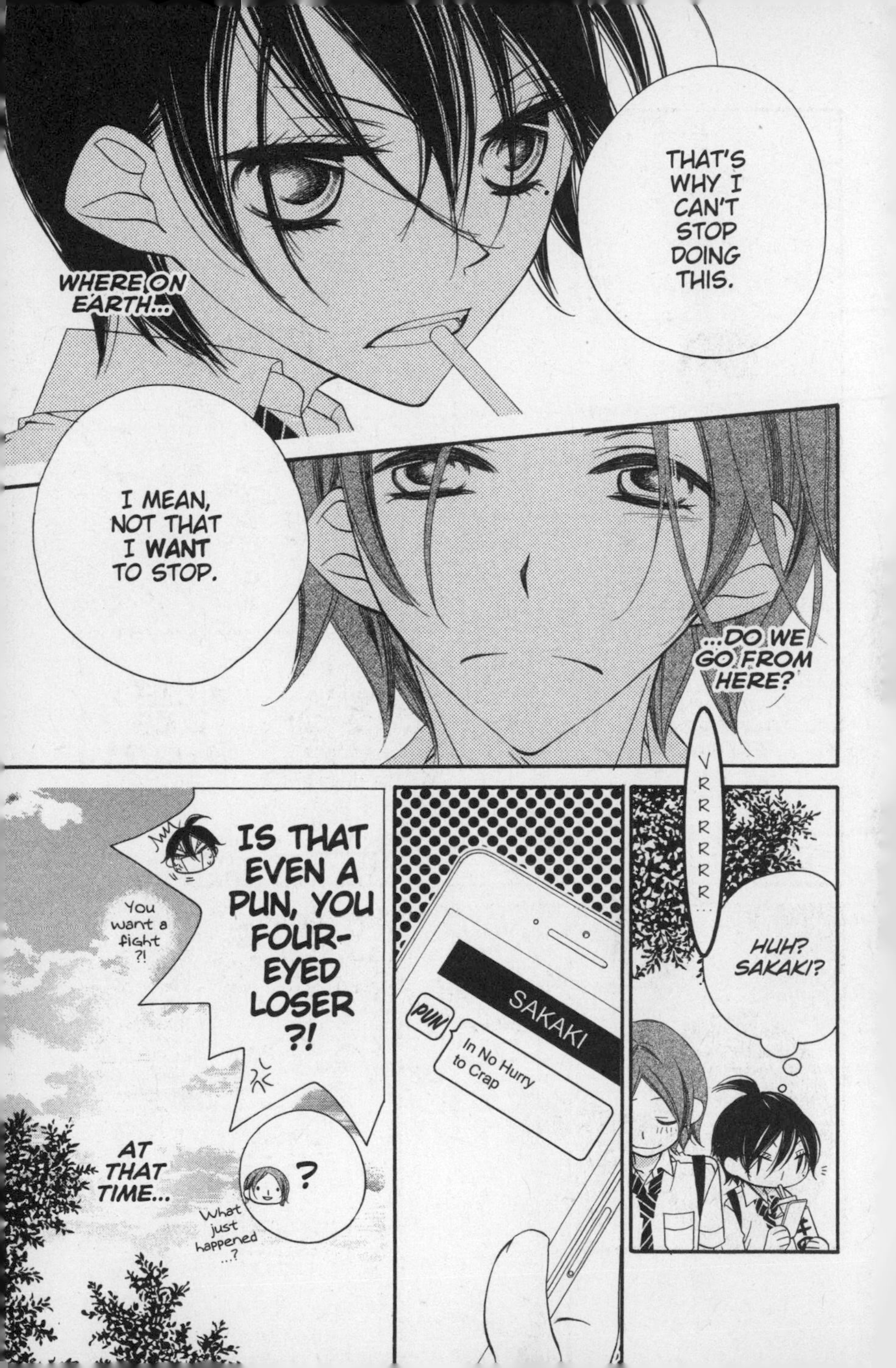
THAT'S WHY I CAN'T STOP DOING THIS.
WHERE ON EARTH...
I MEAN, NOT THAT I WANT TO STOP.
...DO WE GO FROM HERE?
VRRRRRR...
HUH? SAKAKI?
SAKAKI
PUN
In No Hurry to Crap
IS THAT EVEN A PUN, YOU FOUR-EYED LOSER?!
You want a fight?!
?
What just happened...?
AT THAT TIME...

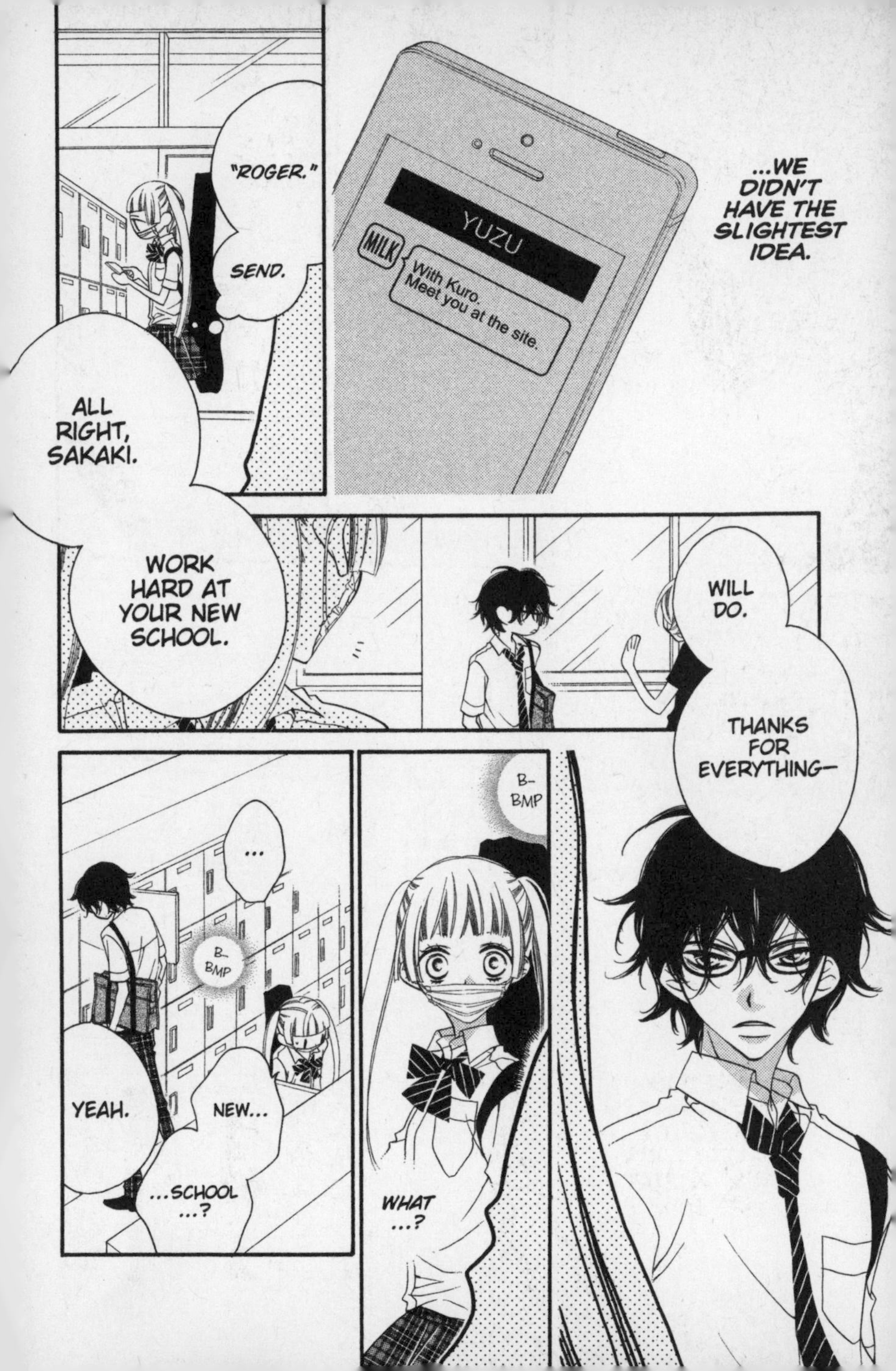
...WE DIDN'T HAVE THE SLIGHTEST IDEA.
YUZU
MILK
With Kuro.
Meet you at the site.
"ROGER."
SEND.
ALL RIGHT, SAKAKI.
WORK HARD AT YOUR NEW SCHOOL.
WILL DO.
THANKS FOR EVERYTHING—
B-BMP
WHAT ...?
...
B-BMP
YEAH.
NEW...
...SCHOOL ...?

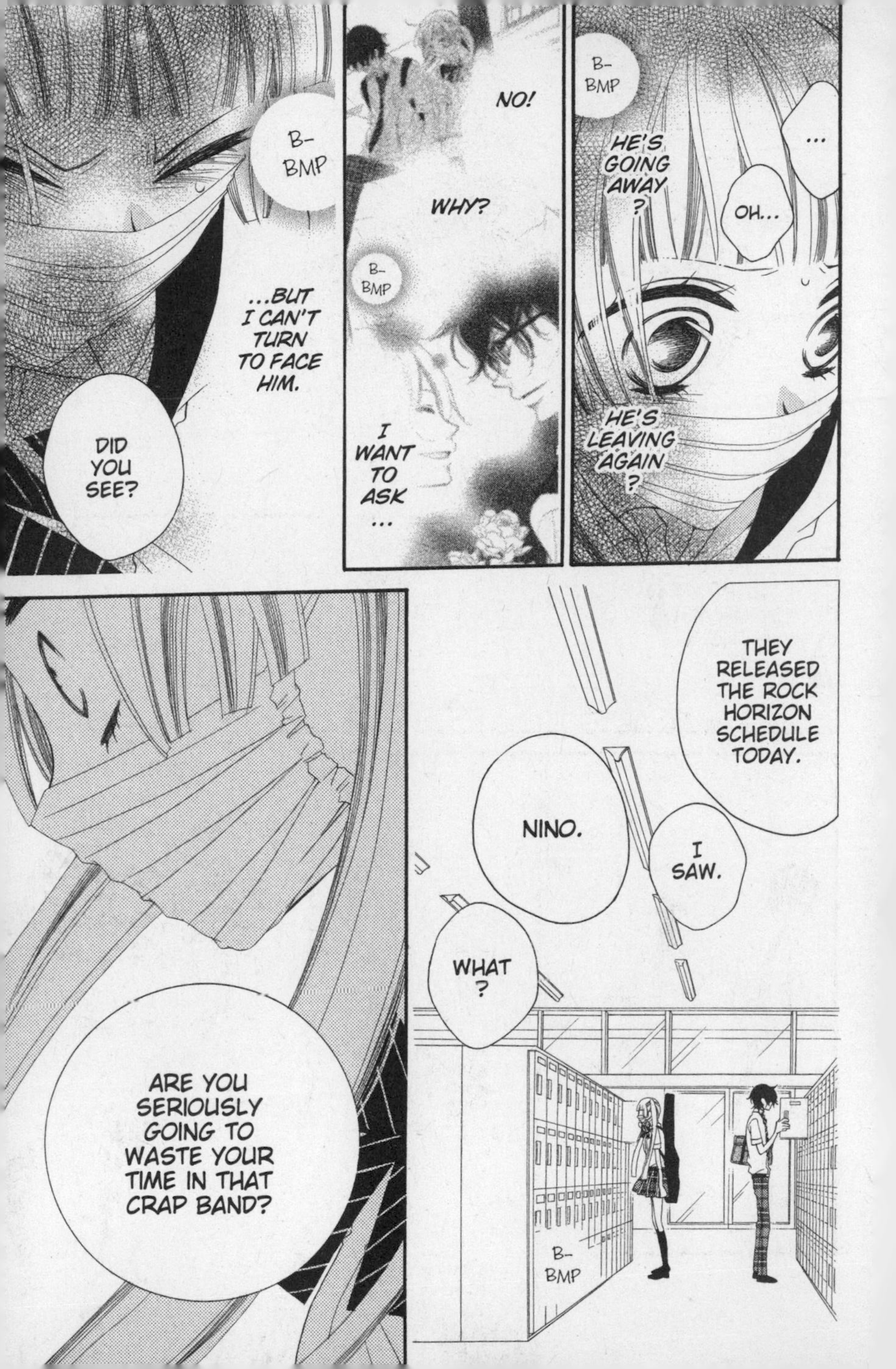
...
B-BMP
OH...
HE'S GOING AWAY?
HE'S LEAVING AGAIN?
NO!
WHY?
B-BMP
I WANT TO ASK...
B-BMP
...BUT I CAN'T TURN TO FACE HIM.
DID YOU SEE?
THEY RELEASED THE ROCK HORIZON SCHEDULE TODAY.
I SAW.
NINO.
WHAT?
B-BMP
ARE YOU SERIOUSLY GOING TO WASTE YOUR TIME IN THAT CRAP BAND?

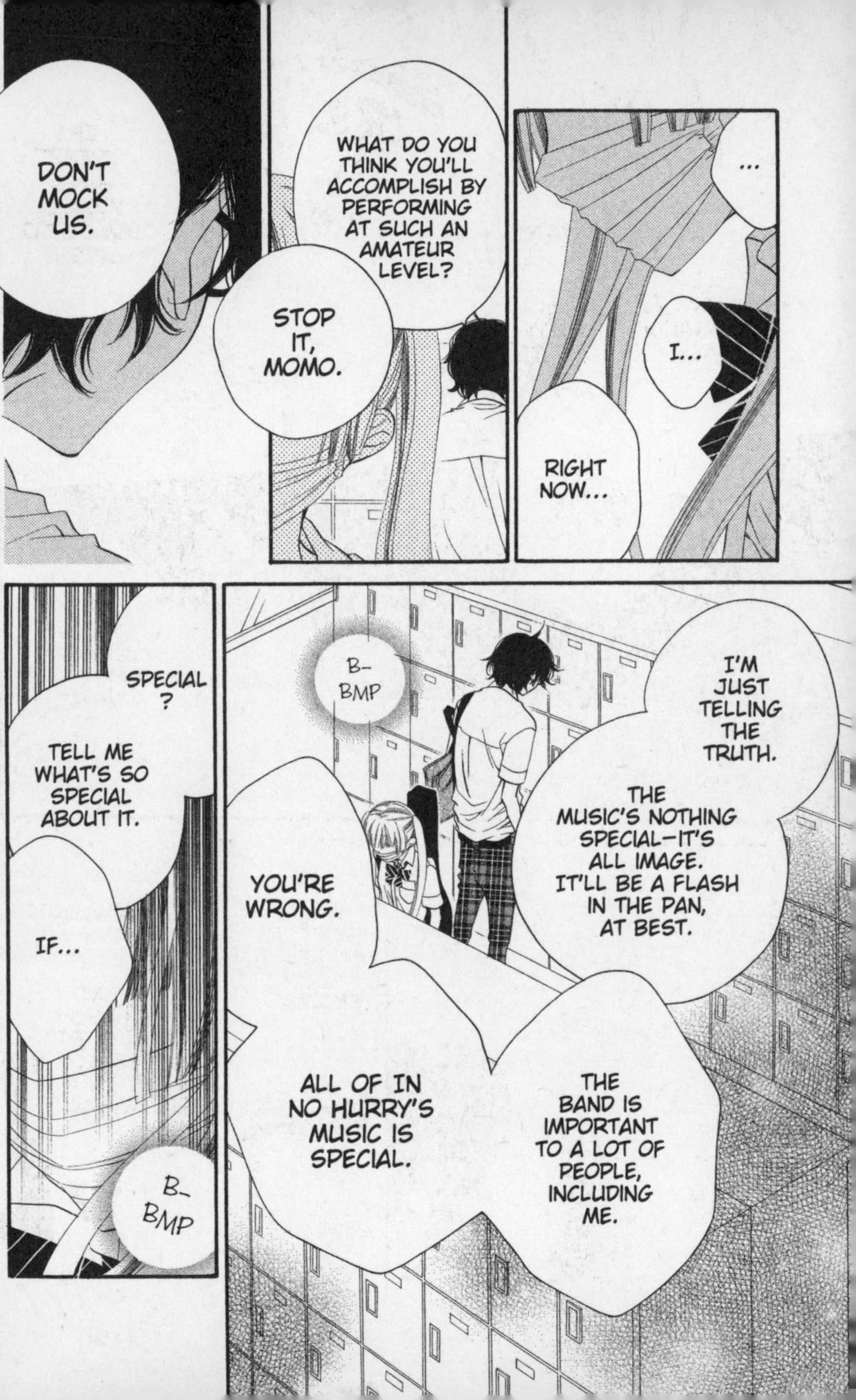
...
I...
RIGHT NOW...
WHAT DO YOU THINK YOU'LL ACCOMPLISH BY PERFORMING AT SUCH AN AMATEUR LEVEL?
STOP IT, MOMO.
DON'T MOCK US.
I'M JUST TELLING THE TRUTH.
B-BMP
THE MUSIC'S NOTHING SPECIAL—IT'S ALL IMAGE. IT'LL BE A FLASH IN THE PAN, AT BEST.
YOU'RE WRONG.
THE BAND IS IMPORTANT TO A LOT OF PEOPLE, INCLUDING ME.
ALL OF IN NO HURRY'S MUSIC IS SPECIAL.
SPECIAL?
TELL ME WHAT'S SO SPECIAL ABOUT IT.
IF...
B-BMP

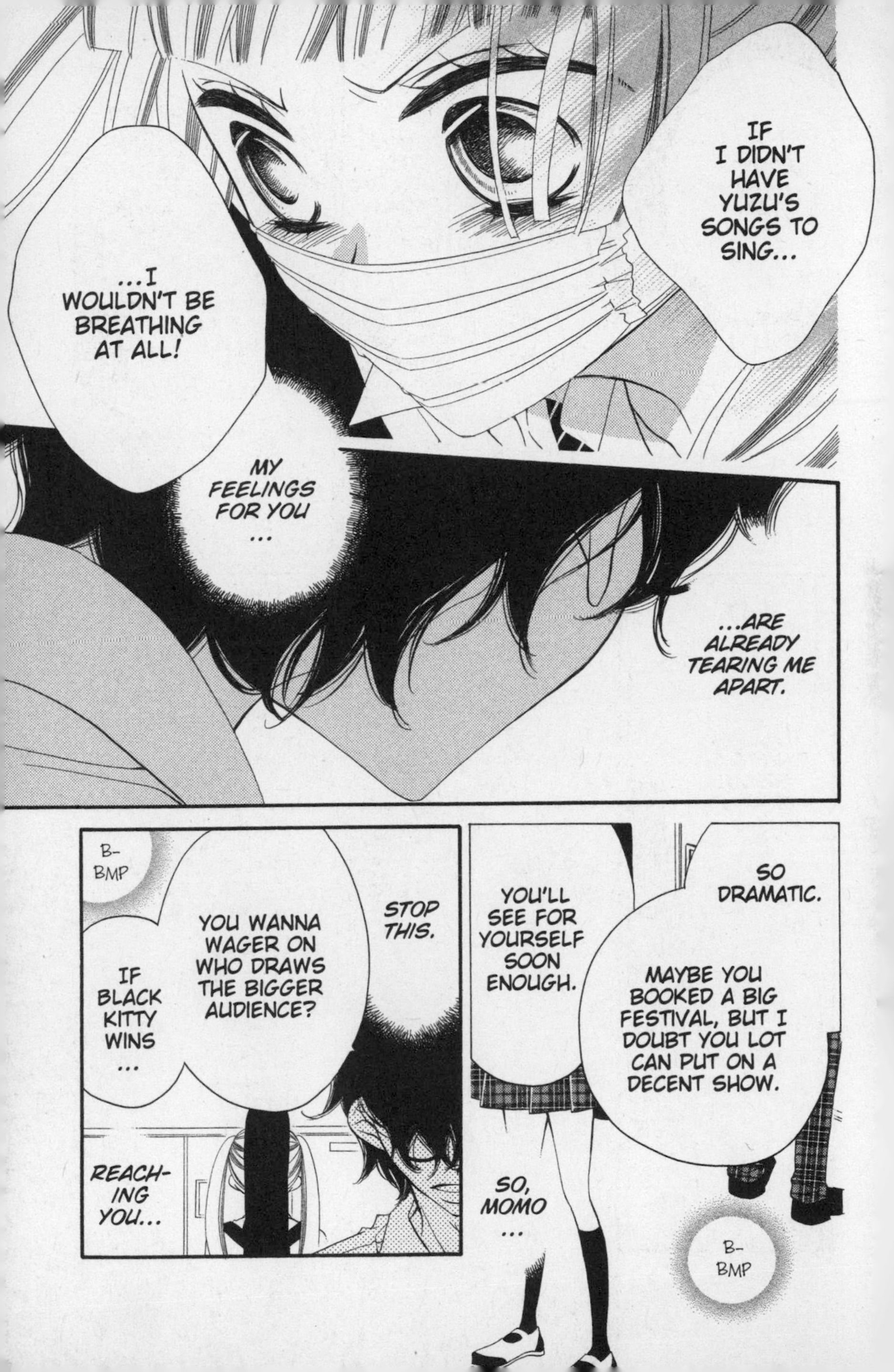
IF I DIDN'T HAVE YUZU'S SONGS TO SING...
...I WOULDN'T BE BREATHING AT ALL!
MY FEELINGS FOR YOU ...
...ARE ALREADY TEARING ME APART.
SO DRAMATIC.
MAYBE YOU BOOKED A BIG FESTIVAL, BUT I DOUBT YOU LOT CAN PUT ON A DECENT SHOW.
YOU'LL SEE FOR YOURSELF SOON ENOUGH.
SO, MOMO ...
B-BMP
STOP THIS.
YOU WANNA WAGER ON WHO DRAWS THE BIGGER AUDIENCE?
B-BMP
IF BLACK KITTY WINS ...
REACHING YOU...

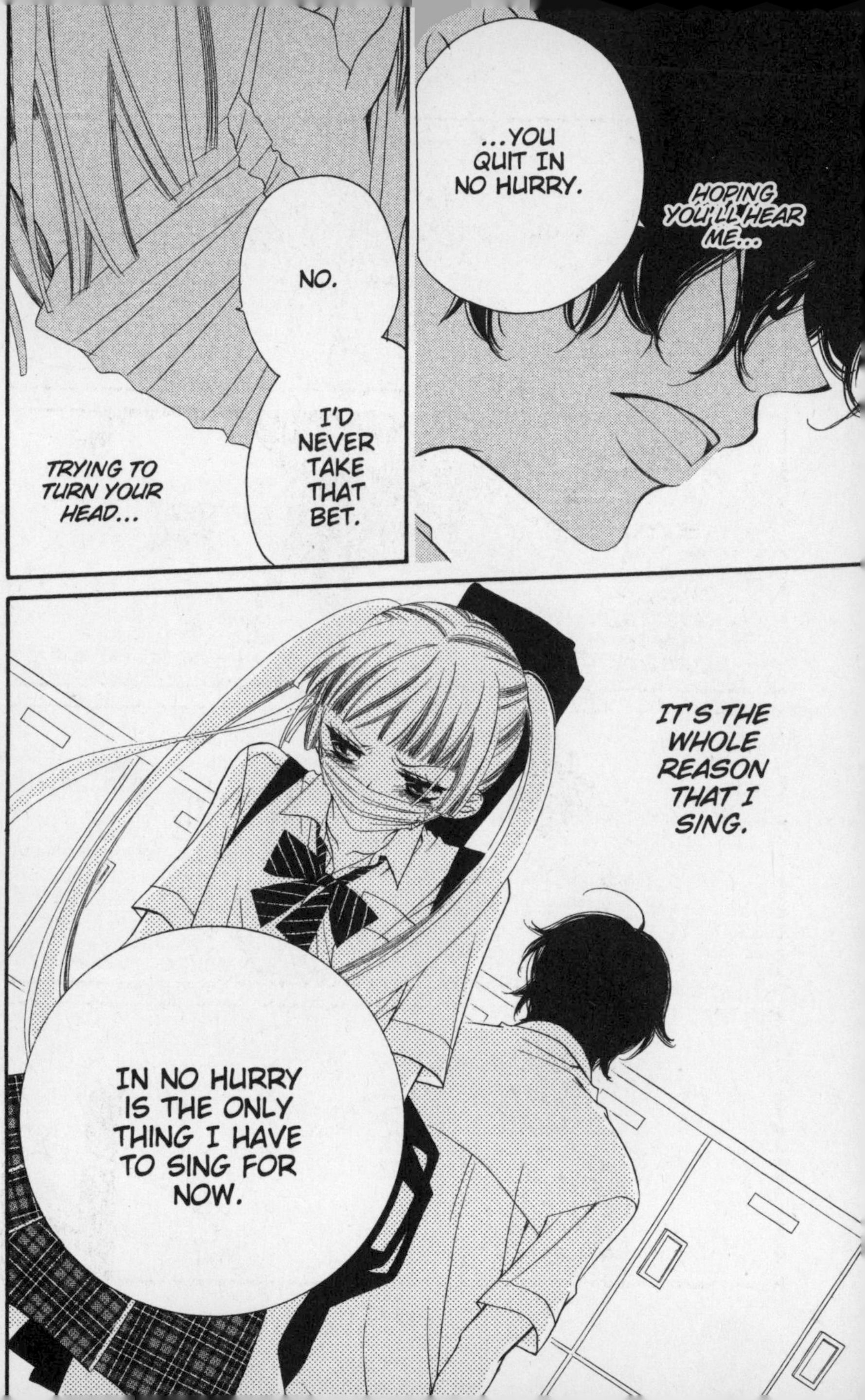

...YOU QUIT IN NO HURRY.
HOPING YOU'LL HEAR ME...
NO.
I'D NEVER TAKE THAT BET.
TRYING TO TURN YOUR HEAD...
IT'S THE WHOLE REASON THAT I SING.
IN NO HURRY IS THE ONLY THING I HAVE TO SING FOR NOW.

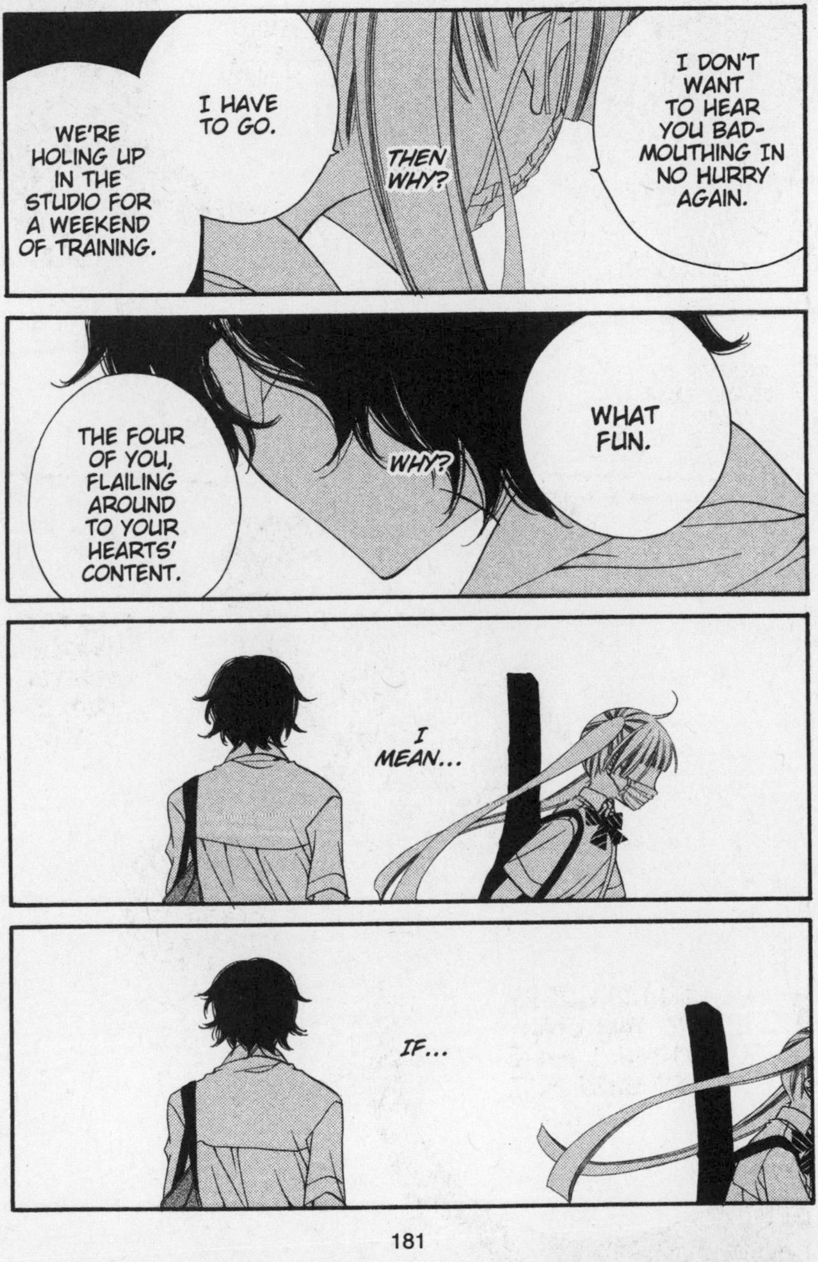
I DON'T WANT TO HEAR YOU BAD-MOUTHING IN NO HURRY AGAIN.
THEN WHY?
I HAVE TO GO.
WE'RE HOLING UP IN THE STUDIO FOR A WEEKEND OF TRAINING.
WHAT FUN.
WHY?
THE FOUR OF YOU, FLAILING AROUND TO YOUR HEARTS' CONTENT.
I MEAN...
IF...

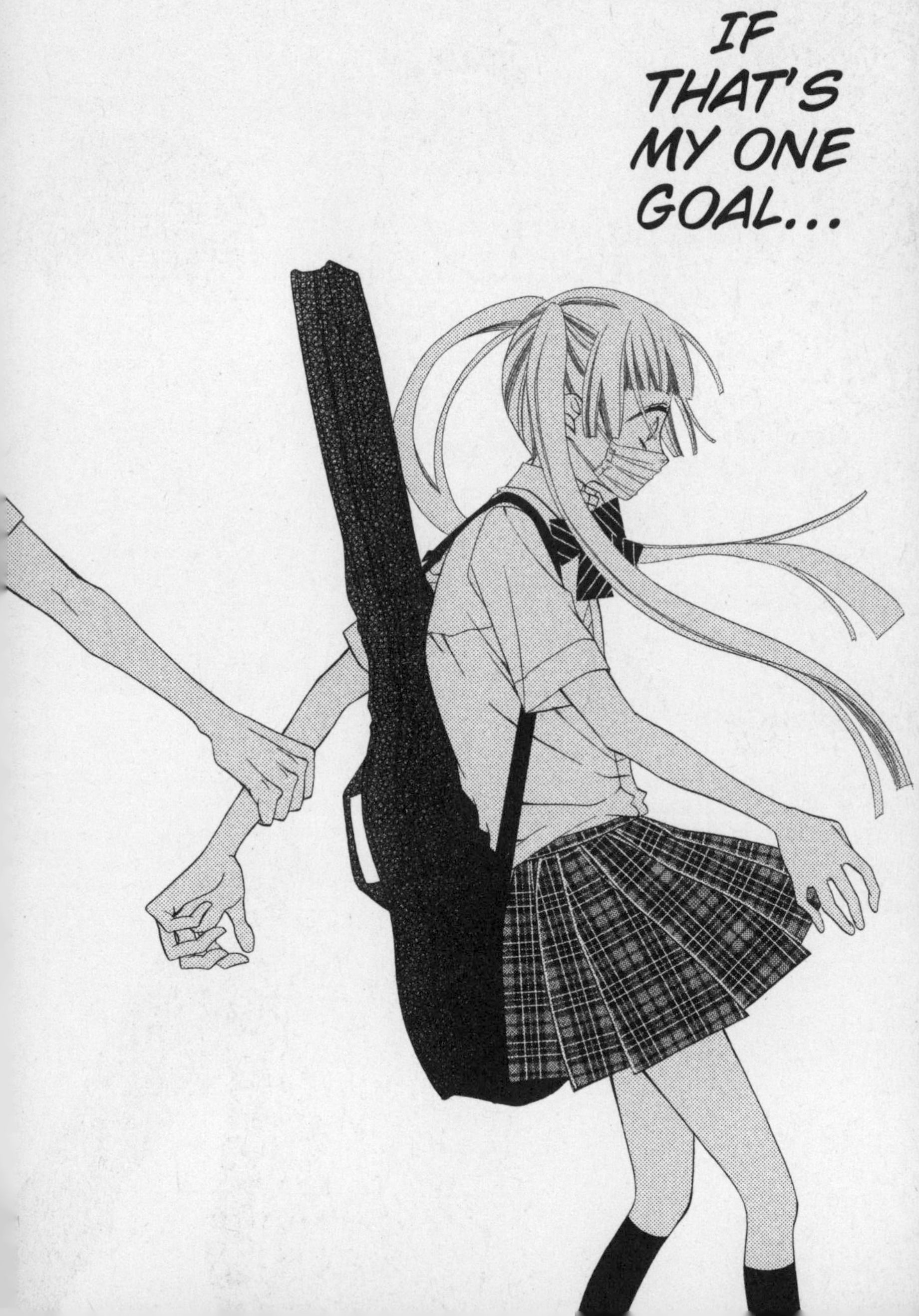
IF THAT'S MY ONE GOAL...

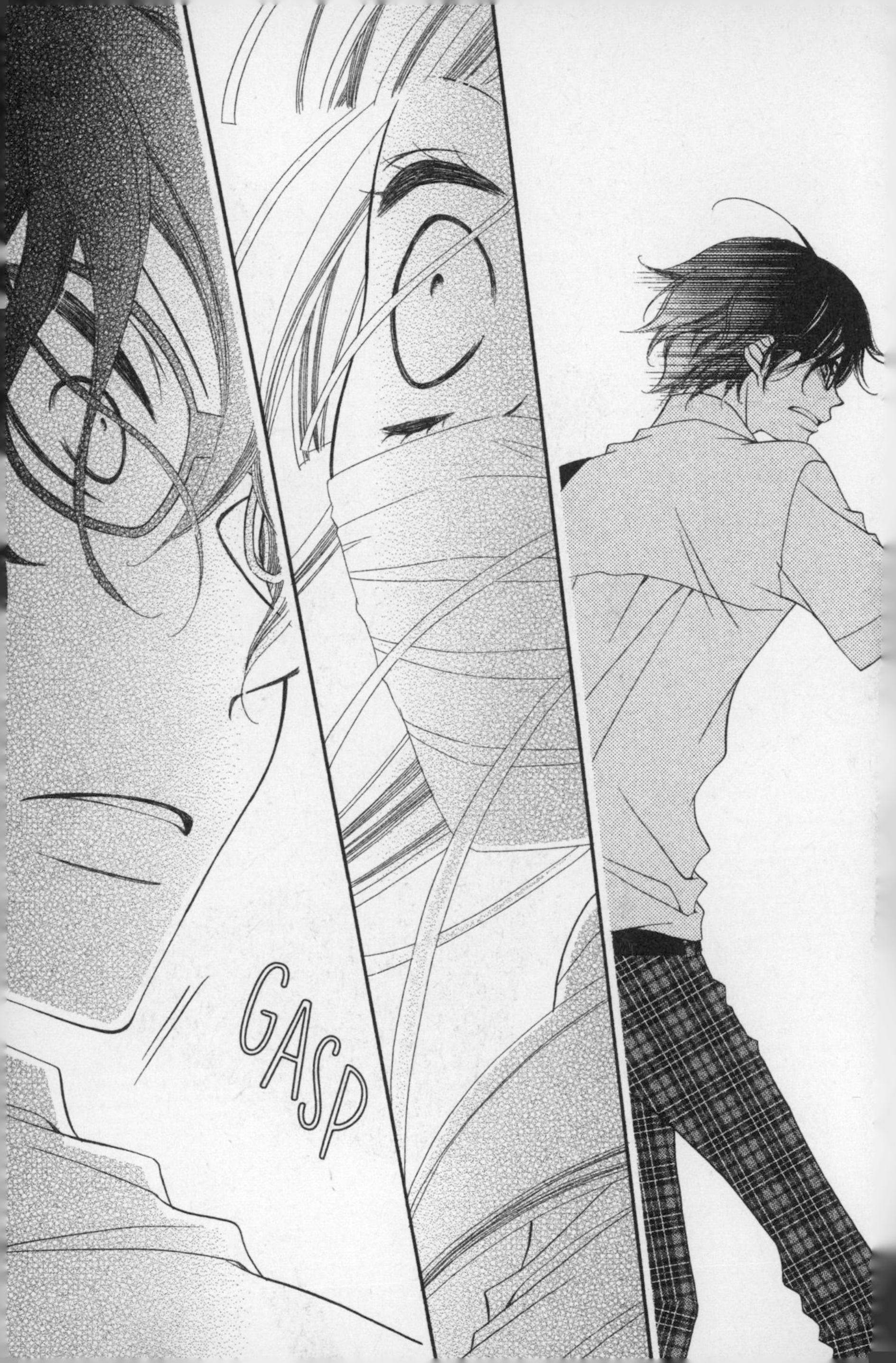
GASP

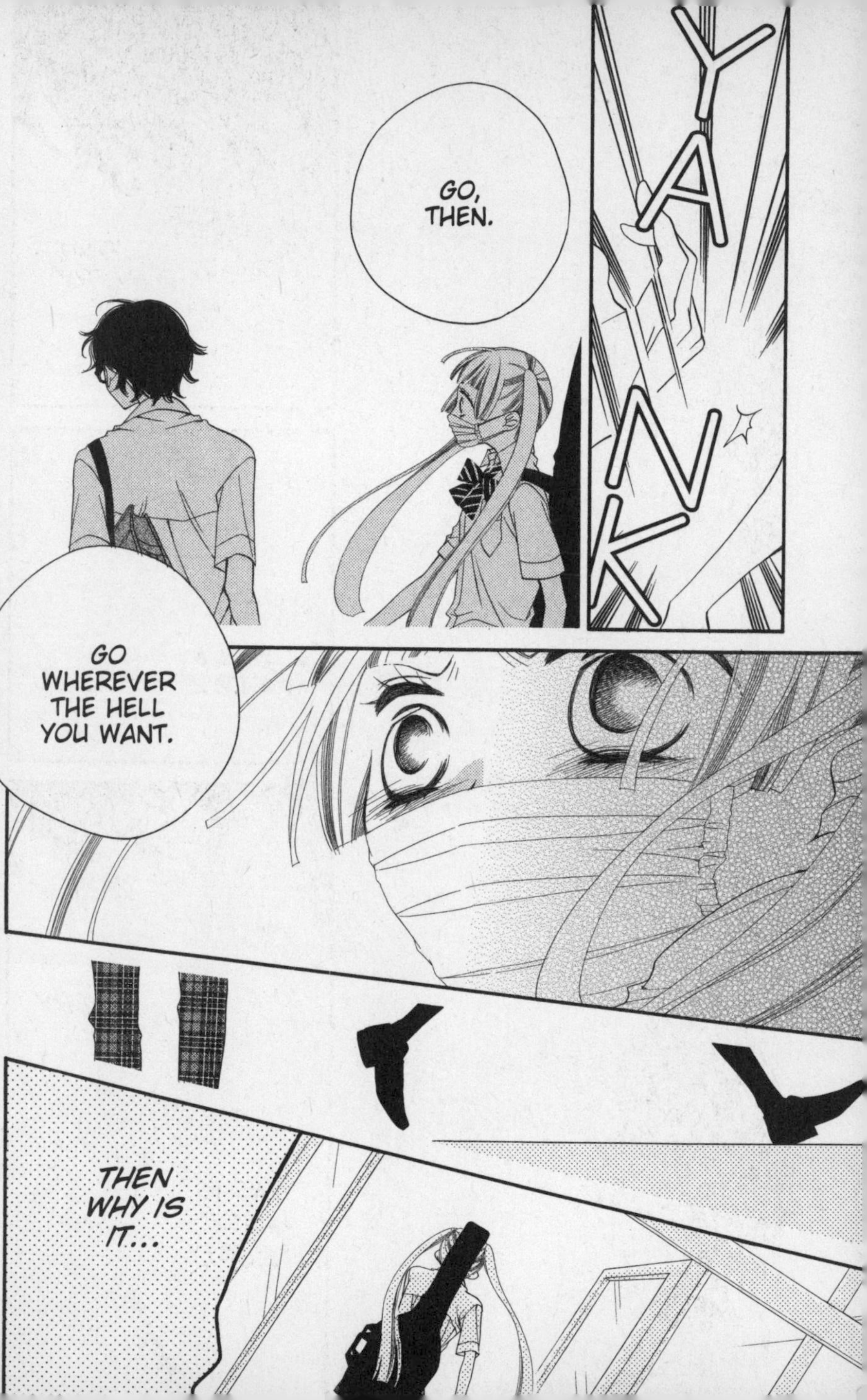
YANK
GO, THEN.
GO WHEREVER THE HELL YOU WANT.
THEN WHY IS IT...

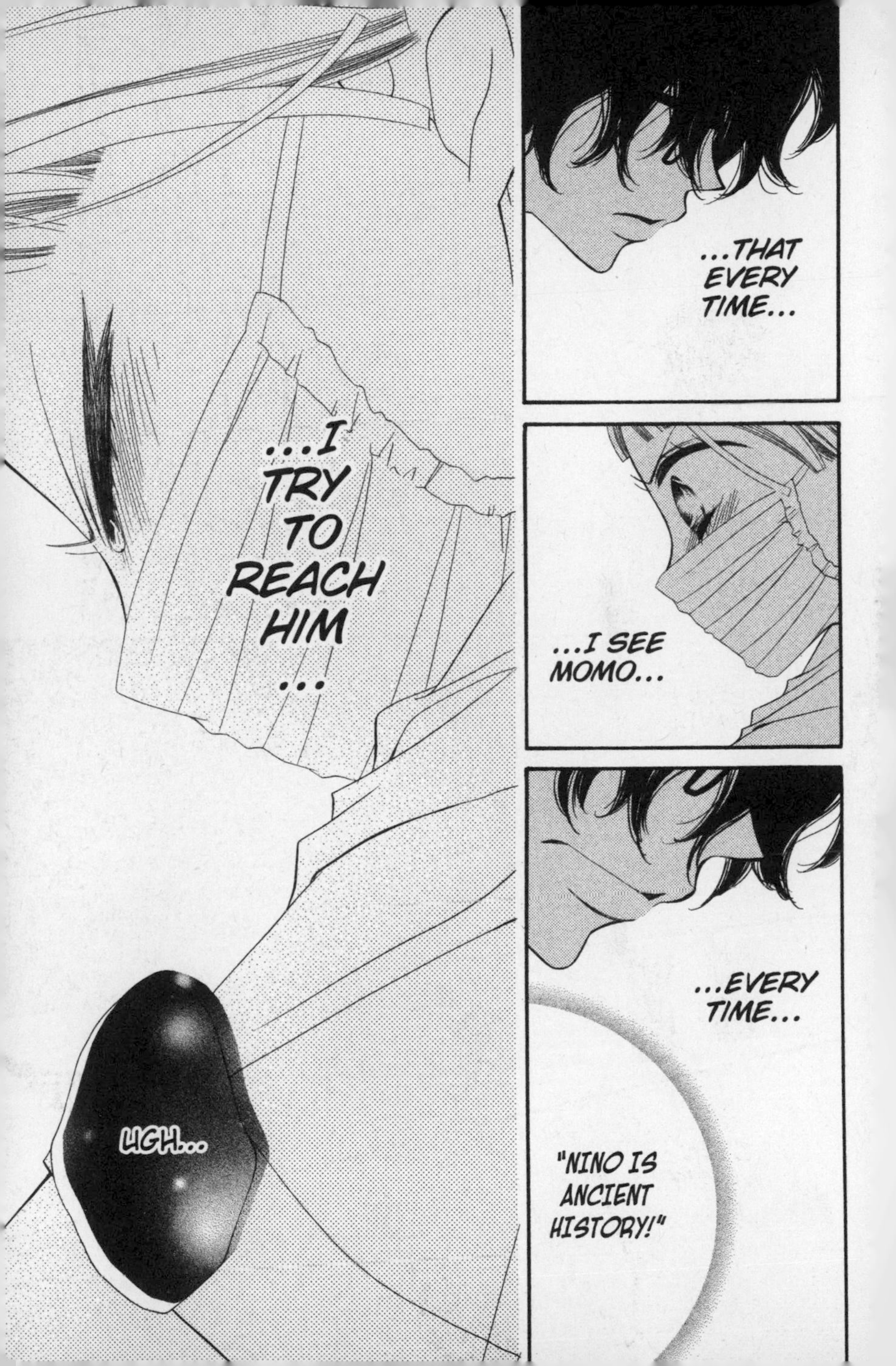
...THAT EVERY TIME...
...I SEE MOMO...
...EVERY TIME...
"NINO IS ANCIENT HISTORY!"
...I TRY TO REACH HIM...
UGH...

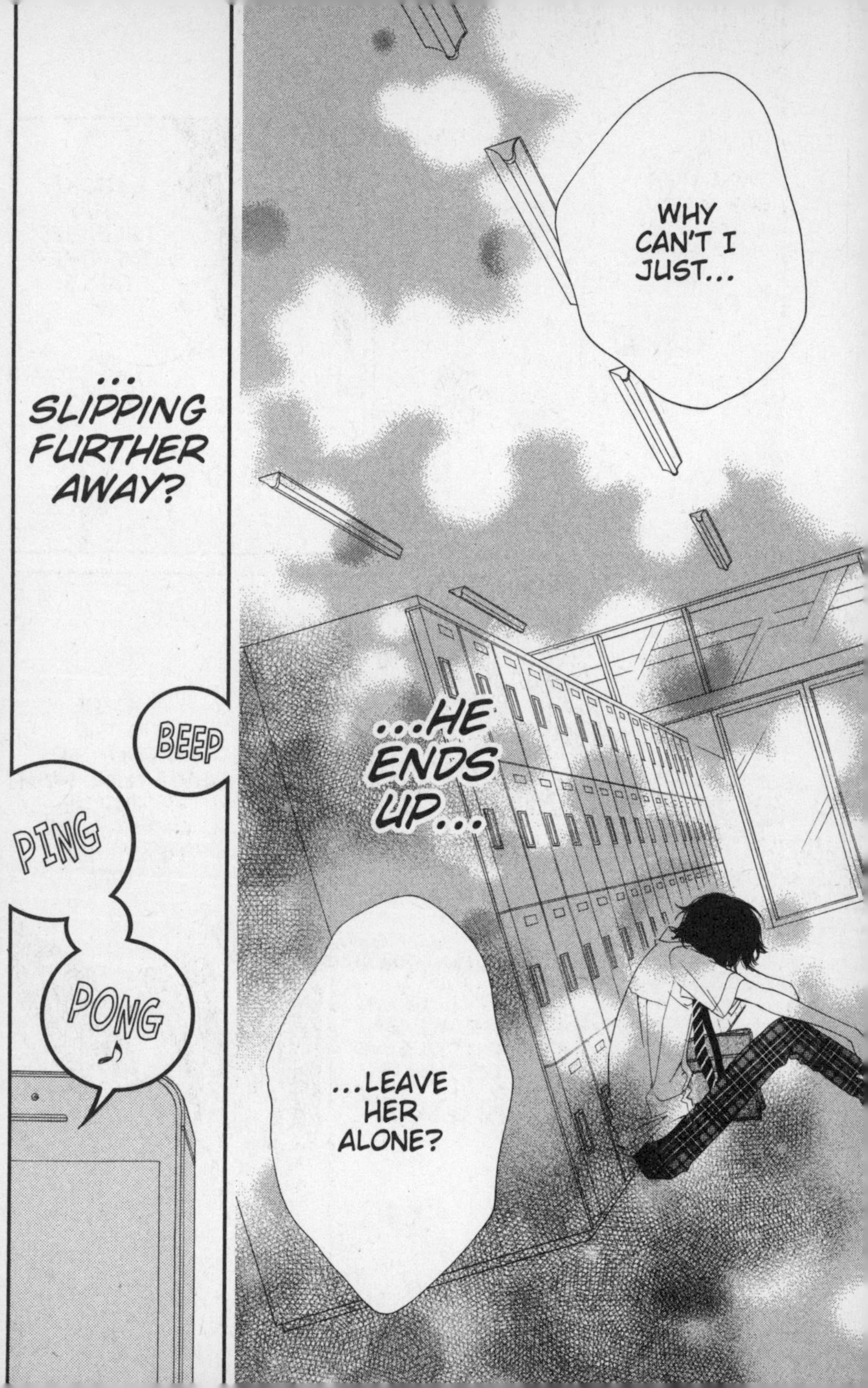
WHY CAN'T I JUST...
...HE ENDS UP...
...LEAVE HER ALONE?
...SLIPPING FURTHER AWAY?
BEEP
PING
PONG ♪

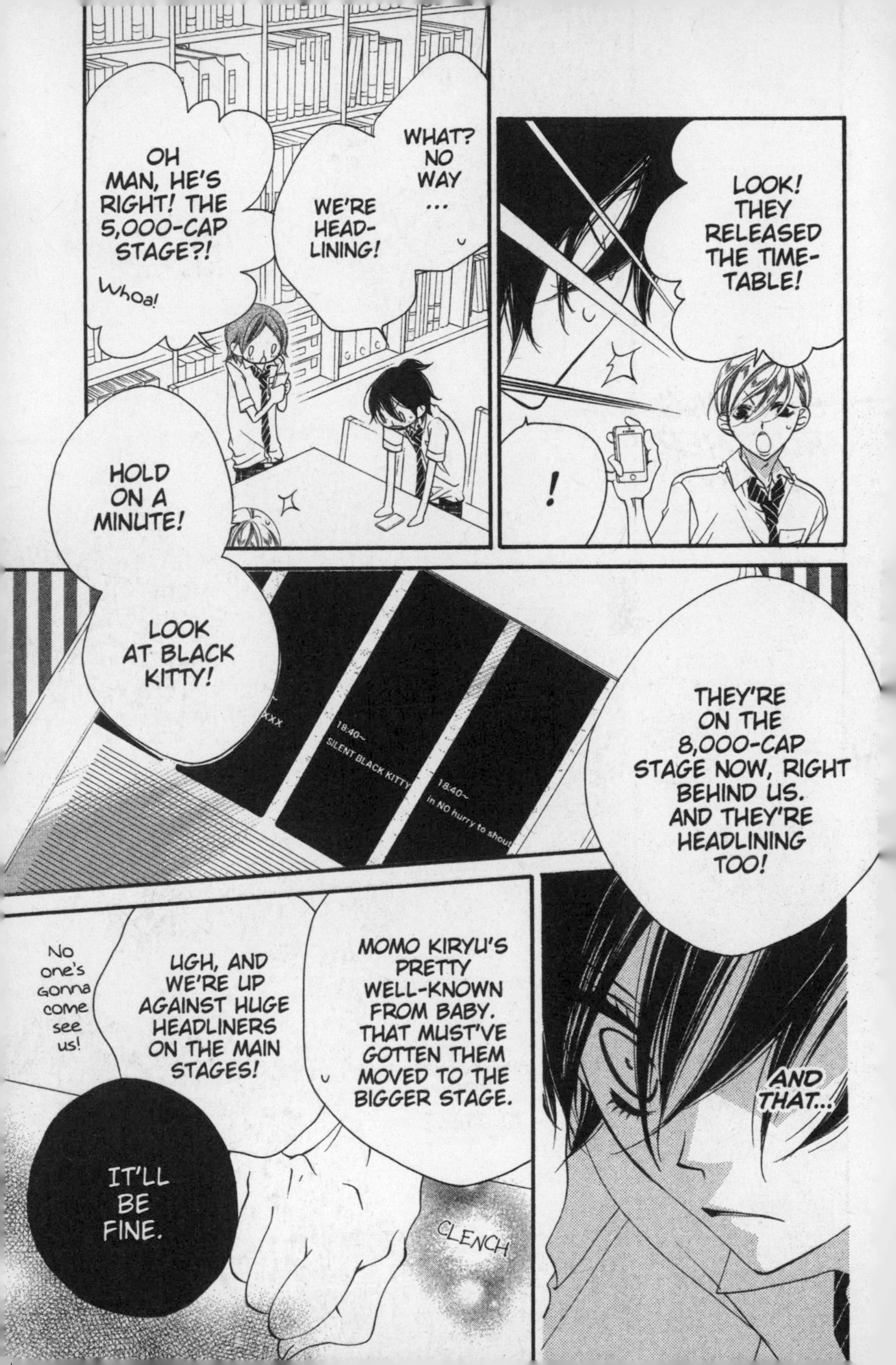
LOOK! THEY RELEASED THE TIME-TABLE!
!
WHAT? NO WAY ...
WE'RE HEADLINING!
OH MAN, HE'S RIGHT! THE 5,000-CAP STAGE?!
Whoa!
HOLD ON A MINUTE!
LOOK AT BLACK KITTY!
18:40~
SILENT BLACK KITTY
18:40~
in NO hurry to shout
THEY'RE ON THE 8,000-CAP STAGE NOW, RIGHT BEHIND US. AND THEY'RE HEADLINING TOO!
AND THAT...
MOMO KIRYU'S PRETTY WELL-KNOWN FROM BABY. THAT MUST'VE GOTTEN THEM MOVED TO THE BIGGER STAGE.
UGH, AND WE'RE UP AGAINST HUGE HEADLINERS ON THE MAIN STAGES!
No one's gonna come see us!
IT'LL BE FINE.
CLENCH

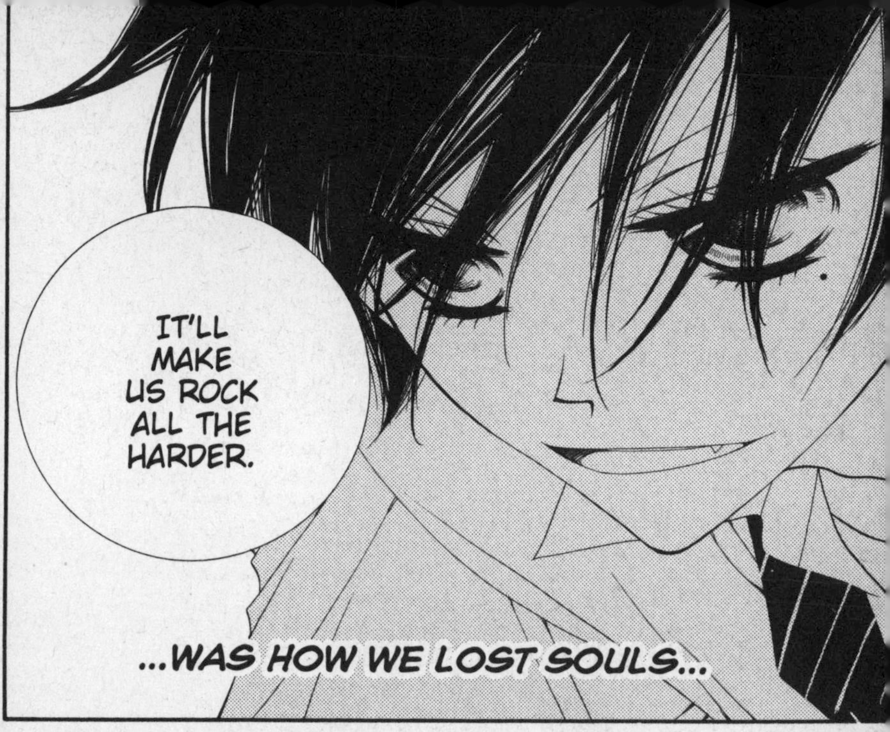
IT'LL MAKE US ROCK ALL THE HARDER.
...WAS HOW WE LOST SOULS...

...BEGAN OUR SUMMER.

ANONYMOUS NOISE ④ / THE END

TO BE CONTINUED IN ANONYMOUS NOISE 5

I closed down the official site that I'd
been using for ten years and started
a Tumblr account instead. Tumblr
has all the features that I'd been
wanting, so it felt weird that I hadn't
been using it all along. Please drop
by and take a look sometime!

- Ryoko Fukuyama

Born on January 5 in Wakayama Prefecture in
Japan, Ryoko Fukuyama debuted as a manga
artist after winning the Hakusensha Athena
Shinjin Taisho Prize from Hakusensha's *Hana
to Yume* magazine. She is also the author of
Nosatsu Junkie. *Anonymous Noise* was adapted
into an anime in 2017.